Acclaim for Robert Bauval and Graham Hancock:

THE KEEPER OF GENESIS

'The book reads like a detective story, with the reader
enthusiastically trying to outguess the writers'
Literary Review

'*Keeper of Genesis* is an exciting book, highly topical and
deservedly a best-seller'
Spectator

'The trick is to keep reading. Start the book in the early evening
and continue uninterrupted till you complete it in the small
hours. The effect is wonderful . . . Your entire world view has
been shifted a hundred yards to the right. You fall asleep
thinking that nothing will ever be the same again'
Sunday Telegraph

FINGERPRINTS OF THE GODS

'One of the intellectual landmarks of the decade'
Literary Review

'Part travelogue, part sensation, part unravelling, a fascinating
story'
Catholic Herald

'Hancock has invented a new genre: an intellectual whodunnit
by a do-it-yourself sleuth with whom we can all identify'
The Guardian

'[Hancock's] sweep through the ancient world is arresting and
audacious'
Daily Mail

THE ORION MYSTERY

'Absorbing and fascinating . . . highly and compulsively
readable'
Sunday Times

'A discovery about the pyramids that could change our view of
human history'
Evening Standard

'Persuasive and scholarly'
Observer

Keeper of Genesis

Robert Bauval is a construction engineer with a long-standing interest in the astronomy of the pyramids, having lived in Egypt and elsewhere in the Middle East for much of his life. *The Orion Mystery* was his first book.

Graham Hancock is a former East African correspondent for *The Economist* and has travelled widely round the world. He is the author of *Fingerprints of the Gods, The Sign and the Seal* and *Lords of Poverty*.

Diagrams by Robert G. Bauval and R. J. Cook.

Jacket photograph and photographs 2, 3, 4, 5, 6, 8, 9, 10, 17, 18, 19, 20, 22, 24, 25, 26, 27, 28, 30, 31 and 32 by Santha Faiia.

Photographs 11, 12, 15 and 16 courtesy of Rudolph Gantenbrink.

Photograph 29 by Robert Bauval.

Photograph 7 courtesy of *Venture Inward* magazine.

Photograph 13 Spiegel TV. Photograph 14 Antoine Boutros. Photograph 1 The Lady Sophia Schilizzi.

Keeper of Genesis

A Quest for the Hidden Legacy of Mankind

ROBERT BAUVAL
GRAHAM HANCOCK

ARROW

Reprinted in Arrow Books, 1997

7 9 10 8 6

First published in the United Kingdom in 1996 by William Heinemann

This edition first published in 1997 by Mandarin Paperbacks, reprinted twice

Arrow Books
The Random House Group Limited
20 Vauxhall Bridge Road, London SW1V 2SA

Random House Australia (Pty) Limited
20 Alfred Street, Milsons Point, Sydney, New South Wales 2061, Australia

Random House New Zealand Limited
18 Poland Road, Glenfield, Auckland 10, New Zealand

Random House South Africa (Pty) Limited
Endulini, 5a Jubilee Road, Parktown 2193, South Africa

The Random House Group Limited Reg. No. 954009

www.randomhouse.co.uk

A CIP catalogue record for this book is available from the British Library

Papers used by Random House are natural, recyclable
products made from wood grown in sustainable
forests. The manufacturing processes conform to the
environmental regulations of the country of origin

Typeset by Deltatype Ltd, Birkenhead, Merseyside
Printed and bound in the United Kingdom by
Cox & Wyman Ltd, Reading, Berkshire

ISBN 0 7493 2196 2

To the memory of my father Gaston Bauval,
who rests in the land of Egypt.

Robert G. Bauval

To my friend, John Anthony West,
for his twenty years of courageous work
to prove the geological antiquity of the Sphinx,
and for the vast implications of the evidence
that he has put before the public.
'The truth is great and mighty,' as the
ancient texts say. 'It hath never been broken
since the time of Osiris.'

Graham Hancock

Contents

Line Illustrations

Acknowledgements

Robert G. Bauval:

Foremost, a special thanks to the readers. In the last two years I have received hundreds of letters of encouragement and good-will and it's sure nice to know you're all out there sharing in this common quest for truth.

I am immensely grateful for the patience and understanding of my wife Michele, and my two children, Candice and Jonathan.

Particular gratitude goes to the following relatives, friends and colleagues for their support: John Anthony West, Chris Dunn, Bill Cote, Roel Oostra, Joseph and Sherry Jahoda, Joseph and Laura Schor, Niven Sinclair, Marion Krause-Jach, Princess Madeleine of Bentheim, James Macaulay, Robert Makenty, Linda and Max Bauval, Jean Paul and Pauline Bauval, my mother Yvonne Bauval, Geoffrey and Thérèse Gauci, Patrick and Judy Gauci, Denis and Verena Seisun, Colin Wilson, Mohamed and Amin El Walili, Julia Simpson, Sahar Talaat, Professor Karl-Klaus Dittel and his wife Renate, Hani Monsef, Mark Ford, Peter Zuuring, Richard Thompson, Adrian Ashford, Dave Goode, Okasha El Daly, Mohamad Razek, Heike Nahsen, Ilga Korte, Gundula Schulz El Dowy, Antoine Boutros, Professor Jean Kerisel, Roy Baker, Murry Hope, William Horsman and Charlotte Ames.

I would like to convey my warm thanks to Bill Hamilton and Sara Fisher of A.M. Heath & Co., Ltd, for putting up with my pleonastic ways, Tom Weldon and all the staff at William Heinemann Ltd, Peter St Ginna and Brian Belfiglio at Crown Publishing Inc., Melanie Walz and Doris Janhsen at Paul List Verlag, and Udo Rennert of Wiesbaden.

Finally, I want to pay tribute to the engineer and my friend Rudolf Gantenbrink for opening the way for all of us with his bold and daring exploration in the Great Pyramid.

Robert G. Bauval,
Beaconsfield, February 1996

Graham Hancock:

Special thanks and love to Santha, my wife and partner, my best and dearest friend. Love and appreciation to our children: Gabrielle, Leila, Luke, Ravi, Sean and Shanti. Special thanks also to my parents, Donald and Muriel Hancock, who have given me so much, and for the help, advice and adventurous spirit of my uncle, James Macaulay. Many of the individuals named in Robert's acknowledgements likewise deserve my thanks: they know who they are. In addition I take this opportunity to send my personal good wishes to Richard Hoagland, Lew Jenkins, Peter Marshall, and Ed Ponist.

Graham Hancock,
Lifton, February 1996

Part I

Enigmas

Chapter 1

Horizon Dweller

'There is scarcely a person in the civilized
world who is unfamiliar with the form and
features of the great man-headed lion that
guards the eastern approach to the Giza
pyramids.'

Ahmed Fakhry, *The Pyramids*, 1961

A gigantic statue, with lion body and the head of a man, gazes east
from Egypt along the thirtieth parallel. It is a monolith, carved out of
the limestone bedrock of the Giza plateau, two hundred and forty feet
long, thirty-eight feet wide across the shoulders, and sixty-six feet
high. It is worn down and eroded, battered, fissured and collapsing.
Yet nothing else that has reached us from antiquity even remotely
matches its power and grandeur, its majesty and its mystery, or its
sombre and hypnotic watchfulness.

It is the Great Sphinx.

Once it was believed to be an eternal God.

Then amnesia ensnared it and it fell into an enchanted sleep.

Ages passed: thousands of years. Climates changed. Cultures
changed. Religions changed. Languages changed. Even the positions
of the stars in the skies changed. But still the statue endured, brooding
and numinous, wrapped in silence.

Often sand engulfed it. At widely separated intervals a benevolent
ruler would arrange to have it cleared. There were those who
attempted to restore it, covering parts of its rock-hewn body with
blocks of masonry. For a long period it was painted red.

By Islamic times the desert had buried it up to its neck and it had
been given a new, or perhaps a very old, name: 'Near to one of the
Pyramids,' reported Abdel-Latif in the twelfth century, 'is a colossal

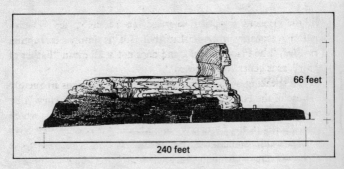

66 feet

240 feet

1. Profile of the Great Sphinx from the south showing restoration blocks along the paws and flanks and extensive weathering on the core limestone body.

head emerging from the ground. It is called Abul-Hol.' And in the fourteenth century El-Makrizi wrote of a man named Saim-ed-Dahr who 'wanted to remedy some of the religious errors and he went to the Pyramids and disfigured the face of Abul-Hol, which has remained in that state from that time until now. From the time of this disfigurement, also, the sand has invaded the cultivated land of Giza, and the people attribute this to the disfigurement of Abul-Hol.'

Enduring memories

Abul-Hol, the Arabic name for the Great Sphinx of Egypt, is supposed by most translators to mean 'Father of Terror'.

An alternative etymology, however, has been proposed by the Egyptologist Selim Hassan. During the extensive excavations that he undertook on the Giza plateau in the 1930s and '40s he uncovered evidence that a colony of foreigners – 'Cananites' – had resided in this part of Lower Egypt in the early second millennium BC. They were from the sacred city of Harran (located in the south of modern Turkey near its border with Syria) and they may perhaps have been pilgrims. At any rate artefacts and commemorative stelae prove that they lived in the immediate vicinity of the Sphinx – worshipping it as a god under the name *Hwl* .[1]

In the Ancient Egyptian language, *bw* means 'place'. Hassan therefore reasonably proposes that Abul-Hol, 'is simply a corruption of *bw Hwl*, "the Place of *Hwl*", and does not at all mean "Father of Terror", as is generally supposed'.[2]

When speaking of the Sphinx, the Ancient Egyptians frequently made use of the Harranian derivation *Hwl*, but they also knew it by many other names: *Hu*,[3] for example, and *Hor-em-Akhet* – which means 'Horus in the Horizon'.[4] In addition, for reasons that have never been fully understood, the Sphinx was often referred to as *Seshep-ankh Atum*, 'the living image of *Atum*,[5] after *Atum-Re* the self-created sun-god, the first and original deity of the ancient Egyptian pantheon. Indeed, the very name 'Sphinx' that has haunted the collective subconscious of the Western world since Classical times, turns out to be no more than a corruption – through Greek – of *Sheshep-ankh*.

In this way, with subtlety, a number of very archaic ideas, once held by the ancient Egyptians, have survived for thousands of years.[6] Would we not be foolish, therefore, to ignore entirely the lingering tradition that associates the Sphinx with a great and terrible riddle?

Stillness and silence

Crouching in the massive horseshoe-shaped trench of bedrock out of which it was carved, the statue looks old: a fierce and raddled towering monster, higher than a six-storey building and as long as a city block. Its flanks are lean, deeply scalloped by erosion. Its paws, now covered with modern repair bricks, are substantially worn away. Its neck has been clumsily shorn up with a cement collar intended to keep its grizzled head in place. Its face, too, is bruised and battered, and yet it somehow seems serene and ageless, unpredictably portraying different moods and expressions at different times and seasons, coming alive with patterns of light and shadow cast by scudding clouds at dawn.

Wearing the elegant *nemes* head-dress of an Egyptian Pharaoh, it gazes patiently into the east, as though waiting for something – waiting and watching, lost in its 'stillness and silence' (in the words of the Roman naturalist Pliny), and targeting for ever the equinoctial rising point of the sun.

How long has it stood here inspecting the horizon?

Whose image does it portray?

What is its function?

In our search for answers to these questions we have found ourselves drawn into strange and unexpected areas of research. Like souls on the way of the dead, we have had to pass through the dark kingdom of the ancient Egyptian afterworld, to navigate its narrow corridors, flooded passageways and hidden chambers, and to confront the fiends and demons lurking there. Using computer simulations we have journeyed back in time to stand beneath skies more than 12,000 years old, and watched Orion cross the meridian at dawn as Leo rose resplendent in the east. We have immersed ourselves in archaic rebirth texts and myths and scriptures and found amongst them the veiled remnants of a remarkable 'astronomical language' that can, without too much difficulty, be read and understood today.

Through clues expressed in this language we believe that we are able to identify with certainty who and what the Sphinx really is. Moreover, as we shall see in Parts III and IV, this identification appears to open a window on a forgotten episode in human history when the waters of a great deluge were ebbing and men sought to transform themselves into gods. In our opinion the stakes are high. Indeed we think it possible that the Sphinx and the three great Pyramids may offer knowledge of the genesis of civilization itself. Our immediate aim in Parts I and II, therefore, is to undertake a complete re-evaluation of all these titanic monuments, of the scholarship that has surrounded them during the past century or so, and of their numerous neglected, geodetic and geological and astronomical qualities.

Once these factors are taken into account a new Rosetta Stone begins to emerge, expressed in architecture and time, in allegories and symbols, and in specific astronomical directions and co-ordinates that tell the seeker where to look and what he might hope to find.

Meanwhile the Great Sphinx waits patiently.

Keeper of secrets.

Guardian of mysteries.

Chapter 2

The Riddle of the Sphinx

'*Sphinx*, mythological creature with a lion's
body and human head . . . The earliest and
most famous example in art is the colossal
recumbent Sphinx at Giza, Egypt, dating
from the reign of King Khafre (4th dynasty,
*c.*2575–2465 BC). This is known to be a
portrait statue of the King . . .'

Encyclopaedia Britannica

There is a belief that the Great Sphinx of Giza was fashioned during
that period of Egyptian history classified as the 'Old Kingdom' on the
orders of the Fourth Dynasty Pharaoh named Khafre whom the
Greeks later knew as Chephren and who reigned from 2520–2494 BC.
This is the orthodox historical view and readers will find it reported in
all standard Egyptological texts, in all encyclopaedias, in archaeological journals and in popular scientific literature. In these same sources
it is also repeatedly stated as fact that the features of the Sphinx were
carved to represent Khafre himself – in other words, its face is his
face.

Thus, for example, Dr I. E. S. Edwards, a world-renowned expert
on the monuments of the Giza necropolis, tells us that although the
face of the Sphinx has been 'severely mutilated': 'it still gives the
impression of being a portrait of Khafre and not merely a formalised
representation of the king.'[1]

In a similar vein Ahmed Fakhry, professor of ancient history at
Cairo University, informs us that: 'as it was first conceived, the
Sphinx symbolised the king, and its face was carved in Khafre's
likeness.'[2]

The only problem – at any rate without access to a time machine –

is that none of us, not even distinguished Egyptologists, is really in a position to say whether or not the Sphinx is a portrait or likeness of Khafre. Since the Pharaoh's body has never been found we have nothing to go on except surviving statues (which might or might not have closely resembled the king himself). The best known of these statues, an almost unsurpassable masterpiece of the sculptor's art carved out of a single piece of black diorite, now reposes in one of the ground-floor rooms of the Cairo Museum. It is to this beautiful and majestic representation that the scholars make reference when they tell us – with such confidence – that the Sphinx was fashioned in Khafre's likeness.

This confidence was particularly apparent in an article in the prestigious *National Geographic* magazine which appeared in the US in April 1991, and a similar one that appeared in Britain in the *Cambridge Archaeological Journal* in April 1992.[3] The articles were written by Professor Mark Lehner, of Chicago University's Oriental Institute, who used 'photogrammetric data and computer graphics' to 'prove' that the face of the great Sphinx was that of Khafre:

> Zahi Hawass, Director General of the Giza Pyramids, invited me to join his excavation [around the Sphinx] in 1978. During the next four years I led a project to map the Sphinx in detail for the first time. We produced front and side views with photogrammetry, a technique using stereoscopic photography ... Computers have taken the records further. Maps were digitized to make a 3-D wireframe model; some 2.6 million surface points were plotted to put 'skin' on the skeleton view. We have constructed images of the Sphinx as it may have looked thousands of years ago. To create the face, I tried matching views of other sphinxes and pharaohs to our model. With the face of Khafre, the Sphinx came alive . . .[4]

It all sounds technically very impressive and persuasive. After all, who in their right mind is going to argue with '2.6 million surface points' based on 'stereoscopic photography' and 'photogrammetry'?

Behind the technical jargon, however, the truth is rather less awe-inspiring. A close reading shows that all that Lehner did in order to 'reconstruct' the face of the Sphinx was to prepare a computerized three-dimensional wireframe skeleton on which he then superimposed the face of Khafre. This is admitted in the *National Geographic* article, which reproduces a photograph of the diorite statue of Khafre above the following caption: 'The author [Lehner] used this face for the computer reconstruction of the Sphinx.'[5]

So what Mark Lehner really did was to *remodel* the face of the Sphinx on a computer according to his own preferences – in much the same way that some ancient Egyptians had probably done several times before him on the face of the statue itself. The present features of the Sphinx, in other words, are no more likely to be those of Khafre than they are to be those of a number of other Pharaohs – Thutmosis IV, for example, or Amenhotep, or Ramesses II (who is last known, as Lehner admits, to have 'extensively reworked' the monument at around 1279 BC).[6] The simple, honest truth is that during the thousands of years of the Sphinx's existence, often with only its head protruding above the sand, almost anyone could have worked on its face at almost any time. Moreover, Lehner's own photogrammetric study has thrown up at least one piece of evidence which is highly suggestive of major recarving: the Sphinx's head, he writes, is 'too small' in proportion to the body. He tells us that this is because it is an early prototype of the later very popular (and always proportionate) sphinx form, and speculates that 'the Fourth Dynasty Egyptians may not [yet] have worked out the canon of proportions between the royal head with the *nemes* headdress on the lion body'.[7] He does not consider the equally valid and more intriguing possibility that the head was once much larger – and perhaps even leonine, and that it was reduced in size by recarving.

Probably relevant in this regard is an additional observation that Lehner has made: 'a subtle discrepancy' exists 'between the axis of the head [of the Sphinx] and that of the facial features'[8] – the head being orientated perfectly to due east, and the features swivelled somewhat to the north of east.

Once again this is an error that is consistent with the recarving of a much older and heavily eroded statue. And it is consistent, too, as we shall see later in this chapter, with new geological evidence concerning the Sphinx's antiquity. Setting these matters aside for the moment, however, it seems clear that the mere fact that Mark Lehner is able to graft an image of Khafre onto the battered visage of the Sphinx by means of the 'ARL (Advanced Research Logic) Computer and the

AutoCad (release 10) graphics application',[9] proves nothing more than that with good computer graphics you can make anyone's face look like anyone else's face. 'The same computer technique,' in the words of one outspoken critic, 'could be used to "prove" the Sphinx was really Elvis Presley . . .'[10]

It was partly in an attempt to resolve this impasse that a group of independent researchers took the unusual step of bringing a detective to Egypt in 1993. The detective in question was Lieutenant Frank Domingo, a senior forensic artist with the New York Police Department, who has been preparing 'identikit' portraits of suspects for more than twenty years. As a man who knows and works with faces every day of his professional life, he was commissioned to make a detailed study of the points of similarity and difference between the Sphinx and the Khafre statue. Months later, after returning to his lab in New York where he undertook careful comparisons of hundreds of photographs of the two works, Domingo reported:

> After reviewing my various drawings, schematics and measurements, my final conclusion concurs with my initial reaction, i.e. that the two works represent two separate individuals. The proportions in the frontal view, and especially the angles and facial protrusion in the lateral views convinced me that the Sphinx is not Khafre . . .'[11]

So on the one hand we have a top forsenic expert, Frank Domingo, telling us that the Sphinx's face does not represent Khafre's face. And on the other we have Mark Lehner, the Egyptologist computer buff, saying that only with Khafre's face does the Sphinx 'come alive'.

Undatable, anonymous

Why is there room for such widely varying opinions concerning the world's best known and most intensively studied ancient monument?

In 1992, in two different forums, Mark Lehner made somewhat contradictory statements which hint at the answer to this question:

1 At the annual meeting of the American Association for the Advancement of Science he said: 'There is no direct way to date the Sphinx itself because the Sphinx is carved right out of natural rock.'[12]

2 In the *Cambridge Archaeological Journal* he wrote: 'Although we

are certain that the Sphinx dates to the Fourth Dynasty, we are
confronted by a complete absence of Old Kingdom texts which
mention it.'[13]

To deal with the first point first, it is a simple matter of fact that no
objective test presently exists for the accurate dating of rock-hewn
monuments.[14] Many people are under the erroneous impression that
the radio-carbon technique could be used, but this is not so: it is only
applicable to organic materials (in which it measures the quantity of
the isotope Carbon-14 that has decayed since the death of the
organism in question). Since the Sphinx is made of carved rock it
cannot be dated by this method.

This brings us to the second point. Stone monuments *can* be dated
with reasonable accuracy if there are contemporary texts which refer
to their construction. Ideally, in the case of the Sphinx, what one
would require would be an inscription carved during the Fourth
Dynasty and directly attributing the monument to Khafre. As Mark
Lehner admits, however, no contemporary text referring to the
Sphinx has ever been found.

In all honesty, therefore, what confronts us at Giza is an entirely
anonymous monument, carved out of undatable rock, about which, as
the forthright Egyptologist Selim Hassan wrote in 1949, 'no definite
facts are known'.[15]

One syllable

Why, therefore, do Mark Lehner and other influential modern
scholars continue to link the Sphinx to Khafre and to insist that 'The
Old Kingdom Fourth Dynasty date for [its] origin . . . is no longer an
issue'[16]?

One reason is a single syllable carved on the granite stela which
stands between the monument's front paws and which has been taken
as proof that Khafre built the Sphinx. The stela, which is not
contemporary with the Sphinx itself, commemorates heroic efforts by
the Pharaoh Thutmosis IV (1401–1391 BC) to clear the Sphinx
completely of encroaching sand and describes the lion-bodied statue
as the embodiment of 'a great magical power that existed in this place
from the beginning of all time'.[17] The inscription also contains, in line

13, the first syllable – *Khaf* – of the name Khafre. The presence of that syllable, in the words of Sir E. A. Wallis Budge, is: 'very important for it proves that . . . the priests of Heliopolis who advised Thutmosis to undertake the work of clearing away the sand from the Sphinx believed that it was fashioned by Khafre . . .'[18]

But does the syllable *Khaf* really prove so much?

When the stela was excavated by the Genoese adventurer Gian Battista Caviglia in 1817, line 13 – which has now entirely flaked away – was already badly damaged. We know of its existence because, not long after the excavation, the British philologist Thomas Young, a leading expert in the decipherment of ancient Egyptian hieroglyphs, was able to make a facsimile of the inscription. For line 13 his translation reads as follows: '. . . which we bring for him: oxen . . . and all young vegetables; and we shall give praise to Wenofer . . . Khaf . . . the statue made for Atum-Hor-em-Akhet. . . .'[19]

On the assumption that Khaf was Khafre's name, Young added the syllable *Re* between square brackets to show that a lacuna had been filled in.[20] In 1905, however, when the American Egyptologist James Henry Breasted studied Young's facsimile he concluded that a mistake had been made: 'This mention of King Khafre has been understood to indicate that the Sphinx was the work of this king – a conclusion which does not follow; [the facsimile of] Young has no trace of a cartouche . . .'[21]

In all the inscriptions of ancient Egypt, from the beginning to the end of Pharaonic civilization, the names of kings were always inscribed inside oval-shaped signs or enclosures known as 'cartouches'. It is therefore extremely difficult to understand how on the granite stela between the paws of the Sphinx the name of as powerful a king as Khafre – or indeed of any other king – could have been written without its pre-required cartouche.

Besides, even if the syllable Khaf was intended to refer to Khafre, its presence does not necessarily imply that he *built* the Sphinx. It is equally possible that he was being commemorated for some other service. For example, like many Pharaohs after him (Ramesses II, Thutmosis IV, Ahmoses I, etc., etc.[22]) – and perhaps like many before him too – is it not possible that Khafre was a *restorer* of the Sphinx?

As it happens, this perfectly logical deduction and others like it were favoured by a number of the leading scholars who pioneered the discipline of Egyptology at around the end of the nineteenth century. Gaston Maspero, for example, Director of the Department of Antiquities at the Cairo Museum, an acclaimed philologist of his time, wrote in 1900:

> The stela of the Sphinx bears, on line 13, the [name] of Khafre in the middle of a gap . . . There, I believe, is an indication of [a renovation and clearance] of the Sphinx carried out under this prince, and consequently the more or less certain proof that the Sphinx was already covered with sand during the time of his predecessors . . .[23]

This view is supported by the text of another roughly contemporary stela, the so-called 'Inventory Stela' – also found at Giza but arbitrarily assumed by the majority of modern Egyptologists to be a work of fiction – which states that Khufu saw the Sphinx. Since Khufu, the supposed builder of the Great Pyramid, was Khafre's predecessor, the obvious implication is that Khafre could not have built the Sphinx.[24] Encouraged by this testimony, Maspero at one point went so far as to propose that the Sphinx could have existed since the times of the 'Followers of Horus', a lineage of pre-dynastic, semi-divine beings whose members were believed by the ancient Egyptians to have ruled for thousands of years before the 'historical' Pharaohs.[25] Later in his career, however, the French Egyptologist modified his opinion to conform with the general consensus and stated that the Sphinx 'probably represents Khafre himself '.[26]

That Maspero should have felt compelled to recant his heretical views on the Sphinx tells us more about the power of peer pressure within Egyptology than it does about the quality of evidence concerning the antiquity and attribution of the monument itself. Indeed, the evidence underpinning the prevailing consensus is extremely slim, resting not so much on 'facts' as on the *interpretation* that certain authorities have chosen at one time or another to give to particular and usually highly ambiguous data – in this case the solitary syllable of Khafre's name on the Thutmosis stela.

Very few senior members of the profession have been as honest about such matters as Selim Hassan. In his classic 1949 study of the Sphinx, from which we have already quoted, he issued this pertinent warning:

> Excepting for the mutilated line on the granite stela of Thothmosis IV, which proves nothing, there is not a single ancient inscription which connects the Sphinx with Khafre. So sound as it may appear, we must treat this evidence as circumstantial until such a time as a lucky turn of the spade will reveal to the world definite reference to the erection of this statue . . .[27]

Context

Since Hassan wrote there has been no such 'lucky turn of the spade'. Nevertheless the conventional wisdom that the Sphinx was built by Khafre, *circa* 2500 BC, remains so strong and so all-pervasive that one assumes there must be something else behind it other than the disputed resemblance to the statue of Khafre in the Cairo Museum and the contradictory opinions of scholars concerning a half-ruined stela.

According to Mark Lehner, there is indeed something else – a kind of magic bullet which he clearly regards as powerful enough to kill any niggling doubts and questions. Today the Director of the Koch-Ludwig Giza Plateau Project, and former Director of the now completed Giza Mapping Project, Lehner is recognized as a world expert on the Sphinx. Whenever he fires his magic bullet at the occasional 'heretics' who have suggested that the monument might be a lot older than 2500 BC, therefore, he does so from a position of great influence and authority.

The name of his magic bullet is context and, at the 1992 annual meeting of the American Association for the Advancement of Science, where he was selected as the official spokesman of Egyptology to put the orthodox point of view in a debate on the true age of the Sphinx, he made extensive use of this 'bullet':

> The Sphinx does not sit out alone in the desert totally up for grabs as to 'how old is the Sphinx?'. The Sphinx is surrounded by a vast

architectural context which includes the Pyramid of Khufu [better known as the Great Pyramid], the Pyramid of Khafre ['the second Pyramid'] and the Pyramid of Menkaure,[28] pharaohs of the Fourth Dynasty. Each pyramid has a long causeway running from a Mortuary Temple on its eastern side, down to the level of the Nile flood-plain, where a Valley Temple served as an entrance to the pyramid complex . . .

Officials and relatives of the pharaohs built their tombs in cemeteries east and west of the Khufu Pyramid, and southeast of the pyramids of Khafre and Menkaure respectively. Digging at Giza for nearly two centuries, archaeologists have retrieved an abundance of material [dating to the Fourth Dynasty]. Hundreds of tombs have yielded the mortal remains and artifacts of people who composed the state administration of the Pyramid Age . . . We are discovering evidence of the working class and everyday life of the society that built the Sphinx and pyramids . . . We have evidence of the ruins of an ancient city spread out along the valley for the entire length of the Giza Plateau. All this is part of the archaeological context of the Sphinx . . .[29]

Lehner goes on to say that there are several specific reasons why this context persuades him that 'the Sphinx belongs to Khafre's Pyramid complex':

The south side of the Sphinx ditch forms the northern edge of the Khafre causeway as it runs past the Sphinx and enters Khafre's Valley Temple. A drainage channel runs along the northern side of the causeway and opens into the upper south-west corner of the Sphinx ditch, suggesting the ancient quarrymen formed the ditch after the Khafre causeway was built. Otherwise they would not have had the drain empty into the ditch. Khafre's Valley Temple sits on the same terrace as the Sphinx Temple. The fronts and backs of the Temples are nearly aligned, and the walls of both are built in the same style . . .[30]

The evidence for the two Temples, the causeway and the second Pyramid all being part of one architectural unit with the Sphinx is indeed compelling. But using this evidence to support the conclusion that Khafre built the Sphinx is rather less so. What it ignores is the possibility that the entire 'unit' could have been built long before

Khafre's time by as yet unidentified predecessors and then *reused* – perhaps even extensively restored – during the Fourth Dynasty.

It is this possibility – not precluded by any inscriptions and not ruled out by any objective dating techniques – that has made the Sphinx the subject of an increasingly virulent controversy during the 1990s . . .

Water erosion

The origins of this controversy go back to the late 1970s when John Anthony West, an independent American researcher, was studying the obscure and difficult writings of the brilliant French mathematician and symbolist R. A. Schwaller de Lubicz. Schwaller is best known for his works on the Luxor Temple, but in his more general text, *Sacred Science* (first published in 1961), he commented on the archaeological implications of certain climatic conditions and floods that last afflicted Egypt more than 12,000 years ago:

> A great civilization must have preceded the vast movements of water that passed over Egypt, which leads us to assume that the Sphinx already existed, sculptured in the rock of the west cliff at Giza that Sphinx whose leonine body, except for the head shows indisputable signs of aquatic erosion.[31]

Schwaller's simple observation, which nobody appeared to have taken any notice of before, obviously challenged the Egyptological consensus attributing the Sphinx to Khafre and to the epoch of 2500 BC. What West immediately realized on reading this passage, however, was that, through geology, Schwaller had also offered a way 'virtually to prove the existence of another, and perhaps greater civilization antedating dynastic Egypt – and all other known civilizations – by millennia'.[32]

> If the single fact of the water erosion of the Sphinx could be confirmed, it would in itself overthrow all accepted chronologies of the history of civilization; it would force a drastic re-evaluation of the assumptions of 'progress' – the assumption upon which the whole of modern education is based. It would be difficult to find a single, simple question with graver implications . . .[33]

Not floodwaters

West is right about the implications. If the weathering patterns on the Sphinx can be proved to have been caused by water – and not by wind or sand as Egyptologists maintain – then there is indeed a very serious problem with established chronologies. In order to understand why, we need only remind ourselves that Egypt's climate has not always been as bone dry as it is today and that the erosion patterns to which West and Schwaller are drawing our attention are unique to the 'architectural unit' that Lehner and others define as the 'context' of the Sphinx. From their common weathering features – which are not shared by the other monuments of the Giza necropolis – it is obvious that the structures making up this unit were all built in the same epoch.

But when was that epoch?

West's initial opinion was that:

> There can be no objection in principle to the water-erosion of the Sphinx, since it is agreed that in the past, Egypt suffered radical climatic changes and periodic inundations – by the sea and (in the not so remote past) by tremendous Nile floods. The latter are thought to correspond to the melting of the ice from the last Ice Age. Current thinking puts this date at around 15,000 BC, but periodic great Nile floods are believed to have taken place subsequent to this date. The last of these floods is dated around 10,000 BC. It follows, therefore, that if the great Sphinx has been eroded by water, it must have been constructed prior to the flood or floods responsible for the erosion . . . [34]

The logic is indeed sound 'in principle'. In practice, however, as West was later to admit, 'flood or floods' could not have been responsible for the peculiar kind of erosion seen on the Sphinx:

> The problem is that the Sphinx is deeply weathered up to its neck. This necessitates 60-foot floods (at a minimum) over the whole of the Nile Valley. It was difficult to imagine floods of this magnitude. Worse, if the theory was correct, the inner limestone core-blocks of the so-called Mortuary Temple at the end of the causeway leading from the Sphinx had also been weathered by water, and this meant floods reaching to the base of the Pyramids – another hundred feet or so of floodwaters . . . [35]

Floodwaters, then, could not have eroded the Sphinx. So what had?

Rainfall

In 1989 John West approached Professor Robert Schoch of Boston University. A highly respected geologist, stratigrapher and paleontologist, Schoch's speciality is the weathering of soft rocks very much like the limestone of the Giza plateau. Clearly, says West, he was a man who 'had exactly the kind of expertise needed to confirm or rebut the theory once and for all'.[36]

Schoch was at first sceptical of the idea of a much older Sphinx but changed his mind after making an initial visit to the site in 1990. Although he was unable to gain access to the Sphinx enclosure he could see enough from the tourist viewing platform to confirm that the monument did indeed appear to have been weathered by water. It was also obvious to him that the agency of this weathering had not been floods but 'precipitation'.

'In other words', West explains, 'rainwater was responsible for weathering the Sphinx, not floods . . . Precipitation-induced weathering took care of the problem in a single stroke. The sources I was using for reference talked about these floods in conjunction with long periods of rains, but it hadn't occurred to me, as a non-geologist, that the rains, rather than the periodic floods, were the actual weathering agent . . .'[37]

As we have noted, Schoch got no closer to the Sphinx on his 1990 visit than the tourist viewing platform. At this stage, therefore, his endorsement of West's theory could only be provisional.

Why had the geologist from Boston not been allowed inside the Sphinx enclosure?

The reason was that since 1978 only a handful of Egyptologists had been granted that privilege, with all public access closed off by the Egyptian authorities and a high fence built around the site.

With the support of the Dean of Boston University, Schoch now submitted a formal proposal to the Egyptian Antiquities Organization, requesting permission to carry out a proper geological study of the erosion of the Sphinx.

A rude interruption

It took a long time, but because of his eminent institutional backing, Schoch's proposal was eventually approved by the EAO, creating a brilliant opportunity to get to the bottom of the Sphinx controversy once and for all. John West immediately set about putting together a broadly based scientific team, including a professional geophysicist, Dr Thomas L. Dobecki, from the highly respected Houston consulting firm of McBride-Ratcliff & Associates.[38] There were also to be others who joined 'unofficially': an architect and photographer; two further geologists; an oceanographer and a personal friend of John West's, film-producer Boris Said.[39] Through Said, West had arranged to 'record the ongoing work in a video documentary which would have wide public appeal':[40]

> Since we could expect nothing but opposition from academic Egyptologists and archaeologists a way had to be found to get the theory to the public, if and when Schoch decided the evidence warranted full geological support. Otherwise it would simply be buried, possibly for good . . .[41]

As a way of getting the theory of an ancient rainfall-eroded Sphinx to the public, West's film could hardly have been more successful. When it was first screened on NBC television in the United States in the autumn of 1993 it was watched by 33 million people.

But that is another story. Back in the Sphinx enclosure the first interesting result came from Dobecki, who had conducted seismographic tests around the Sphinx. The sophisticated equipment that he had brought with him picked up numerous indications of 'anomalies and cavities in the bedrock between the paws and along the sides of the Sphinx'.[42] One of these cavities he described as:

> a fairly large feature; it's about nine metres by twelve metres in dimension, and buried less than five metres in depth. Now the regular shape of this – rectangular – is inconsistent with naturally occurring cavities . . . So there's some suggestion that this could be man-made.[43]

With legal access to the enclosure, West recalls, Schoch, too:

> was swiftly dropping conditionals . . . The deeply weathered Sphinx and its ditch wall, and the relatively unweathered or clearly wind-

weathered Old Kingdom tombs to the south (dating from around Khafre's period) were cut from the same member of rock. In Schoch's view it was therefore geologically impossible to ascribe these structures to the same time period. Our scientists were agreed. Only water, specifically precipitation, could produce the weathering we were observing . . .[44]

It was at this crucial moment, while the members of the team were putting together the first independent geological profile of the Sphinx, that Dr Zahi Hawass, the Egyptian Antiquities Organization's Director-General of the Giza Pyramids, fell upon them, suddenly and unexpectedly, like the proverbial ton of bricks.

The team had obtained their permission from Dr Ibrahim Bakr, then the President of the Egyptian Antiquities Organization. What they had not known, however, was that relations between Bakr and Hawass were frosty. Neither had they reckoned with Hawass's energy and ego. Fuming that he had been bypassed by his superior, he accused the Americans of tampering with the monuments:

> I have found out that their work is carried out by installing endoscopes in the Sphinx's body and shooting films for all phases of the work in a propaganda . . . but not in a scientific manner. I therefore suspended the work of this unscientific mission and made a report which was presented to the permanent commission who rejected the mission's work in future . . .[45]

This was putting it mildly. Far from 'suspending' their work, Hawass had virtually thrown the American team off the site. His intervention had come too late, however, to prevent them from gathering the essential geological data that they needed.

When did it rain?

Back in Boston, Schoch got down to work at his laboratory. The results were conclusive and a few months later he was ready to stick his neck out. Indeed to John West's delight he was now prepared fully to endorse the notion of a rain-eroded Sphinx – with all its immense historical implications.

Schoch's case, in brief – which has the full support of palaeo-climatologists – rests on the fact that heavy rainfall of the kind required to cause the characteristic erosion patterns on the Sphinx had stopped falling on Egypt thousands of years before the epoch of 2500 BC in which Egyptologists say that the Sphinx was built. The geological evidence therefore suggests that a *very conservative* estimate of the true construction date of the Sphinx would be somewhere between '7000 to 5000 BC minimum'.[46]

In 7000 to 5000 BC – according to Egyptologists – the Nile valley was populated only by primitive neolithic hunter-gatherers whose 'toolkits' were limited to sharpened flintstones and pieces of stick. If Schoch is right, therefore, then it follows that the Sphinx and its neighbouring temples (which are built out of hundreds of 200-ton limestone blocks) must be the work of an as yet unidentified advanced civilization of antiquity.

The Egyptological reaction?

'That's ridiculous', scoffed Peter Lecovara, assistant curator of the Egyptian Department in Boston's Museum of Fine Arts. 'Thousands of scholars working for hundreds of years have studied this problem and the chronology is pretty much worked out. There are no big surprises in store for us . . .'[47]

Other 'experts' were equally dismissive. According to Carol Redmont, for example, an archaeologist at the University of California's Berkeley campus: 'There is no way this could be true. The people of that region would not have had the technology, the governing institutions or even the will to build such a structure thousands of years before Khafre's reign.'[48]

And the redoubtable Zahi Hawass, who had tried to nip the geological research in the bud in the first place, had this to say about the Schoch–West team and their unorthodox conclusions concerning the antiquity of the Sphinx:

American hallucinations! West is an amateur. There is absolutely no scientific base for any of this. We have older monuments in the same area. They definitely weren't built by men from space or Atlantis. It's nonsense and we won't allow our monuments to be exploited for personal enrichment. The Sphinx is the soul of Egypt'.[49]

John West was not in the least bit surprised by the rhetoric. In his long and lonely quest to mount a proper investigation into the age of the anonymous Sphinx many such brickbats had been thrown at him before. This time, with Schoch's heavyweight support – and the massive exposure of the whole matter on NBC television – he felt vindicated at last. Furthermore it was clear that the Egyptologists were rattled by the intrusion of an empirical science like geology into their normally cosy and exclusive academic territory.

West, however, wanted to take the matter a good deal further than Schoch was prepared to go and felt that the geologist had been too conservative and lenient in his 'minimum' estimate of 7000 to 5000 BC for the age of the Sphinx: 'Here Schoch and I disagree, or rather interpret the same data somewhat differently. Schoch very deliberately takes the most conservative view allowed by the data . . . However I remain convinced that the Sphinx must predate the break-up of the last Ice Age . . .'[50]

In practice this means any time before 15,000 BC – a hunch that West says is based on the complete lack of evidence of a high culture in Egypt in 7000 to 5000 BC. 'If the Sphinx was as recent as 7000–5000 BC,' he argues, 'I think we probably would have other Egyptian evidence of the civilization that carved it.'[51] Since there is no such evidence, West reasons that the civilization responsible for the Sphinx and its neighbouring temples must have disappeared long before 7000–5000 BC: 'The missing other evidence is, perhaps, buried deeper than anyone has looked and/or in places no one has yet explored – along the banks of the ancient Nile perhaps, which is miles from the present Nile, or even at the bottom of the Mediterranean, which was dry during the last Ice Age . . .'[52]

Despite their 'friendly disagreement' as to whether the erosion of the Sphinx indicated a date of 7000 to 5000 BC, or a much more remote period, Schoch and West decided to present an abstract of their research at Giza to the Geological Society of America. They were encouraged by the response. Several hundred geologists agreed with the logic of their contentions and dozens offered practical help and advice to further the investigation.[53]

Even more refreshing was the reaction from the international media. After the GSA meeting articles appeared in dozens of newspapers, and the issue of the Sphinx's age was widely covered by television and radio. 'We were over the fifty-yard line and heading downfield,' recalls West.[54]

As for the matter of his difference of opinion with Schoch about the dating of the monument, he honestly concedes that 'only further research will resolve the question'.[55]

Jury still out

Since 1993 the Egyptian government, on the advice of Western Egyptologists, has not permitted any further geological research or seismic investigations to be undertaken around the Sphinx. This is surprising in view of the momentous implications of Schoch's findings and all the more surprising because his original evidence has not yet been convincingly challenged in any forum. On the contrary, as the years have gone by, the Boston geologist has withstood the rigours of scientific peer review, several times successfully defending his contention that the distinctive weathering visible on the Sphinx, and on the walls of its enclosure – a combination of deep vertical fissures and rolling, undulating, horizontal coves – is 'a classic, textbook example of what happens to a limestone structure when you have rain beating down on it for thousands of years . . .'[56] When set in the context of our knowledge of ancient climates at Giza, he adds, this represents abundant evidence 'that the Great Sphinx predates its traditional attribution of *circa* 2500 BC . . . I'm just following the science where it leads me, and it leads me to conclude that the Sphinx was built much earlier than previously thought.'[57]

Of course it cannot be said that Robert Schoch has *proved* that the monument dates back to the epoch of 7000 to 5000 BC. Nor has John West *proved* the even earlier date that he favours. But then again neither has orthodox Egyptology *proved* that the Sphinx belongs to Khafre and to the epoch of 2500 BC.

In other words, by any rational and reasonable criteria, the jury is still out on the true attribution and antiquity of this extraordinary monument.

The riddle of the Sphinx is still unsolved. And as we see in the next chapter, it is a riddle that encompasses the entire Giza necropolis.

Chapter 3

Mystery Piled upon Mystery

'It is said that the stone [used in the
construction of the Pyramids of Giza] was
conveyed over a great distance . . . and that
the construction was effected by means of
mounds . . . The most remarkable thing is
that, though the constructions were on such
a great scale and the country round about
them consists of nothing but sand, not a
trace remains either of any mound or of the
dressing of the stones, so that they do not
have the appearance of being the slow
handiwork of men but look like a sudden
creation, as though they had been made by
some god and set down bodily in the
surrounding sand.'

Diodorus Siculus, *Book I*, first century BC

The Giza necropolis, site of the Great Sphinx and the three great
Pyramids of Egypt, is, by any standards, an extraordinary architectural and archaeological puzzle. This is not only because of the many
remarkable physical and engineering characteristics of the principal
Pyramids and temples, but also because all of these monuments are
essentially uninscribed and anonymous. Like the Sphinx, therefore,
they are difficult to date by objective means. Like the Sphinx, too,
their attribution to specific Pharaohs by Egyptologists is necessarily
based upon a somewhat arbitrary interpretation of contextual clues.

The three great Pyramids, for example, are conventionally
assigned as the tombs of Khufu, Khafre and Menkaure – three
Pharaohs of the Fourth Dynasty. Yet no Pharaoh's body has ever been
found in any of these monuments and while there are some so-called

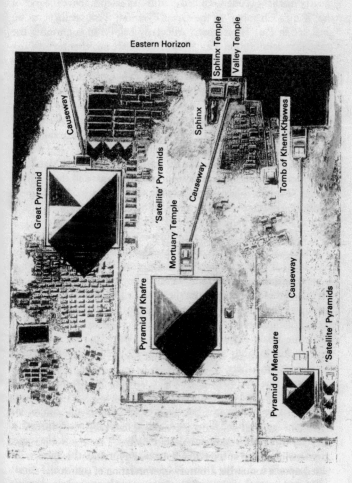

Eastern Horizon

Sphinx Temple

Valley Temple

Causeway

Sphinx

Causeway

Great Pyramid

'Satellite' Pyramids

Mortuary Temple

Tomb of Khent-Khawes

Pyramid of Khafre

Causeway

Pyramid of Menkaure

'Satellite' Pyramids

2. Overhead view of the principal monuments of the Giza necropolis.

'quarry marks' – crudely daubed graffiti – in cavities above the roof of the 'King's Chamber' in the Great Pyramid, these writings, as we shall see in Part II, are not particularly helpful in confirming the orthodox identification with Khufu. There are no other texts of any kind in the Great Pyramid, or in the Pyramids attributed to Khafre and Menkaure. The three small 'satellite' Pyramids lined up along the eastern face of the Great Pyramid, and the three other satellite Pyramids lying near the south-western edge of the site, are similarly bereft of inscriptions. Some Fourth Dynasty artefacts were found inside these six 'satellite' structures but there is no guarantee that these artefacts are contemporary with the monuments.

The same problem applies to the statues of Khafre and Menkaure that were found in the latter's 'Mortuary' Temple and the former's 'Valley' Temple. These statues are the only evidence supporting the attribution of these otherwise anonymous and uninscribed edifices to the two Pharaohs in question. In all logic, however, they only suggest that attribution. They certainly do not confirm it. Khafre and Menkaure, in other words, *might* have built the temples. But it is also possible that they took over pre-existing structures which they had inherited from an earlier time, and that they adapted, renovated and furnished these structures with their own statues in order to suit their own purposes. After all, we do not attribute the building of London's Trafalgar Square to Nelson just because his statue stands there. By the same token Egyptologists could be going too far when they attribute the building of the Valley Temple to Khafre on the basis of his statue found there.

Indeed, this is an observation that is true for the Giza necropolis as a whole. The undoubted connection that it has with the Fourth Dynasty is not in dispute, but the precise nature of this connection remains unproven. To be sure, there are huge quantities of unmistakable and heavily inscribed Fourth Dynasty *mastaba* tombs lying east and west of the Great Pyramid and west of the Sphinx, but the contention that the Pyramids themselves are 'tombs and tombs only' is guesswork. It could be the case, as has happened elsewhere in the world, that an ancient and sacred site designed and built for one purpose was subsequently taken over and re-used for another rather different purpose. We might imagine, for example, that the Pyramids and the other principal monuments surrounding them were originally intended to fulfil purely ritual, ceremonial and religious functions and that the practice of burying the dead there – principally Fourth Dynasty queens and nobles judging by the identifiable remains that have survived – was a later adaptation effected by people who were unconnected to the genesis of the site but who sought to be interred in a place that was imbued with ancient prestige and sanctity. A Western analogy is the practice of burying the remains of particularly favoured individuals under the flagstones of medieval cathedrals – a practice that continues to this day, but that does not lead us to conclude that these cathedrals are tombs or even that they were built primarily for the purposes of burial.

Impossible engineering

Approaching Giza from the east, through the modern Arab village of Nazlet-el-Sammam, one comes first to the Great Sphinx – which rears its grizzled head above an ugly bus-park and a crowd of tourist shops and cafés. Fortunately the ground has been cleared for a distance of about two hundred metres in front of the monument, giving an open view of the enormous and unusual architectural complex that has surrounded it since time immemorial.

This complex consists of the so-called 'Sphinx Temple' and the 'Valley Temple of Khafre', the former lying immediately to the east of the Sphinx, and directly overlooked by it, the latter lying a little to the south of the Sphinx Temple, separated from it by a narrow corridor but in direct alignment – a bit like two chunky, detached houses standing side by side.

The layout of these monuments, and the relationship that both of them have to the Sphinx and its enclosure, are best appreciated from the plans and photographs reproduced herewith. The Valley Temple is the larger of the two, being almost square and measuring approximately 130 feet along each side; the Sphinx Temple is more pronouncedly rhomboidal with side lengths of about 100 feet.

Originally around 40 feet high, both monuments are built out of massive limestone core-blocks and both were at one time fitted with inner and outer casings of granite. These casings and much of the core masonry have been removed from the Sphinx Temple, leaving it in a very dilapidated state. By contrast the Valley Temple is still largely intact. Both monuments are roofless, lacking their original ceiling beams. In the case of the Valley Temple, however, sixteen original interior columns and architraves remain in place in the T-shaped central hall, creating graceful patterns of light and shadow.

The unifying features of these ancient and anonymous structures are the stark, undecorated austerity of the building style, and the use throughout of ponderous megaliths – many of which are estimated to weigh in the range of 200 tons apiece.[1] There are no *small* blocks here at all: every single piece of stone is enormous – the least of them weighing more than 50 tons – and it is difficult to understand how such monsters could have been lifted and manoeuvred into place by the ancient Egyptians. Indeed, even today, contractors using the latest construction technology would face formidable challenges if they were commissioned to produce exact replicas of the Sphinx Temple and the Valley Temple.

The problems are manifold but stem mainly from the extremely large size of the blocks – which can be envisaged in terms of their dimensions and weight as a series of diesel locomotive engines stacked one on top of the other. Such loads simply cannot be hoisted by the typical tower and hydraulic cranes that we are familiar with from building sites in our cities. These cranes, which are pieces of advanced technology, can generally 'pick' a maximum load of 20 tons at what is called 'minimum span' – i.e. at the closest distance to the tower along the 'boom' or 'arm' of the crane. The longer the span the smaller the load and at 'maximum span' the limit is around 5 tons.

Loads exceeding 50 tons require special cranes. Furthermore, there are few cranes in the world today that would be capable of picking 200-ton blocks of quarried limestone. Such cranes would normally have to be of the 'bridge' or 'gantry' type, often seen in factories and at major industrial ports where they are used to move large pieces of equipment and machinery such as bulldozers, military tanks, or steel shipping containers. Built with structural steel members and powered with massive electric motors, the majority of these cranes have a load limit of under 100 tons. In short, a commission to put together a temple out of 200-ton blocks would be a

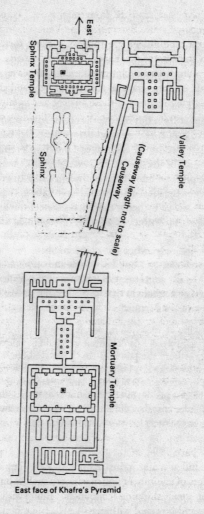

3. The Great Sphinx and the architectural complex that surrounds it:
Sphinx Temple, Valley Temple, Causeway (foreshortened and not to
scale) and Mortuary Temple.

most unusual and very taxing job, even for modern heavy-load and crane specialists.

In the United States there are presently only two land-based cranes of the 'counterweight and boom' type able to handle loads in the 200-ton range. Recently one was brought in to a Long Island construction site to lift a 200-ton boiler into a factory. The crane has a boom 220 feet long (at one end of which is 160-ton concrete counterweight which keeps it from tipping over). A crew of 20 men had to work for six weeks to prepare the ground before the boiler could be lifted.[2]

The biggest technical challenge of building a replica of the Valley Temple would be the need to lift *hundreds* of such weights and to do so within the physical limitations of the Giza site. In order to overcome that challenge the ideal crane would have to be of the gantry or bridge type, made *mobile* by being mounted on steel tracks – which would have to be set up within, or around, the confined area of the temple structure itself.

Not surprisingly, when the crane engineer responsible for lifting the 200-ton boiler on Long Island was shown photographs and given technical details concerning the blocks of the Valley Temple – and asked whether he thought that he could hoist similar blocks into place with his crane – he replied:

> I'm looking at what you're showing me here, and looking at the distances involved. I don't know if we would be able to pick the 200-ton blocks from the positions that I see available to us . . . In my business we pick heavy loads, and we look to see how heavy loads were picked by other people before us. And seeing how they moved these heavy blocks, 200-ton blocks, thousands and thousands of years ago, I have no idea how they did this job. It's a mystery and it'll probably always be a mystery to me, and maybe to everybody.[3]

How, why, when?

Mystery or not, the Valley Temple and the Sphinx Temple stand at Giza as mute testimony to the fact that certain builders in antiquity did know how to pick 200-ton loads, and did have the technical wherewithal to do the job. Furthermore, although it is reasonably certain that they did not do it with gantry or any other such cranes, we are in darkness as to how they did do it. Confronted by such questions

Egyptologists tend to speak in vague and general terms of 'earth ramps' and 'unlimited manpower'.[4] Engineers, however are required to be more specific and to address themselves to the issues of the precise kinds of ramps that would have been required – up which such big blocks could have been dragged – and the precise numbers of men that would have been needed to drag them.

No detailed technical studies have ever been undertaken at Giza concerning the logistics of building the Sphinx and Valley Temples. The Pyramids, however – which Egyptologists also believe were built with ramps – have been studied quite closely by a number of highly qualified architects and engineers.[5] What these studies have indicated is that the maximum feasible gradient for a construction ramp up which heavy loads could be hauled by men on foot is 1 in 10.[6] In the case of the Great Pyramid, which originally reached a height of 481 feet, this would have called for a ramp 4800 feet long and almost three times as massive as the Pyramid itself.[7]

Of course, such a problem does not apply where the Sphinx Temple and the Valley Temple are concerned because their original constructed height was much lower than that of the Pyramids and they therefore could have been approached by relatively short 1-in-10 ramps. The fearsome mass and weight of the many 200-ton blocks found in these temples, however, rules out the use of *any* ramp made of materials less stable than the limestone ashlars of the temples themselves.[8]

Let us assume, then, that solid stone ramps were used and then later dismantled and cleared away. The question now becomes: how many men would be required to haul hundreds of 200-ton blocks up such ramps? To get this problem into perspective it is helpful to realize that a block of 200 tons represents a load roughly equivalent to 300 family-sized automobiles (each with an average weight of three-quarters of a ton).

Again, we do not have a technical study on the Sphinx and Valley Temples to refer to. Fortunately, however, a relevant study has been undertaken at the Great Pyramid where the French master engineer Jean Leherou Kerisel, a consultant for the building of the Cairo Metro, worked out the logistics of hauling into place the 70-ton blocks that were used in the construction of the so-called King's Chamber.

According to his calculations the job could just about have been done – although with enormous difficulty – with teams of 600 men arranged in ranks across a very wide ramp buttressed against one face of the Pyramid.[9] From this it follows that teams 1800 men strong would have been required to haul the Valley Temple blocks. But could 1800 men have been effectively harnessed to such dense and relatively compact loads (the maximum dimensions of each block are 30 feet by 10 feet by 12 feet)? And more to the point, since the temple walls do not exceed 130 feet along each side, how likely is it that such large teams could have been organized to work efficiently – or at all – in the limited space available? Assuming a minimum of three feet of horizontal space per man, each rank of haulers could not have contained more than fifty men. To make up the total of 1800 men needed to move a 200-ton block, therefore, would have called for no less than thirty-six ranks of men pulling in unison, to be harnessed to each block.

The potential complications that might have arisen are mind-boggling. Even assuming they could all have been overcome, however, the next question that presents itself is perhaps the most intriguing of all.

Why?

Why bother?

Why specify temples built out of unwieldy 200-ton blocks when it would have been much easier, much more feasible and just as aesthetically pleasing, to use smaller blocks of say two or three tons each?

There are really only two answers. Either the people who designed these hulking edifices had knowledge of some technique that made it *easy* for them to quarry, manipulate and position enormous pieces of stone, or their way of thinking was utterly different from our own – in which case their motives and priorities are unlikely to be fathomable in terms of normal cross-cultural comparisons.

We also need to ask *when* the work was done.

As noted earlier, the Sphinx Temple and the Valley Temple are both anonymous monuments. And although it is certain that use was made of the latter for Khafre's funerary rituals, there is no proof that he built it. On the contrary, if Professor Robert Schoch's geological evidence is correct, then it is quite certain that Khafre did *not* build either of these structures. This is so because the Sphinx itself was made by hewing a deep horseshoe-shaped trench out of the bedrock of the Giza plateau, leaving a central core which was then carved into shape, and because geologists have been able to prove that the limestone megaliths used in both temples came from the trench and were thus quarried at the same time as the Sphinx.[10] It therefore follows, if the Sphinx is indeed thousands of years older than Egyptologists think it is, that the temples must also be thousands of years older.

What we may be looking at here are the fingerprints of highly sophisticated and perhaps even technological people capable of awe-inspiring architectural and engineering feats at a time when no civilization of any kind is supposed to have existed anywhere on earth.

Supportive of this possibility is the fact that the megaliths of the temples demonstrate precisely the same apparent precipitation-induced weathering features as the Sphinx itself. And it is of interest to note that the surviving granite casing blocks seem to have been carved on their inner faces to fit over the limestone core-blocks *at a time when these were already heavily marked by erosion.* Since the granite casing has the look of other Old Kingdom Egyptian architecture (while the limestone core-blocks do not) this may be taken as further evidence of the theory that an ancient, revered and much-eroded structure was restored and renovated by the Old Kingdom Pharaohs. Robert Schoch certainly favours this view. 'I remain convinced,' comments the Boston University geology professor, 'that the backs of the Old Kingdom granite facing stones were carved to match or complement the earlier weathering features seen on the surfaces of the core limestone blocks of the temples.'[11]

Memorials mighty

The famous black diorite statue of Khafre that now stands in the Cairo Museum was found upside down in a twenty-foot deep pit in the floor of the antechamber that leads into the Valley Temple's T-shaped central hall. Walking through this hall, hemmed in by immensely strong and thick limestone and granite walls, the visitor will eventually come to a high, narrow passageway on the north-western side of the structure. This passage leads out of the rear of the temple, along the southern side of the Sphinx trench – where it overlooks the Sphinx – and thence joins with the massive 'causeway' that runs for more than 1000 feet up the slope of the Giza plateau linking the Valley Temple to the Mortuary Temple and thence to the eastern face of the second Pyramid.

The causeways – one for each of the three Pyramids – are important features of the Giza necropolis, though all have fallen into an advanced state of disrepair. Some 20 feet wide, and varying in length from quarter of a mile up to half a mile, they each originally linked a Mortuary Temple to a Valley Temple. Today, however, the only relatively intact complex is that attributed to Khafre described above. In the case of the third Pyramid, the Valley Temple is now completely gone but the megalithic ruins of the Mortuary Temple are still in place. In the case of the Great Pyramid the only remaining part of the Mortuary Temple is its basalt floor, while the ruins of the Valley Temple – if any survive – are buried under the village of Nazlet-el-Sammam.

The three causeways, like the Mortuary and Valley Temples, are fashioned out of huge blocks of limestone. Indeed all of these prodigious structures are clearly 'of a piece' from a design point of view and seem to have been the work of builders who thought like gods or giants. There is about them an overwhelming, weary, aching sense of antiquity and it is certainly not hard to imagine that they might be the leavings of a lost civilization. In this regard we are reminded of *The Sacred Sermon*, a 'Hermetic' text of Egyptian origin that speaks with awe of lordly men 'devoted to the growth of wisdom' who lived 'before the Flood' and whose civilization was destroyed: 'And there shall be memorials mighty of their handiworks upon the earth, leaving dim trace behind when cycles are renewed . . .' [12]

There is another feature of the causeways, of intense interest to us, which we shall explore in detail in Parts III and IV – their orientation. The causeway of the Third Pyramid, like the gaze of the Sphinx, is targeted due east. The causeway of the second Pyramid points 14 degrees south of due east. The causeway of the Great Pyramid points 14 degrees north of due east. The arrangement is precise, geometrical,

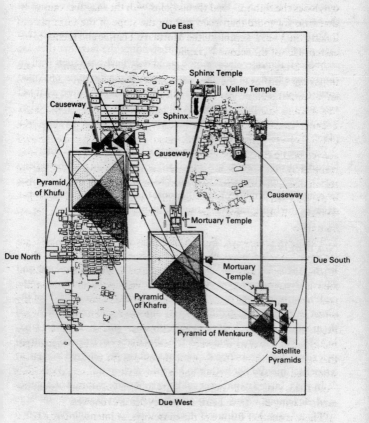

4. The artificial 'Horizon of Giza'.

obviously deliberate, with each significant structure bearing a designed relationship to every other structure – and the whole contained within a large, circular artificial 'horizon' that is apparently centred on the apex of the second Pyramid with its rim lying just to the west of the rump of the Sphinx.

Orthodox Egyptological opinion concerning the causeways is that they were ceremonial roads. Notwithstanding the fact that they are technological masterpieces which could only have been built with an enormous expense of ingenuity and effort at the direction of skilled surveyors and architects, the assumption is that they were used *just once* for the funerary journey of the Pharaoh's corpse from Valley Temple to Mortuary Temple where his final embalming rituals took place.

Perhaps so. As we shall show in Parts III and IV, however, there are features of these causeways which suggest that they may have been used many times by many different Pharaohs and that they have their technical and symbolic origins in events that occurred long before the dawn of the historical civilization of Egypt.

Not purely symbolic boats

In the 1850s Sir Richard Francis Burton, the British explorer and adventurer, visited Egypt and the Pyramids of Giza. He noted some odd 'rhomboidal depressions' lying parallel to the eastern side of the Great Pyramid, close to the end of its causeway, and made sketches of them which are now kept in the British Museum.[13] Some years later, in 1881, Sir William Flinders Petrie, the 'Father of British Egyptology', also saw these strange depressions but simply referred to them as 'trenches' and did not bother to have them cleared.[14]

In 1893, buried in pits near a relatively obscure pyramid on another site, the famous French Egyptologist de Morgan discovered six large wooden boats, but little was made of this. In 1901 another French Egyptologist, Chassinat, discovered a 'rhomboidal pit' near the pyramid of Djedefra at Abu Roash. After noting that it very much resembled the pits at Giza near the Great Pyramid, he wrote: 'their purpose is unknown, as is the case here.'[15]

Ancient Egyptian funerary texts are strewn with references to boats

– notably the various solar and divine vessels on which the deceased hoped to voyage in the cosmic afterlife (the 'boat of millions of years' for example, the 'bark of Osiris', and the 'bark of Ra'). Carvings, drawings and paintings of such 'boats' and 'barks', with their characteristic high prows and sterns, adorn the walls of many an ancient tomb in Egypt and their symbolic and religious functions were understood well before the close of the nineteenth century. Nevertheless it was only when the German archaeologist Ludwig Borchardt excavated an obvious and unmistakable boat made of bricks near the sun-temple and pyramids at Abusir, that it was recognized that the mysterious 'rhomboidal pits' were in fact boats – or at any rate representations of boats, or graves for boats.

Since Borchardt's time, several other boat pits have been found – by Selim Hassan in 1933, for example, and by Walter Emery in 1937. Finally, in 1954, Kamal el-Mallakh discovered something quite breathtaking – a partially disassembled cedarwood boat, more than 143 feet long, buried in a pit on the south side of the Great Pyramid. Much more recently another vessel of similar dimensions has been located in an adjacent pit. As yet unexcavated, it is apparently to be studied by a Japanese consortium.

The fact that Egyptologists took a long time to notice that there were large boats buried at Giza does not necessarily mean that their analysis of the function of these boats is completely wrong. The idea is that the majestic vessels were intended in some 'primitive', 'magical', 'superstitious', 'half-savage' way to serve as symbolic vehicles on which the souls of dead Pharaohs could sail into Heaven. This interpretation is consistent with the ancient Egyptian funerary texts and there can be little doubt that the boats – 'solar boats' as the Egyptologists call them – were indeed intended to play a part in symbolic celestial journeys. As we shall see in Parts III and IV, however, it is possible that the precise nature and purpose of those journeys may have been much more complex and significant than has hitherto been recognized.

Meanwhile, standing in front of the 'solar boat' excavated from beside the south face of the Great Pyramid in 1954 it is hard not to note the marks of wear and tear on the keel and gangplank and the numerous other clear signs that this elegant cedarwood vessel, with its high curving prow and stern, was sailed many times on water.[16]

If it was purely symbolic, why was it used?

And why was it necessary to have such an elaborate and technically accomplished[17] craft for symbolic purposes? Wouldn't a symbolic vessel – such as the brick boats and boat 'graves' found at other Pyramids – have done just as well?

The Pyramids

The dominant features of the Giza necropolis are, of course, its three great Pyramids – those conventionally attributed to Khufu, Khafre and Menkaure. In a sense they are what the entire, vast enterprise proclaims itself to be all about, what the causeways lead towards, what the 'solar boats' are buried beside. Sprawling diagonally across the meridian axis of the site, it is they, above all else, that the geometrical 'Horizon of Giza' appears to have been designed to circumscribe. Nothing about them is accidental: their original constructed heights, their angles of slope, the measurement of their perimeters, even the pattern in which they are carefully laid out on the ground – all of these things are purposive and laden with meaning.

Because we have described the Pyramids in such detail in other publications[18] – where we have also looked in depth into many of their technical and engineering puzzles – we will not trouble the reader with superfluous details here. Some basic statistics and a few points of analysis are, however, unavoidable at this stage.

The Great Pyramid was originally 481.3949 feet in height (now reduced to just a little over 450 feet) and its four sides each measure some 755 feet in length at the base. The second Pyramid was originally slightly lower – with a designed height of 471 feet – and has sides measuring just under 708 feet in length. The third Pyramid stands some 215 feet tall and has a side length at the base of 356 feet.

When they were built the second Pyramid and the Great Pyramid were both entirely covered in limestone facing blocks, several courses of which still adhere to the upper levels of the former. The Great Pyramid, by contrast, is today almost completely bereft of its casing. We know from historical accounts, however, that it was once clad from bottom to top with smoothly-polished Tura limestone which was shaken loose by a powerful earthquake that devastated the Cairo area in AD 1301. The newly exposed core masonry was then used for some years as a crude local quarry to rebuild the shattered mosques and palaces of Cairo.

All the Arab commentators prior to the fourteenth century tell us that the Great Pyramid's casing was a marvel of architecture that caused the edifice to glow brilliantly under the Egyptian sun. It consisted of an estimated 22 acres of 8-foot-thick blocks, each weighing in the region of 16 tons, 'so subtilly jointed that one would have said that it was a single slab from top to bottom'.[19] A few surviving sections can still be seen today at the base of the monument. When they were studied in 1881 by Sir W. M. Flinders Petrie, he noted with astonishment that 'the mean thickness of the joints is 0.020 of an inch; and, therefore, the mean variation of the cutting of the stone from a straight line and from a true square is but 0.01 of an inch on a length of 75 inches up the face, an amount of accuracy equal to the most modern opticians' straight-edges of such a length.'

Another detail that Petrie found very difficult to explain was that the blocks had been carefully and precisely cemented together: 'To merely place such stones in exact contact at the sides would be careful work, but to do so with cement in the joint seems almost impossible . . .'[20]

Also 'almost impossible', since the mathematical value pi (3.14) is not supposed to have been calculated by any civilization until the Greeks stumbled upon it in the third century BC,[21] is the fact the designed height of the Great Pyramid – 481.3949 feet – bears the same relationship to its base perimeter (3023.16 feet) as does the circumference of any circle to its radius. This relationship is $2\,pi$ (i.e. 481.3949 feet $\times 2 \times 3.14 = 3023.16$ feet).

Equally 'impossible' – at any rate for a people like the ancient Egyptians who are supposed to have known nothing about the true shape and size of our planet – is the relationship, in a scale of 1:43,200, that exists between the dimensions of the Pyramid and the dimensions of the earth. Setting aside for the moment the question of whether we are dealing with coincidence here, it is a simple fact, verifiable on any pocket calculator, that if you take the monument's original height (481.3949 feet) and multiply it by 43,200 you get a quotient of 3938.685 miles. This is an underestimate by just 11 miles of the true figure for the polar radius of the earth (3949 miles) worked out by the best modern methods. Likewise, if you take the monument's perimeter at the base (3023.16 feet) and multiply this figure by 43,200 then you get 24,734.94 miles – a result that is within 170 miles of the true equatorial circumference of the earth (24,902 miles). Moreover, although 170 miles sounds quite a lot, it amounts, in relation to the earth's total circumference, to a minus-error of only three quarters of a single per cent.

High precision

Such fine errors are within the general margins of tolerance found at the Great Pyramid. Indeed, although it has a footprint of over 13 acres, and consists of some six and a half million tons of limestone and granite blocks, the sheer mass and size of this monster of monuments are not its most impressive characteristics. More astounding by far is the incredible high-tech precision that is built into every aspect of its design.

Before going into the details, let us consider the implications of very fine precision in very large monuments.

An analogy with the simple wrist-watch helps. If you are after an accuracy of, say, a few seconds per week, then an ordinary quartz watch costing fifty dollars or less will do the trick. If you want accuracy to within a fraction of a second per year, however, then the quartz watch will no longer serve and you will have to turn to something of the order of an atomic clock.

A similar situation applies in the construction industry. If you are building a brick wall that is to appear straight within plus or minus 1 degree per 100 metres and the whole roughly directed due north, then any good bricklayer should be able to meet your specification. However, if your requirement is for a wall that is straight within 1 arc minute per 100 metres and directed *exactly* due north, then you are going to need a laser theodolite, an ordnance survey map accurate to 10 metres, and a highly qualified team of professionals including an expert setting-out engineer, an astronomer, a surveyor, several master-masons and a week or so to ensure that the precision you are aiming for has in fact been achieved.

Such 'atomic clock' precision was achieved by the builders of the Great Pyramid more than 4500 years ago. This is not a matter of historical speculation, or of theory, but of plain, measurable facts.

For example the earth's equatorial circumference of 24,902 miles works out at around 132 million feet, with the result that a degree of latitude at the equator is equivalent to approximately 366,600 feet (i.e. 132 million feet divided by 360 degrees). Each degree is divided into 60 arc minutes, which means that 1 arc minute represents just over 6100 feet on the earth's surface, and each arc minute is then further subdivided into 60 arc seconds – with the result that 1 arc second is equivalent to a distance of about 101 feet. This system of measuring by degrees is not a modern convention but rather an *inheritance* of scientific thinking, connected to 'base 60' mathematics, that dates back to the remotest antiquity.[22] Nobody knows where, or when, it originated.[23] It seems, however, to have been employed in the geodetic and astronomical calculations that were used to locate the Great Pyramid – for the monument is positioned barely a mile to the south of latitude 30, i.e. almost exactly one third of the way between the

5. Geodetic location of the Great Pyramid of Giza on latitude 30 degrees north (one third of the way between the equator and the north pole) and at the centre of the world's habitable landmasses.

north pole and the equator.[24]

It is unlikely that this choice of location could have come about by chance. Moreover, because no suitable site for such a massive structure exists a mile or so to the north, it would be inadvisable to assume that the fractional offset from the thirtieth parallel could have been caused by a surveying error on the part of the Pyramid builders.

This offset amounts to 1 arc minute and 9 arc seconds – since the Pyramid's true latitude is 29 degrees 58' 51″. Interestingly, however, as a former Astronomer Royal of Scotland has observed:

> 'If the original designer had wished that men should see with their bodily, rather than their mental eyes, the pole of the sky from the foot of the Great Pyramid, at an altitude before them of 30 degrees, he would have had to take account of the refraction of the atmosphere; and that would have necessitated the building standing not at latitude 30 degrees, but at latitude 29 degrees 58' 22″.'[25]

In other words the monument turns out to be situated less than half an arc minute to the north of *astronomical* latitude 30, uncorrected for atmospheric refraction. Any 'error' involved is thus reduced to less than half of one-sixtieth of one degree – a hair's breadth in terms of the earth's circumference as a whole.

The same obsessive concern with accuracy is found in the orderly evenness of the Pyramid's base:

Length of West side:	755 feet 9.1551 inches
Length of North side:	755 feet 4.9818 inches
Length of East side:	755 feet 10.4937 inches
Length of South side:	756 feet 0.9739 inches[26]

The variation between the longest and shortest sides is therefore less than 8 inches – about one tenth of 1 per cent – quite an amazing feat when we consider that we are measuring a distance of over 9000 inches carpeted with thousands of huge limestone blocks weighing several tons each.

There is no sign that the ancient Pyramid builders were in any way daunted by the task of maintaining such fastidious standards of symmetry on such a grand scale. On the contrary, as though willingly seeking out additional technical challenges, they went on to equip the monument with corners set at almost perfect right-angles. The variation from 90 degrees is just 0 degrees 00' 02" at the north-west corner, 0 degrees 03' 02" at the north-east corner, 0 degrees 03' 33" at the south-east corner, and 0 degrees 00' 33" at the south-west corner.[27]

This, it must be conceded, is not just 'atomic clock' accuracy but the Rolex, BMW, Mercedes Benz, Rolls-Royce and IBM of building engineering all rolled into one.

And there is more.

It is fairly well known that the Pyramid was aligned by its architects to the cardinal points (with its north face directed north, its east face directed east, etc., etc.). Less well known is just how eerily exact is the *precision* of these alignments – with the average deviation from true being only a little over 3 arc minutes (i.e. about 5 per cent of a single degree).[28]

Why such meticulousness?

Why such rigour?

Why should even the most megalomaniacal of Pharaohs have cared whether his massive 'tomb' was aligned within 3 arc minutes of true north – or indeed within a whole degree of true north? To the naked-eye observer it is virtually impossible to determine such a deviation. Indeed most of us could not spot a misalignment within 3 whole degrees (180 arc minutes), let alone within 3 arc minutes (and some people have trouble telling the general direction of north at all). So the question has to be asked: what was all this incredible precision for? Why did the builders burden themselves with so much extra work and difficulty when the effects of their additional labours would not be visible to the naked eye anyway?

They must, one assumes, have had a powerful motive to create what is truly a miracle of the surveyor's art.

And what makes this miracle all the more remarkable is the fact that it was not performed on a perfectly flat area of ground, as one might expect, but with a massive natural mound, or hill, left exactly in the middle of the site on which the Great Pyramid was being erected. Estimated to be almost 30 feet high – as tall as a two-storey house – and positioned dead centre over the base area (of which it occupies approximately 70 per cent), this primeval mound was skilfully incorporated into the lower courses of the growing edifice. No doubt its presence has contributed down the epochs to the structure's legendary stability. It is extremely difficult, however, to understand how the ancient surveyors were able to square the base of the Pyramid in its early and most important stages with the mound so solidly in the way (squaring the base normally involves taking repeated diagonal measurements across the corners).[29] All that we can say for sure is that the base *is* square and that the monument *is* locked into the cardinal axes of our planet with great care and precision.

Chambers and passageways

The second and third Pyramids have relatively simple internal chambers and passageway systems – the former having one principal chamber just below ground level, positioned centrally under the apex of the monument, the latter having three main chambers, cut a little more deeply into the bedrock but again positioned centrally under the apex of the monument. The entrances to both Pyramids are in their north faces and take the form of cramped passageways sloping downwards at an angle of 26 degrees, before levelling off to join horizontal corridors under the monument.

The internal structure of the Great Pyramid, by contrast, is much more complex, with an elaborate arrangement of passageways and galleries – sloping up and down again at 26 degrees – and with three principal internal chambers. Of these latter only one, the 'Subterranean Chamber', is below ground level. The other two – the so-called 'Queen's Chamber' and 'King's Chamber' – are both located in the heart of the monument's superstructure at substantial altitudes above the ground.

The layout of these internal features is best appreciated from the diagram printed on page 45. Chief amongst them, surmounted only by Davison's Chamber (and above that by the four so-called 'relieving chambers' which contain the 'quarry marks' mentioned earlier) is the rectangular red-granite room, now famous as the 'King's Chamber'. It proved to be completely devoid of either treasures or inscriptions, or the body of a king, when it was first entered by Calif Al Mamoun in the ninth century AD. Measuring 34 feet 4 inches in length, 17 feet 2 inches in width, and 19 feet 1 inch in height it is located about 150 feet vertically above the base of the Pyramid. Its many mysteries are too

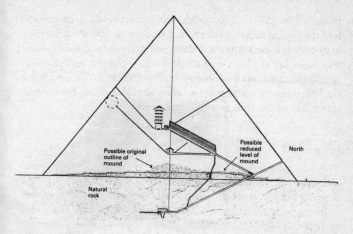

6. Cross-section of the Great Pyramid of Egypt showing the natural mound of bedrock that is known to be built into its lower courses.

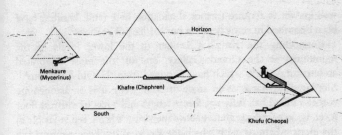

7. Internal corridors and passageways of the three Pyramids of Giza.

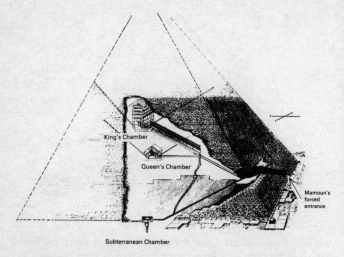

8. Principal internal features of the Great Pyramid. The entrance in the
north face known as 'Mamoun's Hole' was forced by Arab explorers in the
ninth century AD. At this time the exterior facing blocks of the Pyramid
were still intact, hiding the true entrance from sight.

well known to require further elucidation here (and, besides, have
been described in some detail in our earlier publications[30]).

Connecting the King's Chamber to the lower levels of the
monument is the Grand Gallery, one of 'the most celebrated
architectural works which have survived from the Old Kingdom'.[31]
Sloping downwards at an angle of 26 degrees, it is an astonishing
corbel-vaulted hall fully 153 feet in length and 7 feet in width at floor
level. Its lofty ceiling, 28 feet above the visitor's head, is just visible in
the electric lighting with which the Pyramid has been equipped in
modern times.

At the base of the Grand Gallery a horizontal passage, 3 feet 9
inches high and 127 feet long, runs due south into the 'Queen's
Chamber'. Again found empty by Mamoun, this is a smaller room
than the King's Chamber, measuring 18 feet 10 inches from east to
west and 17 feet 2 inches from north to south. Reaching a height of 20

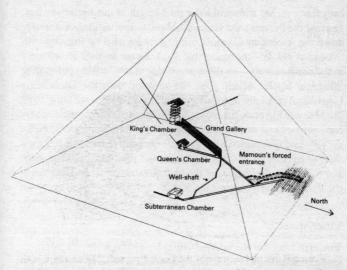

King's Chamber Grand Gallery

Queen's Chamber

Mamoun's forced
entrance

Well-shaft

Subterranean Chamber

North

9. Detail of the corridors, chambers and shafts of the Great Pyramid.

feet 5 inches, the ceiling is gabled (whereas it is flat in the King's
Chamber) and there is a large corbelled niche of unknown function
just south of the centre line in the east wall.

Returning along the horizontal passageway to its junction with the
base of the Grand Gallery the visitor will note, behind a modern iron
grille, the narrow and uninviting mouth of the 'Well-Shaft' – a near
vertical tunnel, often less than 3 feet in diameter, that eventually joins
up with the Descending Corridor, almost 100 feet below ground level.
How the tunnelers, encysted in solid rock, were able to home in so
accurately on their target remains a mystery. Mysterious, too, is the
true function of all these odd systems of interconnecting 'ducts' which
lead busily hither and thither inside the body of the monument, like
the circuits of some great machine.

Sloping downwards from the Grand Gallery, and extending it in
the direction of the ground at the continuing angle of 26 degrees, is
another corridor. Known (from the point of view of those entering the
Pyramid) as the Ascending Corridor, it measures 3 feet 11 inches high

by 3 feet 5 inches wide and has a total length of just under 129 feet. Leaving the Pyramid, the visitor is obliged to ape-walk uncomfortably down the Ascending Corridor until the point where it joins up with 'Mamoun's Hole' – the tunnel that the Arabs cut for their forced entry in the ninth century – on the western side of two hulking red-granite 'plugging blocks' which mask the junction with the Descending Corridor. At the bottom of this 350-foot-long corridor, off limits to all but *bona fide* Egyptologists (and those willing to bribe the increasingly hard-pressed and demoralized Inspectors and *ghafirs* responsible for the day-to-day adminstration of Giza) is a truly remarkable feature – the Subterranean Chamber that nestles in solid bedrock more than 100 feet below the surface of the plateau (and almost 600 feet below the Pyramid's lofty summit platform).

Inner space

The first thing that the interpid visitor should do, after gaining access to the Descending Corridor, is to climb up it a few feet in the direction of the Pyramid's true entrance. Now covered with an iron grille, this entrance is located in the monument's north face, nine courses above and 24 feet to the east of 'Mamoun's Hole' (through which all members of the public enter the Pyramid today).

Here, at the point in the ceiling of the Descending Corridor where the mouth of the Ascending Corridor was hewn upwards, it is possible to inspect the bottom end of the lowermost of the two plugging blocks. It is as firmly jammed in place today as it was when Mamoun's diggers first encountered it in the ninth century, and it is easy to understand why its presence there encouraged them to tunnel round it into the softer limestone, seeking a way past the obstacle and into the upper reaches of whatever lay beyond.

Perhaps this was exactly what the Pyramid builders had 'programmed' those early explorers to do. After all, if you see that a huge chunk of granite has been hauled into place to block what is obviously an upwards-sloping corridor, then it is only human nature to try to get into that corridor – which Mamoun's men did.

More than a thousand years later, tourists and archaeologists still follow the trail that those pioneering Arabs blazed around the plugging blocks into the main north-south axis of the Pyramid's system of passageways. And though there have been all manner of hackings and tunnellings in search of further passageways (in the floors and walls of the King's and Queen's Chambers, for example), the plugs at the base of the Ascending Corridor have never subsequently been disturbed.

This is an understandable oversight if one is satisfied that the sole function of these plugs was to block the Ascending Corridor in a north-south direction. Why, however, has no one ever tried to find out if anything lies behind their *eastern* aspect?[32] As well as having the same height and width as the Ascending Corridor, thus filling it completely, each of the plugs is about four feet in length – and thus easily long enough to conceal the entrance to a second and completely separate passageway system branching off at right angles towards the east.

There is certainly room for such a second system inside the Great Pyramid – and for much else besides. Indeed it has been calculated that as many as 3700 fully constructed chambers, each the size of the existing King's Chamber could be accommodated within the monument's vast 'inner space' of 8.5 million cubic feet.[33]

The stones of darkness and the shadow of death

Having examined the plugging blocks, the visitor is faced by a long climb down the full 350-foot length of the Descending Corridor, initially through masonry and thence into bedrock. As the journey proceeds, the rays of sunlight penetrating the barred entrance to the north grow progressively weaker and one has the sense of dropping like a deep-sea diver into the dark depths of a midnight-black ocean.

The corridor, which every intuition proclaims to be a remotely ancient, prehistoric feature, is 3 feet 11 inches high by 3 feet 6 inches wide and may originally have been cut into the 30-foot-tall rocky mound that occupied this site millennia before the Pyramid was built. It is unsettling, therefore, to discover that it is machine-age straight from top to bottom. According to Flinders Petrie, the variation along the whole passage 'is under $\frac{1}{4}$ inch in the sides and $\frac{3}{10}$ inch on the roof'.[34] In addition there is one segment of the corridor, 150 feet in length, where 'the average error of straightness is only one fiftieth of an inch, an amazingly minute amount.'[35]

With hunched back, the visitor continues down this long, straight corridor sloping due south into the bedrock of the Giza plateau at the now familiar angle of 26 degrees. As ever greater depths are plumbed it is hard not to grow increasingly conscious of the tremendous mass of limestone that is piled above and of the heavy, dusty, unfresh fug of the subterranean air – like the exhalation of some cyclopean beast. Looking back apprehensively towards the entrance, one notices that the penetrating light has been reduced to a glimmering star-burst, high up and far away. And it is normal, at this point, to feel a concomitant glimmer of apprehension, a slight tug of anxiety at the extent of one's separation from the world above.

On the west side of the corridor, quite near the bottom, is an alcove, again covered by an iron grille, that gives access to the vertical Well-Shaft and thence to the Grand Gallery and the upper chambers. Soon afterwards the 26-degree descending slope levels off into a low horizontal passageway, running 29 feet from north to south, through which the visitor is obliged to crawl on all fours. Near the end of this passageway, again on the west side, is another alcove, 6 feet long and 3 feet deep, that has been roughly hewn out of the bedrock and that ends in a blind, unfinished wall. Then, after a further 4 feet of crawling, the horizontal passageway opens at a height of about 2 feet above floor level into the Subterranean Chamber.

Were it not for a single low-wattage electric bulb installed in modern times, the visitor would now be in complete darkness. The light that the bulb casts has a greenish, sepulchral hue, and what it reveals is a most peculiar room, considerably larger than the King's Chamber, measuring 46 feet along its east-west axis, and 27 feet 1 inch from north to south, but with a maximum height of just 11 feet 6 inches.[36] In the approximate centre of the floor, on the east side, is a railing surrounding a square pit reaching a depth of about 10 feet, and beyond that, penetrating the south wall, is a second horizontal

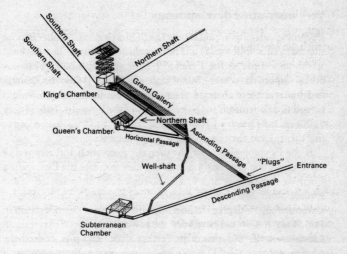

10. The complex internal design of the Great Pyramid. It is possible that many other passageways and chambers remain to be discovered within the gigantic monument.

corridor, 2 feet 4 inches square, running due south into the bedrock for a further 53 feet and terminating in a blank wall. Looking to the right, one notes that the floor of the western side of the Chamber rises up into a kind of chest-high platform. This has been irregularly trenched, creating four parallel 'fins' of limestone running east to west, almost touching the relatively flat roof at some points but with a clearance of up to six feet in others.

All these strange features conspire to create an oppressive, claustrophobic atmosphere in the room that reminds the visitor of how far beneath the ground he has burrowed, and of how inescapably he could be entombed here if there were to be any serious collapse of the millions of tons of limestone above his head.

Very interesting developments

Egyptological opinion concerning the Subterranean Chamber may be summarized as follows: (1) it is not a prehistoric feature, but was built at the same time as the Pyramid (i.e. around 2500 BC); (2) it was initially intended to be the burial place of Khufu; (3) then the Pharaoh and his architects changed their minds, stopped work on it, and turned their attentions to the main body of the Pyramid – where they built first the Queen's Chamber (also later 'abandoned' according to this theory) and then finally the King's Chamber.[37]

If the Egyptologists are right then the excavation and removal of more than 2000 tons of solid rock in order to create the Descending Corridor – rock that first had to be mined and then hauled to the surface from increasingly greater depths through that cramped, unventilated, 26-degree channel – would all have been undertaken in vain. Vain, too, would have been the hewing out of the Subterranean Chamber itself, and also of its further shafts and pits. Indeed the whole enterprise would, in retrospect, have been entirely pointless if the end result had merely been to leave, at a depth of more than 100 feet below the Giza plateau, an unfinished, rough-walled, low-ceilinged crypt – 'resembling a quarry'[38] – for which nobody would ever have any use.

This obviously defies common sense. An alternative scenario does exist, however, which has stimulated the curiosity of a number of investigators during the last two centuries. According to this scenario the Chamber was deliberately left unfinished so as to hoodwink treasure hunters into *believing* that it had been abandoned and thus convince them of the pointlessness of further explorations there – a pretty effective means of keeping casual intruders away from any other cavities or concealed passageways that might be connected to it.

With such suspicions in mind, the Italian explorer Giovanni Battista Caviglia and the British adventurer Colonel Howard Vyse both felt inspired (between 1830 and 1837) to drill holes into the bottom of the pit at the centre of the Subterranean Chamber. They extended its original depth of 10 feet by a further 35 feet (now largely filled in).

More recently the French archaeologist, André Pochan, has drawn attention to a curious passage from the Greek historian Herodotus who visited Egypt in the fifth century BC and spent much time interviewing priests and other learned men there. Herodotus reports that he was told quite specifically of the existence of 'underground chambers on the hill on which the Pyramids stand ... These chambers King Cheops [Khufu] made as burial chambers for himself in a kind of island, bringing in a channel from the Nile . . .'[39]

Pochan has calculated that if there really is a chamber fed by Nile water under the Pyramid, then it would have to be at a great depth – at least 90 feet below the pit. Likewise the Danish architect Hubert Paulsen has argued on the basis of geometry that the most probable place for any further chamber to be found in the Great Pyramid is underneath the pit[40] – a view that is also supported by the calculations of the British geometer Robin Cook.[41]

It is a French engineer, however, Professor Jean Kerisel, who has most vigorously pursued the quest for concealed subterranean chambers. The current President of the Association France-Egypte, he was in the pit with his assistants on 12 October 1992 when a major earthquake occurred, demolishing large parts of Cairo. This experience, he stated later, gave the researchers 'a few very unpleasant moments some 35 metres under the plateau'.[42]

Happily, the Subterranean Chamber did not collapse and Kerisel and his team were able to finish their work. This involved the use of two non-destructive techniques: ground-penetrating radar and microgravimetry. The results were inconclusive in the chamber itself but extremely promising in the horizontal passageway that connects it to the end of the Descending Corridor. In Kerisel's own words: 'a structure was detected under the floor of the passageway, which could be a corridor oriented SSE–NNW whose ceiling is at the depth that the Descending Corridor would have reached had it been prolonged.'[43]

Nor was this all. A second very clear anomaly, a 'mass defect' as Kerisel calls it, 'was detected on the western side of the passageway six metres before the chamber entrance. According to our calculations, this anomaly corresponds to a vertical shaft at least five metres deep with a section of about 1.40 × 1.40 metres very close to the western wall of the passageway.'[44]

In short, what Kerisel believes he has identified off the Subterranean Chamber's entrance corridor is something that looks very much like a completely separate passageway system, terminating in a vertical shaft. His instruments may have misled him, or, as he himself admits, he may merely have picked up the traces of 'a large volume of limestone dissolved by the action of underground water – in other words a deep cave'.[45] Alternatively, however, if the 'mass defect' turns out to be a man-made feature, as he strongly suspects, then 'it may lead to very interesting developments'.[46]

Labyrinth

It should be obvious that a civilization that could build *up* to the height of the Great Pyramid's summit platform, that could create giant stone statues more than 240 feet long, and that could lift the 200-ton blocks of the Valley and Mortuary Temples into place (forming intricate jigsaw-puzzle patterns at heights of 40 feet and more above the ground) would not have experienced any unsurmountable difficulty in building *down* as well. On the contrary, such a civilization could, if it had so wished, have hewn out underground complexes of immense size, connected to one another by labyrinths of tunnels.

The possibility therefore cannot be ruled out that the Subterranean Chamber under the Great Pyramid could be just one of many such deeply buried features. Indeed, as the reader will recall, the seismological work carried out at Giza in the early 1990s by the American geophysicist Thomas Dobecki did indicate the presence of a large and apparently man-made hypogeum in the bedrock beneath the Sphinx. Ultimately only further excavations and research can shed further light on these matters. Meanwhile, however, there is a great deal of evidence from all parts of the necropolis which suggests that the creation of ambitious rock-hewn structures – both above and below the ground – was, indeed, part of the standard repertoire of the Pyramid builders. They also quite frequently chose to mingle rock-hewn and built-up structures – as in the case of the tomb of Khent-Khawes, a supposed Queen of Menkaure, which consists of a natural outcropping sculpted in pyramidial form surmounted by a curious sarcophagus-shaped temple.

A more spectacular and conspicuous mixture of rock-hewn and built-up features occurs at the Pyramid of Khafre. It stands on an artificially levelled 12-acre platform cut bodily out of the plateau – which slopes steeply from north-west to south-east at this point (i.e. it is higher in the west and lower in the east). In consequence the north and west sides of the Pyramid are enclosed within a trench that decreases steadily in height from about 20 feet at the north-west corner to about 10 feet at the south-west corner – and to zero at the north-east and south-east corners. The lower courses of the Pyramid itself on the north and west sides are contoured out of the central mound of bedrock that the builders left in place after hollowing out the trench. On the east and south sides, however, the slope of the plateau falls below the level chosen for the base of the Pyramid. The builders solved this problem by bringing thousands of enormous filling blocks to the site – average weight about 100 tons each – to create an unshakable horizontal foundation. They then went on to lay the first few courses of the monument on the eastern and southern sides using the same unwieldy megaliths. Thereafter they reverted to smaller blocks and in consequence a clear demarcation line is visible between the two types of construction. Like some of the characteristics of the Sphinx and Valley Temples referred to earlier, this demarcation gives the impression not just of different building techniques but actually of two distinctly different *stages* of building separated by an unknown interval of time.

The mystery of the shafts

There is one other anomalous feature of the Giza necropolis which we have not yet mentioned but with which we shall close this chapter as it leads us on to the next stage of our investigation. This feature is confined to the Great Pyramid and is unique in ancient Egyptian architecture. It takes the form of four narrow shafts – usually described by Egyptologists as 'ventilation channels' – two of which emanate respectively from the northern and southern walls of the King's Chamber and the other two from the northern and southern walls of the Queen's Chamber.

The four shafts have an average cross-section of 23 × 22 cms and lengths that vary from about 24 metres (northern shaft of the Queen's Chamber) to about 65 metres (northern shaft of the King's Chamber). They are all inclined to the horizontal plane of the Pyramid and their angles of slope vary from 32 degrees 30 minutes (northern shaft of the King's Chamber) to 45 degrees 15 minutes (southern shaft of the King's Chamber). The shafts were constructed in a step-by-step manner as the Pyramid rose in height (i.e. they were not drilled through the masonry as some have supposed) and they reveal the use of very complex and sophisticated engineering and levelling techniques.

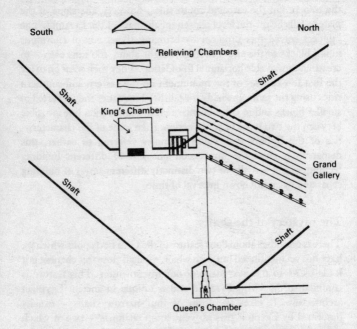

11. The King's and Queen's Chambers and their four shafts. Note that the shafts of the Queen's Chamber were not originally cut through into the chamber but stopped short several inches from the inner walls. The shafts were opened in 1872 by the British engineer Waynman Dixon.

It has been suggested that the reason for their inclination was to find the 'shortest route' to the outside of the Pyramid and this has been taken to imply that the ancient builders wanted to 'save' work and time. However, such geometrical logic goes very much against *engineering logic* – for the simple reason that building shafts on an incline would not save time or work at all. Quite the contrary: no construction engineer or builder could possibly agree that the 'shortest route' is the best route in this case – even though it may seem so to those looking only at the geometry. The truth, as Egyptian architect Dr Alexander Badawy first noted in the 1960s, is that to build inclined shafts rather than to have simple horizontal channels leading to the outside of the Pyramid would create many difficulties – and especially so when we consider the high precision and rigid consistency of the inclinations.[47]

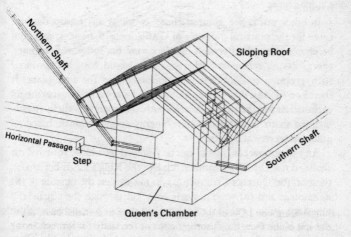

12. Details of the Queen's Chamber and its shafts.

To build inclined shafts rather than horizontal ones entails five tedious operations. First, the base course must be prepared; this calls for the shaping of special blocks with their upper faces sloping to serve as the 'floor' of each shaft. Secondly, more special blocks have to be prepared with U-shaped inner faces to form the profile, i.e, the 'walls' and 'ceilings' of the shafts. Thirdly, yet more special blocks have to be cut with their undersides inclined in order to cover the sides of the shafts. Fourthly, the tops of the shafts must be covered with other special blocks with sloping undersides. Fifthly, the main masonry courses of the Pyramid have to be integrated with these special design features along the entire lengths of the shafts.

If ventilation was really the objective then the question that must be asked is this: why opt for such complications and difficulties when an effective flow of air could have been provided for the chambers in a much simpler way? From an engineer's point of view the obvious solution would have been to leave a masonry joint open – say 20 cms – running horizontally from the top of each chamber right to the outside of the monument. In this case no special cutting of blocks would have been necessary, nor indeed any tedious alignments or levelling work.

In other words the 'shortest route' is not by any means the best route for the practical purposes of ventilation and, besides, it should be obvious that the Pyramid builders were not interested in time/energy-saving schemes – otherwise they would not have favoured such gigantic, multimillion-ton monuments in the first place. It therefore follows that we are unlikely to be rewarded in seeking an explanation for the precise north-south alignments of these steeply inclined shafts in terms of a time/energy-saving rationale based on quaint geometrical figures.

Any doubt over this issue can be resolved by a close study of the shafts of the Queen's Chamber. Unlike the King's Chamber shafts, those in the Queen's Chamber (a) do not exit on the outside of the monument and (b) were not originally cut through the Chamber's limestone walls. Instead the builders left the last five inches intact in the last block over the mouth of each of the shafts – thus rendering them invisible and inacccessible to any casual intruder. With the help of a steel chisel, they were finally discovered in 1872 by the British

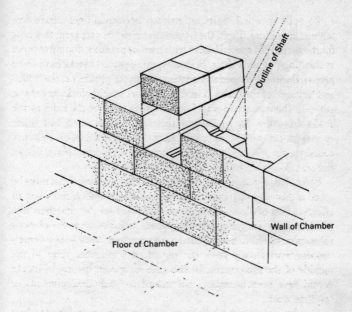

13. Queen's Chamber wall and shaft mouth.

engineer Waynman Dixon, a Freemason whose curiosity had been aroused by the shafts in the King's Chamber and who decided to look for similar features in the Queen's Chamber.

In later chapters we will be considering the implications of Dixon's 1872 discovery, and the follow-up to it. The point that we wish to make here, however, is the obvious one that shafts which were originally closed at both ends could not possibly have been used, or intended, for ventilation. They must, therefore, have had some higher purpose – one that was thought by the builders to justify the enormous care, skill and effort involved in constructing them.

As we shall see, that 'higher purpose' can now be identified with certainty.

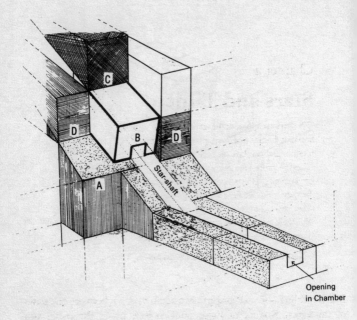

14. Construction details of the Great Pyramid's shafts. At least four different kinds of blocks (A, B, C and D), continuing the full length of the shafts, were required for the successful completion of these mysterious features of the Pyramid. The engineering problems would have been immense. The notion that the primary purpose of the shafts was for ventilation is disproved by the fact that the Queen's Chamber shafts were originally closed at both ends and by the complexity of the design – which would not have been necessary if simple ventilation had been the objective.

Chapter 4

Stars and Time

'The various apparent movements of the
heavenly bodies which are produced by the
rotation and revolution of the earth, and the
effects of precession, were familiar to the
Egyptians . . . They carefully studied what
they saw, and put their knowledge together
in the most convenient fashion, associating it
with their strange imaginings and their
system of worship . . .'

J. Norman Lockyer, *The Dawn Of Astronomy*, 1894

It is humbling and awe-inspiring to stand at dawn between the paws of the Great Sphinx of Egypt and to look up as the rising sun illuminates its face. The colossal statue *seems* ancient – almost as old, one might imagine, as time itself. And, as we saw in Chapter 2, a mounting body of geological evidence suggests that it *is* ancient – vastly older than the 4500 years allocated to it by Egyptologists and perhaps dating back as far as the last Ice Age when no civilization capable of fashioning such a monument is supposed to have existed.

Such notions are of course controversial and hotly disputed. Moreover, as should be obvious by now, geology is incapable of providing us with a precise chronology and is particularly limited by the present state of our knowledge of palaeo-climatology. Indeed, the most we can say, on the sole basis of the monument's erosion patterns, is that it does appear to have been carved at a much earlier date than Egyptologists believe but that its antiquity could range anywhere between 15,000 BC and 5000 BC.

There is, however, another science which, provided one essential

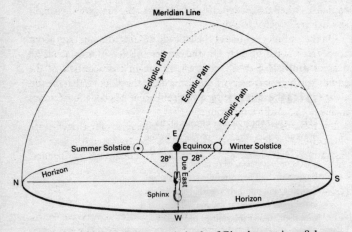

15. On the summer solstice at the latitude of Giza the sun rises 28 degrees north of east, on the winter solstice it rises 28 degrees south of east and on the equinoxes it rises due east. The Great Sphinx of Giza is an astronomical monument orientated perfectly towards due east and thus serves as a superb equinoctial marker or 'pointer'.

precondition is fulfilled, can provide a much more accurate dating – to within a few decades – of uninscribed ancient stone monuments. This is the science of archaeoastronomy. The precondition upon which it depends for its successful functioning is that the monuments studied should have been accurately aligned to the stars or to the rising points of the sun by their builders.

The Great Sphinx fulfils this precondition. It lies exactly along the east-west axis of the Giza necropolis with its patient and eternal gaze set perfectly towards due east. It is, therefore, a superb 'equinoctial marker': its eyes target the exact position of sunrise at dawn on the spring equinox.

To clarify matters a little, astronomers speak of four 'cardinal moments' in the year: the summer solstice – the longest day in the northern hemisphere – when the earth's north pole points most directly at the sun, the winter solstice, the shortest day, when the pole points most directly away from the sun, and the spring and autumn equinoxes when the earth lies broadside-on to the sun and when night and day are of equal length.

On the summer solstice at the latitude of Giza, the sun rises about 28 degrees north of east. On the winter solstice it rises about 28 degrees south of east. By contrast, the main characteristic of the equinoxes (here and everywhere else around the globe) is that the sun always rises *due east* providing a sure and accurate geodetic reference to one of the cardinal directions.

It is towards this reference point, with high precision, that the gaze of the Sphinx is set – not by accident, but by design, and as part of a vast, archaic astronomical plan of uncanny accuracy and intelligence.

Observatory

Thousands of years ago, under the clear skies of a younger world, Egypt's Giza plateau must have been the ultimate observatory. From the high ground half a mile to the west of the Sphinx on which the three principal Pyramids stand, there would have been a faultless 360-degree view around an enormous circular horizon – a prospect that would have invited observations of the rising and setting points of the sun throughout the year, and also of the rising and setting points of the stars. It is certain, furthermore, whatever the other functions of the necropolis, that it was indeed used for practical and precise observational astronomy of the kind developed by navigators to pinpoint the positions of ships on the open ocean. Like the ability to keep strictly to a chosen course, the fabulous accuracy with which the principal monuments of Giza are aligned to true north, south, east and west could not have been achieved by any other science.[1]

Details of these alignments have already been given in Chapter 3. It is therefore sufficient here to remind ourselves that the Great Pyramid stands at a point on the earth's surface exactly one third of the way between the north pole and the equator (i.e. astride latitude 30) and that its 'meridional' (i.e. north-south) axis is aligned to within three-sixtieths of a single degree of true north-south. It is a small but significant point that this alignment is more accurate than that of the Meridian Building at the Greenwich Observatory in London – which is offset by an error of nine-sixtieths of a degree. In our opinion, such

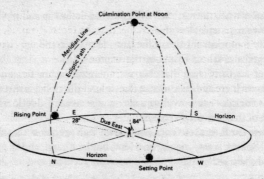

16. The trajectory of the sun on the summer solstice, with its culmination point (highest altitude) being attained at meridian transit.

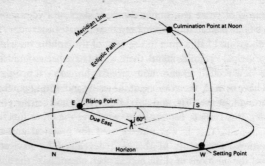

17. The trajectory of the sun on the equinox.

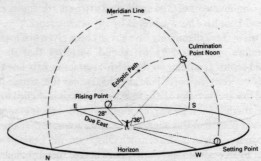

precision constitutes a 'fact' which archaeologists and Egyptologists have never seriously considered, i.e. that the Great Pyramid, with its 13-acre footprint and six million tons of mass, could *only* have been surveyed and set out by master astronomers.[2]

It is our conviction that this 'astronomical factor' deserves to be given much greater prominence than it has hitherto been accorded by Egyptologists. Moreover, thanks to the recent development of sophisticated star-mapping computer programs, it is possible for us to simulate the skies over Giza in any epoch during the past 30,000 years and thus to recreate the celestial environment in which the Pyramid builders worked.

Standing as it were beneath those ancient skies, initiated by microchip into the cosmic secret of the changing positions of the stars, certain features of the key monuments – features that are of no significance from the purely archaeological or Egyptological perspective – begin to take on a peculiar meaning.

Targeting Stars

Let us begin with the four mysterious shafts emanating from the King's and Queen's Chambers of the Great Pyramid, the engineering

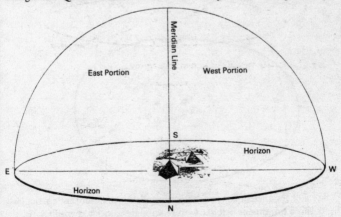

19. The horizon of Giza and the meridian of the Great Pyramid.

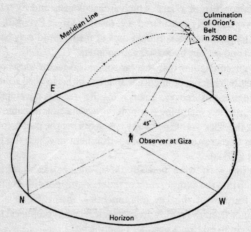

20. Culmination (meridian-transit) of Orion's belt *circa* 2500 BC. In this epoch the belt stars crossed the meridian at altitude 45 degrees, targeted by the southern shaft of the King's Chamber.

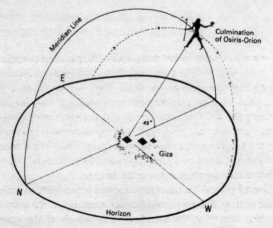

21. For the ancient Egyptians the constellation of Orion, and particularly its three prominent belt stars, were strongly associated with Osiris, the god of resurrection and rebirth.

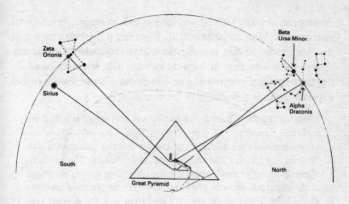

22. The stellar alignments of the Great Pyramid's four shafts in the epoch of 2500 BC.

aspects of which we considered at the end of the previous chapter. As we have seen, two of these shafts are aligned perfectly to due north and the other two perfectly to due south. They thus target, at varying altitudes, what astronomers refer to as the 'meridian' – an imaginary line 'dividing the sky' that is best envisaged as a hoop connecting the north and south poles and passing directly over the observer's head. It is as they cross this imaginary line ('transit the meridian') that the stars (and also the sun, moon and planets) are said to 'culminate' – that is, reach their maximum altitude above the horizon.

The Great Pyramid has numerous features which leave us without any doubt that its designers paid careful attention to the stars and tracked their transit at the meridian. The mouth of the original entrance corridor, for example, targets the meridian with the precision of the barrel of an artillery piece. All the internal passageways, too, run perfectly north-south, thus making the whole monument, as many astronomers have noted, an obvious 'meridional instrument'.[3] Most conclusive of all, however, is the fine accuracy of the four shafts. Recent investigations have established beyond any shadow of doubt that in *circa* 2500 BC – the era recognized by Egyptologists as the 'Pyramid Age' – each one of these shafts targeted a special star as it culminated at the meridian:

> From the Queen's Chamber, the northern shaft is angled at 39 degrees and was aimed at the star *Kochab* (Beta Ursa Minor) in the constellation of the Little Bear – a star associated by the ancients with 'cosmic regeneration' and the immortality of the soul. The southern shaft, on the other hand, which is angled at 39 degrees 30', was aimed at the bright star *Sirius* (Alpha Canis Major) in the constellation of the Great Dog. This star the ancients associated with the goddess Isis, cosmic mother of the kings of Egypt.[4]
>
> From the King's Chamber, the northern shaft is angled at 32 degrees 28' and was aimed at the ancient Pole star, *Thuban* (Alpha Draconis) in the constellation of the Dragon – associated by the Pharaohs with notions of 'cosmic pregnancy and gestation'. The southern shaft, which is angled at 45 degrees 14', was aimed at *Al Nitak* (Zeta Orionis), the brightest (and also the lowest) of the three stars of Orion's belt – which the ancient Egyptians identified with Osiris, their high god of resurrection and rebirth and the legendary bringer of civilization to the Nile Valley in a remote epoch referred to as *Zep Tepi*, the 'First Time'.[5]

Because we can reconstruct the ancient skies over Giza with modern computers we can demonstrate the spot-on alignments of the four shafts to the four stars *circa* 2500 BC. What the same computers also show us is that these alignments were rare and fleeting, only valid for a century or so, before the continuous gradual change effected in stellar altitudes by the passage of time altered the positions at which the stars transited the meridian.

This phenomenon, the result of a slow and stately wobble in the axis of the earth, is known technically as precession. Over a cycle of 25,920 years it causes the infinitely-extended north pole of our planet's spin axis to trace out a great circle in the heavens. The main astronomical effects of this motion are:

1 an equally slow and stately change in the celestial north pole –

which sometimes coincides with a 'pole star' (and sometimes with empty space) as it progresses eternally around its 25,920-year cycle;

2 changes in the altitude of all stars above the horizon as they cross the observer's meridian at any given latitude;

3 changes in the constellations against the background of which the sun rises due east at dawn on the spring equinox (naturally precession also changes the constellations that mark the autumnal equinox – and the winter and summer solstices as well).

The *rate* of precessional change is constant and predictable for each of these key astronomical effects and can be calculated backwards and forwards in time across the entire star-field. This means, for example, that if we were to observe a specific bright star – say *Al Nitak* in Orion's belt – from a given place today, and if we were to record its altitude at the meridian, then provided such a record was to be found and understood thousands of years hence it could be used to determine the epoch or 'time' when the original observation was made.

The same logic can be applied to the four meridional shafts emanating from the King's and Queen's Chambers. Their alignments at 2500 BC – on four stars that were of ritual importance within the 'Osiris cycle' of beliefs – cannot possibly have been accidental. On the contrary, it is obvious that we are confronted here by the products of a conscious and careful design. This in turn makes it equally obvious that the Great Pyramid must have some extremely strong connection with the epoch of 2500 BC – the approximate date at which all orthodox Egyptologists and archaeologists in fact believe it to have been built.

In short, the four star-shafts serve as precise time-markers by which, in theory at least, we should be able once and for all to confirm the date for the construction of the last-surviving wonder of the ancient world. This would be highly desirable since, in the absence of other objective means of dating the monument, controversy continues to linger over its exact age. However, the archaeoastronomical picture is rather more complicated than it seems.

The Companions of Osiris

The complication arises from the strong correlation, first demonstrated in *The Orion Mystery*, between the three belt stars of the Orion constellation and the ground-plan of the three Pyramids of Giza. An overhead view shows that the Great Pyramid and the second Pyramid stretch out along a diagonal running 45 degrees to the south and west of the former's eastern face. The third Pyramid, however, is offset somewhat to the east of this line. The resulting pattern mimics the sky where the three stars of Orion's belt also stretch out along a 'faulty' diagonal. The first two stars (*Al Nitak* and *Al Nilam*) are in direct alignment, like the first and second Pyramids, and the third star (*Mintaka*) lies offset somewhat to the east of the axis formed by the other two.[6]

The visual correlation, once observed, is obvious and striking on its own. Additional confirmation of its symbolic significance, however, is provided by the Milky Way, which the ancient Egyptians regarded as a kind of 'Celestial Nile' and which was spoken of in archaic funerary texts as the 'Winding Waterway'.[7] In the heavenly vault the belt stars of Orion lie to the west of the Milky Way, as though overlooking its banks; on the ground the Pyramids stand perched above the west bank of the Nile.[8]

Faced by such symmetry, and by such a complex pattern of interlocking architectural and religious ideas, it is hard to resist the conclusion that the Pyramids of Giza represent a successful attempt to build Orion's belt on the ground. This makes all the more sense when we recall the firm identification of the Orion constellation with the high god Osiris.

But bearing in mind the changes induced by the phenomenon of precession we must also ask: 'Orion's belt *when*?' 'Orion's belt in what epoch?'

A perfect match

From the evidence of the shafts we have seen how the Great Pyramid is 'precessionally anchored' to Orion's belt in 2500 BC (because in this epoch the southern shaft of the King's Chamber targeted the meridian-transit of *Al Nitak*, the Great Pyramid's celestial

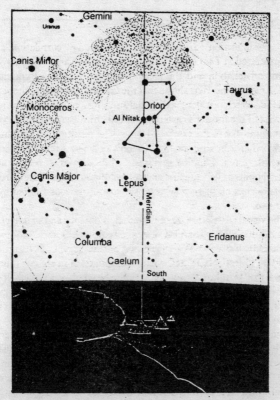

23. Orion's belt crossing the meridian of the Great Pyramid in 2500 BC with the star *Al Nitak*, the Great Pyramid's celestial counterpart, in perfect alignment with the southern shaft of the King's Chamber at an altitude of 45 degrees. However, note how the belt stars and the Milky Way appear out of kilter and askew in relation to the ground plan of the three Pyramids and the Nile. The sky–ground images are, of course, similar, but there is a sense that the sky image needs somehow to be 'twisted' in an anti-clockwise direction to get the perfect match. This can only be achieved by going back in time – by looking at the sky above Giza in a far earlier epoch . . .

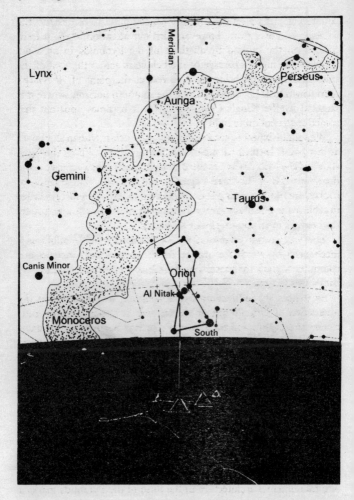

24. The perfect match of sky–ground images is achieved in 10,500 BC when the pattern of the Milky Way and of the three stars of Orion's belt at meridian transit is precisely matched by the course of the Nile and the pattern of the three great Pyramids on the ground.

counterpart). If we set our precessional computer to reconstruct the ancient skies over Giza, however, turn our attention to the pattern formed on the ground by all three of the Pyramids in 2500 BC, simulate the nightly passage of the belt stars across the roof of the celestial sphere and bring them to rest at the point of *Al Nitak's* meridian-transit (45 degrees above the southern horizon, where it is targeted by the King's Chamber shaft), it becomes apparent that something is not quite right.

We should expect to see a perfect meridian-to-meridian alignment at this point. Instead we notice that the dominant axis of the three stars and the Milky Way lies tilted conspicuously askew relative to the dominant axis of the three Pyramids and the Nile. These latter, of course, are fixed in their places. What is required, therefore, in order to achieve the 'ideal' sky–ground arrangement, is somehow to 'rotate' the heavens in an anti-clockwise direction.

The vast cosmic engine of the earth's axial wobble offers us a mechanism by which this can be done: we need only instruct our computer to track the precessionally induced movements of the stars backwards in time.

As it does so, millennium by millennium, we observe that the orientation of Orion's belt at culmination is slowly rotating anti-clockwise and thus approaching ever closer to our desired meridian-to-meridian match. It is not until 10,500 BC, however – 8000 years *before* the 'Pyramid Age' – that the perfect correlation is finally achieved with the Nile mirroring the Milky Way and with the three Pyramids and the belt stars identically disposed in relation to the meridian.[9]

Rising stars

There is a feature of this 10,500 BC correlation which suggests strongly that coincidence is not involved. The pattern that is frozen into monumental architecture in the form of the Pyramids marks *a very significant moment* in the 25,920-year precessional cycle of the three stars of Orion's belt – one that is unlikely to have been randomly selected by the Pyramid builders.

To get a clear grasp of what is involved here let us call up a computer simulation of the skies over Giza in our own epoch, *circa* AD 2000. Looking due south at dawn we note that *Al Nitak* crosses the meridian at an altitude of 58 degrees 06' above the horizon. This, as it happens, is within 8 minutes of the highest altitude that this star will attain in its precessional cycle, i.e. 58 degrees 14' (to be reached at around AD 2500).[10]

Let us now project our simulation backwards in time and recreate the sky as we would see it if we were standing in the same position at around 10,500 BC – i.e. just under 13,000 years, or half a precessional cycle, earlier. In this remote epoch we discover that *Al Nitak* crosses the meridian at an altitude of only 9 degrees 20' above the horizon.[11]

It will never fall lower: the epoch of 10,500 BC marks the nadir of the star's precessionally induced slide up and down the meridian (just as the epoch of AD 2500 marks its zenith). Like a slowly moving lever in a narrow vertical slot, it takes 12,960 years to descend from top to bottom, and a further 12,960 years to ascend from bottom to top again.[12]

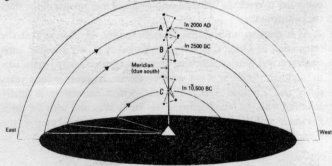

25. By mimicking the sky pattern of Orion's belt in 10,500 BC the three great Pyramids of Giza mark a very significant moment in the 26,000-year precessional cycle of these stars – the lowest point in their slide up and down the meridian, when (as seen from the latitude of Giza) they culminated at an altitude of 9 degrees 20 minutes above the horizon (C). In 2500 BC they culminated at altitude 45 degrees (B). In our own epoch, 2000 AD (A) they are approaching the highest altitude that they will attain in their precessional cycle – 58 degrees 06 minutes above the horizon at meridian transit.

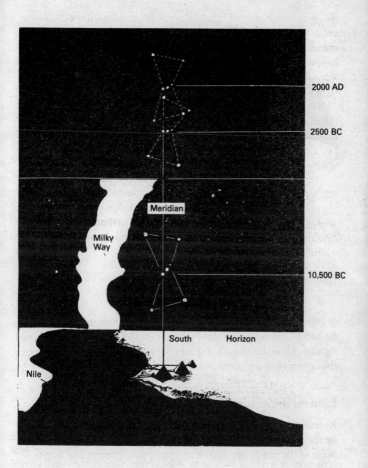

26. Artist's impression showing the precessional cycle of Orion's belt up and down the meridian. The pattern of the stars in 10,500 BC marks the beginning, or 'First Time', of the cycle. It is this pattern that is reproduced on the ground by the three great Pyramids of Giza.

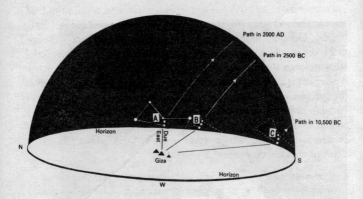

27. The rising points and trajectory of Orion's belt in (A) 2000 AD, (B) 2500 BC, (C) 10,500 BC.

By exactly mimicking the disposition of the belt stars in the sky in 10,500 BC the layout of the Pyramids on the ground thus not only signifies a specific epoch but also rather precisely and surgically marks the *beginning* of a precessional half-cycle.

Lion on the ground, lion in the sky

As was pointed out in *Fingerprints of the Gods*, the same role is played by the Great Sphinx – which gazes directly at the equinoctial rising point of the sun in any and every epoch, past, present and future, for ever.

This orientation provides us with an astronomical basis for dating the monument because it is known that the attention of astronomers in ancient times was particularly focused on the zodiacal constellation – considered to define the astrological 'Age' – that rose just ahead of the sun in the eastern sky at dawn on the spring equinox.[13] The same phenomenon of the earth's axial precession that affects the altitude of stars at the meridian also affects these famous constellations – Leo, Cancer, Gemini, Taurus, Aries, Pisces, Aquarius, etc., etc – the co-ordinates of which, in relation to the rising point of the equinoctial sun, undergo slow but continuous precessionally induced changes. The result is a hard-to-observe astronomical phenomenon, known as the precession of the equinoxes, which manifests as a gradual circulation of the equinoctial point around all twelve 'houses' of the zodiac. In the words of historians of science Giorgio de Santillana and Hertha von Dechend, whose essay *Hamlet's Mill* is a ground-breaking study of archaic precessional mythology:

> The constellation that rose in the east just before the sun (that is, rose heliacally) marked the 'place' where the sun rested . . . It was known as the sun's 'carrier', and as the main 'pillar' of the sky . . . .The sun's position among the constellations at the vernal [spring] equinox was the pointer that indicated the 'hours' of the precessional cycle – very long hours indeed, the equinoctial sun occupying each zodiacal constellation for just under 2200 years.[14]

In our own epoch the sun on the spring equinox rises against the stellar background of the constellation of Pisces, as it has done for approximately the last 2000 years. The 'Age of Pisces', however, is now approaching its end and the vernal sun will soon pass out of the sector of the Fishes and begin to rise against the new background of Aquarius. To be precise, it takes exactly 2160 years for the equinoctial point to pass completely through one constellation or 'house' of the zodiac.

With this process in mind, let us now reverse Santillana and von Dechend's 'precessional clock'. Passing back through the Age of Pisces (and the Age of Aries that preceded it) we find that in the epoch of 2500 BC, when the Sphinx is conventionally assumed to have been built, it was the constellation of Taurus that housed the sun on the spring equinox.

It is here that the crux of the problem lies. To state the case briefly:
1 The Sphinx, as we have seen, is an equinoctial marker – or 'pointer'.
2 On a site that is as profoundly *astronomical* as Giza one would naturally expect an equinoctial monument dating from the 'Age

of Taurus' either to have been built in the shape of a bull, or at any rate to symbolize a bull. The Sphinx, however, is emphatically *leonine* in form.

3 It is a simple fact of precession that one must go back to the 'Age of Leo' beginning at around 10,500 BC, in order to obtain the 'correct' sky–ground symbolism. This, as it turns out, is the only epoch in which the due–east–facing Sphinx would have manifested exactly the right symbolic alignment on exactly the right day – watching the vernal sun rising in the dawn sky against the background of his own celestial counterpart.[15]

To clarify this latter notion, let us return to our computer simulation of the skies over Giza in 10,500 BC, instructing the program to recreate the positions of the sun and stars just before dawn on the spring equinox in that epoch. And let us set our direction of view due east in line with the gaze of the Sphinx. Indeed, with the aid of a little virtual reality and poetic licence, let us imagine that we are standing between the paws of the Sphinx itself at that date – a date that we already know accords rather well with the *geology* of the monument.

What we would see, occupying the portion of the sky into which the sun is about to rise, would be the splendid zodiacal constellation of Leo – a constellation that very strongly resembles its namesake the lion and thus also the leonine Sphinx.

The minutes pass. The sky begins to lighten. Then, at the exact moment at which the top of the solar disc breaks over the horizon directly ahead of us we make a 90–degree right turn – so that we are now looking due south. There, culminating at the meridian at altitude 9 degrees 20', we observe the three stars of Orion's belt forming a pattern in the sky that is identical to the ground plan of the Giza Pyramids.

The question reduces to this: is it a coincidence, or more than a coincidence, that the Giza necropolis as it has reached us today out of the darkness of antiquity is still dominated by a huge equinoctial lion statue at the east of its 'horizon' and by three gigantic Pyramids disposed about its meridian in the distinctive manner of the three stars of Orion's belt in 10,500 BC?

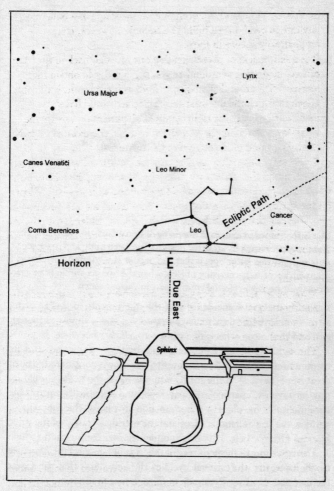

Labels in image: Lynx, Ursa Major, Canes Venatici, Leo Minor, Coma Berenices, Leo, Ecliptic Path, Cancer, Horizon, E, Due East, Sphinx

28. In the pre-dawn on the vernal equinox in 10,500 BC, with the sun some 12 degrees below the horizon, the Great Sphinx would have gazed directly at his own celestial counterpart, the constellation of Leo – which experienced what astronomers call its 'heliacal rising' at this moment.

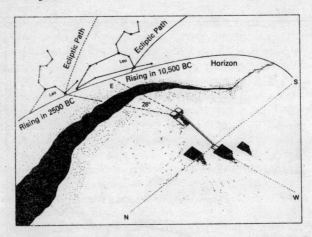

29. Superimposed images of the rising of Leo in 2500 BC, when the Great Sphinx is presumed by archaeologists to have been built, and in 10,500 BC. It is only in this latter epoch that the perfect sky–ground correlation is attained, at the heliacal rising of Leo, when the Sphinx would have gazed directly at his own celestial counterpart in the pre-dawn.

And is it also a coincidence that the monuments in this amazing astronomical theme park manage to *work together* – almost as though geared like the cog-wheels of a clock – to *tell the same 'time'*?

Throughout the ancient world the moment of sunrise, and its conjunction with other celestial events, was always considered to be of great importance.[16] At the spring equinox in 10,500 BC, as should by now be obvious, a particularly spectacular and statistically improbable conjunction took place – a conjunction involving the moment of sunrise, the constellation of Leo and the meridian transit of the three stars of Orion's belt. It is this unique celestial conjunction (which furthermore marks the *beginning* of the 'Age of Leo' and the *beginning* of the upwards precessional cycle of the belt stars) that the Great Sphinx and the three Pyramids of Giza appear to model.

But why should the ancients have sought to create a simulacrum of the skies on the ground at Giza?

Or, to put the question another way, why should they have sought to bring down to earth an image of the heavens?

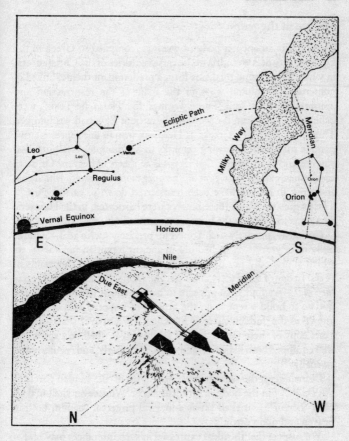

30. The moment of sunrise on the vernal equinox in 10,500 BC. At the exact moment that the top of the solar disc broke over the horizon due east in direct alignment with the gaze of the Sphinx the three stars of Orion's belt culminated at the meridian in the pattern that is mimicked on the ground by the three great Pyramids. Sphinx and Pyramids thus appear to 'work together' as an architectural representation of this unique celestial conjunction.

Motive in the texts

There exists an ancient body of writings, compiled in Greek in the Egyptian city of Alexandria in the early centuries of the Christian era, in which sky–ground dualisms form a predominant theme, linked in numerous convoluted ways to the issue of the resurrection and immortality of the soul. These writings, the 'Hermetic Texts', were believed to have been the work of the ancient Egyptian wisdom god Thoth (known to the Greeks as Hermes), who in one representative passage makes the following remarks to his disciple Asclepius: 'Do you not know, Asclepius, that Egypt is an image of heaven? Or, so to speak more exactly, in Egypt all the operations of powers which rule and work in heaven have been transferred down to earth below?'[17] The purpose to which these powers were harnessed, in the Hermetic view, was to facilitate the initiate's quest for immortality.

Curiously, precisely such a quest for precisely such a goal – 'a life of millions of years' – is spelled out in ancient Egyptian funerary texts which supposedly pre-date the Hermetic writings by thousands of years. In one of these texts, *Shat Ent Am Duat* – the *Book of What is in the Duat* – we find what appears to be an explicit instruction to the initiate to build a replica on the ground of a special area of the sky known as the 'hidden circle of the Duat': 'Whosoever shall make an exact copy of these forms . . . and shall know it, shall be a spirit and well equipped both in heaven and earth, unfailingly, and regularly and eternally.'[18]

Elsewhere in the same text we hear again of 'the hidden Circle in the *Duat* . . . in the body of Nut [the sky]': 'Whosoever shall make a copy thereof . . . it shall act as a magical protector for him both in heaven and upon earth.'[19]

We suspect that the ideas expressed in such utterances may hint at the true motive for the construction of the huge astronomical monuments of the Giza necropolis and may help us to find a coherent explanation for their precise alignments to the cardinal directions of the sky, their unique 'star shafts', and their intense celestial symbolism. At any rate, as we shall demonstrate in Parts III and IV, it is a fact that the *Duat* sky-region described in the ancient Egyptian texts was dominated by the constellations of Orion and Leo – both of which appear to have been 'imaged' on the ground at Giza (with the former additionally targeted by the southern shaft of the King's Chamber in the Great Pyramid) – and by the star Sirius, which was targeted by the southern shaft of the Queen's Chamber. We also note in passing that the internal corridor, passageway and chamber systems of the Pyramids very closely resemble surviving vignettes (painted on Eighteenth Dynasty tomb walls) of various regions of the *Duat*. Of particular interest in this regard is the mysterious 'Kingdom of Sokar' in the 'Fifth Division of the *Duat*' in which 'travellers upon the way of the holy country . . . enter into the hidden place of the *Duat*.' [20]

As we shall also see in Parts III and IV, there are the repeated references in the *Book of What is in the Duat*, and in numerous other funerary and rebirth texts, to *Zep Tepi*, the 'First Time' – the remote epoch when the gods were believed to have come to earth and established their kingdom in Egypt. [21] Those gods included Thoth-Hermes, the 'Thrice-Great' master of wisdom, the goddess Isis whose celestial counterpart was the star Sirius, and Osiris, the 'once and future king', who was killed, revenged by his son Horus, and then reborn to live for ever as the 'Lord of the *Duat*'. [22]

The celestial counterpart of Osiris was Orion – a constellation that the ancient Egyptians knew as *Sah*, the 'Far-Strider' and most frequently depicted by means of the three characterstic belt stars. And since Osiris was said to have ruled in the 'First Time' we wonder whether this could be the reason why the three great Pyramids of Giza depict the three stars of Orion's belt as they looked 12,500 years ago at what might reasonably be defined as their astronomical 'First Time' – i.e. at the beginning of their current upwards precessional cycle?

An even bigger question, upon which much of our investigation hinges, concerns the identification of the Sphinx with the constellation of Leo – and specifically with the constellation of Leo when it marked the spring equinox in 10,500 BC. In Parts III and IV we will follow astronomical clues, laid out in the ancient Egyptian texts, which strongly support this identification and which offer intriguing hints as to its implications.

South

31. Artist's impression of the 'First Time' of Orion-Osiris.

32. The celestial counterpart of Osiris was Orion, a constellation that the ancient Egyptians knew as *Sah*, the 'Far Strider', and depicted (as in the central register of this vignette from the tomb of an ancient Egyptian architect named Senmut) by means of the three characteristic belt stars.

Fundamental questions

If the monuments of the Giza necropolis were of no significance in the human story then problems in the study and interpretation of these monuments would be of no significance either. But this site could hardly be more significant. Indeed, there is a sense in which it has always been with us. It is a marker of our history – a memorial to the genesis of our civilization – and it may still have vital information to give us about ourselves. More than any other ancient place, in other words, Giza raises, and might possibly answer, all the old, fundamental questions: who we are, where we came from, perhaps even where we are going. For these reasons we can hardly afford to be indifferent to the Great Sphinx and the three great Pyramids. For these reasons the quality of research that has been carried out around them – and that has defined and explained them – really does matter.

As we shall see in Part II this research has become strangely tangled up with an ancient tradition of quest for hidden chambers and lost records at Giza . . .

Part II

Seekers

Chapter 5

The Case of the Psychic, the Scholar and the Sphinx

'There has been one systematic search, a sort
of direct shot at finding the Hall of Records,
when the Edgar Cayce Foundation funded
SRI International . . .'

Dr Mark Lehner, Edgar Cayce Foundation
and ARE Magazine *Venture Inward*, 1985

There is a tradition which asserts that the Giza monuments stand as a
last and grand memorial to a highly advanced antediluvian civilization
that was destroyed by a 'Great Flood'. This tradition also holds that
somewhere at Giza, either beneath the Great Sphinx or within the
Great Pyramid itself, is concealed a 'Hall of Records' in which is
preserved the entire knowledge and wisdom of the lost civilization.

Such ideas may be of very archaic origin[1] and have continued
throughout history to inspire investigations at Giza. In the fourth
century AD, for example, the Roman Ammianus Marcellinus directed
treasure-hunters to search for 'certain underground galleries in the
Pyramids', constructed as repositories for scrolls and books of past
ages and intended 'to prevent the ancient wisdom from being lost in
the Flood.'[2]

Likewise, many of the Arab chroniclers from about the ninth
century AD onwards seem to have had access to a common source of
information which caused them to agree that the Great Pyramid was
built 'before the Flood' as a repository for scientific knowledge.
Caliph Al Mamoun, who forced a tunnel into the northern face of the
monument in AD 820, did so out of a conviction that he was entering a
relic from antediluvian times which had been charged by its maker

with the secrets of 'all profound science', which could 'convey knowledge of both history and astronomy',[3] and which would be found to contain 'a secret chamber with maps and terrestrial spheres'.[4]

In a similar vein, a number of ancient Egyptian inscriptions and papyri make tantalizing statements about hidden chambers – the Chamber of Archives, the Hall of Records, etc., etc. – which have been interpreted as references to a hypogeum beneath or close by the Sphinx.[5] And Coptic legends report that 'there exists a single subterranean chamber under the Sphinx with entrances to all three Pyramids ... Each entrance is guarded by statues of amazing abilities.'[6]

In modern times, ideas such as these have been kept very much alive in the doctrines of speculative Freemasonry[7] and in the teachings of esoteric schools like the AMORC Rosicrucians of California and the Theosophical Society of London and Madras. In addition, from the 1920s to the 1940s, almost identical notions were expressed with curious vehemence by the American psychic Edgar Cayce, known to some as the 'Sleeping Prophet'.

Since an examination of 'psychic intuitions' would take us far beyond the intended scope of this book we shall offer no opinions on the merits or the sources of Cayce's information. What we do find relevant to our investigation, however, is that his pronouncements concerning a supposed Atlantean 'Hall of Records' at Giza have quietly spawned a multimillion-dollar New Age industry that has embroiled itself deeply with mainstream Egyptological research into the Pyramids and the Sphinx.

We first learned about this unexpected involvement – unexpected because psychics and Egyptologists are normally about as hard to mix as chickens and polecats – when reviewing the numerous studies and excavations undertaken at Giza by the American Egyptologist, Mark Lehner. As the reader will recall from Part I, Professor Lehner has gone on record several times during the 1990s to oppose the theory of a 12,500-year-old Sphinx – and any notion of a Hall of Records beneath it. During the 1970s and 1980s, however, he was directly involved with the followers of Edgar Cayce and with their distinctive beliefs about the secrets and mysteries of Giza.

Trancing the Hall of Records

The management of the Edgar Cayce 'industry' is largely entrusted to a corporation known as the Edgar Cayce Foundation (ECF), and to the affiliated Association for Research and Enlightenment (ARE), both of which are headquartered in the US coastal town of Virginia Beach. The first impression that most visitors get on arrival here is of a sort of medical clinic or retirement home located with a calming view of the ocean in mind. The windows of the principal building, which are made of opaque glass, are a little disconcerting. But reassurance is provided by a large black-and-white sign, visible from the parking lot, which reads:

A.R.E.

EDGAR CAYCE FOUNDATION

Atlantic University Visitor Center

School of Massage

Bookstore

Edgar Cayce was born in Hopkinsville in Kentucky in 1877. At the age of twenty he suffered from a speech impediment. After fruitless attempts to have it diagnosed by local doctors, he discovered that he could put himself into a deep trance and somehow diagnose the disorder and dictate a remedy. Cayce was urged to try his technique on others – with results that were so spectacularly successful that within months he had gained an immense reputation as a 'healer' with the gift of inner vision. All sorts of desperate people flocked to Virginia Beach to be diagnosed by the 'Sleeping Prophet'.

In his trances Cayce would also give psychic 'readings' to his enthusiastic followers – readings that were taken down in shorthand by a secretary.[8] Cayce would always claim to have absolutely no recollection of what happened during these trances, but the 'readings' show that he frequently spoke to his followers about their 'past lives' in a remote epoch – the epoch of 'Atlantis', before and after the terrible deluge which supposedly destroyed that fabled continent. Altogether some 700 of Cayce's 'life readings' – now available on CD-ROM – expound in one way or another on the so-called 'Atlantean' story which begins with 'humankind's arrival on earth some ten million years ago, and ends with the sinking of the last remnants of Atlantis [prior to] 10,000 BC'.[9]

The essential message of these readings is that a number of 'Atlanteans' escaped the destruction of their continent and somehow reached the Nile Valley in Egypt in the eleventh millennium BC. Cayce himself claimed to be the reincarnation of their high priest Ra-Ta. According to Dr Douglas G. Richards, director and researcher at the Atlantic University (which is part of the Edgar Cayce Foundation): 'many who received life readings [from Cayce] were said to have been associated with him in this past life' in prehistoric Egypt.[10]

One of the most persistent accounts given by Edgar Cayce during his deep trances concerned:

> References and clues [which] indicate Egypt as a repository for records – records of Atlantis and ancient Egypt during the time of Ra-Ta, which may some day be found. They also mention again and again tombs and pyramids yet to be uncovered in Egypt, and give specific dates for the building of the Great Pyramid.[11]

The chronology that Cayce gave for this latter enterprise was '10,490 to 10,390 BC'.[12] He also stated: '. . . some 10,500 [years] before the coming of the Christ . . . there was first that attempt to restore and add to that which had been begun and what is called the Sphinx . . .' Also at around 10,500 BC the Cayce readings state that a vast underground repository was established containing a library of wisdom from the lost civilization of Atlantis: 'This in position lies, as the sun rises from the waters, the line of shadow (or light) falls between the paws of the Sphinx . . . Between, then, the Sphinx and the river . . .'[13] In another reading Cayce gave even more specific directions: 'There is a chamber or passage from the right forepaw [of the Sphinx] to this entrance of the record chamber . . .'[14]

According to the readings, the Hall of Records is to be rediscovered and re-entered when 'the time has been fulfilled' – which, Cayce suggested, would be at or just before the close of the twentieth century, perhaps in 1998.[15] The readings allude frequently to the Old and New Testaments of the Bible, contain numerous references to Jesus, and depict the rediscovery of the Hall of Records as being linked in some way to a series of events that will prelude the 'Second Coming' of Christ.[16]

The Scholar

The corporate history of the Association for Research and Enlightenment (ARE) begins in 1931, when the management of the newly founded institute was entrusted to Edgar Cayce's eldest son, Hugh Lynn Cayce – who had just majored in psychology. His first task was to provide a repository for his father's growing library of psychic 'readings', a sort of modern 'Hall of Records' in Virginia Beach. This task was eventually completed after Edgar Cayce's death in 1945. Meanwhile the ARE continued to expand and today has flourished into a multimillion-dollar organization with over 40,000 members world-wide. Unsurprisingly, however, despite a diversity of interests, its major thrust continues to be to prove the validity of the Edgar Cayce readings. What this involves in practice is a concerted attempt to find the so-called 'Hall of Records' of Atlantis which, as we have seen, is believed to have been preserved at Giza since 10,500 BC under the Sphinx and which, as the prophet said, would be opened before the year 2000. As two of Cayce's own children recently confirmed:

> Over twenty years ago the ECF began to lay the groundwork for what would later become actual fieldwork in Egypt. The specific areas of interest were the Sphinx, the Great Pyramid, and the immediate surrounding area known as the Giza plateau. The driving force for this research was Hugh Lynn Cayce. Motivated by his father's psychic readings, as well as a personal interest in archaeology, he turned his energies and enthusiasm to initiating solid archaeological research that might validate them . . .[17]

In 1973 Hugh Lynn managed to round up a group of sponsors who were ready to finance a long-term strategy in Egypt. First and foremost this entailed providing an 'academic scholarship . . . plus a small stipend' to a 'gifted individual' who could become a respected Egyptologist and gain the confidence of the leading lights of this stern profession.[18]

The 'gifted individual' chosen to receive the stipend was Mark Lehner,[19] until 1995 a Professor of Egyptology at the University of Chicago's world-famous Oriental Institute. Often referred to in Edgar Cayce literature as 'the scholar', it appears that some time in

1973 Lehner was earmarked by Hugh Lynn Cayce for a mission in Egypt which was envisaged as follows:

> The scholar could complete a degree in Cairo and gain first-hand experience and make contacts in his field. For the ECF [Edgar Cayce Foundation], such support could create a realistic perspective on research efforts in Egypt, produce contacts, and lead eventually to research involvement in this area. Although the scholar would be independent of the ECF, his presence in Egypt would serve as an effective liaison or channel for the ECF to develop long-term involvement there.[20]

Lehner arrived in Cairo in the fall of 1973 and studied at the American University near Al Tahrir Square – from whence he graduated in 1975 with high honours:

> After graduation the Edgar Cayce Foundation supported him as a research fellow for several years in the department of anthropology. During this time, the student not only continued his academic studies, but also made contacts with people and organizations well known for their research. These contacts made it possible for the ECF to sponsor – directly in some cases, and partially in others – actual field research.[21]

Proof under the paws

In 1974 Lehner published a book, *The Egyptian Heritage*, which is copyrighted to the Edgar Cayce Foundation and which bears the subtitle 'Based on the Edgar Cayce Readings'. Its prime objective is to substantiate Cayce's statements about the supposed 'Atlantean connection' in the prehistory of Egypt and the 'Hall of Records' established at Giza in 10,500 BC:

> According to the [Edgar Cayce] readings, it is a legacy which will soon be rediscovered, and will bear profound determinations – not only for the history of dynastic Egypt, but for the entire physical and spiritual epic of our evolution on this planet, and for the years yet to pass.[22]

In *The Egyptian Heritage* Lehner also informs us that:

> There are 1159 Edgar Cayce readings which contain references and information on the Ra–Ta period in Egypt. The story presented here

has been culled from approximately 300 of these readings . . . In presenting correlative Egyptological data I will attempt to demonstrate that there are good empirical reasons for believing that the Ra-Ta story is, in fact, rooted in truth. Of course, the final confirmation lies beneath the paws of the Sphinx at Giza . . .[23]

Anomalies

Naturally the prime area of interest of the ECF/ARE in terms of 'actual field research' was – and remains – scanning, drilling and excavation in the vicinity of the Sphinx where the Cayce readings say that the 'Hall of Records' is located.

In 1973-4, while Mark Lehner was still a student at the American University in Cairo, the first in a series of serious pioneering projects was launched, using ground-penetrating radar and other high-tech remote sensing equipment to locate 'anomalies' under the bedrock beneath the Sphinx. These projects were channelled through well-established academic institutions – the Ain Shams University in Cairo and the prestigious Stanford Research Institute (SRI) in the USA.[24]

In 1977 the US National Science Foundation funded a project at Giza again involving the SRI. This time use was made of several new techniques such as resistivity measurements (from metal rods driven into the rock across which an electric current was passed), magnetometry, and also the latest aerial photography and thermal infrared image-enhancing techniques. According to the SRI team's official report: 'Several anomalies were observed as a result of our resistivity survey at the Sphinx . . . Behind the rear paws (north-west end) we ran two traverses. Both traverses indicate an anomaly that could possibly be due to a tunnel aligned north-west to south-east . . .'[25]

Two other 'anomalies' were noted, deep in the bedrock 'in front of the paws of the Sphinx'.[26]

According to ECF/ARE historians the 1973-4 and 1977 projects 'paved the way for work . . . that would succeed in discovering hidden chambers'.[27] Exactly how and where is not made clear. At any rate in 1978 the ECF/ARE collaborated with the SRI and provided funds (to the tune of about US $50,000[28]) for a more detailed survey of the Sphinx enclosure and the nearby Sphinx Temple. The survey was recorded in the SRI's own records as 'The Sphinx Exploration Project'. It entailed an extensive resistivity scan of the entire floor of the Sphinx and Sphinx Temple enclosures. Should any 'anomalies' be found, it was agreed that the SRI was to confirm them with acoustic sounding techniques. The next step was to have holes cut into the bedrock with precision drills through which borescope cameras could then be inserted.

Several anomalies beneath the bedrock were indeed identified and inspected in this way but proved to be just natural cavities.

A falling out

Also in 1978, US drilling experts from a company called Recovery Systems International (RSI) arrived at Giza with a telescopic diesel-powered drill and official permits, under the direction of an American named Kent Wakefield, to bore a number of holes deep beneath the Sphinx.[29] There was more of a connection between the SRI and the RSI than the anagram formed by their initials. Recovery Systems International, like the Edgar Cayce Foundation, apparently funded some of the SRI's programme at Giza, and made use of the SRI's resistivity readings to guide the placement of their drill holes. According to Mark Lehner, who was there at the time, Recovery Systems International was probably organized 'just for this project'.[30]

The equipment for RSI's work was air-freighted to Egypt and brought to the site where it was positioned in the Sphinx Temple, directly in front of the paws of the Sphinx itself. One hole was bored, uneventfully. A second hole was then drilled. Mark Lehner and Kent Wakefield examined this hole with a borescope and saw only 'Swiss-cheese–like solution cavities' which form naturally in limestone. The solid bottom of the hole was tapped with a plumb-bob by Lehner who concluded that there was nothing unusual about it.[31]

Immediately afterwards the project was stopped. According to Mark Lehner this abrupt halt was 'due to lack of time, funds, and falling out between RSI and SRI'.[32] Also it seems that Recovery Systems International 'did not appreciate at all the Cayce component of the project' and that this eventually led to a 'serious falling out between RSI and SRI'.[33]

Granite structures

Shortly after this episode, in 1979, as we shall see in further detail below, Mark Lehner got involved with the American Research Center in Egypt (ARCE for short) – which is the officially registered American Egyptological mission in Egypt.[34] At about the same time, Zahi Hawass, today the Director-General of the Giza Pyramids, was supervising excavations 165 feet to the east of the Sphinx Temple and hit bedrock at a depth of only six feet. A few months later, however – in 1980 – Egyptian irrigation specialists checking for groundwater drilled in the same area, less than 100 feet away from the Hawass dig, and were able to go down more than 50 feet without impediment before their drill-bit suddenly collided with something hard and massive. After freeing the drill, much to their surprise, they found that they had brought to the surface a large lump of Aswan granite.[35]

No granite occurs naturally anywhere in the Nile Delta area where Giza is located, and Aswan – the source of all the granite used by the ancients at Giza – is located 500 miles to the south. The discovery of what appears to be a substantial granite obstacle – or perhaps several obstacles – 50 feet below ground level in the vicinity of the Sphinx is therefore intriguing to say the least.

Adding to the intrigue were further discoveries that the SRI made around the Sphinx in 1982 as a result of yet another project financed by the Edgar Cayce Foundation.[36] Mark Lehner, who was once again present throughout, described what the SRI did as follows:

> They brought a very powerful acoustical sounder, which is a long pencil-shaped thing. They put it down a drill hole. This is called Immersion Downhole Acoustics. You have to be in water. So they put it down into the water table and it sent out sound waves in all directions. Then they put down a listener, like a stethoscope, and you get a signal on an oscilloscope if sound waves are coming through; if they're not, you don't. You discover fissures this way – on one side of the fissure there's no signal and on the other side there is.
>
> They put the sounder underneath the paw [of the Sphinx] and always got a good, clear signal – there's no underground cavity blocking it. And they put it along the paw between the elbow and that box on the side, around the outside of the box and into the corner, and there was always a good signal.

But, at my prompting, they put it on the bedrock floor inside the box – and it was dead three places where they put it down, as though there is some kind of opening or empty space underneath that was blocking the signal. That was the very last day of the SRI project, and they never checked that out.[37]

Since 1982, we were suprised to learn, almost no further research has been officially authorized to investigate the numerous tantalizing hints of deeply buried structures and chambers in the vicinity of the Sphinx. The single exception was Thomas Dobecki's seismic work in the early 1990s. As reported in Part I, this resulted in the discovery of what appears to be a large, rectangular chamber beneath the forepaws of the Sphinx. Dobecki's investigations were part of the wider geological survey of the Sphinx led by Professor Robert Schoch of Boston University – a survey, as the reader will recall, that was brought abruptly to a halt in 1993 by Dr Zahi Hawass of the Egyptian Antiquities Organization.

The mapping surveys

The American Research Center in Egypt (ARCE) has several times received ECF–ARE financing for its programme of investigations at Giza.[38] In 1979, for example, a proposal was made to the ARCE for a full-scale mapping survey involving the Great Sphinx and its enclosure in which use would be made of modern photogrammetric techniques to record every detail, crack, fissure, contour and outline of the monument. When the survey went ahead, Mark Lehner was appointed as its Field Director. Funders were the Edgar Cayce Foundation, the Chase National Bank of Egypt and the Franzhein Synergy group.[39]

Mark Lehner completed the mapping survey in 1983 and by 1984 his reputation was sealed as America's leading expert on the Sphinx. He was then appointed Director of the newly established and much more extensive and ambitious Giza Mapping Project, again under the auspices of the ARCE, and with some funding – again – coming from the Edgar Cayce Foundation and ARE. The major financial contributors were the Yale Endowment for Egyptology, General Dynamics, the multimillionaire David Koch, and a Los Angeles real-estate tycoon named Bruce Ludwig.[40] More recently the Giza Mapping Project has been superceded by the Giza Plateau Project which also numbers David Koch and Bruce Ludwig amongst its funders and which is also directed by Mark Lehner.[41]

Pulling away

When, exactly, Professor Lehner began to pull away from the influence of the Edgar Cayce Foundation and cross over into the mainstream of professional Egyptology and its orthodoxy is not especially clear. However, some light may be shed on the matter by an interview that he gave in August 1984 to Robert Smith, editor of the ARE magazine *Venture Inward*. The interview was published in two parts in the January–February issues of 1985. Asked about his work at Giza, Lehner explained:

> The history of my involvement began in 1972 when I went on an ARE tour. We stopped in Egypt for a week and I went out to the Giza plateau with a group, and then I went out to the Giza Pyramids again by myself and sat for awhile in the King's Chamber of the Great Pyramid. I wandered around the cemeteries that are outside the Pyramid, and something plugged into me about this place. I vowed that I would be back in a year, and so I was. I went back to study at the American University in Cairo. During that year before returning to Cairo, I enthusiastically researched the Cayce readings on Egypt and put together the book, *The Egyptian Heritage*. The readings describe not only a civilization in Egypt in 10,500 BC, but also, preceding that, the lost civilization of Atlantis, which was in its final days, according to the Cayce information, when the Sphinx and the Pyramids were built . . .[42]

Lehner then explained how he had come to realize that 'there's a great disparity between the dating of the monuments by professional scholars and that given in the Cayce readings'. He added that for him investigating the Sphinx was 'just a focus of a general metaphysical and spiritual quest'. This had led him to work, he elaborated, 'with the bedrock realities [and] ground truth' – realities that had made him bracket all his expectations and ideas and 'just deal with what the site has to offer'.[43]

In *Venture Inward* magazine of May–June 1986, Robert Smith published an illuminating report about a meeting that took place at the Edgar Cayce Foundation attended by Mark Lehner, Charles Thomas Cayce (President of the ARE), James C. Windsor (President of the Edgar Cayce Foundation), Edgar Evans Cayce, and other ARE officials. On the agenda was the evaluation of future ECF/ARE activities at Giza. Setbacks and mounting scientific evidence against the Cayce prophesies had caused some to question whether it was still worthwhile funding projects there. Ironically, much of the adverse evidence was being turned up by Lehner's research.[44] Robert Smith recounts the discussion that took place:

> 'What do we do next?' asked Edgar Evans Cayce, the younger son of Edgar Cayce and a member of the Board of Trustees.
>
> 'Should we drill more holes?' asked Charles Thomas Cayce, president of the ARE, and grandson of Edgar Cayce.
>
> Neither has given up the search for Ra-Ta. Lehner, the young archaeologist who has led the search at Giza for the past decade, wants to press on with it too.
>
> 'You are not as optimistic now about the prospects of vindicating some of the things that were said about this area in the readings,' noted James C. Windsor, President of the Edgar Cayce Foundation. 'Do you have any interest in the Hall of Records? Is it worth looking for?'
>
> 'Oh, absolutely,' replied Lehner. 'I think it is, but not in as tangible a way as I used to think.'[45]

Lehner went on to explain at length why various archaeological and scientific tests had frustrated his hopes that the Cayce readings might be linked to a suitably 'tangible' reality. 'Why then continue the search?' wondered Robert Smith.

'I have a sort of gut feeling that something is under the Sphinx and that something is out there at the pyramids in the way of a mystery,' said Lehner. 'I like to think of it as something kind of pulsating.'[46]

During the meeting at the Edgar Cayce Foundation, Charles Thomas Cayce reportedly asked Lehner whether it would be possible to drill holes at regular intervals in order to locate underground passages near the Sphinx, but Lehner felt that the Egyptians would 'balk' at this idea. He suggested in passing, however, that a certain American oil company official, who at that time was apparently working for an American museum might be interested in using his 'crack geophysical prospecting team' for explorations beneath the Sphinx.[47]

Since making these statements and proposals – because, he says, of what the site has taught him – Lehner has veered further and further away from the Edgar Cayce influence. Today he repudiates any notion of an earlier civilisation in 10,500 BC. Indeed, so complete does his conversion appear to have been that in a recent denunciation of John West's geological theories concerning the Sphinx he felt compelled to state: 'I believe we have a professional responsibility to respond to notions – like those of Cayce and West – that would rob the Egyptians of their own heritage by assigning the origins and genius of Nile Valley civilization to some long-lost agent like Atlantis.'[48]

Lehner does not attempt to deny his own former involvement with the Edgar Cayce Foundation, or with ideas about Atlantis, but seeks instead to find ways to reconcile the origins of his former interests in 'mystical interpretations of the Pyramids and the Sphinx' with his present hard-core commitment to 'bedrock realities'. Lehner compares his situation to that of Sir W. M. Flinders Petrie, who had come to Egypt in the 1880s 'to test the mystical "pyramid inch" against the stone of Khufu's pyramid' – and found the 'pyramid inch' wanting.[49] Petrie, as we shall see in the next chapter, had followed in the footsteps of his father, William, and the notorious Astronomer Royal of Scotland, Piazzi Smyth – both of whom passionately believed that the Great Pyramid had been built under divine inspiration by the Israelites during their bondage in Egypt.[50]

Lunch with Mr Cayce

In May 1994 we flew to New York and made our way by car to Virginia Beach in Norfolk, Virginia, where the headquarters of the Edgar Cayce Foundation, and its partner organization the Association for Research and Enlightenment, are located. We wanted to explore the unexpected connections that this organization had at one time enjoyed with Mark Lehner, and were curious to know how – if at all – the Egyptian Antiquities Organization and Zahi Hawass, Lehner's colleague at Giza, fitted into all this.

Mutual friends arranged a meeting for us with the current President of the ARE and the Edgar Cayce Foundation, Mr Charles Thomas Cayce, the grandson of Edgar Cayce. We were also to meet two prominent ARE members who, we were informed, had contributed to various projects at Giza in the 1970s and 1980s and to the more recent geological investigations carried out by John West and Robert Schoch.

The venue was the Edgar Cayce Foundation and ARE headquarters on Atlantic Avenue. There we were greeted by cheerful and friendly staff. It was a normal busy day and we saw visitors of all ages browsing in the well-stocked library and bookshop and making their way to various lectures and meditation classes. The general atmosphere was a bit like that of the campus of a small university or college.

We were taken for lunch by Mr Cayce at the nearby Ramada Oceanfront Hotel. There we were joined by the two senior ARE members who had come from New York and Washington to meet us. The discussion at the table ranged widely and included what seemed to be a completely open and honest review of the ARE's various initiatives at Giza over the previous two decades. Everyone seemed to know Mark Lehner well, and both the man from Washington and the man from New York also spoke of Zahi Hawass in extremely personal and friendly terms.

At this point we could not avoid bringing up the matter of John West's recent sensational NBC television documentary, *Mystery of the Sphinx* which, as we saw in Part I, Lehner had treated with disfavour and which had also provoked the following vigorous rebuttal from Zahi Hawass:

> The film indicates an attempt by these pretenders to prove that the age of the Sphinx dates back to fifteen thousand years . . . [and that] the builders of the Sphinx, and consequently the Pyramids and other great antiquities, were not the ancient Egyptians but other people of higher culture and education that came from the 'Atlantis' continent after its destruction and put beneath the Sphinx the scientific records of the lost continent! It is evident that this John West represents nothing but a continuation of the cultural invasion of Egypt's civilization. Before him was Edgar Cayce in Virginia who pretended he lived in Atlantis fifteen thousand years ago and then fled to Egypt

with the records which he buried near the Sphinx before the destruction of the continent! . . .[51]

Presented late in 1993 by the Hollywood actor Charlton Heston, *Mystery of the Sphinx* had been partially financed by the ECF/ARE and their supporters, and had very strongly endorsed the view that the Sphinx, and a number of the other monuments on the Giza necropolis, must date back to at least the eleventh millennium BC.[52] As we reported in Part I, it was this same documentary that had also broken the news of Thomas Dobecki's seismic surveys around the Sphinx and his discovery of a large rectangular chamber buried deep in the bedrock beneath its front paws. This, of course, had suggested to the ECF/ARE that there could be a connection with Cayce's 'Hall of Records'. As Charlton Heston remarked in his commentary: 'the unexpected cavity detected by the seismograph was located precisely where Edgar Cayce said it would be – under the front paws of the Sphinx.'[53]

We asked Charles Cayce and his two colleagues how they felt about Hawass's angry and dismissive reaction to the film and his talk of 'pretenders'.

The ARE men simply smiled and shrugged their shoulders. They were very confident, they informed us, that everything was working for the best: no matter what anybody said or did, the truth about Giza was going to emerge and the 'Hall of Records' was going to be discovered, just as Edgar Cayce had prophesied.[54] On this note we parted company.

Correspondence

On 15 October 1995, Mark Lehner wrote us a five-page letter in response to a draft of this chapter that we had asked him to review.[55] In the same letter he informed us that he had recently resigned from Chicago University's Oriental Institute to 'devote more time to research and writing'. He also notified us that he intended to publish a book on 'New Age beliefs and Ancient Egypt' which, he said, would expound, in greater detail than we have done here, on his involvement with work funded by the Edgar Cayce Foundation.[56]

Our correspondence with Lehner was care of the Harvard Semitic

Museum in the state of Massachussets. As we write these words his colleague in Egypt, Dr Zahi Hawass, is supervising the excavation of a newly discovered 'Old Kingdom' temple complex with underground tunnels immediately to the south-east of the Great Sphinx of Giza.[57] Interviewed in December 1995 for a possible television documentary concerning the mysteries of the Sphinx, Hawass led the film crew into a tunnel beneath the Sphinx itself. 'Really,' he said, 'even Indiana Jones will never dream to be here. Can you believe it? We are now inside the Sphinx in this tunnel. This tunnel has been never opened before. No one really knows what's inside this tunnel. But we are going to open it for the first time.'

POSTSCRIPT: Further correspondence with Mark Lehner, giving his comments on this chapter, is reproduced on pages 307–14 as Appendix 3

Chapter 6

The Case of the Iron Plate, the Freemasons, the Relics and the Shafts

'I am more than convinced of the . . .
existence of a passage and probably a
chamber (in the Great Pyramid) containing
possibly the records of the ancient
founders . . .'

John Dixon. Letter to Piazzi Smyth dated 25
November 1871, commenting on the
Queen's Chamber in the Great Pyramid

'Deep inside the Great Pyramid lies a dead
end [in the southern shaft of the Queen's
Chamber]. Rudolf Gantenbrink could
explore beyond it, but no one will let him.'

Sunday Telegraph, London, 1 January 1995

Perhaps the most exotic researcher ever to have pronounced on the mysteries of the Pyramids was Charles Piazzi Smyth, a nineteenth-century Astronomer Royal of Scotland. Like Edgar Cayce, he believed the Great Pyramid to be somehow linked to Biblical prophecies concerning the 'Second Coming' of Christ. And like Edgar Cayce, too, his name turns up most unexpectedly in connection with recent remarkable discoveries at Giza.[1]

We will see why, later in this chapter. Meanwhile, as many readers will recall from the international news coverage it received at the time, high hopes were raised in March 1993 of a possible hidden chamber deep within the Great Pyramid. Rudolf Gantenbrink, a Munich-based German engineer, had used a tiny, hi-tech robot camera to explore the long narrow shafts emanating from the northern and southern walls of the Queen's Chamber and, at the end of the southern shaft (the one targeted on the star Sirius) had discovered a small portcullis door complete with copper handles. Immediately after the find was made, Dr Zahi Hawass enthused to a German television team 'in my opinion this is THE discovery in Egypt' and expressed the hope that 'records' on papyrus scrolls to do with the 'religion' of the builders and maybe the 'stars', might be stashed away behind the tantalizing door.[2] Similar hopes were also raised in *The Times* of London which, in addition, noted a curious link with Edgar Cayce and the 'Hall of Records':

> SECRET PASSAGE POSES PYRAMID MYSTERY: In the 1940s Edgar Cayce, the American clairvoyant, prophesied the discovery, in the last quarter of the 20th century and somewhere near the Sphinx, of a hidden chamber containing the historical records of Atlantis. Whether recent discoveries in the Great Pyramid of Cheops [Khufu] have anything to do with that is far from certain, but the discovery of a small door at the end of a long, hitherto unexplored, 8-inch square shaft has set many speculating about what, if anything, might lie behind it . . .[3]

As we write these words, almost three years after Rudolf Gantenbrink made his amazing discovery, no further exploration has been permitted inside the southern shaft of the Queen's Chamber and the mysterious portcullis door remains unopened. During this period we note that Dr Zahi Hawass (rather like his friend Mark Lehner over the issue of 10,500 BC) has executed a radical volte-face. Gone are the eulogies and the great expectations and he now asserts: 'I think this is not a door and nothing is behind it . . .'[4]

Double standard

The story of the Great Pyramid's shafts, and the oddly contradictory Egyptological responses to whatever is discovered in them – or whatever new ideas are proposed concerning them – goes back to the late 1830s when the British explorer Colonel Howard Vyse 'sat down before the Great Pyramid as at a fortress to be besieged'. This comment, from one of his contemporaries, alludes to Vyse's renowned use of dynamite to 'explore' the Great Pyramid.[5] It might have been more appropriate, though less polite, to say that he confronted the last surviving wonder of the ancient world as though it were a woman to be raped. Nevertheless, the fact remains that during a hectic season of explorations and intrusive excavations (1836–7), Vyse and his team did manage to make what looked like two extremely important discoveries:

1 A section of flat iron plate, about one eighth of an inch thick, a foot long and four inches wide, extracted from the masonry of the southern face of the Pyramid at the exit point of the southern shaft of the King's Chamber (the shaft targeted on Orion's belt).

2 'Quarry marks' daubed inside the so-called relieving chambers above the King's Chamber. These hieroglyphs are the first and only 'inscriptions' ever found inside the Great Pyramid. They take the form of loosely scrawled graffiti and include the name of Khufu, the Fourth Dynasty Pharaoh whom Egyptologists suppose to have been the builder of the monument.

The second find – the appearance of Khufu's name – has been repeatedly hailed by Egyptologists during the past 160 years as proof positive that the otherwise anonymous Pyramid was indeed built by the Pharaoh Khufu. The first – the iron plate – has been dismissed as a fraud and the plate itself now lies in a narrow drawer in the British Museum, as ignored and forgotten as the skull of Piltdown Man.[6]

Suppose, however, that the Egyptologists have got things the wrong way round?

Suppose that it is the 'quarry marks' that are forged and the iron plate that is genuine?

In this case the tidy and well-worked-out chronology of the evolution of Egyptian society, which appears in all the standard textbooks, would be shown to rest on frighteningly insecure foundations, the attribution of the Great Pyramid to Khufu would revert to undocumented speculation, and the orthodox date of the Iron Age in Egypt – placed by Egyptologists as being not earlier than 650 BC[7] – would have to be pushed back almost 2000 years.

We have argued elsewhere, and at length, that the quarry marks inside the Great Pyramid could have been forged – and specifically that Howard Vyse, who had spent £10,000 on his 1836–7 excavations (a princely sum in those days) had both the motive and the opportunity to forge them.[8] Briefly:

1 It is notable that the marks were only discovered in the four 'relieving chambers' opened by Vyse himself, and not in the chamber immediately below these (and immediately above the ceiling of the King's Chamber) which had been opened by a previous explorer, Nathaniel Davison, in 1765. It is also notable that Vyse's diary entry for the day on which he first opened and accessed the lowest of 'his' four chambers (i.e. the one above Davison's Chamber) reports a thorough examination but makes no mention whatsoever of any hieroglyphs prominently daubed on the walls in red paint. On the very next day, however, when Vyse returned to the chamber with witnesses, the hieroglyphs were suddenly there – almost as though they had been painted overnight.[9]

2 As one of Vyse's critics has perceptively pointed out, 'the perspective and angles at which the inscriptions were made shows that they were painted not by the quarry masons before the blocks were moved, but rather by someone working in the cramped quarters of the [relieving] chambers after the blocks had been placed in the Pyramid. Instructions for locating blocks in a construction project [which is what the quarry marks purport to be] serve no purpose after the fact has been accomplished. Clearly they were added by someone else and not by the builders themselves.'[10]

3 There are horrendous 'orthographic' problems with the hieroglyphs. These problems were first pointed out in the nineteenth century by Samuel Birch, a British Museum expert on the ancient Egyptian language. Although nobody either then or now has paid any attention to his comments, he made the important observation that the styles of writing expressed in the 'quarry marks' are a strange anomalistic hotchpotch of different eras. Some of the cursive forms and titles used in these supposedly Fourth Dynasty inscriptions are found nowhere else in Egypt until the Middle Kingdom, about 1000 years later

(when they become plentiful). Others are unknown until the Twenty-sixth Dynasty (664–525 BC). Perhaps most telling of all, however, is the use of certain words and phrases in a completely unique and zany way that occurs nowhere else in the entire sprawling corpus of writings that has come down to us from ancient Egyptian times. To give an example, the hieroglyph for 'good, gracious' appears where the number 18 is meant.[11]

4 There are difficulties with the name Khufu itself as it is given in the quarry marks. It contains a mistake (a dot surrounded by a circle instead of a simple filled-in circle) that – like the usage of the 'good, gracious' hieroglyph – is repeated on no other ancient Egyptian inscription. Interestingly, however, this same mistake in the writing out of the name Khufu occurs in the only two source books on hieroglyphs that would have been available to Vyse in 1837: Leon de Laborde's *Voyage de l'Arabie Petree* and Sir John Gardner Wilkinson's *Materia Hieroglyphica*.[12]

5 Last but not least, even if the quarry marks were not forged by Vyse, what do they really prove? Isn't attributing the Great Pyramid to Khufu on the basis of a few lines of graffiti a bit like handing over the keys of the Empire State building to a man named 'Kilroy' just because his name was found spray-painted on the walls of the lift?

We are frankly puzzled that such questions are never asked and, in general, that Egyptologists are so ready to accept the quarry marks as 'proof' of Khufu's ownership of the Pyramid. Their own credulity on such matters is of course their business. Nevertheless we think that it verges on intellectual chicanery for the same dubious attribution to be regurgitated again and again, in all the standard texts, without any cautionary notes about the many problems, anachronisms and inconsistencies that cast doubt on the authenticity and significance of Vyse's 'discovery'.[13]

Strangely, however, his other 'discovery', which Egyptologists today unhesitatingly write off as a forgery, gives every indication of being genuine – and highly significant. This was the discovery of a flat iron plate embedded in the masonry of the Pyramid's southern face.

The iron plate affair

As we have seen, the two main chambers in the superstructure of the Great Pyramid – the King's Chamber and the Queen's Chamber – are each equipped with two long, narrow shafts which bore deep into the solid masonry, one directed northward and the other to the south. Those emanating from the King's Chamber cut right through to the outside. Those emanating from the Queen's Chamber stop somewhere within the core of the monument.

The existence of the King's Chamber shafts was first recorded by Dr John Greaves, a British astronomer, in 1636. It was not until 1837, however, that they were investigated thoroughly – by Colonel Howard Vyse with the assistance of two civil engineers, John Perring and James Mash. Another member of Vyse's team was Mr J. R. Hill, an obscure Englishman living in Cairo, who in May of 1837 was put in charge of clearing the mouth of the southern shaft (which emerges at the 102nd course of masonry on the south face of the Pyramid). In accord with Vyse's methods elsewhere, Hill was instructed to use explosives and was thus responsible for the ugly vertical scar which may be seen to this day running up the centre of the south side of the Great Pyramid.

On Friday, 26 May 1837, after a couple of days of blasting and clearing, Hill discovered the flat iron plate mentioned above. Vyse was soon afterwards to trumpet it in his monumental opus, *Operations Carried on at the Pyramids of Gizeh* as 'the oldest piece of wrought iron known',[14] but Hill at the time was content to write up the discovery in the proper, sober manner:

> This is to certify that the piece of iron found by me near the mouth of the air-passage [shaft], in the southern side of the Great Pyramid at Gizeh, on Friday, May 26th, was taken out by me from an inner joint, after having removed by blasting the two outer tiers of the stones of the present surface of the Pyramid; and that no joint or opening of any sort was connected with the above mentioned joint, by which the iron could have been placed in it after the original building of the Pyramid. I also shewed the exact spot to Mr. Perring, on Saturday, June 24th.[15]

John Perring, a civil engineer, thus examined the exact spot of the find. With him was James Mash, also a civil engineer, and both were 'of the opinion that the iron must have been left in the joint during the building of the Pyramid, and that it could not have been inserted afterwards'.[16] Ultimately Vyse sent the mysterious artefact, together with the certifications of Hill, Perring and Mash, to the British Museum. There, from the outset, the general feeling was that it could not be a genuine piece, because wrought iron was unknown in the Pyramid Age, and that it must therefore have been 'introduced' in much more recent times.

In 1881 the plate was re-examined by Sir W. M. Flinders Petrie who found it difficult, for a variety of cogent reasons, to agree with this analysis:

> Though some doubt has been thrown on the piece, merely from its rarity, [he noted] yet the vouchers for it are very precise; and it has a cast of a nummulite [fossilized marine protozoa] on the rust of it, proving it to have been buried for ages beside a block of nummulitic limestone, and therefore to be certainly ancient. No reasonable doubt can therefore exist about its being a really genuine piece . . .[17]

Despite this forceful opinion from one of the oddball giants of Egyptology in the late Victorian Age, the profession as a whole has been unable to cope with the idea of a piece of wrought iron being contemporary with the Great Pyramid. Such a notion goes completely against the grain of every preconception that Egyptologists internalize throughout their careers concerning the ways in which civilizations evolve and develop.

Scientific analysis

Because of these preoccupations, no further investigations of any significance were undertaken into the iron plate for another 108 years and it was not until 1989 that a fragment from it was at last subjected to rigorous optical and chemical tests. The scientists responsible for the work were Dr M. P. Jones, Senior Tutor in the Mineral Resources Engineering Department at Imperial College, London, and his colleague Dr Sayed El Gayer, a lecturer in the Faculty of Petroleum and Mining at Egypt's Suez University, who gained his Ph.D. in extraction metallurgy at the University of Aston in Birmingham.[18]

They began their study by checking on the nickel content of the iron plate. Their reason for doing this was to exclude the faint possibility that it might have been manufactured from meteoritic iron (i.e. iron from fallen meteorites – a material that is known, very rarely, to have been used during the Pyramid Age). Ready-made meteoritic iron of this sort, however, is always extremely easy to identify because it invariably contains a significant proportion of nickel – typically seven per cent or more.[19] On the basis of their first test Jones and El Gayer noted: 'The iron plate from Giza is clearly not of meteoritic origin, since it contains only a trace of nickel.' The metal, therefore, was man-made. But how had it been made?

Further tests proved that it had been smelted at a temperature between 1000 and 1100 degrees centigrade. These tests also picked up the odd fact that there were 'traces of gold on one face of the iron plate'.[20] Perhaps, Jones and El Gayer speculated, it might originally have been 'gold-plated, and this gold may be an indication that this artefact . . . was held in great esteem when it was produced'.[21]

Finally, when was it produced?

After completing an extremely careful and detailed study, the two metallurgists reported as follows: 'It is concluded, on the basis of the present investigation, that the iron plate is very ancient. Furthermore, the metallurgical evidence supports the archaeological evidence which suggests that the plate was incorporated within the Pyramid at the time that structure was being built.'[22]

When Jones and El Gayer submitted their findings to the British Museum, they were in for quite a surprise. Instead of being excited, officials fobbed them off: 'The structure of the iron plate is unusual,' conceded Paul Craddock and Janet Lang. 'We are not sure of the significance or origin of this structure but it is not necessarily indicative of great age.'[23]

The British Museum's view

Because the iron plate appeared to have been removed originally from within or near the mouth of the King's Chamber's 'Orion' shaft it was of great interest to us. We decided to take a look at it. Through Dr A.

J. Spencer, Assistant Curator of the Egyptian Antiquities Department at the British Museum, we arranged a viewing on 7 November 1993. We were permitted to handle the plate and were intrigued by its unusual weight and texture. We could also hardly fail to notice that under its surface patina the internal metal possessed a brilliant shine – which was revealed at the point where the fragment had been cleanly sliced off for El Gayer's and Jones's analysis. Dr Spencer repeated the British Museum's official line – that the plate was not old but had been introduced, probably deliberately, in Vyse's time – and that El Gayer and Jones's conclusions were 'highly dubious'.[24]

How and why could the conclusions of such eminent metallurgists be deemed 'highly dubious', we asked?

Dr Spencer had no answer and Dr Craddock, whom we spoke to on the phone, did not wish to elaborate.

A few days later we called Dr M. P. Jones and heard from him how he and Dr El Gayer had examined the plate in the laboratories at Imperial College London in 1989. Dr Jones is now retired and lives in Wales. When we asked him what he thought of the British Museum's view of his conclusions he was, understandably, rather irritated. He insisted that the iron plate was 'very old' and, like us, he felt – since there were two opposing views – that the best way to resolve this matter would be further testing in an independent laboratory.

After all, the implications of man-made iron in 2500 BC are tremendous. And this isn't just a matter of redating the so-called Iron Age. Perhaps in a way more intriguing are the questions raised as to the *function* that an iron plate might have had, inside the southern shaft of the main chamber in the Great Pyramid, many thousands of years ago. Could there be a relationship between this plate and the stone portcullis door with copper 'handles' that Rudolf Gantenbrink had so recently discovered at the end of the southern shaft of the Queen's Chamber – a shaft directed to 'Sirius-Isis', the consort of 'Orion-Osiris'?

In their 1989 report, El Gayer and Jones noted that the plate was probably a fragment coming from a larger piece which might originally have composed a square plate that would have fitted, like a sort of 'gate', neatly over the mouth of the shaft.

Stargate

In later chapters we will make detailed reference to the so-called 'Pyramid Texts' of ancient Egypt. These texts take the form of extensive funerary and rebirth inscriptions carved on the tomb walls of certain Fifth- and Sixth-Dynasty pyramids at Saqqara, about ten miles south of Giza. Egyptologists agree that much if not all of the content of the inscriptions predates the Pyramid Age.[25] It is thus unsettling to discover in these ancient scriptures, supposedly the work of neolithic farmers who had hardly even begun to master copper, that there are abundant references to iron.

The name given to it is *B'ja* – 'the divine metal' – and we always encounter it in distinctive contexts related in one way or another to astronomy, to the stars and to the gods.[26] For example *B'ja* is frequently mentioned in the texts in connection with the 'four sons of Horus' – presumably related in some way to strange beings called the *Shemsu Hor*, the 'Followers of Horus' and 'Transfigured Ones', whom we shall also be discussing in later chapters. At any rate, these very mysterious 'sons of Horus' seem to have been made of iron or to have had iron fingers: 'Your children's children together have raised you up, namely [the four sons of Horus] . . . your mouth is split open with their iron fingers . . .'[27]

Iron is also mentioned in the texts as being necessary for the construction of a bizarre instrument called a *Meshtyw*. Very much resembling a carpenter's adze or cutting tool, this was a ceremonial device which was used to 'strike open the mouth' of the deceased Pharaoh's mummified and embalmed corpse – an indispensable ritual if the Pharaoh's soul were to be re-awakened to eternal life amidst the cycles of the stars.

In the Pyramid Texts we thus find a high priest making this cryptic statement:

> Your mouth is in good order for I split open your mouth for you . . . O king, I open your mouth for you with the adze of iron of *Upuaut*, I split open your mouth for you with the adze of iron which split open the mouths of the gods . . . Horus has split open the mouth of this king with that wherewith he split open the mouth of his father, with that wherewith he split open the mouth of Osiris . . .[28]

From such utterances, and many more like them, it is clear that iron was somehow seen by the composers of the Pyramid Texts as being imperative in the rituals aimed at ensuring new life – cosmic and stellar life – to the dead king. More importantly the above verse also connects the metal and its uses to the ancient prototype of all such rituals by means of which Osiris himself, Egypt's 'Once and Future King', died and was then restored to immortal life as Lord of the sky-region of Orion. This region, as we shall see in Part III, was known as the *Duat*. In it all the Pharaohs of Egypt hoped that they would reside eternally after their own deaths:

> The gate of the earth is open for you . . . may a stairway to the *Duat* be set up for you to the place where Orion is . . .[29]
>
> O king . . . the sky conceives you with Orion . . . the sky has borne you with Orion . . .[30]
>
> O king, be a soul like a living star . . .[31]
>
> The gate of the earth-god is open . . . may you remove yourself to the sky and sit upon your iron throne . . .[32]
>
> The aperture of the sky window is opened for you . . .[33]
>
> The doors of iron which are in the starry sky are thrown open for me, and I go through them . . .[34]

What seems to be envisaged here, taken literally and reduced to the basic common denominators running through all the above utterances, appears to be nothing less than an iron 'stargate' intended to admit Osiris, and all the dynasties of dead kings after him, into the celestial realms of the belt of Orion. But if the Pyramid Texts are describing a stargate then they are also describing a timegate – for they express no doubt that by passing through the iron-doored portals of the sky the soul of the deceased will attain a life of millions of years, navigating eternity in the vessels of the gods. Naturally, therefore, by virtue of its original position at or near the end of the southern shaft of the King's Chamber, we are tempted to wonder whether the neglected iron plate in the British Museum might have been connected with such amazingly sophisticated concepts and beliefs about immortality and about the ability of 'the equipped spirit' to gain a complete mastery over death and time.

We wonder, too, what might have been the function of other mysterious objects that were discovered in the shafts of the Queen's

Chamber when these were first opened in 1872 by Waynman Dixon, an enterprising engineer from Newcastle-upon-Tyne.

Unknown dark distance

Unlike the King's Chamber shafts, those in the Queen's Chamber (a) do not exit on the outside of the monument and (b) were not originally cut through the chamber's limestone walls. Instead the builders left the last five inches intact in the last block over the mouth of each of the shafts – thus rendering them invisible and inaccessible to any casual intruder.

The reader will recall the mention of Charles Piazzi Smyth and his prophetic theories about the Great Pyramid at the start of this chapter. In the early 1860s, when he was formulating these theories, he befriended a certain William Petrie, an engineer, whose son, W. M. Flinders Petrie, was later to be universally acclaimed as the founder of the academic discipline of Egyptology.[35]

William Petrie was amongst the first 'Pyramidologists' of the Victorian Age to give strong support to Piazzi Smyth's notion that the Great Pyramid might be some sort of prophetic monument to Mankind encoding a Messianic blueprint designed to serve as an advance-warning mechanism for the 'Second Coming' of Christ.[36] 'There had been a time', wrote Professor Hermann Bruck and Dr Mary Bruck in their authoritative biography of the Astronomer Royal, 'when Flinders Petrie and his father had wholeheartedly concurred with most of Piazzi Smyth's ideas.'[37] Indeed as these two eminent astronomers and authors point out, the young Flinders Petrie set out to Egypt in 1880 on his famous study of the Great Pyramid precisely because he wanted to 'continue Piazzi Smyth's work'.[38]

Returning now to the shafts in the Queen's Chamber, we were interested to learn that their discoverer, the engineer Waynman Dixon – together with his brother John – had also maintained very close ties with Piazzi Smyth. Indeed, it had been through the Astronomer Royal's direct influence that the Dixons were able to explore the Great Pyramid in 1872 and discover the previously concealed entrances to the northern and southern star-shafts in the Queen's Chamber.[39]

Waynman Dixon's curiosity had been aroused by the shafts in the King's Chamber which provoked him to look for similar features in the Queen's Chamber. This search, which took place some time early in 1872, was undertaken with the full knowledge of Piazzi Smyth, who later described the whole matter in his book. The story goes that after noticing a crack in the southern wall of the Queen's Chamber – roughly where he thought that he might find shafts – Waynman Dixon set his 'carpenter and man-of-all-work', a certain Bill Grundy 'to jump a hole with a hammer and steel chisel at that place. So to work the faithful fellow went, and with a will which soon began to make a way into the soft stone at this point when lo! after a comparatively very few strokes, flop went the chisel right through into something or other.'[40]

The 'something or other' Bill Grundy's chisel had reached turned out to be 'a rectangular, horizontal, tubular channel, about 9 inches by 8 inches in transverse breadth and height, going back 7 feet into the wall, and then rising at an angle into an unknown dark distance . . .'[41]

This was the southern shaft.

Next, measuring off a similar position on the north wall, Waynman Dixon 'set the invaluable Bill Grundy to work there with his hammer and steel chisel; and again, after a very little labour, flop went the said chisel through into somewhere; which somewhere was presently found to be a horizontal pipe or channel of transverse proportions like the other, and, at a distance within the masonry of 7 feet, rising at a similar angle, but in the opposite direction, and trending indefinitely far . . .'[42]

Together with his brother John, Waynman Dixon made efforts to probe both the northern and southern shafts – using a jointed rod, something like a chimney-sweep's rod, for this purpose.[43] Late-nineteenth-century technology was not up to the job and a segment of the rod became wedged in the northern shaft, where it still remains.[44] Before this happened, however, the Dixons found three small relics in the shafts.

These objects – a rough stone sphere, a small two-pronged hook

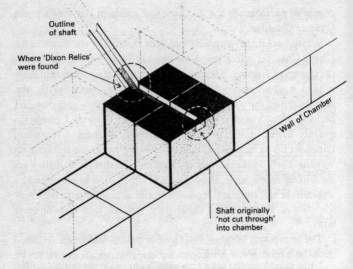

33. Detail of Queen's Chamber shaft.

made out of some form of metal, and a fine piece of cedar wood some 12 centimetres long with strange notches cut into it[45] – were exported from Egypt in the summer of 1872 and arrived safely in England a few weeks later.[46] During the next year or so they were commented upon in books, and even illustrated in scientific and popular magazines such as *Nature* and the *London Graphic*.[47] Before the turn of the century, however, they had disappeared.[48]

Links

A curious series of links exists involving all of the following:

- the discovery of Queen's Chamber shafts with their constituent relics;
- the formation of the Egyptian Exploration Society (the EES,

British Egyptology's most prestigious organization);
- the foundation, at University College, London, of Egyptology's most prestigious Chair;
- British Freemasonry.

In 1872, whilst the Dixon brothers were exploring the Great Pyramid, a well-known Freemason and parliamentarian, Sir James Alexander, proposed a motion to bring to Britain the incorrectly named 'Cleopatra's Needle' – a 200-ton obelisk of Pharaoh Thutmosis III which had originally been erected some 3500 years ago in the sacred city of Heliopolis.[49] Funding for the project came from the personal fortune of another Freemason, the eminent British dermatologist, Sir Erasmus Wilson,[50] and Sir James Alexander recommended that the civil engineer John Dixon – also a Freemason – should be engaged to collect the obelisk from Egypt. On this basis Sir Erasmus Wilson promptly recruited John Dixon – and also his brother, Waynman, who was then living in Egypt.[51]

A few years later the same Erasmus Wilson was responsible for the creation of the Egyptian Exploration Society (the EES) and served as its first president.[52] Then in 1883, Wilson and the Victorian author Emelia Edwards co-founded the important Chair in Egyptology at University College London – and it was through Wilson's personal recommendation that the young Flinders Petrie became the first scholar to occupy it.[53]

Perhaps all such connections are nothing more than quaint coincidences. If so, then it is probably also a coincidence that in the seventeenth century the founder of the Ashmolean Museum in Oxford, one of the most prestigious of today's Egyptological research centres (which holds the coveted 'Petrie Chair'), was none other than Elias Ashmole – the first man ever, according to Masonic historians, to be openly initiated on British soil into the hitherto secret society of Freemasonry.[54]

We have no evidence that the Brotherhood is still a significant influence in Egyptology today. Our researches into the pedigree of this insular discipline, however, did, in a rather oblique way, lead to the rediscovery of two of the three missing 'Dixon' relics.

The British Museum and the missing cigar box

These three items are the *only relics ever to have been found inside the Great Pyramid*. Moreover the *place* in which they were found, i.e. the star-shafts of the Queen's Chamber, links them directly to one of the key aspects of our own research. In the summer of 1993, therefore, 121 years after they had been discovered, we resolved to try to find out what had happened to them.

Going back through press reports, and the private diaries of the figures involved, we found out that John and Waynman Dixon had brought the relics to England in a cigar box. We also learned, as noted earlier, that the Dixons had been involved in bringing to England Cleopatra's Needle. The obelisk was erected on the Thames Embankment, where it stands to this day. John Dixon was at the inauguration ceremony and was on record as having buried 'a large cigar box, contents unknown' beneath the pedestal of the monument.[55]

The logic looked persuasive. John Dixon brought the relics to England in a cigar box. John Dixon brought Cleopatra's Needle to England. And John Dixon buried a cigar box beneath Cleopatra's Needle. Around that time the relics disappeared. The strong Masonic link in this affair called to mind a well-known practice in operative and speculative Freemasonry which involves certain rituals when placing the corner-stones of Masonic monuments and edifices. This practice suggested the possibility that the relics from the Great Pyramid could have been hidden under Cleopatra's Needle along with the other Masonic paraphernalia and memorabilia known to have been installed there.[56]

At any rate, the relics did genuinely seem to have disappeared and the experts whom we consulted at the British Museum said they had no idea where they could have gone to. We also consulted Professor I. E. S. Edwards, the Museum's former Keeper of Egyptian Antiquities (1954–74) and a former vice-president of the EES. Edwards is Britain's foremost authority on Giza and the author of a definitive text, *The Pyramids of Egypt*, first published in 1946 and reprinted virtually every year since then. In all editions of this book we found that he had mentioned Waynman Dixon and reported how the shafts in the Queen's Chamber were discovered, but had made absolutely no reference to the relics. This, he told us, was because he had no recollection of them and therefore, of course, no idea concerning what their ultimate fate might have been.

Like ourselves, however, Professor Edwards knew of the link between Flinders Petrie, Piazzi Smyth and the Dixons, and knew that Petrie's exploration of the Great Pyramid had immediately followed that of the Dixons.

Oddly enough, Petrie, too, makes no mention of the relics in his own famous book *Pyramids and Temples of Gizeh* – though he does speak of the Dixons and the shafts. But could he have referred to them elsewhere in his voluminous publications? Edwards suggested that we ask Petrie's biographer, the Egyptologist Mrs Margaret Hackford-Jones, to research the matter in Petrie's diaries and private papers. If he had made any mention of the Dixon relics then she would definitely be able to find it. But a thorough search by Mrs Hackford-Jones brought no results.[57]

In the absence of viable alternatives, therefore, we wondered whether it might not be worth looking to see whether the three curious objects might not still be in Dixon's cigar box underneath Cleopatra's Needle.

The story was picked up by the *Independent*, a British national newspaper, on 6 December 1993. Interviewed in the report, Professor Edwards stated categorically that neither he nor anyone else he knew had heard of these relics before.[58] We were therefore taken by surprise on 13 December 1993 – only a week after the article containing Edwards's quote was published – when Dr Vivian Davies, the Keeper of Egyptian Antiquities at the British Museum, casually announced in a letter to the *Independent* that the relics, still in the cigar box, were in his Department's keep.[59]

So why had his Department not admitted to having them before?

'I think there has been a lot of misunderstanding about this whole business,' soothed a Museum PR spokesman a few days later. 'We didn't say we did not have them, we said we were not aware of having them.'[60]

After doing some more digging we discovered what had happened. The relics (or rather two of them because the only carbon-datable item, the piece of wood, was missing) had not been placed under

Cleopatra's Needle as we had at first conjectured. Instead they had remained in the hands of the Dixon family for exactly a hundred years. Then, in 1972, Dixon's great-granddaughter had taken them along to the British Museum and had generously donated them to the Egyptian Antiquities Department. Their receipt was recorded in the meticulous hand of the Keeper himself – Dr I. E. S. Edwards.[61] Thereafter the relics seemed simply to have been forgotten and only resurfaced in December 1993 because an Egyptologist named Dr Peter Shore happened to read the *Independent*'s story about our search for them. Now retired in Liverpool, Shore had been Edwards's assistant in 1972. He remembered the arrival of the relics at the British Museum and now promptly notified the relevant authorities that they had a potentially embarrassing incident on their hands.

We naturally wondered how it was possible that mysterious relics recovered from unexplored shafts inside the Great Pyramid of Egypt could have been treated with such indifference by professional Egyptologists. To be completely honest we found it very difficult to accept that they really could just have been forgotten for twenty-one years by the British Museum's Egyptian Antiquities Department. What we could not understand at all, however, was how they could have stayed forgotten during most of 1993 after a robot had explored the very same shafts and found a much publicized closed 'door' deep within one of them. Indeed more than two weeks before the article in the *Independent* came out, Rudolf Gantenbrink, the discoverer of the 'door', had visited London and given a full lecture at the British Museum to a large group of Egyptologists – including Professor Edwards, Dr Vivian Davies and many others who knew of our search for the 'Dixon' relics. During the lecture, Gantenbrink showed and explained detailed video footage, taken by his robot, of the interior of the Queen's Chamber shafts – i.e. the shafts in which the relics had been found. As well as the 'door' at the end of the southern shaft, the footage also clearly showed, still lying on the floor of the *northern* shaft, but at higher levels than the Dixons had been able to reach, at least two distinct objects – a metallic hook, and an apparent baton of wood.[62]

In the next chapter we shall take a look at Gantenbrink's exploration, and at the events that led up to and followed it.

Chapter 7

The Case of the Robot, the Germans and the Door

> '*Upuaut*, a wolf deity . . . He was chiefly
> revered for his role as Opener of the Ways to
> the Underworld, showing the dead souls the
> path through that dark realm . . .'
>
> Veronica Ions, *Egyptian Mythology*, 1982

The introduction of a robot-camera into the narrow mouth of the southern shaft of the Queen's Chamber in March 1993, and the subsequent spectacular discovery of a closed portcullis 'door' 200 feet along that shaft, are not events that occurred in a vacuum. On the contrary, although mainstream Egyptologists profess little interest in the Queen's Chamber (which they generally regard as an 'unfinished', 'abandoned' and unimportant feature of the Great Pyramid), quite a lot of activity had taken place around it during the previous decade.

In 1986, for example, two French architects, Gilles Dormion and Jean-Patrice Goidin, somehow managed to obtain a scientific licence to conduct a spectacular exploration inside the Great Pyramid. Dormion and Goidin had persuaded certain senior officials at the Egyptian Antiquities Organization that a 'hidden chamber' could lie behind the west wall of the horizontal corridor leading to the Queen's Chamber. In a rare move, the EAO gave permission for the drilling of a series of small holes to test the theory. Apparently some evidence was found of a large 'cavity' which was filled with unusually fine sand – nothing more – but this was enough to send the world media into a frenzy and to turn Dormion and Goidin into hot media properties for a while. Egyptologists fumed on the quiet. The project was eventually stopped and Dormion and Goidin were never to resume their work in the Great Pyramid.[1]

The same thing happened again in 1988 when a Japanese scientific team from Waseda University took up the challenge. They were led by Professor Sakuji Yoshimura. This time the Japanese used 'non-destructive techniques' based on a high-tech system of electromagnetic waves and radar equipment. They, too, detected the existence of a 'cavity' off the Queen's Chamber passageway, some three metres under the floor and, as it turned out, very close to where the French had drilled. They also detected a large cavity behind the north-west wall of the Queen's Chamber itself, and a 'tunnel' outside and to the south of the Pyramid which appeared to run underneath the monument. Before any further exploration or drilling could be done, the Egyptian authorities intervened and halted the project. Yoshimura and his team were never to return to complete their work in the Queen's Chamber.[2]

It seems odd, despite all the buzz concerning hidden chambers in the vicinity of the Queen's Chamber, that nobody should have taken a closer look into the Queen's Chamber's mysterious and hitherto unexplored shafts. Disappearing as they do, one northwards and the other southwards, into the bowels of the monument, one would have thought that somebody would have had the gumption to investigate them (using video-camera reconnaissance instead of all these unsatisfactory and inconclusive drillings and radar scanning probes). Indeed, as we have argued elsewhere, there is much about their construction and design that could almost have been deliberately contrived to stimulate and invite such investigations.[3] Throughout the 1980s, however, the consensus of senior Egyptologists was that the shafts, like the Queen's Chamber itself, were 'abandoned' features of the Great Pyramid. No doubt it was the power of this consensus, and the built-in reluctance to challenge it, that discouraged individual Egyptologists from interesting themselves in the shafts. After all, what would be the point of exploring obscure parts of the Pyramid that everyone knew had been 'abandoned' during construction.

As a non-Egyptologist, the German robotics engineer Rudolf Gantenbrink did not suffer from such inhibitions. Early in 1991 he submitted a proposal for the videoscopic examination of the shafts to the German Archaeological Institute in Cairo.

Planning an adventure

Gantenbrink's story, as he reported it to us in many hours of documented conversations, goes back to August 1990 when the Egyptian Antiquities Organization commissioned the German Archaeological Institute in Cairo to install a ventilation system inside the Great Pyramid. This project would mainly involve the 'cleaning' of the two shafts of the King's Chamber which (unlike those in the Queen's Chamber) emerge on the outside faces of the pyramid and thus could be of some conceivable use for ventilation. After cleaning, powerful electric fans would be installed in their mouths to boost the natural air-flow through them.

A few months after accepting the EAO's commission for the ventilation project Rainer Stadelmann, the Director of the German Archaeological Institute, received Rudolf Gantenbrink's proposal for the exploration of the Queen's Chamber shafts using a high-tech miniature robot. This proposal, a copy of which Gantenbrink has kindly supplied to us, is entitled *Videoscopische Untersuchung der sog. Luftkanale der Cheopspyramide* (Videoscopic Investigation of the so-called Air Shafts in the Pyramid of Cheops).[4]

The proposal outlines Gantenbrink's plans to build a special robot equipped with two powerful lamps and a 'CCD Farbvideokamera' with a special fixed-focus lens giving a full 90-degrees angle of vision. The specifications of the robot would include a powerful electric motor in order for it to be able to tackle the steep slopes of the shafts. The video camera and the motor would be controlled from a console and monitor unit stationed inside the chamber and linked to the robot by electric cables. Caterpillar tracks would be fixed above and below the robot's chassis and adjusted with two sets of powerful hydrolic-suspension units in order to ensure a good grip on the ceiling and floor of the shafts.

There is nothing in the *Videoscopische* study about ventilation. What it describes is unambiguously an exploration into the unchartered regions of the Great Pyramid, an adventure in the Queen's

Chamber shafts – a 'robot's journey into the past'.[5] Nevertheless the next move was logical enough: Stadelmann passed over the EAO's 'ventilation' scheme to Rudolf Gantenbrink.

Nor did Gantenbrink object. He had intended, in any case, to examine the King's Chamber shafts at some point during his project and saw no difficulty in fitting these shafts with the electric fans called for by the ventilation scheme. Indeed the idea of getting involved in ventilating the Pyramid as well as exploring it rather appealed to him since it added a 'conservation and restoration' element to his work.

Diversion and delay

As planned, however, Gantenbrink began with the exploration of the Queen's Chamber shafts. Assigned by the German Archaeological Institute to assist Gantenbrink, and to serve as the Institute's official representative on site, was Uli Kapp (who, coincidentally, had also assisted Mark Lehner on the ARCE Sphinx Project in 1979–80).[6] The start date was February 1992 and the decision was made to tackle the southern shaft first[7] – the very shaft in which, in March 1993, the 'door' would be discovered.

The initial exploration of the shaft was not as simple as Gantenbrink had supposed. He had to adapt to the rather oppressive conditions within the Queen's Chamber and found that manoeuvring the sturdy little robot inside the confined space of the narrow and steeply sloping shaft was difficult and extremely slow work. By mid-May 1992, however, he had made considerable progress, penetrating to a depth of 70 feet. Furthermore, as he peered curiously into his monitor screen, he could see the shaft disappearing into the deep, dark distance beyond. Where did it lead to? Was it really 'abandoned' as the majority of Egyptologists maintained,[8] or did it serve some yet unknown and greater function? Hitherto Egyptologists had theorized that this shaft would not be more than 30 feet long but now Gantenbrink had proved them wrong. What could possibly lie ahead?

The desire to continue was irresistible. But at this nail-biting stage he was called to attend to the secondary ingredient of his project – the 'ventilation' of the Great Pyramid using the shafts of the King's Chamber.

Since these extend from the Chamber's northern and southern walls right through to the outside of the Pyramid, Gantenbrink was able to investigate them with a much simpler device than that required for the Queen's Chamber shafts. This device he named *Upuaut I*. Resembling a crude, miniature sledge, and mounted with a video camera, it could be hauled up and down the shafts by means of cables with pulleys at both ends.

Upuaut I could only look at the King's Chamber shafts – where it found little of interest. The cleaning job was done in a quainter manner. Gantenbrink made use of an old axle from the wreck of an abandoned truck in the nearby village of Nazlet-el-Sammam, which he attached to a cable and yanked up and down the shafts to push out the debris and sand that had piled up inside them. This done he arranged for sponsors to supply and install electric fans and then informed the German Archaeological Institute that he would now prepare for the continuation of his exploration of the much more promising and mysterious 'blind-ended' shafts of the Queen's Chamber.

Upuaut II

Gantenbrink enthusiastically proposed to Stadelmann that he would develop an even more powerful robot, to be named *Upuaut II*, in order to launch the final assault on the cramped and inaccessible shafts. This new machine would be specially designed to overcome the difficulties encountered by its predecessor (the prototype robot, used in early 1992, now discarded and jocularly named 'the father of *Upuaut*') in the first attempt to explore these shafts. *Upuaut II*, Gantenbrink had decided, would be smaller, smarter, and much stronger. He opted to design it from scratch and to this end brought together a team of engineering and electronic experts, mostly volunteers, in a special laboratory in Munich.

What they were to come up with during the course of the next year was a marvel of the space age. The body of the robot was made of a particularly light but robust aluminium used in aircraft components. A sophisticated laser was included which could probe any small and

inaccessible regions within the shaft. Hundreds of electronic components were used to form the electronic 'brain' and guidance system of
the robot. Specially designed motors and gears were fitted to the front
and rear of the main body, and steel struts were added for extra
stability. Even hydraulic high-pressure pistons were included,
capable of generating a thrust of 200 kilograms to ensure that the robot
could brace itself tightly within the shaft. A new camera unit was also
designed that could swivel not only horizontally but also vertically to
catch every conceivable angle of view. Two powerful high-intensity
bulbs, fitted on each side of the camera, would illuminate the way
ahead. Finally a special eight-wheel drive system – four gripping the
floor and four gripping the roof of the shaft – would ensure that the
robot could reach its final destination.

Problems with permits

During the latter part of 1992 and the early part of 1993, while *Upuaut
II* was being designed and built in Munich, Rudolf Gantenbrink
arranged for a television crew to come with him to Egypt to film his
forthcoming exploration of the Queen's Chamber shafts. When he
and the crew (including the film-maker Jochen Breitenstein and an
assistant, Dirk Brakebusch) arrived in Cairo on 6 March 1993,
however, the exploration and filming were delayed by something that
at first appeared to be only a minor administrative problem: the
German Archaeological Institute had not yet obtained the necessary
filming permits from the Egyptian Antiquities Organization. When
no permits were forthcoming, Gantenbrink reports that first Dr
Stadelmann and then he himself approached Zahi Hawass, the EAO's
Director-General of the Giza Pyramids, who granted 'verbal permission' for the filming to go ahead.[9]

Accordingly, the exploration began.

Discovery

Mid-March 1993 was a crucial period for Rudolf Gantenbrink in his
work inside the Great Pyramid – all the more crucial because: (a) the
whole operation had cost him a great deal of money (including

$250,000 in research-and-development costs for the robot alone); (b) it was being filmed at personal expense for a commercial documentary and (c) a deadline for the completion of the film had been set for the last week of March.

It was at around this time, says Gantenbrink, that Stadelmann recalled Uli Kapp and withdrew the official support that the German Archaeological Institute had previously accorded to the exploration of the shafts.

Perhaps other men would have stopped and gone meekly home at this point. Gantenbrink is far from meek. Feeling that he was on the verge of a breakthrough, he decided that he was going to forge on – with or without Stadelmann's support.

The crucial figure was now Zahi Hawass, whose personal authority on the site provided the whole 'official' sanction and backing for Gantenbrink's work. However, Hawass's undocumented 'verbal permission' actually counted for a great deal on the Giza plateau. Indeed it was as good as a signed and sealed mandate to the lowly *ghafirs* guarding the entrance to the Great Pyramid and was taken at face value not only by Gantenbrink and his team but also by a young inspector from the EAO, Muhammad Shahy, who had been assigned to work with the Germans.[10]

So Gantenbrink reasoned that he would still be able to go in and out and work undisturbed in the Queen's Chamber. This he successfully did, making rapid progress with the robot in the exploration of both the northern and the southern shafts.

Early on the morning of 21 March 1993, just before starting the day's work as usual, he paid a visit to Zahi Hawass at his office on the Giza plateau. There, to his consternation, he learned that the Director of the Giza Pyramids had been suspended from his post on account of an unrelated scandal concerning a missing Fourth-Dynasty statue.[11] (Hawass was not to be reinstated as Director of the Giza Pyramids until April 1994.)

This unexpected turn of events could not have come at a more vital moment – for by 21 March 1993 *Upuaut II* was deep inside the southern shaft of the Queen's Chamber and was, in Gantenbrink's opinion, very close to whatever lay at the end. The exploration, however, was to go on. Destiny had fixed an amazing rendezvous for

Gantenbrink on the next day, 22 March, coincidentally the spring equinox.

With him in the Queen's Chamber on that fateful day were Jochen Breitenstein, Dirk Brakebusch and Muhammad Shahy.[12] By 10 a.m. Gantenbrink had managed to manoeuvre *Upuaut II* a distance of 170 feet up the shaft. At about 180 feet a sharp settlement in the floor of the shaft created a dangerous obstacle that threatened to halt progress but that was eventually surmounted. Then, barely an hour later, at 11.05 a.m., after crawling a total distance of 200 feet into the shaft, the floor and walls became smooth and polished and the robot suddenly – and one might almost say 'in the nick of time' – reached the end of its journey.

As the first images of the 'door' with its peculiar metal fittings appeared on the small television monitor in the Queen's Chamber, Rudolf Gantenbrink immediately realised the massive implications of his find. This was archaeological history in the making[13] – an exciting and significant new discovery inside the world's most famous and most mysterious ancient monument. And it was interesting to note that under the lower western corner of the 'door' there was a little gap beneath which the red laser spot projected by *Upuaut* was seen to disappear. The urge to look under the 'door' and see whatever might lie beyond it must have been almost unbearable. The gap, however, was far too small for *Upuaut*'s camera to be able to peer into. A fibre-optic lens would need to be added if that was to be done, but rigging it would take days, perhaps even weeks, to organize.

After the initial excitement had died down, Gantenbrink's first instinct was to make doubly certain that the unique video images that he had been looking at on the screen had been properly recorded. Once he was satisfied that the recordings were excellent, he and his team packed the tapes, together with the rest of their gear, and returned to their base at the Movenpick Hotel.

For several days after 22 March nothing happened, with no official announcement of any kind being made to the press by the German Archaeological Institute. The reason, it seems, was that Dr Stadelmann could not make up his mind as to what form, exactly, such an announcement should take. During this hiatus, Gantenbrink and the film crew decided to return to Munich. They naturally took along all their equipment, including the twenty-eight videotapes shot during the exploration. A few days later, at the beginning of April 1993, Gantenbrink sent us a copy of the tape showing the discovery of the 'door'.

We passed this tape on to the British media.

Much ado, then nothing

The first major story appeared on the front page of the London *Independent* on 16 April 1993:

> Archaeologists have discovered the entrance to a previously unknown chamber within the largest of Egypt's Pyramids. Some evidence suggests it might contain the royal treasures of the Pharaoh Cheops [Khufu], for whom the Great Pyramid was built 4500 years ago. The contents of the chamber are almost certainly intact. The entrance is at the end of a sloping passage 65 metres long but only eight inches (20 cms) wide and eight inches high ... According to the Belgian Egyptologist Robert Bauval, the passage points directly at the Dog star Sirius, held by the ancient Egyptians to be the incarnation of the goddess Isis. Other small passages in the Pyramid appear to point to other heavenly bodies – the Belt of Orion and the star Alpha Draconis, which at the time was in the area now occupied by the Pole Star ...

The reaction to the *Independent*'s front-page splash was electrifying. Dozens of reporters from all over the world wanted to interview Gantenbrink within hours and that same evening Britain's Channel 4 TV News covered the story in depth. Dr I. E. S. Edwards made a rare appearance in this report and created something of a sensation by telling millions of excited viewers that 'a statue of the king gazing towards the constellation of Orion' might be found behind the mysterious 'door'. 'But it's a wild guess – we have no precedents,' he was quick to add.

But wild guess or not, and still with no clear statement emanating from Cairo, the international media had a field day:

'PYRAMID MAY HOLD PHARAOH'S SECRETS' ran the front page of *The Age* in Melbourne; 'SECRET CHAMBER MAY SOLVE PYRAMID RIDDLE' shouted *The Times* in London; 'NOUVEAU MYSTERE DANS LA PYRAMIDE' *Le Monde* announced excitedly in Paris; 'PYRAMID MYSTERY' reported the *Los Angeles Times*; 'VIVE LA TECHNIQUE: PORTE POUR KHEOPS!' cried *Le Matin* in Switzerland.[14]

It was almost as though the cult of the Pyramid had suddenly come to life again. At any rate the story continued to run for many more weeks in dozens of regional newspapers and several international magazines.[15] Everyone, it seemed, wanted to know what was behind the little 'door', and why the Pyramid's shafts were directed towards the stars . . .

The first official riposte came from the German Archaeological Institute, through Reuters in Germany, on 16 April 1993. Mrs Christine Egorov, Stadelmann's secretary – here presented as the *Institutsprecherin* – firmly pronounced that the very idea of a possible chamber at the end of the shaft was nonsense. The Queen's Chamber's 'air-channels', she explained, did not head in the direction of anything at all and the purpose of Gantenbrink's robot had been solely 'to measure the humidity of the Pyramid'.[16]

Soon afterwards, a second report went out on the Reuters wire, this time quoting Dr Stadelmann: 'I don't know how this story happened but I can tell you this is very annoying,' he fumed. 'There is surely no other chamber . . . there is no room behind the stone.'[17]

Political games

In the years that followed Gantenbrink made repeated efforts to get his exploration of the Queen's Chamber shafts restarted, arguing that there was no need to speculate as to whether or not the 'door' was really a door, or whether there might or might not be a chamber concealed behind it:

> I take an absolutely neutral position. It is a scientific process, and there is no need whatsoever to answer questions with speculation when questions could be answered much more easily by continuing the research . . . We have a device (ultrasonic) that would discover if there is a cavity behind the slab. It's nonsensical to make theories when we have the tools to discover the facts.'[18]

One of the main problems that Gantenbrink faced was that he did not belong to the Egyptological profession but was regarded by the leading academics at Giza as a hired technician – which meant, by definition, that his views were assumed to have no merit. He explained how, after discovering the slab-door in March 1993, he had been all but ignored and the find handled with indifference: 'I was scheduled to meet the Minister of Culture about the discovery, but it never happened. A press conference was scheduled. It never happened.' [19]

In late 1994, Gantenbrink announced in Paris that he was willing to supply the robot to the Egyptians and even train an Egyptian technician at his own expense so that the exploration could resume, but a few weeks later he was politely rebuffed by the EAO's Chairman, Dr Nur El Din: 'Thank you for your offer to train the Egyptian technician [Nur El Din had written] . . . unfortunately we are very busy for the time being, therefore we will postpone the matter.' [20]

'The search for truth', Gantenbrink commented in January 1995, 'is too important to be ruined by a silly political game. My only hope is that they will soon reach the same conclusions.' [21]

Breakfast with Gantenbrink

On 19 February 1995 we arrived in Egypt and the next morning had breakfast with Rudolf Gantenbrink at the Movenpick Hotel in Giza.

He had been in Egypt for most of the previous week, still trying to obtain permission to resume his exploration of the Queen's Chamber shafts, and was returning to Munich later that morning. During his visit, he told us, he had finally managed to have a face-to-face meeting with Dr Nur El Din.

'What was the response?' we asked.

Gantenbrink shrugged his shoulders: 'Encouraging.' But he looked less than encouraged.

We then asked if he had been back inside the Queen's Chamber on this visit.

'No,' he replied, 'I prefer not to go there.'

He could not bear the thought, he told us, of returning to the site of his great discovery without his robot, purposelessly, like a tourist. 'I will go back in the Queen's Chamber with *Upuaut* and complete the exploration of the shafts,' he said proudly, 'or I won't go back there at all.'

Select groups

That same month – February 1995 – one of the most prosperous and active members of the Association for Research and Enlightenment spoke to us by telephone from the United States about plans that were in hand for furthering the quest for the Hall of Records at the Giza necropolis:

> The next three years are going to be super years . . . We sort of have '96 set up for our little expedition to the Sphinx – with underground radar. 1996 was when Zahi said we'd be able to go. We'll do more ground-scanning and most of all we're going to get to love and understand the people around us, and the various groups, and work with them . . . and I figure that by '98 we'll hit something.[22]

We learnt in the same conversation that the same individual had been keeping a close watch on events surrounding the hidden door in the Great Pyramid during the two years since Rudolf Gantenbrink's project had ground to a halt. He claimed to have been informed that the Egyptian authorities would soon make an attempt to reach the door with their own robot in order to insert a fibre-optic camera beneath it and to see whatever lies beyond. Our informant also said that he had been invited by 'Zahi' to be amongst the select group of witnesses present inside the Pyramid when this moment eventually comes: 'He promised me a one-month's advance notice before they do anything . . . Something's definitely going to happen. He's not sure when. He had delays – I think with the robot – but they'll get it done . . .'[23]

One thing at any rate seems certain: Rudolf Gantenbrink, whose inventiveness and daring led to the original discovery of the door at the end of the Queen's Chamber's mysterious southern shaft, is unlikely to be present. In September 1995 it was reported to us that the Egyptian Antiquities Organization had issued notification to the German authorities advising that they did not wish to pursue the exploration in the Great Pyramid.[24]

Burial

After reviewing the scholarly goings on concerning the possible geological antiquity of the Sphinx and the 'anomalies' located in the bedrock beneath it, the case of the iron plate in the southern shaft of the King's Chamber, and the case of the relics found in the shafts of the Queen's Chamber, we are frankly not surprised by the case of Gantenbrink's 'door'. Here, too, orthodox academics have participated in the burial of research that promises new insights into the Giza monuments and – to this day – the 'door' remains unopened.

We have no opinion as to whether or not it might lead to a 'Hall of Records' – 'records' on papyrus scrolls to do with the 'religion' of the builders as Zahi Hawass speculated in 1993 during his year of absence from his post as Director of the Giza Pyramids.[25] Our own research has convinced us, however, that the shaft in which Rudolf Gantenbrink made his remarkable discovery is linked to an archaic system of beliefs and rituals that envisaged the monuments of the Giza necropolis as an 'image of heaven'.

In Parts III and IV we will attempt to decode this image and learn its meaning.

Part III
Duality

Chapter 8

The Clues of Duality

'Newton . . . was the last of the magicians . . .
Why do I call him a magician? Because he
looked at the whole universe and all that is in
it as a riddle, as a secret that could be read by
applying pure thought to certain evidence,
certain mystic clues which God had laid
about the world to allow a sort of
philosopher's treasure hunt to the esoteric
brotherhood. He believed that these clues
were to be found partly in the heavens . . .
partly in certain papers and traditions
handed down by the bretheren . . . By pure
thought, by concentration of mind, the
riddle, he believed, would be revealed to the
initiate . . .'

John Maynard Keynes, The Royal Society,
Newton Tercentenary Celebrations, 1947

We saw in Parts I and II how the astronomical character of the
architecture of the Sphinx and of the Giza Pyramids has failed to
interest Egyptologists and has not been taken into account in their
analysis of the function and significance of the monuments. This, in
our view, has resulted in a number of serious misinterpretations of the
available evidence – perhaps the most flagrant examples of which, at
the level of physical exploration and research, have been the chronic
neglect of the four astronomically aligned shafts of the Great Pyramid
and the long and shocking period of inactivity over the matter of the
'door' in the southern shaft of the Queen's Chamber.

We hinted at the end of Part I that the logic of all these shafts, and of
the ground-plan and symbolism of the Pyramids and the Sphinx,

appear to be connected to certain very powerful religious and cosmological ideas set out in ancient Egyptian funerary and rebirth texts and in the so-called 'Hermetic' writings. These express the philosophy 'as above, so below' and advocate the drawing down to earth of cosmic powers as an essential step in Mankind's quest for knowledge of the divine and immortality of the soul: 'And I, said Hermes, will make Mankind intelligent, I will confer wisdom on them, and make known to them the truth. I will never cease to benefit thereby the life of mortal men; and then will I benefit each one of them, when the force of nature working in him is in accord with the movement of the stars above.' [1]

In the following chapters we will offer evidence to suggest that the extraordinary monuments of the Giza necropolis are part of a grand and long-forgotten scheme to initiate certain select individuals, the most recent of whom were the Pharaohs of Egypt, into an esoteric cosmic wisdom linking earth to heaven by means of which they sincerely expected to transcend the limits of death:

> All the world which lies below has been set in order and filled with contents by the things which are placed above; for the things below have not the power to set in order the world above. The weaker mysteries must yield to the stronger; and the system of things on high is stronger than the things below. [2]

> Thy protector is the Star-God . . . thy soul passeth on . . . thy body is equipped with power . . . The doors of the hidden land are opened before thee . . . Osiris, conqueror of millions of years, cometh unto thee . . . [3]

Cosmic environment

The world view of the ancient Egyptians, which they appear to have inherited intact and fully formed at the very beginning of their historical civilization some 5000 years ago, was profoundly dualistic and cosmological. The foundation of Pharaonic theocracy, the unification of the 'Two Lands' of Upper and Lower Egypt into one kingdom, the notions that they had of their own past and ancestry, their laws and calendrical measures, the architecture of their temples and pyramid complexes, and even the land of Egypt itself and the Nile – all these were cosmological concepts to them. Indeed, they saw their cosmic environment (the sky, the Milky Way, the sun and the stars, the moon and the planets, and all their cycles) as being bound together in perfect duality with their earthly environment (their land and the Nile, their living king and his ancestors, and the cycles of the seasons and epochs).

We suspect that the history of ancient Egypt, to the extent that it was written down *at all* in papyri and tablets and inscriptions, was frequently expressed in a kind of 'cosmic code' ritualistically and symbolically linked – like the Pyramids themselves – to the ever-changing patterns of the sky. From this it follows that we must look to the sky, just as the Egyptians did, if we wish to understand the ideas that they were trying to communicate in their (on the face of things) extremely strange and problematic religious writings. These writings include mysterious and archaic texts aimed at guiding the afterlife journey of the deceased, such as the *Book of the Dead* (which the ancient Egyptians knew as *Per-Ém-Hru*, the Book of 'Coming Forth By Day'), the *Book of Two Ways*, the *Book of Gates*, the *Book of What is in the Duat* and the *Coffin Texts*. Oldest and most enigmatic of all these funerary and rebirth documents however, are the so-called *Pyramid Texts* which began to be copied and compiled from older sources in the second half of the third millennium BC. These remarkable records have come down to us in the form of lavish hieroglyphic inscriptions on the tomb walls of a number of Fifth- and Sixth-Dynasty pyramids at Saqqara, some ten miles to the south of the Giza necropolis, and offer us a hitherto neglected key by means of which the secrets of the great Pyramids and the Sphinx can be unlocked.

Astronomical essence

All the above-named documents, and many more, have been translated into modern languages during the past hundred years, and all have been studied by scholars – the majority of whom would not dispute that they incorporate a complex network of astronomical references, symbols, allegories and allusions.[4] Only a handful of researchers, however, have considered the possibility that these astronomical characteristics could constitute the *essence* of the texts. In this group the late Giorgio de Santillana and Hertha von Dechend, whose study, *Hamlet's Mill*, we encountered in Chapter 4, have commented on the manner in which the soul of the deceased Pharaoh was thought of as having travelled through the skies:

> . . . well-equipped . . . with his Pyramid Text or Coffin Text, which represented his indispensable timetable and contained the ordained addresses of every celestial individual he was expected to meet. The Pharaoh relied upon his particular text as the less distinguished dead relied upon his copy of chapters from the *Book of the Dead*, and he was prepared to change shape into the . . . semblance of whatever celestial 'station' must be passed, and to recite the fitting formulae to overcome hostile beings . . .[5]

Santillana and von Dechend also comment, somewhat witheringly, on the hopeless inadequacy of many of the translations that scholars work with today – translations which treat the astronomical aspects of the texts as though they are of no particular relevance:

> So the elaborate instructions in the *Book of the Dead*, referring to the soul's celestial voyage, translate into 'mystical' talk, and must be treated as holy mumbo jumbo. But then, modern translators believe so firmly in their own invention, according to which the underworld has to be looked for in the interior of our globe – instead of in the sky – that even 370 specific astronomical terms would not cause them to stumble.[6]

The problem identified here is, we will demonstrate, a large and multi-faceted one which has led scholarly analysis of the texts into a blind alley through a complete and conspicuous neglect of: (a) the most important religious concept of the ancient Egyptians; (b) the most vital feature of their land and sky and (c) the most fundamental element of their spiritual and cosmological beliefs.

Otherworld

In the earliest religious writings that have survived from ancient Egypt a powerful symbolic terminology is used to describe the cosmic 'world of the dead' and its features. This world is referred to as the *Duat*[7] – a concept that is routinely translated by modern Egyptologists as 'the Underworld' (or sometimes as the 'Netherworld').[8] In the Pyramid Texts, however, the *Duat* is clearly a location in the starry sky – as many distinguished Egyptologists of earlier generations such as Selim Hassan, Sir E. A. Wallis Budge and Kurt Sethe were undoubtedly aware.[9] Yet even these pioneers failed to get to grips with the full implications and characteristics of the concept because they lacked familiarity with astronomy.

For example, in his analysis of the various ways in which the word *Duat* was inscribed in hieroglyphic characters throughout the whole span of Egyptian history, Selim Hassan makes the following comment: 'If we consider the evidence afforded by the meaning of its name during the Old Kingdom [the Pyramid Age], we shall see that the original *Duat*, the future Underworld, was localized in the sky.'[10] He then cites the view of Kurt Sethe that 'the *Duat* could be either the red glow of twilight which precedes the dawn (i.e. the "false dawn") or the spacious region in the east of the sky where this glow appears . . .'[11]

Hassan goes on to quote from line 151 of the Pyramid Texts: 'Orion has been enveloped by the *Duat*; while he who lives in the Horizon (i.e. Re [the sun-god]) purifies himself; Sothis [Sirius] has been enveloped by the *Duat* . . . in the embrace of [their] father Atum.'

In Hassan's opinion: 'This clearly shows how, as the sun rises and purifies himself in the Horizon, the stars Orion and Sothis [Sirius], with whom the King is identified, are enveloped by the *Duat*. This is a true observation of nature, and it really appears as though the stars are swallowed up each morning in the increasing glow of the dawn. Perhaps the determinative of the word *Duat*, the star within a circle, illustrates the idea of this enveloping of the star. When on his way to join the stars, the dead king must first pass by (or through) the *Duat* which will serve to guide him in the right direction. Thus we see in Utterance 610 [of the Pyramid Texts]: "The *Duat* guides your feet to the Dwelling-place of Orion . . . The *Duat* guides your hand to the Dwelling-place of Orion." . . .'[12]

Stars rising with the sun

Hassan's assessment of the celestial landscape of the *Duat* is only accurate in as much as he realizes that it is in the east, that the moment of observation is the pre-dawn (which he calls 'false dawn', and that

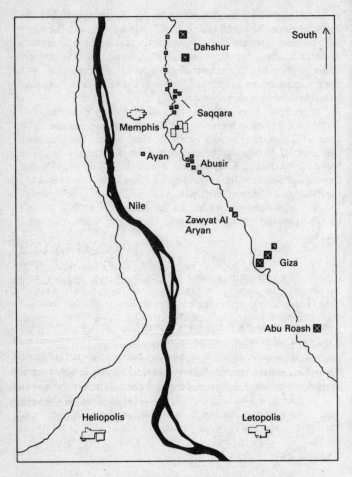

34. The 'Memphite necropolis' – Pyramid fields from Abu Roash to Dahshur.

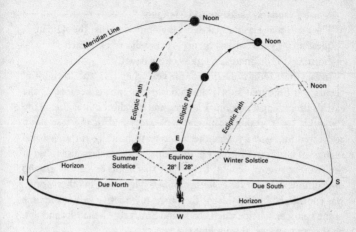

35. Rising points of the sun at the solstices and equinoxes as observed from the Memphite necropolis. In the epoch of 2500 BC – the 'Pyramid Age' – the *Duat* was observed and considered to be active only at the time of the summer solstice when the stars of Orion and Sirius rose heliacally (i.e. just ahead of the sun) at dawn.

the constellation of Orion (Osiris), the star Sirius (Isis), the sun (Re), and some other cosmic feature representing 'Atum' (the 'Father' of the Gods), are all to be found in the *Duat*. Because he is not conversant with basic celestial mechanics, however, and because he fails to set the relevant lines from the Pyramid Texts in the context of their time and their place, he then goes on to make a serious error of interpretation which has subsequently been compounded by numerous other astronomically illiterate scholars:

1 The time the Pyramid Texts were compiled was the epoch of 2800 BC to 2300 BC approximately.[13]

2 The place of observation of the sky was just south of modern Cairo in the so-called 'Memphite necropolis' (named after *Mennefer*, later 'Memphis', the first historically recognized capital of ancient Egypt), where stand the great Pyramids of Giza (and also lesser Old Kingdom pyramids such as those at Abu Roash,

Abusir, Saqqara, Dahshur and Meidum).[14]

3 The error that Hassan makes is his assumption that the stars in question – i.e. Orion and Sirius – are swallowed up 'each morning' in the 'increasing glow of the dawn.'

In fact there is only one time of the year when this 'swallowing-up' occurs – a time that slowly alters down the epochs because of the earth's precessional motion. The long and the short of it is that in the Pyramid Age the specific phenomena described in the texts, and addressed by Hassan (phenomena known technically as the 'heliacal risings' of Orion and Sirius, i.e. the risings of these stars just ahead of the sun at dawn) could only have been observed at around midsummer – i.e. *at the summer solstice.*[15] The *Duat*, in other words, was considered by the ancient Egyptians to be active *only* at the time of the summer solstice when Orion and Sirius rose heliacally and not, as Hassan suggests, throughout the year.

With these facts in mind, let us attempt to reinterpret the cosmic *Duat*, this time placing it in its proper astronomical context.

Cosmic river

One of the most salient features of the *Duat*, as it is described in the ancient Egyptian texts, is its relationship to a great cosmic 'river' called the 'Winding Waterway'. Several studies have confirmed beyond any serious doubt that the 'Winding Waterway' was the magical band of light meandering across the sky that we know as the 'Milky Way'.[16] It is also evident that the ancient priest-astronomers who compiled the Pyramid Texts identified the terrestrial counterpart of this 'Winding Waterway' in the sky as the River Nile and its yearly flood, the 'Great Inundation', which also happened to coincide with the summer solstice:[17]

The Winding Waterway is flooded, the Fields of Rushes are filled with water, and I am ferried over thereon to yonder eastern side of the Sky, place where the gods fashioned me . . . [Orion's] sister is Sothis
. . .[18]

. . . e to my waterways which are in the bank of the Flood of the Great Inundation, to the place of contentment . . . which is in the Horizon . . .[19]

May you lift me and raise me to the Winding Waterway, may you set me among the gods, the Imperishable stars . . .[20]

As Sir E. A. Wallis Budge rightly observed: 'the Egyptians . . . from the earliest times . . . depicted to themselves a material heaven [the *Duat*] . . . on the banks of a Heavenly Nile, whereon they built cities.'[21] And similarly the philologist Raymond Faulkner, who translated the Pyramid Texts and much of the other religious literature of ancient Egypt into English, could not avoid making the obvious correlations between the 'celestial river', the 'Winding Waterway' and the Milky Way.[22]

Kingdom of Osiris in the sky

The stars of Orion and Sirius are located on the right bank of the Milky Way, which – at the summer solstice in the Pyramid Age – would have appeared as a vertical 'cosmic river' in the pre-dawn in the east.

To the ancient Egyptians, therefore, the *Duat* could not possibly have been seen merely as some vague, blank, rose-tinted region somewhere over the eastern horizon. On the contrary, it clearly had an extremely specific address in the sky – the 'Dwelling Place' of 'Orion and Sirius' on the banks of the 'celestial Nile':

Be firm O Osiris-King [Orion] on the underside of the sky with the Beautiful Star [Sirius] upon the bend of the Winding Waterway . . .[23]

Betake yourself to the Waterway . . . May a stairway to the *Duat* be set for you to the place where Orion is . . .[24]

O King, you are this Great Star, the companion of Orion, who traverses the sky with Orion, who navigates [in] the *Duat* with Osiris . . .'[25]

With this starry landscape in mind, we can begin to conjure up a fairly detailed image of the *Duat*, the 'Kingdom of Osiris' in the sky – a distinct pattern of stars, at a specific celestial location, that comes complete with its own 'cosmic Nile'.

But when was this cosmic kingdom 'founded'?

'First Time'

In their most profound and beautiful religious texts, as we noted in Part I, the ancient Egyptians spoke of 'the time of the gods', *Zep Tepi*

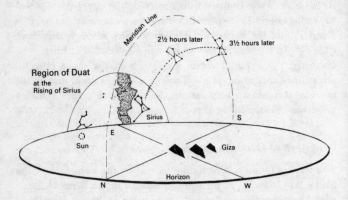

36. The sky region of the *Duat* with the stars of Orion and Sirius rising heliacally just ahead of the sun at dawn on the summer solstice. It was at this time of the year, and at this moment only, that the *Duat* was considered to be 'active'. Note that the Milky Way at this same moment appeared as a vertical 'cosmic river' in the east. Also shown is the trajectory of the Orion stars after their dawn rising until their culmination at the meridian.

(literally the 'First Time') with the unshakeable conviction that there had indeed been such an epoch. In other words, they believed that *Zep Tepi* had been an actual, historical event. In line with their prevailing dualism they also believed that it had been projected and 'recorded' in the catalogue of the starry sky. Indeed it was a story that was re-enacted endlessly in the cosmic setting by the cyclical displays of the celestial orbs and the constellations.

What they had in mind, in other words, was a kind of cosmic 'passion play', expressed in the language of allegorical astronomy, in which each main character was identified with a specific celestial body. Re was the sun, Osiris was Orion, Isis was the star Sirius, Thoth was the moon – and so on and so forth. Nor was the drama only confined to the celestial realms; on the contrary, as one might expect in dualistic ancient Egypt, it was also re-enacted on the ground, amidst the cosmic ambiance of the astronomical Pyramids of Giza, where the events of the 'First Time' were commemorated for millennia in secret rituals and liturgies.[26]

Very little is known about these liturgies, or about the myths they expressed. As the Egyptologist R. T. Rundle Clark explains:

> The creation of the myths was founded on certain principles. These are strange and, as yet, only partially understood. The most important element seems to have been as follows:
>
> (a) The basic principles of life, nature and society were determined by the gods long ago, before the establishment of kingship. This epoch – *Zep Tepi* – 'the First Time' – stretched from the first stirring of the High God in the Primeval Waters to the settling of Horus upon the throne and the redemption of Osiris. All proper myths relate events or manifestations of this epoch.
>
> (b) Anything whose existence or authority had to be justified or explained must be referred to the 'First Time'. This was true for natural phenomena, rituals, royal insignia, the plans of temples, magical or medical formulae, the hieroglyphic system of writing, the calendar – the whole paraphernalia of the civilization . . .[27]

Rundle Clark has also recognized that Egyptian art 'is nearly all symbolism', that 'the architectural arrangements and decoration were a kind of mythical landscape' worked down to the last detail, and that everything had a meaning:

> The shrine [tomb or pyramid complex] of the god [the king], for instance, was the 'Horizon', the land of glorious light beyond the dawn horizon where the gods dwelt. The Temple was an image of the universe as it now existed and, at the same time, the land on which it stood was the Primeval Mound which arose from the waters of the Primeval Ocean at Creation . . . At the close of the daily temple service, the priests raised a small figure of *Maat* (the goddess of Law and Order) in front of the divine image. This act was meant to assert that rightness and order had been re-established, but it was also a repetition of an event that took place at the beginning of the world . . . of some mythical happening in the time of the gods . . .[28]

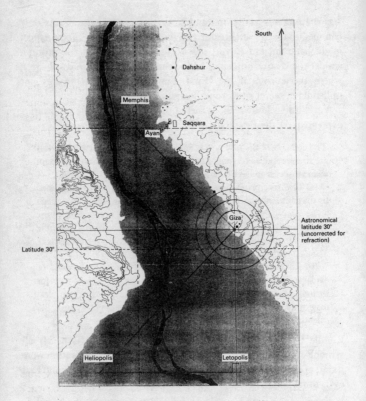

37. The huge triangular region just south of the apex of the Nile Delta encompassing Heliopolis, Memphis and Giza was regarded by the ancient Egyptians as the actual geographical location of the events of the 'First Time' – a sort of geodetic 'Garden of Eden' focused on astronomical latitude 30 degrees north.

Golden Age and the entry of evil

In later chapters we shall be returning to take a closer look at this 'First Time' of the gods. Here, however, it is sufficient to note that *Zep Tepi* was regarded as a mysterious and wonderful golden age that had immediately followed Creation. Furthermore, in the minds of the ancient Egyptians at least, this golden age had not occurred in some hard-to-find never-never land like the Biblical 'Garden of Eden' but in a familiar and unmistakably real physical and historical setting. Indeed it was their emphatic belief that the huge triangular region just south of the apex of the Nile Delta encompassing Heliopolis, Memphis and Giza was the actual geographical location of the events of the 'First Time' – a real 'Garden of Eden', in short, with real geographical features and places. It was here, amidst this sacred landscape, that the gods of the 'First Time' were said in the texts to have established their earthly kingdom.[29]

And what was the cultural character of that Kingdom? Rundle Clark gives the best summary:

> . . . all that was good or efficacious was established on the principles laid down in the 'First Time' – which was, therefore, a golden age of absolute perfection – 'before rage or clamour or strife or uproar had come about'. No death, disease or disaster occurred in this blissful epoch, known variously as 'the time of Re', 'the time of Osiris', or 'the time of Horus' . . .[30]

The gods Osiris and Horus, together with Re (in his composite form as Re-Atum, the 'Father' of the gods) were regarded by the ancient Egyptians as the supreme expressions and exemplars of the 'blissful epoch of the "First Time" '.[31]

Osiris they remembered in particular for having been the first to sit on the throne of this divine Kingdom, which he ruled jointly with his consort Isis.[32] The golden age of plenty over which the royal couple presided (during which agriculture and animal husbandry were taught to humans and laws and religious doctrines were set for them) was however brought to an abrupt and violent halt when Osiris was murdered by his brother, Seth. Left without child, Isis brought the dead Osiris back to life for long enough to receive his seed. As a result of this union she, in due course, gave birth to Horus whose destiny it was to wrangle back the 'kingdom of Osiris' from the clutches of his evil uncle Seth.

Shabaka texts

In all its essential elements this is, of course, the story that we know as Hamlet (which has a far older pedigree than the Shakespeare play[33]), and it is also, in its most recent Hollywood manifestation, the story of the *Lion King* (brother murders brother, bereaved son of the murder victim takes revenge on his uncle and sets the Kingdom to rights).

The original Egyptian version of the story – the so-called 'Memphite Theology' – is found in texts inscribed on a monument known as the 'Shabaka Stone', now in the British Museum.[34] Here we read how, after a great quarrel between Horus and Seth (in which Horus lost an eye and Seth a testicle) Geb, the earth-god (the father of Osiris and Isis), summoned the Great Council of the Gods – the nine-member 'Ennead' of Heliopolis – and with them passed judgement between Horus and Seth:

> Geb, lord of the gods, commanded the Nine Gods to gather to him. He judged between Horus and Seth; he ended their quarrel. He made Seth king of Upper Egypt, up to the place in which he was born, which is Su. And Geb made Horus king of Lower Egypt, up to the place in which his father [Osiris] was drowned[35] which is 'Division-of-the-Two-Lands'. Thus Horus stood over one region, and Seth stood over one region. They made peace over the Two Lands at Ayan. That was the division of the Two Lands . . .[36]

Let us note in passing that Ayan is not a mythical place but was an actual, physical location in ancient Egypt immediately to the north of Memphis, the Early Dynastic capital city.[37] The judgement that was made here was later changed, as the Shabaka Texts go on to tell us:

> Then it seemed wrong to Geb that the portion of Horus was like the portion of Seth. So Geb gave to Horus his [Seth's] inheritance, for he [Horus] is the son of his first born [Osiris] . . .
> Then Horus stood over the two lands. He is the uniter of the Two Lands, proclaimed in the great name: *Ta-tenen*, 'South-of-his-Wall', 'Lord of Eternity' . . . He is Horus, who arose as King of Upper and

Lower Egypt, who united the Two Lands in the [District] of the Wall [Memphis], the place where the Two Lands were united . . .[38]

Treasure trail

What we have in this amazing story is a sort of treasure trail of clues as to how the ancient Egyptians themselves saw the mythical-historical transfer of the 'deeds' or keys of the 'Kingdom of Osiris' to Horus by the Great Ennead and Geb.

It seems clear, for example, that this momentous event was thought to have taken place at Ayan, immediately to the north of Memphis, i.e. about 10 miles or so south of modern Cairo.[39]

And as for the dead Osiris, the Shabaka Texts tell us how the god was taken and buried 'in the land of Sokar':

> This is the land . . . the burial [place] of Osiris in the House of Sokar . . . Horus speaks to Isis and [her sister] Nepthys: 'Hurry, grasp him . . .' Isis and Nepthys speak to Osiris: 'We come, we take you . . .' They heeded in time and brought him to land. He entered the hidden portals in the glory of the Lords of Eternity. Thus Osiris came into the Earth, at the Royal Fortress, to the north of the land to which he had come. And his son Horus as king of Upper Egypt, arose as king of Lower Egypt in the embrace of his father Osiris . . .[40]

Where, what, and whose was the 'land of Sokar'?

It turns out to have been an epithet used by the ancient Egyptians to describe the extensive 'Memphite necropolis' incorporating the Pyramid-field of Giza. According to Sir E. A. Wallis Budge, for example: 'The dominions of Sokar were situated in the deserts round about Memphis and were supposed to cover a large extent of territory.'[41] I. E. S. Edwards tells us that the name 'Sokar' was that of 'the god of the Memphite necropolis' – a predynastic deity of the dead – and that 'by Pyramid times Osiris had become identified with Sokar'.[42] R. T. Rundle Clark then further complicates the picture by speaking of 'Rostau, the modern Giza, the burial place of Memphis and the home of a form of Osiris known as Sokar'.[43]

What confronts us, therefore, appears to be a linked sequence of ideas involving Osiris, Sokar, the 'land of Sokar' (identified with the Memphite necropolis), and now 'Rostau', the ancient Egyptian name

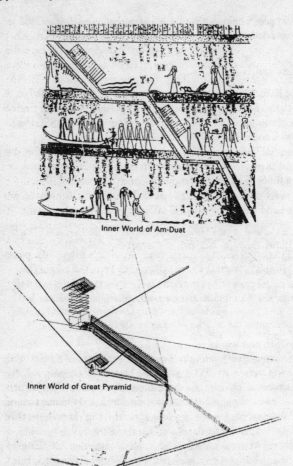

Inner World of Am-Duat

Inner World of Great Pyramid

38. The passageways, chambers and corridors of the 'land of Sokar' in the Fifth Division of the *Duat* as depicted on tomb walls bear a close resemblance to the passageways, chambers and corridors of the Great Pyramid. Could one of the functions of the Pyramid have been to serve as a kind of 'model' or simulation of the afterworld in which initiates underwent trials and ordeals?

for the Pyramid-field at Giza – a name that is in fact carved in hieroglyphs on the granite stela, which we encountered in Part I, that stands to this day between the paws of the Great Sphinx.[44] That same stela also describes Giza in more general terms as 'the Splendid Place of the "First Time" ' and speaks of the Sphinx as standing beside 'the House of Sokar'.[45]

So the clues on the treasure trail, as well as Osiris, Sokar, the land of Sokar and Rostau-Giza, now also include the 'House of Sokar' and lead us back towards *Zep Tepi*, the 'First Time'.

Bearing all this in mind, let us return for a final look at the Memphite theology as it is expressed in the Shabaka Texts.

We find Horus firmly in possesion of the earthly 'Kingdom of Osiris' (which had of course been founded in the 'First Time') and we find the body of Osiris himself safely installed in 'the House of Sokar'.[46] Under these ideal conditions, according to the texts, the spritualized form of Osiris was freed to depart to the sky – and to a specific location in the sky that we have already identified: 'the place where Orion is'.[47] There it was held that he had established the *Duat* – the cosmic 'Otherworld' on the right bank of the Milky Way – as a sort of celestial 'Kingdom of Osiris' for the Dead.[48]

Sphinx god

Selim Hassan actually calls the *Duat* 'the Kingdom of Osiris' and shows how 'Osiris is styled "Lord of the *Duat*" and the Osiris-King [i.e. the deceased Pharaoh] "a companion of Orion" . . .'[49] He then provides a piece of incidental information which adds to our trail of clues when he points out, on the basis of careful textual analysis, that the *Duat* appears in some way to be linked to Rostau.[50]

Like other commentators, Hassan acknowledges that 'the name of Rostau is applied to the Giza necropolis'.[51] But he also, at various points, defines Rostau as 'the Kingdom of Osiris in the tomb',[52] and as 'the Memphite Underworld' – i.e. the Memphite *Duat*.[53] In this context he examines the so–called twelve 'Divisions' (or 'Hours') of the *Book of What is in the Duat* and shows that references to the 'land of Sokar' appear in this text. Indeed, to be a little more specific, he draws our attention to a most intriguing fact. The land of Sokar occupies the Fifth Division of the *Duat*[54] and: 'The centre of the Fifth Division [is] called Rostau.'[55]

So Egyptologists do not dispute that we have a Rostau on the ground in the form of the Pyramid-field at Giza and a Rostau in the sky in the form of the Fifth Division of the *Duat* – a place, as the reader will recall, that was not seen as an 'Underworld' by the ancient Egyptians but rather as a specific celestial location in Orion.

Furthermore, as we noted in passing in Part I, the passageways, chambers and corridors of the land of Sokar – amply protrayed on tomb walls in surviving depictions of the Fifth Division of the *Duat* – uncannily resemble the passageways, chambers and corridors of the Great Pyramid of Giza. Indeed the resemblance is so close that it is permissible to wonder whether one of the functions of the Pyramid may have been to serve as a kind of model or 'simulation' of the afterworld in which initiates underwent trials and ordeals intended to prepare them intellectually and spiritually for the terrifying experiences and judgements that the soul was believed to confront after death.

Here, perhaps, was the testing ground for the ancient Egyptian 'science of immortality' elaborated in every utterance and vignette of the principal funerary and rebirth texts – the purpose of which was to facilitate the journey of the soul through the daunting traps and pitfalls of the *Duat*.

Additional food for thought in this regard is provided by Selim Hassan who does not neglect to mention that one of the distinguishing features of the Fifth Division of the *Duat* is the presence there of a giant 'double-lion' Sphinx-god named Aker, who seemingly protects the 'Kingdom of Sokar'.[56] Hassan also points out that 'above Aker in this scene is a large Pyramid'.[57] He says that this symbolism, when put in 'conjunction with Aker in Sphinx form and the name of Rostau', suggests that 'the Fifth Division was originally a [complete] version of the *Duat* and had its geographical counterpart in the Giza necropolis'.[58]

In support of this idea, Hassan then refers us to another of the ancient Egyptian funerary texts, the so-called *Book of Two Ways*, where mention is made of 'the Highland of Aker, which is the Dwelling Place of Osiris' and also of 'Osiris who is in the Highland of

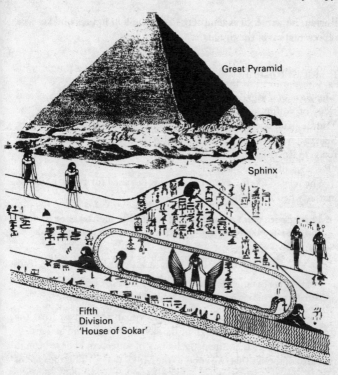

Great Pyramid

Sphinx

Fifth
Division
'House of Sokar'

39. The Fifth Division of the *Duat* features a gigantic 'double-lion' Sphinx-god and a large Pyramid. Compare this symbolic imagery with the Great Sphinx and Great Pyramid seen in profile from the south-east.

Aker'.[59] Hassan suggests that 'highland of Aker' may be a reference to the Giza plateau, 'where is the earthly Rostau'.[60] Exactly the same idea occurred to the American Egyptologist Mark Lehner in his 1974 pamphlet, *The Egyptian Heritage*.[61] Here, after completing a study of

Rostau, he wrote: 'it is tempting to see the lion figures of Aker as a representation of the Sphinx at Giza.'[62]

Roads of Rostau

The *Book of Two Ways* is a text that was copied onto the floors and sides of coffins over a 250-year span (2050–1800 BC) during the Middle Kingdom. According to the archaeo-astronomer Jane B. Sellers it was designed 'to aid the soul of the deceased to pass along the roads to Rostau, the Gate in the necropolis which gives access to the "Passages of the Netherworld" . . .'[63]

The related Coffin Texts (2134–1783 BC) shed further light on the matter when they state:

> I have passed over the paths of Rostau, whether on water or on land, and these are the paths of Osiris, they are [also] in the limit of the sky . . .[64]
>
> I am Osiris; I have come to Rostau to know the secrets of the *Duat* . . .[65]
>
> I shall not be turned back at the gates of the *Duat*; I ascend to the sky with Orion . . . I am one who collects his efflux in front of Rostau . . .[66]

As Sellers points out, many ancient Egyptian texts insist 'that the topography of Rostau, though in the sky, is on water and on land.'[67] She also proposes that 'the paths by way of water' could have been in that area of the sky that 'we know as the Milky Way'.[68] This idea seems highly plausible when we remember that the 'cosmic address' of the *Duat* is the 'Kingdom of Osiris in Orion' on the right bank of the Milky Way. The logic of ancient Egyptian duality therefore suggests that 'the paths by way of land' should be found at the earthly Rostau.

The earthly Rostau is the Giza necropolis,[69] site of the three Pyramids and the Sphinx – so with all this talk of sky-ground dualities it would be almost perverse to ignore the four narrow 'star-shafts' which emanate skywards from the King's and Queen's Chambers inside the Great Pyramid.

The reader will recall that the southern shaft of the King's Chamber was directed at around 2500 BC to the centre of the constellation of Orion – i.e. to Orion's belt at its 'culmination' or 'meridian transit' 45 degrees above the horizon. Strangely, at the

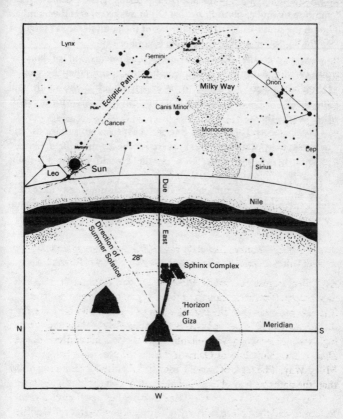

40. Summer solstice in the epoch of 2500 BC: the *Duat* region. Note that Orion's belt at this crucial observational moment was *not* at the meridian but in the south-east and thus far to the left of the point in the sky targeted by the southern shaft of the King's Chamber. The sky seems somehow out of kilter and one has the uncomfortable feeling that the belt stars need to be drawn round to the south, and specifically to the meridian, so that they can interlock with the shaft that targets them.

crucial observational moment in the pre-dawn on the summer solstice – crucial, at any rate, to the ancient Egyptians of the Pyramid Age – computer simulations indicate that Orion was seen *not* at the meridian but in the south-east, i.e. far to the left of the point in the sky targeted by the southern shaft of the King's Chamber.

Looking at the simulation, everything seems out of kilter – dislocated – and one has the uncomfortable feeling that the stars of Orion's belt need somehow to be drawn round to the south, and specifically to the meridian, so that they can interlock with the shaft that targets them.

We suspect that for the ancient Egyptians this curious and unsettling 'dislocation' of the sky served as the stimulus for an esoteric journey which was undertaken on the ground by the Pharaohs themselves following celestial clues.

As we shall see in subsequent chapters their quest may have been for something of immense importance. But in order to understand why, we must first find out who the Sphinx is.

Above: The Great Sphinx of Giza, as this nineteenth-century photograph shows, has spent a large part of its known history covered up to its neck in desert sands. Whilst thus covered, its body has not been subject to wind-erosion, yet the body is heavily weathered. Could there have been some other weathering agency at work? *Below*: The Sphinx was carved by first excavating a large trench around a monolithic central core of limestone which was then shaped into the form of a lion. This photograph, taken from the Great Pyramid, shows the Sphinx in its trench, the remains of the so-called Sphinx Temple (immediately in front, i.e. to the east, of the monument) and Valley Temple (a little to the south). Also shown, running down the south side of the Sphinx, is part of the gigantic causeway of Khafre.

3.

4.

Above: Heavily eroded core body of the Sphinx. The weathering patterns, which have been studied by geologists from Boston University, have been identified as having been caused by prolonged exposure to heavy rains. In 2500 BC, when Egyptologists presume that the Sphinx was built, Egypt was as bone dry as it is today. Between 15,000 BC and 7000 BC, however, the science of palaeo-climatology indicates that Egypt several times passed through periods of wet climate which could have caused weathering patterns such as these. *Left*: The trench surrounding the Great Sphinx, which was created at the same time that the Sphinx was carved, very clearly illustrates the rolling scalloped 'coves' and deep vertical fissures characteristic of precipitation-induced weathering in limestone. The sciences of geology and palaeo-climatology alone, however, can only demonstrate that the Sphinx and its enclosure are much older than previously thought. Archaeo-astronomical analysis provides a far more accurate tool for dating the Sphinx. *Right*: This granite stela between the paws of the Sphinx was erected to commemorate a renovation campaign carried out by Pharaoh Thuthmosis IV (1401 BC–1391 BC). The stela bears the single syllable 'Khaf' which, oddly, has led Egyptologists to conclude that the Sphinx was originally built by the Fourth Dynasty Pharaoh Khafre, *circa* 2500 BC. The stela also states, however, that the Giza necropolis is the 'Splendid Place of the First Time' – associating it with a far earlier epoch.

6.

Above: The Sphinx viewed from the south, over the so-called Khafre causeway. Its heavily eroded lion body lies half-buried in the artificial 'horizon' of Giza from this perspective, mimicking the half-buried constellation of Leo as viewed at the cross-quarter sunrise between the winter solstice and the spring equinox in 10,500 BC (see Chapter Seventeen). *Below*: Professor Mark Lehner (centre), Egyptology's leading expert on the Sphinx, lecturing to senior staff of the Edgar Cayce Foundation at the Association 'for Research in Enlightenment in Virginia Beach, USA (see Chapter Five).

7.

8.

Above: The subterranean chamber of the Great Pyramid of Giza, situated at a depth of 100 feet beneath the plateau, precisely under the apex of the Pyramid. *Below left*: The descending corridor connecting the Pyramid's original entrance in the north face with the subterranean chamber is 350 feet long from top to bottom and does not vary by more than a quarter of an inch from perfectly straight along its entire length. This photograph is taken from the bottom of the corridor, looking up towards the distant sunlight filtering through the entrance. The strange internal corridors and passageways of the Great Pyramid closely resemble ancient Egyptian depictions of the afterlife realm and Kingdom of Osiris, known as the Duat. *Below right*: The authors with John Anthony West in the Queen's Chamber.

11.

12.

13.

14.

Top left: Rudolf Gantenbrink photographed with his equipment during his project to explore the shafts of the King's and Queen's Chambers in the Great Pyramid (see Chapter Seven). *Top right*: Rudolf Gantenbrink, Uli Kapp of the German Archaeological Institute, and the robot *Upuaut* in the Queen's Chamber near the entrance to the southern shaft. *Left above*: Rainer Stadelmann, Director of the German Archaeological Institute in Cairo. *Left below*: Zahi Hawass, Director of the Giza Pyramid Plateau for Egypt's Supreme Council of Antiquities. *Opposite above*: The door, complete with unusual metal fittings, that was filmed by *Upuaut* at the end of the southern shaft of the Queen's Chamber on 22 March 1993 after a journey of some 200 feet along the shaft. *Opposite below*: This photograph, taken from film shot by *Upuaut*, shows the deep interior of the northern shaft of the Queen's Chamber. Lying diagonally across the floor of the shaft can be seen a length of wood which, if retrieved, could be carbon dated (see Appendix 5).

Right: The authors examining the entrance to the northern shaft of the King's Chamber. *Below*: Fragment of the iron-plate, originally coated with gold, that was extracted from the core masonry of the great Pyramid near the exit point of the southern shaft of the King's Chamber in 1837 (see Chapter Six). Egyptologists have dismissed this curious piece of wrought iron as a late intrusion, but all the evidence suggests that it is contemporary with the Great Pyramid (which was, of course, built long before the 'iron age') and that its function may have been related to complex ideas concerning the stellar rebirth of the soul expressed in ancient Egyptian funerary texts.

17.

18.

called Rostau and how Rostau, too, existed in both cosmic and terrestrial realms: in the heavens it was characterized by the three stars of Orion's belt and on earth by the three great Pyramids of Giza. Last but not least, we have seen how the ancient Egyptians of the Pyramid Age particularly observed the *Duat* as it lay along the eastern horizon in the pre-dawn at the time of the summer solstice.

The important word here is 'horizon'. It will prove to be the key to the mystery of who – or what – the Great Sphinx really represents.

Celestial reflections

With the aid of computer simulations, and a little imagination, let us journey to the epoch of 2500 BC, when the Pyramid Texts were compiled, and set our location at Heliopolis on the observatory platform of the astronomer priests. The time of year is the summer solstice, the moment of observation is the pre-dawn, and we are looking in the general direction of the eastern horizon. This means that we have our backs turned to the Giza Pyramids which lie across the Nile some twelve miles to our west.

Looking east also means that we are looking at the *Duat*. And as our computer reconstructs the skies our eyes are drawn to that region of the *Duat* known as Rostau which manifests the celestial counterparts of the three great Pyramids – the three stars of Orion's belt glimmering in the pre-dawn.

Having registered this image we set our direction towards the west, towards the Pyramids. The bodies of the distant monuments are still cloaked in darkness but the first hint of the rising sun lights up their capstones with an astral glimmer . . .

So we can see that there is a sense in which the Giza necropolis is itself a kind of 'horizon' – i.e. that its three pyramids form a reflection in the west of the three 'stars of Rostau' that observers in 2500 BC would have seen on the eastern horizon of Heliopolis in the pre-dawn at the summer solstice. Perhaps this is precisely what was meant by an otherwise cryptic inscription on the granite stela between the paws of the Sphinx which speaks of Giza not only as the 'Splendid Place of the "First Time" ' as we have seen, but also as the 'Horizon of Heliopolis in the West'.[1]

Chapter 9

The Sphinx and its Horizons

'The Sphinx has a Genesis, and that was the
lion . . .'

Egyptologist Selim Hassan, *The Sphinx*,
Cairo 1949

'[The constellation of] Leo resembles the
animal after which it is named. A right
triangle of stars outline the back legs . . . the
front of the constellation, like a giant
backward question mark, defines the head,
mane, and front legs. At the base of the
question mark is Regulus, the heart of the
lion . . .'

Nancy Hathaway, *Friendly Guide to the
Universe*, NY 1994

Even a casual review of the religious texts of the ancient Egyptians
leaves no doubt that they regarded their earthly environment as a
sacred landscape which they had inherited from the gods. It was their
absolute conviction that in the remote golden age called the 'First
Time' Osiris had established a sort of 'cosmic kingdom' in the
Memphite region which had been passed on to his son Horus and
thence through him, down the cycles of the epochs, to subsequent
generations of human 'Horus-Kings' – i.e. to the living Pharaohs of
Egypt.

We have seen that the essence of this sacred 'Kingdom of Osiris'
was the peculiar dualism with which it was connected to an area of the
sky known as the *Duat*, close to Orion and Sirius on the western side
of the Milky Way. We have also seen how the centre of the *Duat* was

Astronomer-priests

When the Pyramid Texts were compiled in the epoch of 2500 BC, the religious centre of the Pharaonic state was at Heliopolis – the 'City of the Sun', called *On* or *Innu* by the ancients, which now lies completely buried under the Al Matareya suburb of modern Cairo.[2] Heliopolis was the earliest cult centre of the sun-god *Re* in his form as *Atum*, the 'Father of the Gods'. The Heliopolitan priests were high initiates in the mysteries of the heavens and their dominant occupation was the observation and recording of the various motions of the sun and the moon, the planets and the stars.[3]

Much leads us to conclude that they benefited from a vast heritage of experience based on such observations, accumulated over enormously long periods of time. At any rate, the ancient Greek and Roman scholars – who were at least two millennia closer to the ancient Egyptians than we are today – were constantly in awe at the high knowledge and wisdom of the Heliopolitan and Memphite priests and especially of their astronomical science.

For example, as early as the fifth century BC, Herodotus (the so-called 'Father of History') displayed great reverence for the priests of Egypt and attributed to them the discovery of the solar year and the invention of the twelve signs of the zodiac – which he says the Greeks later borrowed. 'In my opinion,' he wrote, 'their method of calculation is better than that of the Greeks.'[4]

In the fourth century BC the learned Aristotle – who was tutor to Alexander the Great – similarly recognized that the Egyptians were advanced astronomers 'whose observations have been kept for very many years past, and from whom much of our evidence about particular stars is derived'.[5]

Plato, too, relates how the Egyptian priests observed the stars 'for 10,000 years or, so to speak, for an infinite time'.[6] Likewise Diodorus of Sicily, who visited Egypt in 60 BC, insisted that 'the disposition of the stars as well as their movements have always been the subject of careful observations among the Egyptians' and that 'they have preserved to this day records concerning each of these stars over an incredible number of years . . .'[7]

Perhaps most significantly of all, the Lycian Neoplatonist, Proclus, who studied at Alexandria in the fifth century AD, confirmed that it was not the Greeks but the Egyptians who discovered the phenomenon of Precession: 'Let those, who believe in observations, cause the stars to move around the poles of the zodiac by one degree in one hundred years [meaning the Precession rate] towards the east, as Ptolemy and Hipparchus did before him know . . . that the Egyptians had already taught Plato about the movement of the fixed stars . . .'[8]

Modern historians and Egyptologists, who are unanimous in the view that the Egyptians were poor astronomers,[9] choose to discount such statements as frivolous outcries by misinformed Greeks and Romans. These same scholars all do accept, however, that the priestly centre at Heliopolis was already remotely ancient at the dawn of the Pyramid Age and that it had been sacred since time immemorial to the supreme deity named Atum, the 'Self-Created'.[10]

So who or what exactly was Atum?

Living image of Atum

Addressing the first annual meeting of the prestigious Egypt Exploration Fund on 3 July 1883, the eminent Swiss Egyptologist Edouard Naville had this to say about Atum: 'there can be no doubt that the lion or the sphinx is a form of Atum . . .'[11]

Naville went on to cite what he considered as sufficient evidence for such a conclusion:

> I will cite only one proof, this is the deity Nefer-Atum. This deity can be represented with the head of a lion . . . normally he has a human form, and wears on his head a lotus from which emerge two straight plumes. Sometimes the two emblems [lion and human] are united and between the head of the lion and the plume there is the bird [hawk] of Horus.[12]

Though initially a confusing element, we shall see that the hawk symbolism of Horus crops up frequently in connection with this mystery and gradually begins to take its place in the overall pattern that will emerge. Meanwhile, much else confirms that Atum, the primordial creator god, was regarded by the ancient Egyptians as being primarily leonine or sphinx-like in form.

In the Pyramid Texts, for example, we frequently encounter the designation *Rwty*, normally translated as the 'double-lion'[13] because the hieroglyphic sign shows two lions either side by side or one above the other.[14] It is generally accepted, however, that a finer meaning for the term is 'the creature who has the form of a lion' or 'he who resembles the lion', and that the significance of the double-lion hieroglyph is that it emphasizes the dual and cosmic nature of *Rwty*.[15] The Egyptologist Le Page Renouf wrote that *Rwty* represents 'a single god with a lion's face or form'.[16] And for Selim Hassan '*Rwty* was a god in the form of a lion'. In Hassan's view the choice of the double-lion hieroglyph was very probably linked in some way to the fact that: 'sphinxes are always found in pairs when guarding temple door-ways, and the function of *Rwty* is also that of a guardian.'[17]

Moreover, in line 2032 of the Pyramid Texts, as Hassan points out: 'it is said of the King: "He is taken to *Rwty* and presented to Atum" . . . [and] in the so-called *Book of the Dead* . . . it says (Ch. 3, line 1): "O Atum, who appears as master of the lake, who shines as *Rwty*" . . .'[18]

Indeed, there are many such places in the texts where *Rwty* and Atum are linked. One typical passage states: 'O Atum, spiritualize me in the presence of *Rwty* . . .'[19] And elsewhere we read: 'Lift up this king's double to the god, lead him to *Rwty*, cause him to mount up to Atum . . . The King's rank is high in the Mansion of *Rwty*.'[20]

Such syncretism with *Rwty* strongly supports a 'lion-like' or 'sphinx-like' appearance for Atum. We should therefore not be surprised to discover that in ancient Egyptian religious art Atum is often depicted as a sphinx wearing the characteristic headgear of this god – a tall crown with a plume and lotus.[21] From such depictions many leading Egyptologists have concluded that the Great Sphinx at Giza, though allegedly bearing the face of Khafre, may also have been regarded as an image of Atum.[22] Indeed, as we saw in Part I, one of the most enduring of the many titles by which the Sphinx was known to the ancient Egyptians was *Shesep-ankh Atum* (literally 'living image of Atum')[23] – so we need be in little doubt about this identification.

Atum, Re and Horakhti

Despite all of Atum's well-known Lion-Sphinx characteristics, modern Egyptologists have a tendency to ignore his intense leonine symbolism when discussing his cosmic attributes. More often than not they confine themselves to dishing out certain vague generalities to the effect that Atum was the 'sun-god and creator of the universe', and that his name: '. . . carries the idea of "totality" in the sense of an ultimate and unalterable state of perfection. Atum is frequently called "The Lord of Heliopolis", the major centre of sun worship. The presence of another solar deity on this site, Re, leads to a coalescence of the two gods into *Re-Atum* . . .' [24]

Egyptologist Rosalie David informs us that at the opening of the Pyramid Age 'the god Re [or Ra] had taken over the cult of an earlier god Atum . . . [thus] *Re-Atum* was now worshipped as the creator of the world according to the Heliopolitan theology, and his priests sought to distinguish his various characteristics'. [25]

One of these important characteristics, Davies adds, was Re's manifestion as '*Re-Horakhti*'. [26] Since the literal meaning of *Horakhti* is "Horus-of-the-Horizon", [27] it would seem that what we are to envisage in this latest piece of ancient Egyptian syncretism is a coalescence of the sun's disc with such a deity. Furthermore, as astronomers and astrologers are well aware, the disc of the sun does, in fact, 'coalesce' with (or 'enter the house' of) certain star groups – the twelve constellations of the zodiac – at regular intervals throughout the year. So it is reasonable to wonder whether 'Horus-of-the-Horizon' i.e. Horakhti, could in fact be one of these zodiacal constellations.

The Egyptologist Hermann Kees also gave consideration to the subjects of Heliopolis and Horakhti. In the light of what is about to follow, his remarks are extremely relevant: 'The particular worship peculiar to Heliopolis was that of the stars. From the worship of the stars evolved the worship of Re in the form of 'Horus-of-the-Horizon . . .' [28]

We suggest that this conclusion is in the main correct, though not quite in the manner Kees saw it. We believe that it was not merely from a general 'worship of the stars' but rather from an ancient stellar image – that of a specific zodiacal constellation – that the composite deity *Re-Horakhti* was derived.

Horakhti is represented in ancient Egyptian reliefs as a man with a hawk's head, on top of which rests the solar disc. [29] In this way both the god Horus (symbolized by the hawk) and the sun in the 'horizon' are

41. The path of the sun (the ecliptic) passing through the twelve zodiacal constellations as they are depicted in the famous Denderah Zodiac from Upper Egypt. The sun's disc 'coalesces' with (and is said to be 'housed by') each of these constellations, one after the other, month by month, during the course of the solar year.

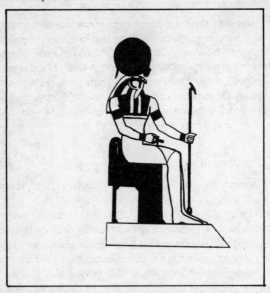

42. Horakhti, 'Horus-of-the-Horizon', was frequently depicted in ancient Egyptian reliefs as a man with a hawk's head on top of which rests the solar disc.

identified with the Pharaoh-King – regarded as the living embodiment of Horus.[30] The Orientalist Lewis Spence noted additionally that the lion 'was identified to the solar deities, with the sun-god Horus [and] Re'.[31] Frequently, too, we find composite lion-hawk representations of the King in ancient depictions. For example, there is a relief from the sun-temple of Pharaoh Sahure at Abusir (Fifth Dynasty, *circa* 2350 BC) which shows the King as a winged lion and also as a lion with a hawk's head.[32]

In summary, therefore, we seem to be looking at the various symbolic expressions of a lengthy process: in prehistoric times a primordial god, Atum, whose form was the lion or the Sphinx, was worshipped by the Heliopolitan priests; then, in the Pyramid Age, Atum was 'coalesced' with Re, whose form was the sun's disc, and finally with Hawk-headed Horakhti – Horus-of-the-Horizon – symbolizing the Horus-King.

The result was the syncretized deity *Atum-Re-Horakhti* whose combined symbolism originated from the leonine or Sphinx-like image of Atum. Somehow this composite or 'coalesced' image was then made manifest in the 'Horizon' in the early Pyramid Age.

In that epoch, as the reader will recall, the focus of the astronomer-priests was on the summer solstice, when the *Duat* was active in the eastern sky. In what zodiacal sign, seen on the eastern horizon, did this all important 'coalescence' take place?

Horus, Dweller-in-the-Horizon

When Edouard Naville was excavating certain New Kingdom remains in Egypt's delta region north of Cairo in 1882–3, he was struck by the fact that a large number of the monuments he uncovered were dedicated to a composite deity he called '*Atum-Harmarchis*'. Associated with these monuments there would always be a *naos*, or sanctuary, containing 'a sphinx with a human head' which Naville states was 'a well-known form of the god Harmarchis'.[33]

We are by now familiar with Atum. But who is this 'Harmarchis'? Naville noted that in addition to his Sphinx form he was often represented as 'a god with a hawk's head, or as a hawk with a solar disc' – symbols with which we are also familiar – and that '*Atum-Harmachis* was the god of Heliopolis, the most ancient city of Egypt'.[34]

'Harmachis' is a Graecianized rendering of the ancient Egyptian name, *Hor-em-Akhet*, which means 'Horus-in-the-Horizon' or 'Horus-Dweller-in-the-Horizon'.[35] In other words, as should be obvious by now, it is a concept that is extremely close to Horakhti, or 'Horus-*of*-the Horizon' – as close, at any rate, as the nuance between 'of ' on the one hand and 'in' on the other . . .

Both deities are called horizon-dwellers. Both are sometimes depicted as a man with the head of a hawk. Both have a solar disc on their heads.[36] Indeed there is no real difference between them at all except, as we shall see, in the nature of the 'Horizon' in which they are said to dwell.

There is one other thing about Hor-em-Akhet and Horakhti, however, that we need to take account of first. The names of these curiously composite and syncretized lion-hawk-solar deities were both frequently, directly and interchangeably applied to the Great Sphinx at Giza.

The 'Two Horizons' of Heliopolis

The earliest surviving references to Hor-em-Akhet date from the New Kingdom, *circa* 1440 BC, and are found on a limestone stela of Pharaoh Amenhotep II, the builder of a small temple that can still be seen on the north side of the Sphinx enclosure. On the stela Amenhotep makes reference to the 'Pyramids of Hor-em-Ahket'

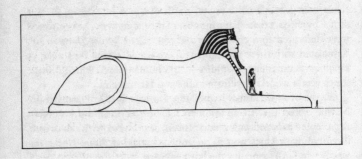

43. Artist's impression of 'reconstructed' Sphinx showing south profile.

which Selim Hassan takes as a sign, 'that he considered the Sphinx to be older than the Pyramids'.[37] Hassan also notes that the stela specifically names the Great Sphinx both as Hor-em-Akhet and as Horakhti.[38]

In a similar vein, in line 9 of its inscription, the granite stela of Thutmosis IV – which stands between the paws of the Sphinx – refers to the Sphinx itself as '*Hor-em-Akhet-Khepri-Re-Atum*', and subsequently, in line 13, as '*Atum-Hor-em-Akhet*',[39] but also refers to Thutmosis as the 'Protector of Horakhti'.[40] And it is on this same stela, as the reader will recall, that Giza is described as 'the "Horizon" [*Akhet*] of Heliopolis in the West' – i.e. as a 'reflection' in the West of what viewers in Heliopolis would have seen on their eastern horizon in the pre-dawn of the summer solstice.

It may also be of relevance that the son of Thutmosis IV, Amenhotep III, is remembered in ancient Egyptian annals as having built a temple in honour of Re-Horakhti, and that Amenhotep's son, the notorious and enigmatic Pharaoh Akhenaten, raised a great obelisk at Luxor in honour of Re-Hor-em-Akhet.[41] Akhenaten was also to name his famous solar-city *Akhet Aten*, the 'Horizon of the sun disc'.[42] And as Selim Hassan points out the *Aten* or sun disc was frequently identified by the ancient Egyptians with the image of the Sphinx.[43] Last but not least, when Akhenaten ascended the throne of Egypt he chose as his most prominent epithet the impressive title of 'High priest of Re-Horakhti '.[44]

It is therefore legitimate to inquire into what exactly is meant by the term 'Horizon' (*Akhet*) in the names Hor-em-Akhet and Horakhti. Are these twin beings known as Horus-in-the-Horizon and Horus-of-the-Horizon to be associated with the celestial horizon – where sky meets land? Or are they to be associated with the 'Horizon' of Heliopolis in the West, i.e. the Giza necropolis?

Or is it not more likely that the texts are prompting us to consider two 'horizons' at the same time?

Interestingly, Egyptologists often translate the names Hor-em-Akhet and Horakhti as meaning 'Horus-of-the-Two-Horizons'. Sir E. A. Wallis Budge, for example, identifies Re-Horakhti to Re-Harmachis [Hor-em-Akhet] and translates both names as 'Ra + Horus-of-the-Two-Horizons'.[45] Likewise the orientalist Lewis Spence writes: 'Horus-of-the-Two-Horizons, the Harmachis [Hor-em-Akhet] of the Greeks, was one of chief forms of the sun-god . . . thus we find Harmachis worshipped principally at Heliopolis . . . his best-known monument is the famous Sphinx, near the Pyramids of Giza.' [46]

So if Hor-em-Akhet is the Great Sphinx in the *western* 'Horizon of

Giza', then should we not look for Horakhti, his 'twin', in the eastern horizon of the sky?

These are questions that we shall continue to pursue. Meanwhile, as Egyptologist Ahmed Fakhry confirms, the various stelae that we have reviewed, and numerous other inscriptions, leave no doubt that the Pharaohs of ancient Egypt knew and worshipped the Sphinx (and obviously, too, his celestial counterpart) under the names Hor-em-Akhet and Horakhti.[47] Fakhry also points out something else of relevance: both names are 'appropriate' since 'the ancient necropolis [of Giza] was called *Akhet Khufu*, the "Horizon" of Khufu'.[48]

Strange silence

Because the earliest surviving texts containing the term Hor-em-Akhet date from the New Kingdom, it is the present consensus of scholars that the ancient Egyptians of the Old Kingdom never spoke of the Sphinx. According to Jaromir Malek of Oxford University, for example: 'Old Kingdom sources are strangely and surprisingly silent about the Great Sphinx of Giza. It was only some 1000 years after the Sphinx had been made . . . that it was mentioned . . .'[49]

Could this really be so? How could the Old Kingdom Egyptians, having taken the trouble to construct the huge Giza necropolis and the rest of the Memphite monuments, fail to make any mention of the Great Sphinx?

One possibility which deserves to be taken seriously is that they did not mention it because they did not build it – but rather *inherited* it from a far earlier epoch. Even on this scenario, however, it strains credulity to suppose, in all their prolific texts, carved on the walls of nine royal Pyramids of the Fifth and Sixth Dynasties, that they would not make a single reference to so magnificent a statue occupying so crucial a site.

The other possibility which has to be considered, therefore, is that Egyptologists could somehow have *failed to recognize* the name given to the Sphinx in the Pyramid Texts.

There is one very obvious contender.

As we have seen, the Sphinx in the New Kingdom was known not only as Hor-em-Akhet but also as Horakhti. And although the name

Hor-em-Akhet definitely does *not* appear in the Pyramid Texts it is a simple fact that the name Horakhti does, many times over. Indeed these archaic scriptures contain hundreds of direct mentions of Horakhti, 'Horus-of-the-Horizon',[50] all of which refer, as scholars agree, 'to the god rising in the east at dawn'.[51] What they have never suspected is the possibility that they may be confronted here by the ancient Egyptian dualistic way of referring to an earthly counterpart by means of its celestial twin.

Searching for Horakhti

'The doors of the sky are thrown open for Horakhti,' states one typical passage in the Pyramid Texts, 'the doors of the sky are thrown open at dawn for Horus of the East . . .'[52] Elsewhere, in line 928, we read: 'go to . . . Horakhti at the horizon . . . I go up on this eastern side of the sky . . .'[53]

Virtually unnoticed by Egyptologists, who write off all such utterances as 'mystical mumbo-jumbo', the Pyramid Texts also provide us with some extremely important astronomical clues when they tell us, again and again, that the dawn rising of Horakhti in the east coincides with the time and place 'where the gods were born'. For example:

> The Winding Waterway is flooded, the Fields of Rushes are filled, that I may be ferried over to the eastern side of the sky, to the place where the gods were born, and I was born there with them, as Horus, as the Horizon Dweller [Horakhti] . . .[54]
>
> go to . . . Horakhti at the horizon . . . on the eastern side of the sky where the gods are born.[55]
>
> . . . the birth of the gods before you [Horus] in the five epagomenal days . . .[56]

Making use of the proper astronomical key, let us try to decode this alleged 'mystical mumbo-jumbo':

1 The 'place where the gods [i.e. the stars] are born' is a specific direction as to where we are to observe Horakhti: the eastern horizon – where all heavenly bodies rise.

2 The time of year at which we are to make our observations is also clearly specified: the so-called 'five epagomenal days', or five

'days upon the year'. To understand this reference we need only remember that the ancient Egyptian calendar was based on 360 days plus five extra or intercalcary days which they called 'the days upon the year' (*epagomenae* in Greek). During these five days five *Neters* or gods were said to have been born, two of whom – Osiris and Isis – were identified by the ancient Egyptians with the constellation of Orion and the star Sirius (also called Sothis).

3 Last but not least the Pyramid Texts also specify the time of day at which the sky is to be observed – clearly dawn, since this was when the birth of the gods was said to have occurred:

> Behold Osiris has come as Orion . . . the dawn-light bears you with Orion . . . your third is Sothis [Sirius] . . .' [57]
>
> Sothis [Sirius] is swallowed up [i.e. fades in the dawn] by the *Duat*, pure and living in the Horizon. [58]
>
> The reed-floats of the sky are brought down to me . . . that I may go up on them to Horakhti at the horizon. I go up on this eastern side of the sky where the gods are born, and I am born as Horus, as 'Him of the Horizon' . . . Sothis is my [companion] . . . [59]
>
> The sky is clear [is lighting up], Sothis lives . . . [60]
>
> It is Sothis . . . who prepares yearly sustenance for you in her name of 'Year' . . . [61]

Geographical and cosmological context

The day on which Sothis-Sirius, after a period of invisibility, was first seen rising with the sun at dawn (i.e. the event referred to by astronomers as the 'heliacal rising' of this star) was taken by the ancient Egyptians as the cosmic marker for the beginning of their New Year.

Furthermore it is certain from the passages quoted above, and from many other references in the Pyramid Texts, that the dawn rising of Sothis-Sirius coincided with the rising of 'Horakhti'. This is an important piece of astronomical information which helps us to identify who Horakhti is – or rather which celestial figure he represents.

We also know from historical records and from computer reconstructions that two major events – one celestial and the other terrestrial – coincided with the heliacal rising of Sirius during the Pyramid Age (*circa* 2500 BC). The celestial event was the summer solstice. And the terrestrial event, as the reader will recall from the previous chapter, was the start of the Nile's annual flood – the 'Great Inundation' that brought fertility to the land.[62]

Once this geographical and cosmological context is fully taken into account we can see exactly what it is that the compilers of the Pyramid Texts were transposing from the ground to the sky when they tell us that the appearance of Horakhti at dawn coincided in their epoch with the start of the 'great flood':

> The Winding Waterway is flooded, that I may be ferried thereon to the horizon, to Horakhti . . . Re has taken me to himself, to the sky, to the eastern side of the sky, as this Horus, as the Dweller in the *Duat*, as this star which illumines the sky [which] is my sister Sothis . . .[63]
>
> This is Horus who came forth from the Nile . . .[64]
>
> They row Horus, they row Horus in the procession of Horus on the Great Flood. The doors of the sky are opened, the doors of the firmament are thrown open for Horus of the East at dawn . . .[65]

Also passage 1172 speaks of 'the Great Flood which is in the sky' in the region of the *Duat*.

So, to summarize, far from being 'mumbo-jumbo', the Pyramid Texts go to great lengths to make it clear that during the epoch of their compilation, *circa* 2500 BC, the rising of Horakhti at dawn coincided with the summer solstice, and with the season of the inundation, at the moment when the *Duat* – the celestial Kingdom of Osiris-Orion – occupied the eastern portion of the sky. We can also deduce from the texts that Re, i.e. the sun's disc, was seen somehow to merge or to unite – or 'coalesce' – with Horakhti at the same time. This is made amply clear by the following reading: 'Re has taken me to himself to the eastern side of the sky as this Horus, as the "Dweller in the *Duat*".'[66]

In other words, what we need to look for in order to identify Horakhti with certainty is an astronomical conjunction during the summer solstice in the Pyramid Age when both the sun and some other significant celestial body would have been seen to occupy the same specific place on the eastern horizon.

As we shall see in the next chapter, computer simulations provide us with the means to search for such a conjunction. They also enable us to relive the drama of the Horus-Kings of ancient Egypt as they participated in an extraordinary ritual, physically re-enacting celestial events observed by the astronomer priests of Heliopolis on their eastern horizon and reflected in the artificial western 'Horizon' of Heliopolis, i.e. amongst the vast and eternal monuments of the Giza necropolis.

Chapter 10

The Quest of the Horus-King

'Egypt . . . considered life to be everlasting
and denied the reality of death . . . Pharaoh
was not mortal but a god. This was the
fundamental concept of Egyptian kingship,
that Pharaoh was of divine essence, a god
incarnated . . . It is wrong to speak of the
deification of Pharaoh. His divinity was not
proclaimed at a certain moment in a manner
comparable to the *concretatio* of the dead
emperor by the Roman senate. His
coronation was not an apotheosis but an
epiphany.'

Henri Frankfort, *Kingship and the Gods*, 1948

'The figure of Osiris is not exclusively at
home in mythology . . . Each king, at death,
becomes Osiris, just as each king, in life,
appears "on the throne of Horus"; each king
is Horus . . . The question whether Osiris
and Horus are . . . gods or kings is, for the
Egyptian, meaningless. These gods are the
late king and his successor; these kings are
those gods . . .'

Henri Frankfort, *Kingship and the Gods*, 1948

The whole force, the impetus and the very *raison d'être* of the
Pharaonic state was to provide all the required ceremonial settings
that would enable the Horus-King to undertake a sort of supernatural
quest – a journey back in time into the earthly and cosmic realms of his
'father' Osiris. Indeed this was the supreme quest in a Pharaoh's

lifetime and at its end lay the ultimate Holy Grail in the form of the astral body of Osiris which the king could encounter only after overcoming many dangers, difficulties and ordeals and after passing through many miracles and terrors. Once in the presence of Osiris the questor would beseech him to 'rise again' and bestow immortality not only on himself, but on the whole land of Egypt.

This great ritual had to be performed by each successive Horus-King, (perhaps even each year) at a specific time preluding the 'rising of Orion'.

Child of the Sun, son of Osiris

In his brilliant study on the Osirian cosmic myth,[1] the late professor of Egyptology at Manchester University, R. T. Rundle Clark, wrote that: 'The king was the mediator between the community and the source of divine power, obtaining it through the ritual and regularizing it through his government. In Egypt there were two sources of power – in the sky and in the tomb with the ancestors. The first location made the king the child of the Sun God; the second location made him Horus, the son of Osiris . . .'[2]

Let us reiterate this important dualistic quality of the Horus-King – 'the child of of the Sun God and the son of Osiris' – for in it lies the true mystery of the great Osirian and Horian rituals of the Pyramid Age. The potential powers of nature within the 'dead' Osiris remained 'inert, asleep or listless, and completely passive' until the Horus-King was able to undertake a 'journey' to the *Duat* and 'visit his father' and 'open his mouth', i.e. bring him back to life.[3] This final and supreme act of filial devotion would then release all the forces of nature which would in turn bring forth the flooding of the Nile and the growth of vegetation – the forces, in short, that would fertilize and regenerate Egypt. In Rundle Clark's words: 'Theologically, the result of Horus's ministration is that Osiris can "send out his soul" or "set himself in motion" . . . The time of Orion in the southern sky after the time of its invisibility is the sign for the beginning of a new season of growth, the revival of nature in all aspects. Osiris has been transformed into a "living soul" . . .'[4]

Sir E. A. Wallis Budge also explains how, from its earliest

beginnings, the Pharaonic state was entirely committed to provide the correct ceremonial setting for each successive Horus-King to be able to perform the 'journey' into the *Duat* to visit the twofold realm of Osiris in the 'horizon':

> [The Egyptians] spared no pains in performing the works which they thought would help themselves and their dead to put on immortality and to arrive in the dominions of him who was 'the King of eternity and the lord of everlastingness'. Every tradition which existed concerning the ceremonies that were performed on behalf of the dead Osiris by Horus and his 'sons' and 'followers', *at some period which even so far back as the IVth Dynasty . . . was extremely remote*, was carefully preserved and faithfully imitated under succeeding dynasties . . . The formulae which were declared to have been recited during the performance of such ceremonies were written down and copied for scores of generations . . .' [5]

The whole emphasis on the King's person, therefore, was that he was seen as the link between the two *Duats*, one in the sky and the other on land, both meant to contain the 'Kingdom of Osiris' as it was in the original 'First Time'. The great 'journeys' of Horus thus took place both in the sky and on the ground and ran, as it were, in parallel. This is how the drama seems to have been conceived:

1 In the sky the Horus-King was the 'son of the Sun' and had to follow the path of the sun disc, cross the 'cosmic river' on the Solar-bark and reach the Gateway that lead into the sky-*Duat* of his 'father Osiris' in the eastern horizon.[6] He then had to travel on one of the 'roads' to Rostau, the centre of the *Duat*, where (then and now) are to be found the three stars of Orion's belt.

2 On the ground the Horus-King was the bodily 'son of Osiris' and had to follow the earthly path, cross the Nile on the solar boat and reach the Gateway (the great Sphinx) that led into the earth-*Duat* of his 'father Osiris' in the western 'horizon', i.e. the necropolis of Giza. He then had to travel on one of the 'roads' to Rostau, the centre of the *Duat*, where (then and now) are to be found the three great Pyramids of Giza.

In both these 'journeys' the Horus-King somehow had to be able to pass through a sort of 'time gateway' which permitted him to enter the twofold *Duat* realms of Osiris – i.e. Rostau-Giza – as they were remembered from the mythical golden age of the gods:

> [The council says to Horus]: Indeed this journey of yours . . . is as when [the first] Horus went to his father Osiris so that he might be a spirit thereby, that he might be a soul thereby . . .[7]
>
> Indeed this journey of yours, indeed these journeys of yours [sky and land] are the journeys of [the first] Horus in search of his father Osiris . . .[8]

From such references it is quite obvious that the events catalogued in the sky and on the land in the 'twofold funeral regions of Osiris' are somehow set or 'frozen' far back in the past in 'the time of the gods', the time of Osiris and Horus – i.e. *Zep Tepi*, the 'First Time'.

Also obvious, as we have seen in previous chapters, is the way in which the twofold funeral regions of Osiris are said to reflect each other at the time of the heliacal rising of Sirius, the 'star of Isis', the sister-wife of Osiris and mother of Horus – an astronomical event which we know coincided in the early Pyramid Age with the appearance of the rising sun at the summer solstice (known as the 'birth of Re').[9] It was at this propitious moment that the Horus-King set out on his quest for the regeneration of Egypt by participating in a grand rebirth ritual simultaneously as the 'son of Osiris' and the 'son of Re'.

As the 'son of Osiris' he emerged from 'the womb of Isis', i.e. the star Sirius,[10] at dawn on the summer solstice, i.e. the day of the 'Birth of Re'. It was then – and there – both at the sky-horizon and on the earth 'horizon' that the Horus-King was meant to find himself in front of the Gateway to Rostau. Guarding that Gateway on the earth-horizon' (i.e. at Giza) he would encounter the gigantic figure of a lion – the Great Sphinx. And guarding that Gateway in the sky-horizon his celestial counterpart would find . . . what?

As usual, once we understand their profoundly astronomical nature, the Pyramid Texts provide us with all the necessary co-ordinates to answer this question. It is simply a matter of realizing that the 'weird' symbolic language used in the texts – far from being mumbo-jumbo – is in fact a precise scientific terminology dressed up in the liturgical clothing of a cosmic drama.[11]

Seventy days from Horakhti

It is well known, and not a matter of controversy even amongst Egyptologists,[12] that the whole emphasis of the ancient Egyptian rebirth cult was on the seventy days of 'invisibility' which Sirius, the star of Isis, endured each year. These seventy days were seen as a cosmic preparation for astral rebirth and, not surprisingly, they were matched to the period of embalming in the mummification rituals of the dead.[13] The culmination and crescendo of this seventy-day period came with the first dawn reappearance, or rising, of Sirius which, as the reader will recall, occurred at around the time of the summer solstice during the Pyramid Age. This was when the astronomer-priests of Heliopolis observed what is technically known as the heliacal rising of Sirius in the east.[14]

Since it was believed that all the potential powers of nature needed to cause the 'rebirth' of the cosmic Horus-King were building up in the 'womb' of the goddess Isis during these crucial seventy days, we can suppose that the beginning of the period marked the beginning of the 'journey' of Horus into the 'underworld' – when the *Duat* was locked, as it were, below the horizon and thus directly 'underneath' the Giza necropolis.

From this it follows that we are invited to find out where the Horus-King's celestial counterpart – i.e. the disc of the sun – stood in the sky some seventy days prior to the heliacal rising of Sirius. The Pyramid Texts again give us the clue. They specify that at this time the Horus-solar-King was to be found on the banks of the Milky Way just about to board the solar bark.[15] Remembering that the astronomical observations in the texts were made during the middle of the third millennium BC, let us try to decode this imagery using computer simulations.

We know, of course, that the 'path' of the sun (which astronomers call the ecliptic) passes through twelve distinct constellations in the course of a complete year – the constellations of the zodiac. *Circa* 2500 BC, therefore, let us see where the sun would have been along the ecliptic path some seventy days before the heliacal rising of Sirius. It would, we discover, have been near the head of Taurus (the Hyades) and poised on the right bank of the Milky Way.[16]

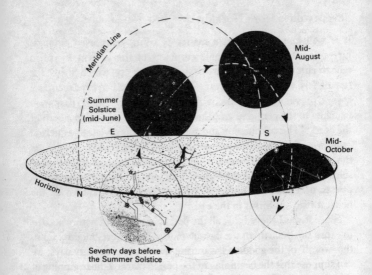

44. Position of the *Duat* sky-region at dawn at various times of the year in the epoch of 2500 BC, the Pyramid Age. The *Duat* was considered to become active only at the summer solstice in mid-June when the stars of Orion and Sirius rose heliacally. Some 70 days prior to this crucial observational moment the *Duat* was 'locked' below the horizon and thus, in a sense, directly 'underneath' the Giza necropolis.

In the ritual or drama performed by the king, is it not possible that this celestial event was the source of the imagery of the cosmic Horus about to 'board' a cosmic 'bark' with the sun-god in order to cross a waterway (the 'Winding Waterway', i.e. the Milky Way):[17]

> The king embarks with Re on this great bark of his, he navigates in it to the horizon with him . . .[18]
> The king shall go aboard the bark like Re on the banks of the Winding Waterway . . .[19]
> The Winding Waterway is flooded . . . you cross thereon to the

horizon, to the place where the gods were born . . . your sister [companion] is Sothis . . .[20]

May you cross the Winding Waterway . . . may you fall in the eastern side of the sky, may you sit in the . . . horizon . . .[21]

He [Horus] goes aboard the bark like Re at the banks of the Winding Waterway . . .[22]

As we wind the ancient skies a little forward in time on our computer we discover that twenty-five days after being stationed near the Hyades-Taurus on the right bank of the cosmic river the sun has indeed 'crossed' the Milky Way and is now 'sailing' eastwards along the ecliptic path in the direction of the great zodiacal constellation of Leo – seen as a huge 'crouching lion' in the sky. We are now just a little over six weeks away from the summer solstice:

The reed-floats of the sky are set down for me that I may cross on them to the horizon, to Horakhti . . . to yonder eastern side of the sky . . . Summons is made to me by Re . . . as Horus, as the Horizon Dweller . . .[23]

The doors of the sky are thrown open for Horakhti . . . the doors of the sky are thrown open at dawn for Horus of the East . . .[24]

go to . . . Horakhti at the horizon . . . on the eastern side of the sky where the gods are born.[25]

Following this extremely clear and specific instruction to 'go to Horakhti' at the horizon (there to meet the sunrise) we continue our eastward journey along the ecliptic path with a sense that we are rapidly converging upon a vital 'station' in the quest of the Horus-King.

The weeks pass in seconds on our computer screen and when we at last 'reach the eastern side of the sky' – at the horizon, at the highly significant moment when 'the gods are born', i.e. at the exact time of rising of the star Sirius – we see that a very powerful celestial conjunction has occurred: the sun (which is now at the summer solstice point) stands exactly between the 'paws' of Leo.[26] The solar disc is positioned near the breast of the cosmic lion where it seems to merge with the bright star Regulus – the 'star of Kings'.[27]

The great celestial 'journey' performed by the cosmic Horus-King along the ecliptic path therefore turns out to lead quite unambiguously to one very specific place in the heavenly landscape: between the

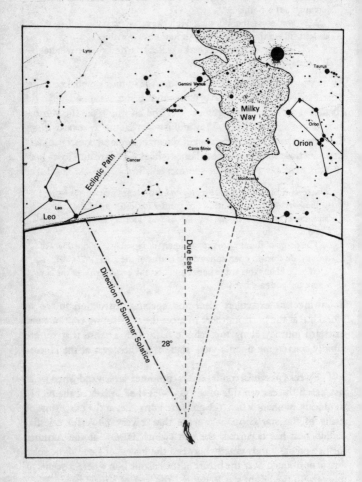

45. Epoch of 2500 BC, the Pyramid Age, seventy days before the summer solstice: an initiate tracking the journey of the 'solar' Horus, the disc of the sun, from its station on the right 'bank' of the Milky Way.

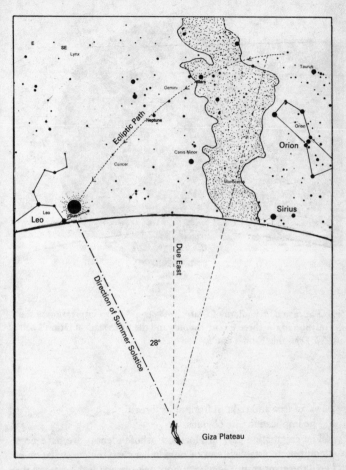

46. Epoch of 2500 BC, the Pyramid Age: an initiate tracking the journey of the 'solar' Horus, the disc of the sun, to its conjunction with Regulus, the heart-star of Leo, at dawn on the summer solstice. The ritual leaves no room for doubt that the enigmatic figure of Horakhti, so frequently referred to in the Pyramid Texts, is none other than the constellation of Leo.

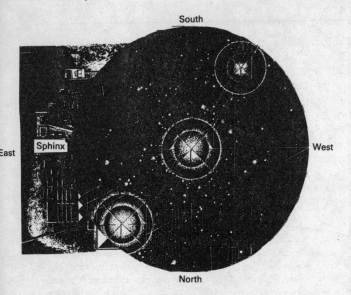

South

East

Sphinx

West

North

47. The 'astral' Kingdom of Osiris in Rostau. Artist's impression of the correlation of the three Giza Pyramids and the three stars of Orion's belt in *Zep Tepi*, the 'First Time'.

'paws' of Leo and right in front of its 'breast'.

The implications are obvious.

The enigmatic figure of Horakhti, whose identity we have been attempting to establish, can be none other than the constellation of Leo – the giant cosmic lion, or sphinx, who stands at the gates of the sky-*Duat* and who assumes the name of 'Horus-of-the-Horizon'.

Let us now transpose the Horus-King to the land and and follow his journey to the earthly 'Horus-in-the-Horizon' – by whom, of course, we mean Hor-em-Akhet, the Great Sphinx in the 'horizon' of Giza.

The High Road and the Low Road

The Horus-King stands on the east bank of the Nile, near the royal residence.[28] After completing certain rituals he boards a great 'solar boat'[29] – perhaps the very boat that was found in 1954 buried in a pit near the south face of the Great Pyramid – and is taken to the west bank of the river in the valley beneath the Giza plateau. He disembarks, makes his way up to the Temple of the Sphinx, and walks between the paws of the great statue to stand in front of its breast.

He is now at the Gateway to Rostau[30] and about to enter the Fifth Division of the *Duat* – the holy of holies of the Osirian afterworld Kingdom. Moreover, he is presented with a choice of 'two ways' or 'roads' to reach Rostau: one which is on 'land' and the other in 'water'.[31]

The eminent German philologist, Adolf Erman, explains:

> Whoever enters the realms of the dead by the sacred place of Rostau has, as we learn from a map of the Hereafter, two routes open to him, which would lead him to the land of the blessed, one by water, the other by land. Both are zigzag, and a traveller cannot change from one to the other, for between them lies a sea of fire . . . Also before entering upon either of these routes there is a gate of fire to be passed . . .[32]

Having made his choice, the Horus-King demands to be taken to see 'his father' Osiris in his astral form. A mediator or priest reports to Osiris and states:

> It is not I who asks that he may see you in this form of yours which has come into being for you; O Osiris, someone asks that he may see you in this form of yours which has come into being for you; it is your son who asks . . . it is Horus who asks that he may see you in this form . . . a loving son . . .[33]

Horus then declares to the council of the gods:

> The sky quivers, the earth shakes before me, for I am a magician, I possess magic. I have come that I may glorify Orion, that I may set Osiris at the head . . .[34]
> I have come to you, my father, I have come to you, Osiris . . .[35]

Next, in a most telling manner, the council of the gods issues the following instruction:

South   North

48. Artist's impression of the original Horus leading the way for the Horus-King initiate into the place where the 'Seat' of Osiris is to be found in the astral Pyramid of final initiation.

> O Horus, the King [your father] is Osiris, this Pyramid of the King is Osiris, this construction of his is Osiris; betake yourself to it . . .[36]

And further light may be shed on the identity of the Osiris-Pyramid by a passage from the *Book of What is in the Duat* which speaks of a mysterious 'district' in the *Duat*: 'which is 440 cubits in length and 440 cubits in breadth'.[37] Can it be a coincidence, since the Egyptian royal cubit is equivalent to 20.6 inches and 440 cubits therefore amounts to just over 755 feet, that the dimensions given are identical to those of the Great Pyramid's square base?[38]

At any rate, after passing through more ordeals and adventures, the questing Horus-King finally reaches Osiris-Orion and finds him listless in the tenebrous underworld of his Pyramid. At this vital juncture, the questor's role is to bid his 'father Osiris' to awake and be reborn – i.e., in dualistic astronomical terms, to rise anew in the east at dawn as Orion: 'Awake for Horus! . . . Raise yourself! . . . The gates of the *Duat* are opened for you . . . Spiritualize yourself . . . May a stairway to the *Duat* be set up for you to the place where Orion is . . .'[39]

Where, then, near or under the Sphinx can we find the 'two ways' or the 'two roads' of Rostau?

And why should the Horus-King be made to choose between them?

Subterranean world

One of the ancient names of the Giza necropolis, as we have seen, was *Akhet Khufu* – *Kherit-Neter-Akhet-Khufu* in full, usually rendered into English as 'the necropolis of the Horizon of Khufu'. In his dictionary of ancient Egyptian hieroglyphs, Sir E. A. Wallis Budge translates the word *Kherit-Neter* as 'cemetery, necropolis'.[40] Selim Hassan, however, points out that *Kherit-Neter* can have the alternative meaning of 'under, or belonging to a God'.[41] And Budge adds that *Kherit* can also mean 'estate' and that the root of the word, i.e. *Kher*, can mean 'under something', 'the lower part' or 'downwards'.[42]

In addition, as Hassan also reminds us, *Kherit* 'may be applied to the Underworld [*Duat*], perhaps as a lingering memory of the conception of Rostau as the Kingdom of Osiris in the tomb'.[43] Could such nuances imply more than a lingering memory? In other words, is it not posible, as we have already suggested in Part I, that under the necropolis-'horizon' of Giza there could be an 'estate' of some kind – perhaps a network of subterranean chambers and passageways?

In his *Handbook of Egyptian Religion*, the German Egyptologist Adolf Erman wrote that: 'the celebrated shrine Rostau, the gates of the ways, led directly to the underworld. It is possible that part of this shrine has survived in the so-called Temple of the Sphinx . . .'[44]

Furthermore, commenting on the word 'Rostau', R. O. Faulkner, the translator of the Pyramid Texts, says that this is also 'the term for a ramp or slide for moving the sarcophagus into a tomb, transferred to a region of the beyond'.[45] Dr I. E. S. Edwards, on the other hand, says that the causeway which links a pyramid complex with its valley temple 'was called "place of the haul" or "entrance of the haul" (Rostau) because it was the way along which sledges bearing the body of the dead king and his personal possessions would be hauled at his funeral'.[46]

Linking the Valley Temple near the Sphinx with the central Pyramid on the Giza plateau, as the reader will recall, are the remains of an enormous causeway. Might not this causeway or 'road' be one of the 'ways' to the heartland of Rostau described in the ancient texts? Such causeways – though now in all cases fallen into ruin – were originally rectangular tunnels roofed over with limestone slabs and decorated with star-spangled ceilings.[47] It is easy to see how symbolism of this kind would have been be appropriate in the context of the Horus-King's cosmic quest to find the astral form of Osiris.

The causeway of the Sphinx runs to the immediate south of the monument at about the level of its shoulder and thence slopes gently upwards in a westerly direction towards the great 'Mortuary Temple' that stands outside the east face of the central Pyramid of Giza. Being in every sense 'dry', it makes sense to consider this causeway as being the 'road by land' to Rostau.

But where might the other 'road' be located – the 'way through water'? There may be an an important clue in the *Book of What is in the Duat*. In this eerie text there is a depiction of the hermetically sealed chamber of the 'Kingdom of Sokar' – Sokar-Osiris – which is also the Fifth Division of the *Duat*. The depiction shows a tunnel filled with water passing *under the paws* of a large Sphinx. The tunnel slopes gently upwards leading, finally, to the Sixth Division.

Interestingly enough, as we saw in Part I, geologists working around the Great Sphinx in the early 1990s identified a large rectangular chamber and other 'anomalies' in the bedrock directly beneath the monument's paws. Interestingly, too, it is well known that far below the Sphinx is an underground watertable which has been constantly replenished since times immemorial by capillary action from the Nile.[48]

Tunnel

Dr Jean Kerisel, the eminent French engineer whose work in the Subterranean Chamber of the Great Pyramid we are already familiar with,[49] has recently taken the geological evidence further by suggesting that the Sphinx may stand over the entrance to a 700–metre-long tunnel leading to the Great Pyramid – a tunnel that was once filled or partially filled with water.[50]

Could such a tunnel be the other 'way' that the Horus-King had to take to 'see the astral form of his Father', i.e. Orion? The fact that inside the King's Chamber of the Great Pyramid is, indeed, a star-shaft pointed directly at Orion's belt – the 'Rostau' in the sky – adds cogency to notions of some sort of underground access route that might have been used by initiates to journey in secret from the Sphinx to the inner passages and chambers of the Pyramid.

Furthermore, in the Pyramid Texts we often hear of a 'Causeway of Happiness' which is in the 'North of the Field of Offerings'. And in the following passage the Horus-King seems to be standing at the entrance of such a 'causeway' at exactly the time Sirius is performing its heliacal rising, i.e. 'Heralding the New Year' 70 days after the sun's crossing of the Milky Way:

> I am the herald of the Year, O Osiris, I have come on business of your father Geb [the earth-god] ... I speak to you, I have made you enduring. 'Causeway of Happiness' is the name of this causeway north of the Fields of Offerings. Stand Up, Osiris, and commend me to those who are in charge of the 'Causeway of Happiness' north of the Field of Offerings just as you commended Horus to Isis on that day on which you made her pregnant ...[51]

The 'Field of Offerings' had a celestial location in the *Duat* somewhere near Orion.[52] Dualistic logic therefore suggests that its earthly counterpart must have been a place where 'offerings' were made by the Horus-King when he was about to enter the Giza necropolis. With this in mind, it is surely of relevance that many of the New Kingdom sphinx stelae found at Giza, including the granite stela of Thutmosis IV that stands between the paws of the Sphinx itself, do in fact show the Horus-Kings making offerings in a temple in front of the monument.[53] Furthermore, as the text quoted above makes clear, the 'Causeway of Happiness' ran to the north of the 'Field of Offerings'. An underground 'causeway' running north-west from the temple of the Sphinx would lead to the Great Pyramid.

So could Kerisel's bold hypothesis be right?[54] Could such an underground system exist at Giza?

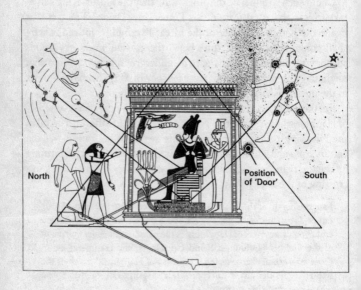

49. Artist's impression of the 'cosmic' Great Pyramid superimposing the star Sirius over the position of the 'gate' in the Sirius star-shaft.

Stargate

These are questions that we shall return to in Part IV. Meanwhile what are we to make of the mention of Isis and her pregnancy that also appears in the above text?

In *The Orion Mystery* it has been shown that the Great Pyramid's so-called Queen's Chamber could have been used for a symbolic 'copulation' or 'seeding' ritual involving the person of the Horus-King on the one hand and the goddess Isis in her astral form (i.e. the star Sirius) on the other. In terms of sky–ground dualism the two might have been thought of as being 'connected' through the Chamber's southern star-shaft, which was targeted on the meridian-transit of Sirius in the Pyramid Age.[55] This hypothesis is strengthened by the fact that such a copulation ritual is found clearly depicted in the Pyramid Texts and that the moment when Osiris supposedly made Isis 'pregnant' is specified as being when Sirius crossed the meridian at dawn.[56] The texts also state of Osiris-Orion: 'Your sister Isis comes to you rejoicing for love of you. You have placed her on your phallus and your seed issues in her, she being ready as "Sothis" [Sirius] . . .'[57]

Was the Horus-King, then, somehow meant to find his way under and into the Great Pyramid and thence to its upper chambers with their star-shafts?

And what might really be the significance of Rudolf Gantenbrink's recent discovery, which we have considered at length in Part II, of a mysterious 'gate' or 'doorway' deep inside one of those shafts – the very shaft that targeted the meridian-transit of Sirius in the Pyramid Age?

Last but not least, is it a coincidence that the ancient Egyptian word *sba*, 'star', also carries the meanings 'gate', 'folding door' and 'great door of heaven'?[58]

Again, these are matters on which we shall have to postpone further conjecture until Part IV. Meanwhile let us return to the quest to unite sky and ground – thus winning the Grail of immortality – in which all the Horus-Kings of ancient Egypt participated.

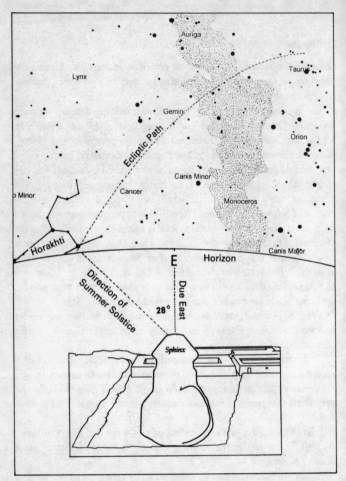

50. Epoch of 2500 BC, the Pyramid Age: the rising of Leo at the summer solstice. Note that in this epoch the gaze of Hor-em-Akhet, 'Horus-in-the-Horizon' – i.e. the Great Sphinx – is not in alignment with Horakhti, 'Horus-of-the-Horizon', i.e. the constellation of Leo. The reader will recall that this same sense of a curious 'dislocation' of the sky–ground images at the summer solstice in 2500 BC also applies to the three great Pyramids and the three stars of Orion's belt.

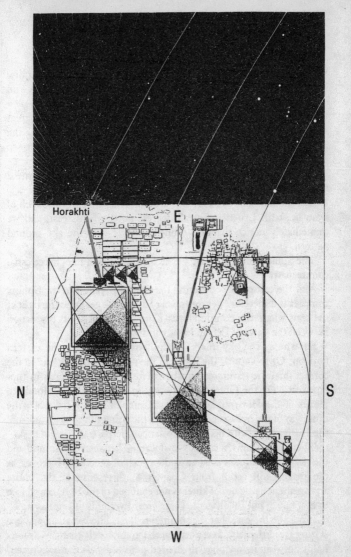

51. Summer solstice in the epoch of 2500 BC. Artist's impression of the *Duat* region as viewed from the Horizon of Giza.

The Splendid Place of the 'First Time'

We left the cosmic Horus-King standing in the sky with the solar disc between the 'paws' of the celestial lion, the constellation of Leo – on the spot marked by the star Regulus.

In the Pyramid Age Regulus rose at approximately 28 degrees north of due east.[59] It is from this spot therefore that the Horus-King in the sky must somehow travel – on one of the 'roads' to Rostau – to reach Orion's belt.

Now we transpose again to the Horus-King in his earthly form at Giza, standing between the paws of the great Sphinx.

It is the moment of dawn on the summer solstice in the epoch of 2500 BC, with Leo rising at 28 degrees north of due east, and we immediately notice that something is wrong with the sky–ground pattern.

The Sphinx gazes due east, i.e. he does not gaze at Leo, his celestial counterpart.

And the causeway connecting the central Pyramid to the Sphinx complex is directed 14 degrees *south* of due east – i.e. far to the right of the spot where the cosmic Horus-King is supposedly at his station between the paws of Leo and ready to travel to Rostau.

So why is the sky-image in the 'wrong place' on the eastern horizon? Or to express the problem the right way round, and in the correct dualistic terminology, why is Hor-em-Akhet, Horus-in-the-Horizon – i.e. the Great Sphinx – not in alignment with Horakhti, Horus-of-the-Horizon, i.e. the constellation of Leo? Why, too, is the causeway of the Sphinx not directed to the rising sun so as to 'link-up' the Horus-King with his cosmic solar counterpart?

There is, it seems, a curious 'dislocation' between the ground and the sky at the summer solstice in the epoch of 2500 BC. Moreover, as the reader will recall from Chapter 8, this sense of the entire arrangement being out of kilter is not confined to the Sphinx and Leo in that epoch but involves the three great Pyramids of Giza as well.

It may be the case that the solution to the riddle has all along been staring us in the face. Inscribed on the granite stela that the Sphinx holds between its own heavily eroded paws – a stela that was placed there in honour of Thutmosis IV, a mighty Horus-King of Egypt – we read the following impressive royal titulary:

The Majesty of Horus, Mighty Bull Begetting Radiance, Favourite of the Two Goddesses, Enduring in Kingship like Atum, Golden Horus, Mighty of Sword, Repelling the Nine Bows, King of Upper and Lower Egypt, Son of Re, Thutmosis ... given life, stability, satisfaction ... for ever. Live the Good God, Son of Atum, Protector of Horakhti, Living Image of the All-Lord, Sovereign . . ., beautiful of Face like His Father, who came forth equipped with the form of Horus upon him . . . Son of Atum, of his body, Thutmosis . . . Heir of Horus Upon His Throne . . .[60]

Does this sound like a man who did not have a clue, as some Egyptologists suggest,[61] as to what the great Sphinx and the other monuments of Giza really represented? Surely not. So what, then, did the majestic Horus-King declare this sacred domain to be?

52. Artist's impression of 'reconstructed' Sphinx showing the statue of a Horus-King, which is known to have once stood between its paws, gazing at the celestial counterpart of the 'Splendid Place of the First Time' in the eastern horizon.

In one simple, powerful phrase, as the reader will recall, he stated that it was 'The Splendid Place of the "First Time" '.[62]

Is it not likely, when he uttered these words, that Thutmosis, 'Heir of Horus Upon His Throne', was repeating what every Horus-King before him had declared the Giza plateau to be?

Is it not likely that he called it 'The Splendid Place of the "First Time" ' because that is exactly what it was remembered to be in traditions that had been handed down from remotest, almost incomprehensible, antiquity?

Could this be why the sky of 2500 BC seems to be so badly out of kilter, somehow skewed and twisted, i.e. 'in the wrong place'? Could it be not so much in the wrong place as *at the wrong time*?

Should we set our computer to search for another time that might match the monuments to the sky, a time long before Thutmosis, long before Khafre and Khufu, the 'time' when Osiris established his kingdom on earth – in other words, the 'First Time'?

When was the 'First Time'?

Part IV

Map

Chapter 11

The Unseen Academy

'The Egyptians believed that in the
beginning their land was ruled by a dynasty
of great gods, of whom Horus, the son of Isis
and Osiris, was the last. He was succeeded
by a dynasty of semi-divine beings known as
the "followers of Horus", who, in turn, gave
place to the historical kings of Egypt.'

Selim Hassan, *The Sphinx*, Cairo, 1949

When was the 'genesis' of civilization in Egypt? When did 'history'
begin?

According to T. G. H. James, formerly Keeper of Egyptian
Antiquities at the British Museum, and a representative voice of
orthodox opinion on these matters: 'The first truly historical period is
that which begins with the invention of writing and it is generally
known as the Dynastic Period. It is a period extending from about
3100 BC to 332 BC and it derives its name from the thirty-one dynasties
into which the successive kings of Egypt were divided in a scheme
preserved in the work of Manetho, a priestly historian who lived
during the [third century BC]. The unlettered cultures which
flourished in Egypt before the beginning of the Dynastic Period, and
which exhibit some of the characteristics which mark the earliest
phases of Egyptian culture in the Dynastic Period, are known as
Predynastic ... Such traces of human life as are found in the Nile
Valley dating from before the Predynastic Period are usually
described in the terms used for European Prehistory – Palaeolithic,
Mesolithic and Neolithic.' [1]

So there we have it. Egyptian history – and civilization with it –
began at around 3100 BC. Before that there were merely 'unlettered

cultures' (admittedly with some 'civilized' characteristics), which were in turn preceded by 'Stone Age' savages ('Palaeolithic' means literally 'Old Stone Age').

The way James puts it, the whole picture seems very clear-cut, orderly and precise. He really makes it sound as though all the facts are now in hand concerning the Predynastic Egyptians and their forebears, and that nothing more remains to be discovered about any of them.

Such anodyne notions of the past are widespread amongst Egyptologists who again and again in their textbooks, and also in mass-market publications like *National Geographic* and Time-Life's misleadingly named *Lost Civilizations* series, convey the comforting impression that the prehistory of Egypt is well understood, organized, categorized and safely put in its place (James even refers us to one specific place in the British Museum where particular enlightenment apparently awaits us: the 'Sixth Egyptian Room' with its definitive display of 'primitive tools made by the Palaeolithic inhabitants of Egypt').[2] Likewise, on the other side of the Atlantic as we saw in Part I, Dr Peter Lecovara, Curator of the Museum of Fine Arts in Boston, assures us that 'thousands of Egyptologists working for hundreds of years have studied this problem [the prehistory of Egypt] and the chronology is pretty much worked out. There is no big surprise in store for us.'[3]

But is everything really as orderly and as well worked out as the 'experts' say? And can we really be so sure that there is 'no big surprise in store for us'?

In our view Lecovara, James, and the many other scholars who share their opinions, would do well to remember the advice of the late Labib Habachi, formerly the Egyptian government's Chief Inspector of Antiquities, who warned in 1984 that 'Egyptology is a field in which chance discovery may disprove an established theory'.[4] In the light of this possibility, Habachi's suggestion was that Egyptologists should avoid making 'unqualified statements' and be honest enough to 'salt their comments with "probably" and "perhaps".'[5]

Certainly a little more 'probably' and 'perhaps' would be in order where the Predynastic and earlier periods of Egyptian history are concerned. Far from the impression conveyed to the public, the truth, as some scholars are prepared to admit, is that 'The state of knowledge of Egyptian prehistory in the late twentieth century is still fragmentary'.[6]

These are the words of Nicholas Grimal, Professor of Egyptology at the Sorbonne University in Paris, who also concedes:

> It has been clear since the Second World War not only that 'prehistory' before the Pharaohs was expanding on a hitherto unsuspected scale, but also that it appeared to be so diverse and self-contained that it was difficult to regard it simply as a 'preparatory' stage for the Dynastic Period . . .[7]

The prevailing Egyptological consensus (to which Grimal in this respect at least is an exception) is unable to offer any coherent theory which explains these 'diverse' and 'self-contained' characteristics of Egyptian prehistory, or that account for the very serious problems of apparent non-continuity between the Predynastic and the Dynastic Periods. The ancient Egyptians themselves, however, passed down records to us which may contain the answer to the whole mystery. These records provide detailed information concerning a period that extends back many thousands of years *before* the sudden emergence of the Pharaonic state in the epoch of 3000 BC.

The only problem is that no one is prepared to take these records seriously. Could this be because they conflict with the modern scholarly consensus on Egyptian chronology? Readers must make up their own minds but, as we shall see below, elements of the same records which *do* conform to the current theory *are* accepted and taken seriously by Egyptologists.

Three eras

As T. G. H. James tells us in his remarks quoted earlier, modern study of ancient Egyptian chronology is largely based on Manetho's *History of Egypt*. The respected Professor Walter Emery puts things much the same way when he reports that the writings of Manetho are of 'immense importance and form the framework on which Egyptian history has been built'.[8]

One of the reasons that Manetho's system is so durable and remains in use by Egyptologists today is that it has again and again proved itself to be accurate. He is known to have based it on 'much older documents, or king-lists, to which, as a learned priest he had access'.[9] Furthermore a number of documents in this category – notably the Palermo Stone, the Turin Papyrus and the Abydos King-List – have been found and translated. In the words of the late Professor Michael Hoffman, a leading expert on Egypt before the Pharaohs: 'Archaeologists and Egyptologists have discovered five such lists which, despite some discrepancies, support Manetho in general.'[10]

Looking at all the surviving sources, it is clear that *three distinct eras of kingship* were remembered:

- The first era was when the *Neteru*, ('*Neters*' or 'Gods') ruled the land of Egypt – an epoch that culminated with the kingship of Horus, the son of Osiris and Isis.
- Then came the era of the 'Followers of Horus', the *Shemsu Hor*, (also known by numerous other titles and epithets) which took the divine Horian lineage across the ages and up to a human Pharaoh named Menes (also known as Narmer or 'King Scorpion'), the legendary 'Unifier of the Two Lands of Upper and Lower Egypt'.
- After Menes came the so-called 'Dynastic' Kings, whose names are individually catalogued in the king-lists.

Egyptologists place the reign of Menes in *circa* 3000 BC and regard him as the first 'historical' king of 'Dynastic' Egypt.[11] They concede that a few Predynastic 'chieftains' must have preceded him in both the north and south of the country but they emphatically reject any suggestion that the '*Neters*' and the 'Followers of Horus' catalogued in the king-lists (and referred to with some prominence by Manetho) could have been historical individuals. On the contrary, the consensus view is that the *Neters*, being 'Gods', are obvious religious fictions and that the *Shemsu Hor* are to be regarded as nothing more than 'mythical kings' who ruled in an equally 'mythical kingdom'.

So, scholars accept as history only the bits of Manetho and the surviving king-lists that fit their theory – i.e. the records of the Dynastic Period from Menes on – and devalue all references in those same records to earlier and more mysterious times.

Writing in the *Cambridge Ancient History*, for example, Professor T. E. Peet groups together all the ancient Egyptian sources concerning the chronology of the 'Gods' and the 'Followers of Horus' and then dismisses the entire corpus of material with the following throwaway remark: 'From the historical point of view there is little to be made of this.' [12]

Likewise, in *Kingship and the Gods*, his detailed study of the Pharaonic state, the eminent Henri Frankfort, Professor of Preclassical Antiquity at the University of London, had this to say about the 'Followers of Horus':

> ... it appears that 'Followers of Horus' is a vague designation for the kings of a distant past ... but it would seem unwise to treat the term as primarily of a historical nature. For each king became at death one of the corporation of 'transfigured spirits' ... [and] merged with that nebulous spiritual force which had supported the living rulers and descendents of the Throne of Horus since time immemorial. [13]

High initiates

We feel obliged to point out that this was not at all how the ancient Egyptians viewed their own history. For them there was never any question of mythical epochs or 'nebulous spiritual forces' lurking in the distant past. For them, to state matters plainly, the 'Followers of Horus', and the geographical landscape in which they had 'ruled', were unquestionable realities to which they were directly and inseverably connected. Indeed, if one takes the Egyptian accounts and traditions seriously what the 'Followers of Horus' begin to sound like is a lineage of real, although 'unnamed' individuals whose function and duty, as Henri Frankfort himself suggested, was to provide the 'spiritual force' behind the monarchy (though by no means in a 'vague' or 'nebulous' manner). The Egyptians' own accounts also invite the conclusion that the role of these 'Followers' may have been to carry down the ages a body of extraordinary knowledge harking back to the even more mysterious 'time of the *Neteru*' – i.e. the 'Gods'.

From available primary sources, in other words, the overall picture that emerges is that the 'Followers of Horus' may not have been 'kings' in the usual sense of the word but rather immensely powerful and enlightened individuals – high initiates who were carefully selected by an élite academy that established itself at the sacred site of

Heliopolis-Giza thousands of years before history began. There is much to suggest, too, that the ancient Egyptian texts are right and that Pharaonic civilization may indeed have owed its unique spark of genius to just such a 'brotherhood' linked to just such an archaic and élite academy.

So who might the *Shemsu Hor* really have been? And what were they 'following'?

Following the Way of Horus

Heliopolis – ancient *On* or *Innu* – was the oldest organized religious centre in Egypt and most probably in the world. Situated some 12 miles north-east of the Giza plateau, and already hoary with age at the

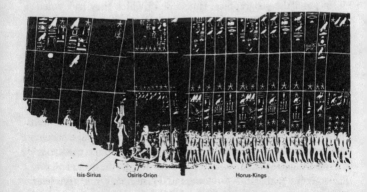

Isis-Sirius   Osiris-Orion   Horus-Kings

53. Osiris-Orion showing the way to his 'Followers', the Horus-Kings, who are the custodians of his dual kingdom in the *Duat*.

dawn of the Pharaonic epoch, it is identified by tradition as the source of the secrets of astral immortality which the Pyramid builders claimed to have inherited. Indeed the title of the High Priest of Heliopolis, as Professor I. E. S. Edwards has recently demonstrated, was 'Chief of the Astronomers', and the regalia of this notable was a ceremonial robe spangled with five-pointed stars.[14]

As we have already hinted in Part III, the dominant concerns of the elitist, 'scientific' priests of Heliopolis were with recording the motions of the stars, measuring and commemorating the passage of time, and peering into the mysteries of the epochs. It has long been known, too, that they carefully studied the cycle of the sun in its perceived yearly circuit along the zodiacal path. And more recently, compelling evidence has emerged that they also followed the far longer cosmic cycle of the 'Great Year' – namely the precessional 'drift' of the stars caused by the earth's axial 'wobble'. The reader will recall that this vast cycle of 25,920 years was measured by the slow rotation of the twelve zodiacal constellations in relation to the point of sunrise on the vernal equinox – in short, the 'precession of the equinoxes' in which a succession of astrological 'Ages', each 2160 years in duration, was believed to have begun to unfold after a kind of spiritual and cultural 'Big Bang' known as *Zep Tepi* – the 'First Time' of the Gods.

To observe and accurately measure the rate of the precession of the equinoxes is a feat that could only have been achieved by scientifically minded, intellectually advanced and highly organized people with a long tradition of precise observational astronomy. Similarly, the building of the three great Pyramids of Giza was not the work of technological primitives only recently emerged from the Stone Age. On the contrary, as historians of science Giorgio de Santillana and Hertha von Dechend have pointed out, such accomplishments 'should be a cogent reason for concluding that serious and intelligent men were at work behind the stage, men who were bound to have used a technical terminology'.[15]

We shall argue that 'serious and intelligent men' – and apparently women too – were indeed at work behind the stage of prehistory in Egypt and propose that one of the many names by which they were known was the 'Followers of Horus'. We propose, too, that their purpose, to which their generations adhered for thousands of years with the rigour of a messianic cult, may have been to bring to fruition a great cosmic blueprint. And we have evidence that the slow unfolding and implementation of this plan somehow entailed tracking two observable 'ways' taken by the celestial bodies across the ages – 'ways' which are both consequences of the earth's axial precession:

- First the 'way' of the stars: these appear to 'drift' in the sense that their place and day of rising at the horizon changes, accompanied by corresponding changes in their altitude at the meridian.
- Secondly the 'way' of the sun, which also appears to 'drift' – in this case 'westwards' along the ecliptic path so that the 'pointer' of the vernal equinox appears to 'sweep' slowly through each one of the twelve zodiacal signs every 2160 years.

In the coded astronomical language of the ancients of Heliopolis, we will argue that the notion of following the sun's westward drift through the zodiac translates as 'Following the Way of Horus (the sun) across the ages'. And we will show that the 'Followers of Horus' are most likely to have acquired their enigmatic title because it described precisely what they did and stood for. They were, we suspect, astrologers and astronomers *par excellence* who had been following and recording the position of the vernal point across the ages from the epoch of the 'First Time' to the epoch of the historical kings of Egypt.

Last but not least, we also propose as a hypothesis for further testing that at a well-defined and predetermined historical moment 'written in the stars' the 'Followers of Horus' may have taken steps to mobilize the native inhabitants of Egypt, unite them into a theocratic state and harness their energies to the further fulfilment of a cosmic blueprint in which the great Pyramids on the west bank of the Nile were to play a pivotal role . . .

Chapter 12

Sages and 'Followers'

'The introduction to the first Edfu
cosmological record discloses the tradition
that the contents of these records were the
"words of the Sages". We are told that this
sacred book was believed to be a "Copy of
the writings which Thoth made according to
the words of the Sages" . . .'

E. A. E. Reymond, *The Mythical Origin of
the Egyptian Temple*, 1969

It is a convention amongst modern scholars that myths do not count as
historical evidence – and, as we saw in the last chapter, this
convention is particularly strongly adhered to by Egyptologists.

Yet there are several well-known cases in archaeology where myths
that have been dismissed as 'unhistorical' were later proved to have
been entirely accurate. One example concerns the world-famous
Troy of Homer's *Iliad* (a great prose-poem compiled from earlier oral
sources *circa* 800 BC). Until not long ago most scholars were convinced
that Troy was a 'mythical city' – i.e. entirely a figment of Homer's
fertile imagination. In 1871, however, the 'buccaneer' German
explorer Heinrich Schliemann proved orthodox opinion wrong when
he followed geographical clues contained in the *Iliad* and discovered
Troy in western Turkey near the Dardanelles (the ancient Helles-
pont) – exactly where Homer had said it was located. Schliemann and
two other intrepid researchers, the Greek scholar Kalokairinos and
the British archaeologist Sir Arthur Evans, then went on to cap this
achievement by following up myths concerning the great 'Minoan'
civilization that was said to have existed on the island of Crete. These
myths, too, were dismissed as unhistorical by orthodox opinion but

were vindicated when Schliemann and his team excavated the remains of a highly advanced culture now firmly identified as that of the 'Minoans'.[1]

Similarly, in the Indian subcontinent, the great body of ancient Sanscrit scriptures known as the Rig-Veda contains repeated references to a high civilization, living in fortified cities, that had preceded the Aryan invasions more than 4000 years ago. Again these references were universally dismissed as 'mythical' – until, that is, the ruins of the great 'Indus Valley' cities such as Harappa and Moenjodaro began to be unearthed in the twentieth century and proved to date back as far as 2500 BC.[2]

In short, the record shows that whole cities and civilizations which were once classified as mythical (and therefore of no historical interest) have a habit again and again of suddenly materializing from the mists of obscurity and becoming historical realities.

Could the same thing be about to happen in Egypt?

Guardians of records

Amongst other peoples such as the Romans and the Greeks, who were considerably closer to ancient Egypt than we are, it was held to be axiomatic that the Pharaohs and their priests were the guardians of accurate records concerning certain highly significant events that had taken place long, long ago. Indeed these records were actually seen and studied, at the sacred city of Heliopolis, by such distinguished visitors as Herodotus (fifth century BC), the Greek lawmaker Solon (640–560 BC) and his fellow countryman the scientist Pythagoras (sixth century BC).[3] From their reports derived the Greek impression of Egypt reported by Plato:[4]

> We Greeks are in reality children compared with this people with traditions ten times older. And as nothing of precious remembrance of the past would long survive in our country, Egypt has recorded and kept eternally the wisdom of the old times. The walls of its temples are covered with inscriptions and the priests have always under their own eyes that divine heritage . . . The generations continue to transmit to successive generations these sacred things unchanged: songs, dances,

rhythms, rituals, music, paintings, all coming from time immemorial when gods governed the earth in the dawn of civilization.[5]

We have already made frequent mention of *Zep Tepi*, the supposedly mythical 'First Time' of the Gods – a remote epoch with which the ancient Egyptians associated the origins of their civilization. And in the last chapter we noted that Manetho's fabled *History*, and a number of inscriptions known as king-lists, also refer back to distant golden ages when the gods, and then subsequently the mysterious 'Followers of Horus', ruled in the Nile Valley. Before immersing ourselves in the next chapter in the truly immense chronology of which all the lists speak, our objective here, as Plato prompts, is to take a look at the 'walls of temples' – specifically at the so-called 'Building Texts' (*circa* 200 BC) inscribed on the walls of the Temple of Edfu that stands in Upper Egypt midway between Luxor and Aswan. These texts, which contain a series of extraordinary references to the 'First Time', are accepted by scholars as the only surviving fragments of a much more ancient, much larger, and much more coherent body of cosmogonical literature – now long lost – that once incorporated a complete 'mythical history' of Egypt, of its gods and of the temples built to honour them.[6] In the texts, the 'Followers of Horus' are equated and merged with other 'mythical' beings, sometimes seemingly divine, sometimes human, who are always portrayed as the bringers and preservers of knowledge down the ages – as an élite brotherhood dedicated to the transmission of wisdom and to the quest for resurrection and rebirth . . .

Memories of the dawn

The Temple of Edfu in its present form was erected over a two hundred-year period between 237 BC and 57 BC but incorporates parts of much earlier structures dating back to the Pyramid Age (for example portions of the inner and outer western enclosure wall). Moreover, like all major temples, it was built 'on hallowed ground' and there attaches to it a recollection of vast antiquity and of momentous antecedents.[7]

Thus, on the face of things, the Building Texts appear to be nothing more than a history of the Edfu Temple itself, together with descriptions of its rooms and halls and of their ritual purpose and significance.[8] A closer look, however, as E. A. E Reymond of Manchester University has demonstrated, reveals a subtext which hints:

> at the existence of certain mythological events ... where the foundation, building and bringing to life of the historical temple [of Edfu] is interpreted as happening in a mythical age. The historical temple is interpreted as the work of the gods themselves, and as an entity of a mythical nature. This ... seems to indicate a belief in a historical temple that was a direct continuation, projection, and reflexion of a mythical temple that came into existence at the beginning of the world ...[9]

Needless to say the 'beginning of the world' is a synonym in the Edfu Texts for the 'First Time', also known as the 'Early Primeval Age'. In this epoch, we learn, the 'words of the Sages' were copied down by the wisdom-god Thoth into a book that codified the locations of certain 'sacred mounds' along the Nile. The title of this lost book, according to the texts, was *Specifications of the Mounds of the Early Primaeval Age*, and it was believed to have contained records not only of all the lesser 'Mounds', or temples, but also of the Great Primeval Mound itself, the place where time had supposedly begun.[10]

Several points of interest arise:

1 The 'Great Primeval Mound' has recently been associated by Professor I. E. S. Edwards with the natural outcropping of rock that is known to lie under the Great Pyramid of Egypt and to have been incorporated into its lower courses of masonry.[11] This analysis appears to reinforce the connections that we have already established in Part I between the Giza necropolis and the 'First Time'.

2 The 'Sages' referred to in the Edfu Building Texts were seven in number. Their special role was as 'the only divine beings who knew how the temples and sacred places were to be created'. And it was they who initiated construction work at the Great Primeval Mound. This work, in which Thoth also participated, involved the setting out and erection of the original 'mythical' temple of the 'First Time'.[12]

3 Also constructed under the direction of the 'Seven Sages' was an

edifice specified as *hwt-ntr*, 'the mansion of the god': ' "Speedy of construction", men called it by name. The sanctuary is within it, "Great Seat" by name, and all its chapels are according to the norm.' [13]

4 When all these works were complete 'the magical protection (*swr mdw*) of that site was made by the Sages'.[14]

5 In the whole corpus of ancient Egyptian writings, the Edfu Building Texts preserve the only references to the 'Seven Sages' that have survived to the present day. Egyptologists have therefore paid little attention to the identity of these beings beyond conceding that that they appear to have played a part in 'a much wider and more general theory concerning the origin of sacred domains and their temples'.[15] In our opinion, however, there is something notable about the context in which the Texts describe the Sages. This context is marked by a preponderance of 'Flood' imagery in which the 'primeval waters' (out of which the Great Primeval Mound emerged) are depicted as gradually receding.[16] We are reminded of Noah's mountain-top on which the Ark settled after the Biblical Deluge, and of the 'Seven Sages' (*Apkallu*) of ancient Babylonian tradition who were said to have 'lived before the Flood' and to have built the walls of the sacred city of Uruk.[17] Likewise is it an accident that in Indian tradition 'Seven Sages' (*Rishis*) are remembered to have survived the Flood, their purpose being to preserve and pass down to future generations the wisdom of the antedeluvian world?[18]

In all cases the Sages appear as the enlightened survivors of a cataclysm that wiped the earth clean, who then set about making a fresh start at the dawn of a new age – which, in ancient Egypt, was referred to as the 'First Time'. As Reymond confirms in her masterly study of the Edfu Texts:

> the first era known by our principal sources was *a period which started from what existed in the past*. The general tone of the record seems to convey the view that an ancient world, after having been constituted, was destroyed, and as a dead world it came to be the basis of a new period of creation which at first was the re-creation and resurrection of what once had existed in the past.[19]

Wisdom and knowledge

According to the Edfu Texts the Seven Sages and the other gods came originally from an island,[20] the 'Homeland of the Primeval Ones'.[21] As noted above, the texts are adamant that the agency that destroyed this island was a flood. They also tell us that it came to its end suddenly[22] and that the majority of its 'divine inhabitants' were drowned.[23] Arriving in Egypt, those few who survived then became 'the Builder Gods, who fashioned in the primeval time, the Lords of Light . . . the Ghosts, the Ancestors . . . who raised the seed for gods and men. . . , the Senior Ones who came into being at the beginning, who illumined this land when they came forth unitedly . . .'[24]

It was not believed that these remarkable beings were immortal. On the contrary, after they had completed their tasks they died and their children took their places and performed funerary rites on their behalf.[25] In this way, just like the 'Followers of Horus', the generations of the 'Builder Gods', or 'Sages', or 'Ghosts' or 'Lords of Light' described in the Edfu Texts could constantly renew themselves – thus passing down to the future traditions and wisdoms stemming from a previous epoch of the earth. Indeed, the similarities between the 'Senior Ones' of Edfu and the *Shemsu Hor* of Heliopolitan tradition are so marked it is hard to escape the conclusion that both epithets, and the numerous others that exist, are all descriptions of the same shadowy brotherhood.

This impression is strengthened by the constant references in the Edfu Texts to the '*wisdom* of the Sages' (wisdom being one of the defining characteristics of the 'Followers of Horus') and the repeated emphasis that their special gift was *knowledge* – including, but not limited to, the knowledge of architecture.[26] Likewise it is noteworthy that the Sages are said to have specified the plans and designs that were to be used for all future temples – a role frequently accorded in other contexts to the 'Followers of Horus'. For example, the temple of Dendera (a little to the north of Edfu) is inscribed with Building Texts of its own which state that the 'great plan' followed by its architects was 'recorded in ancient writings handed down from the "Followers of Horus" '.[27]

Heliopolitan origins

The earliest-surviving references to the 'Followers of Horus' occur in the Pyramid Texts. It is therefore unlikely to be an accident that the notion in the Edfu Texts of the Great Primeval Mound emerging from the waters of a universal deluge coincides exactly with imagery that has also been preserved in the *Pyramid Texts* in which, as E. A. E. Reymond summarizes: 'The Earth in its earliest shape was pictured as a mound which emerged from the primeval water. This mound itself was then considered as a divine being, and as the original terrestrial configuration on which the creator, Atum, dwelt.' [28]

As is well known, the compilation of the Pyramid Texts was undertaken by the priests of Heliopolis.[29] It may therefore be of relevance that ancient Egyptian traditions attribute the founding of Heliopolis to the 'Followers of Horus' – in a period long before the beginning of Dynastic times – and that there is an Egyptian papyrus, now in the Berlin Museum, which clearly suggests that Heliopolis in some way 'existed before the earth was created'.[30] Once again, this interlinks closely with a central proposition of the Edfu Texts, namely that the 'new world' created by the Sages after the Flood was conceived of and designed by its makers as 'the resurrection of the former world of the gods.' [31]

There are other links too. For example what Reymond calls 'the manifestation of the resurrection of the first holy world' took the form in the Edfu Texts of an upright column or rod, 'the Perch' on which a great bird, the Divine Falcon, rested.[32] In Heliopolis there stood a pillar (indeed *Innu*, the Egyptian name for Heliopolis, actually means 'pillar'[33]) on which it was believed that another 'Divine' bird – the *Bennu*, or phoenix – periodically rested.[34] And interestingly the hieroglyph for Heliopolis – a column surmounted by a cross above (or beside) a circle divided into eight parts[35] – is virtually identical to a hieroglyph depicting the Edfu 'Perch' that is reproduced by Flinders Petrie in his *Royal Tombs of the Earliest Dynasties*.[36]

For all these reasons, and many others, Reymond concludes that 'the Edfu documentary sources offer . . . one argument more in favour of the theory that the ritual of the Egyptian temple was Heliopolitan in origin . . . We are of the opinion that the Edfu records preserve the memory of a Predynastic religious centre which once existed near to Memphis, which the Egyptians looked on as the homeland of the Egyptian temple.' [37]

What better candidate is there for that 'Predynastic religious centre near to Memphis' – that 'homeland' of the Egyptian temple – than the sacred city of Heliopolis and its associated Pyramids and other structures on the Giza plateau? Moreover, as the reader will recall, the Giza/Heliopolis complex lies to the north of ancient Memphis. In this light a well-known text on the inner face of the enclosure wall of the temple at Edfu takes on a special meaning, for it tells us that the temple was built 'at the dictates of the Ancestors' according to what was written in a certain 'book' which had 'descended from the sky to the north of Memphis'.[38]

There is of course a sense in which the cosmic monuments of Giza could themselves be said to be a kind of 'book' written in stone and 'descended from the sky' – for, as we now know, the three great Pyramids are the terrestrial counterparts of the three stars of Orion's belt and the Sphinx draws down to earth the regal image of Leo, the celestial lion.

Cycle of the phoenix

The Primeval Mound, identified with the Great Pyramid and with the natural mound of rock that is incorporated into the foundations of that monument, is envisaged in the Pyramid Texts as a place at once of birth and death, and also as a place of rebirth.[39] These ideas fit well with the ancient Egyptian rituals for 'awakening Osiris' and attaining astral immortality – and with the quest of the Horus-King – that we have described in earlier chapters. They also accord with the sense that the texts convey of a cyclical rhythm at work in the universe as the vast 'Mill' of the zodiac grinds out the destiny of world ages.

In Heliopolitan theology, all these processes were grouped together, summarized and expressed in a single image – the *Bennu* bird, the legendary Phoenix which at certain widely separated intervals 'fashioned a nest of aromatic boughs and spices, set it on fire and was consumed in the flames. From the pyre miraculously sprang a new phoenix, which, after embalming its father's ashes in an egg of myrrh, flew with the ashes to Heliopolis where it deposited them in the altar of the Egyptian sun-god, Re. A variant of the story made the dying phoenix fly to Heliopolis and immolate itself in the altar fire, from which the young phoenix then rose . . . The Egyptians associated the phoenix with immortality.' [40]

Sources vary as to the period of the *Bennu*'s return, but in his authoritative study on the subject R. T. Rundle Clark mentions the figure of 12,954 years.[41] Let us note that this figure accords very closely with a half-cycle of precession (where the full cycle, as we have seen, is 25,920 years). As such, 'the return of the phoenix' could be expressed in astronomical terms either as a slow 'sweep' of the vernal point through six houses of the zodiac – for example from the beginning of Leo to the beginning of Aquarius – or, at the meridian, as the number of years required for a star to move between its minimum and maximum altitudes above the horizon.

When considering such co-ordinates in the sky, we are immediately reminded of the Giza necropolis – of how the gaze of the Great Sphinx targets the vernal point on the eastern horizon, and of how the star-shafts of the Great Pyramid lock in to the meridian with machine-age accuracy. Moreover it can hardly be an accident that the capstone or pyramidion placed on top of all pyramids was known in the ancient Egyptian language as the *Benben* and was considered to be a symbol of the *Bennu* bird (and thus also of rebirth and immortality).[42] These capstones were replicas of the original *Benben* stone – perhaps a conical, 'orientated' meteorite[43] – which was said to have 'fallen from heaven' and which was kept in Heliopolis, perched atop a pillar in a Temple called the 'Mansion of the Phoenix'.[44]

Is it not apparent, therefore, that we are confronted here by a tightly knit complex of interwoven ideas, all additionally complicated by masses of Egyptian dualism, in which stone stands for bird, and bird for stone,[45] and both together speak of rebirth and of the 'eternal return'?

The capstone is of course missing from the summit of the Great Pyramid at Giza. And the *Benben* of Heliopolis was already long lost to history by the time of the Greeks . . .[46]

Will these treasures, too, sooner or later 'return'?

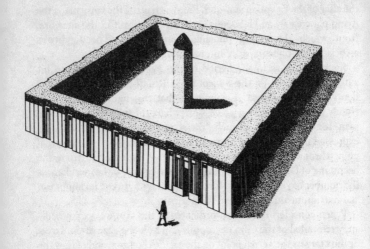

54. Artist's impression of the 'Mansion of the Phoenix' in Heliopolis with its original pillar and pyramid-shaped *Benben* stone.

Ancestor gods

'Underlying all Egyptian speculation', as R. T. Rundle Clark has observed, 'is the belief that time is composed of recurrent cycles which are divinely appointed . . .'[47] There is furthermore a governing moment amongst all these cycles and epochs – the 'genesis event' that the Egyptians called *Zep Tepi*, the 'First Time'.

Zep means 'Time', *Tepi* means 'First'.

But *Tepi* also has other connotations. For example, it is the word for 'the foremost point of a ship' and it can likewise be interpreted as 'the first day of a period of time'. Moreover, according to the astute analysis of Robert K. G. Temple: 'The basic meaning of the word *Tep* is "mouth" . . . and even more fundamentally the "beginning or commencement of anything".' [48]

Perhaps because of this persistent connection with the beginning of things, *Tepi* can also mean 'ancestors'. And the *Tepi-aui-qerr-en-pet* were 'the ancestor-gods of the circle of the sky'.[49] Also in the Pyramid Texts *Tepi-aui* is one of the many titles by which the ancestral deities of the 'early primeval age' were known – the gods and Sages, or 'Followers of Horus', who were supposedly there, at the dawn of civilization, when the phoenix alighted atop the pillar at Heliopolis, uttering a great cry and setting in motion the 'time' of our present epoch of the world . . .

Curiously, the hieroglyphic sign used to determine the *Tepi-aui* is the body of a large, slouching lion, with only the paws, breast and head shown. And we find a similar device being used as the determinative for a very similar class of beings called the *Akeru*, described in Wallis Budge's *Hieroglyphic Dictionary* as a group of gods said to be the ancestors of Re.[50]

The reader will recall from earlier chapters that one of the distinguishing features of the Fifth Division of the *Duat* is the presence there of a giant double-lion Sphinx-god named *Aker* whom Egyptologist Mark Lehner suggests may be 'a representation of the Sphinx at Giza'.[51] Since it is from *Aker* that the *Akeru* derive their name, it is natural that the hieroglyphs should depict them either in the form of slouching lions, or of two lions back to back, or of a double-headed lion.[52]

So the texts seem to invite us to attach leonine characteristics to the 'men or gods of olden times', to the 'Ancestors', and to the Sages. But they also invite something else when, as we shall see in the next chapter, they link the whole concept of ancestral dynasties of gods and spirits with another closely related word, *Akhu*, meaning, variously, the 'Shining Ones', the 'Star People' or the 'Venerables'. In this way they will lead us back to the trail of the 'Followers of Horus' and to the notion that for thousands of years – spanning both the prehistoric and the historic periods – the members of a hidden academy may have been at work behind the scenes in Egypt, observing the stars with scientific rigour and manipulating men and events according to a celestial timetable . . .

Chapter 13

Following the Stars

'The disposition of the stars as well as their
movements have always been the subject of
careful observation among the Egyptians . . .
they have preserved to this day records
concerning each of these stars over an
incredible number of years, this study having
been zealously preserved among them from
ancient times.'

Diodorus Siculus, *Book V*, first century BC

It should be clear by now that the ancient Egyptians had very distinct ideas about the length and scope of their history, and that they set the 'First Time', the 'genesis event' for their civilization, far back in what the Edfu Building Texts call the 'Early Primeval Age'. Just how long ago that event actually took place is not an issue that will be easily resolved because the surviving texts – the king-lists, the very few fragments of Manetho's *History* that have been preserved, and certain travellers' tales – are mostly incomplete and at times mutually contradictory. Moreover we are obliged to cut our way through a luxuriant jungle of diverse terminologies – Sages, Ancestors, Spirits of the Dead, the 'Followers of Horus', etc., etc. – which further complicates the problem of trying to arrive at a coherent picture. Nevertheless, let us see what we can glean from these ancient sources. Let us try to put the jigsaw puzzle together . . .

Shining ones

Amongst the very few king-lists that have survived to the present day, the so-called 'Turin Papyrus' reaches particularly deeply into the dark abyss of the past. Regrettably, more than half of the contents of this fragile document from the second millennium BC have been lost because of the gross incompetence with which it was handled by scholars when it was transferred (in a biscuit tin) from the collection of the King of Sardinia to its present home in the Museum of Turin.[1] The remaining fragments, however, offer occasional tantalising glimpses of an astonishing chronology.

Of the greatest importance amongst these fragments is a badly damaged vertical register in which the names and reigns of ten *Neteru* or 'Gods' were originally given. Although in most cases the durations of these reigns are now illegible or completely broken away, it is possible to read the figure of 3126 years ascribed to the rule of the wisdom-god Thoth and the figure of 300 years ascribed to Horus, the last fully 'divine' king of Egypt.[2] Immediately afterwards comes a second vertical register devoted to the 'Followers of Horus' – the *Shemsu Hor* – the most prominent of that general class of beings variously called 'Ancestors', or 'Sages' or 'Ghosts' or 'Spirits' whom the Egyptians remembered as having bridged the gap between the time of the gods and the time of Menes (the supposed first king of the first historical Dynasty *circa* 3000 BC).[3] Again much of the register is missing, but its last two lines, which seem to represent a summing-up, are of particular interest: 'The *Akhu*, *Shemsu Hor*, 13,420 years; Reigns before the *Shemsu Hor*, 23,200 years; Total 36,620 years.'[4]

The plural word '*Akhu*', is normally translated as 'Venerables'.[5] Yet, as we hinted at the end of the last chapter, a close examination of the full range of meanings that the ancient Egyptians attached to it suggests that another and far more intriguing possibility exists – one that is concealed by so generalized an epithet. To be specific, the hieroglyphs for *Akhu* can also mean 'Transfigured Beings', 'Shining Ones', 'Shining Beings' or 'Astral Spirits' – understandably identified by some linguists with the stars.[6] And there are other shades of meaning, too, that cry out to be taken into account. For example in Sir E. A. Wallis Budge's authoritative *Hieroglyphic Dictionary* the following additional definitions are provided for *Akhu*: 'to be bright', 'to be excellent', or 'to be wise' and 'instructed'.[7] And Budge further informs us that the word was frequently associated with 'those who recite formulae'.[8]

Such data, we suggest, calls for a rethink of the title 'Venerables' as applied to the 'Followers of Horus' in the Turin Papyrus.[9] Rather than merely being 'venerable', is it not possible that what was meant to be conveyed by the word *Akhu* in this context was a picture of vastly enlightened and learned people, apparently with some connection to or interest in the stars – in short an élite of highly initiated astronomer-philosophers?

In support of this notion is the fact that the 'Followers of Horus' were frequently linked in the ancient texts to another equally enlightened and 'shining' class of ancestral beings called the 'Souls of Pe' and the 'Souls of Nekhen'.[10] Now Pe and Nekhen were actual geographical locations in Egypt – the former in the north and the latter in the the south.[11] Interestingly enough, however, as Professor Henri Frankfort has confirmed, the 'Souls' of both these places were also frequently grouped collectively under yet another title, the 'Souls of *Heliopolis*',[12] who were said 'to assist the King's ascent to heaven, a function commonly performed by the Souls of Nekhen and Pe . . . A relief depicting this function shows the Souls of Pe and Nekhen in the act, while the text calls them the "Souls of Heliopolis".'[13]

It is generally accepted that the term 'Soul' – *Ba* – as used by the ancient Egyptians had stellar attributes connected to the notion of eternal life in the *Duat* to which all the historical Pharaohs aspired. Moreover, as Frankfort rightly points out, the Pyramid Texts do indeed define the dominant role of the 'Souls' of Pe and Nekhen – and thus the 'Souls' of Heliopolis – as being to ensure that when a Pharaoh died he would be 'equipped' to ascend to the sky and find his way into the cosmic Kingdom of Osiris.[14] This in turn coincides with what we know of the Sages of Edfu and the 'Followers of Horus', both of whom, as we have seen, may be identified with a single and originally *Heliopolitan* 'brotherhood' of temple-makers whose function was to prepare and initiate the generations of the Horus-Kings in order to bring about the 'resurrection' of what was remembered as 'the former world of the gods'.[15]

Legacy

The notion that some form of invisible college could have established itself at Heliopolis thousands of years before the Pharaohs, and could have been the initiating force behind the creation and unfolding of ancient Egyptian civilization, helps to explain one of the greatest mysteries confronted by Egyptology – namely the extremely sudden, indeed dramatic, manner in which Pharaonic culture 'took off' in the early third millennium BC. The independent researcher John Anthony West, whose breakthrough work on the geology of the Sphinx we reported in Part I, formulates the problem especially well:

> Every aspect of Egyptian knowledge seems to have been complete at the very beginning. The sciences, artistic and architectural techniques and the hieroglyphic system show virtually no signs of a period of 'development'; indeed, many of the achievements of the earliest dynasties were never surpassed or even equalled later on. This astonishing fact is readily admitted by orthodox Egyptologists, but the magnitude of the mystery it poses is skilfully understated, while its many implications go unmentioned.
>
> How does a complex civilization spring full-blown into being? Look at a 1905 automobile and compare it to a modern one. There is no mistaking the process of 'development'. But in Egypt there are no parallels. Everything is right there at the start.
>
> The answer to the mystery is of course obvious, but because it is repellent to the prevailing cast of modern thinking, it is seldom seriously considered. Egyptian civilization was not a 'development', it was a legacy.[16]

Might not the preservers of that legacy, who eventually bequeathed it to the Pharaohs at the beginning of the Dynastic Period, have been those revered and secretive individuals – the 'Followers of Horus', the Sages, the Senior Ones – whose memory haunts the most archaic traditions of Egypt like a persistent ghost?

Gods and heroes

In addition to the Turin Papyrus other chronological records support the notion of an immensely ancient 'academy' at work behind the scenes in Egypt. Amongst these, the most influential were compiled, as we saw earlier, by Manetho (literally, 'Truth of Thoth'), who lived in the third century BC and who 'rose to be high priest in the temple at Heliopolis'.[17] There he wrote his now lost *History of Egypt* which later commentators tell us was divided up into three volumes dealing, respectively, with 'the Gods, the Demigods, the Spirits of the Dead and the mortal Kings who ruled Egypt'.[18]

The 'Gods' it seems, ruled for 13,900 years. After them 'the Demigods and Spirits of the Dead' – epithets for the 'Followers of Horus' – ruled for a further 11,025 years.[19] Then began the reign of the mortal kings, which Manetho divided into the thirty-one dynasties still used and accepted by scholars today.

Other fragments from Manetho's *History* also suggest that important and powerful beings were present in Egypt long before the dawn of its historical period under the rule of Menes. For example Fragment 3, preserved in the works of George Syncellus, speaks of 'six dynasties or six gods who . . . reigned for 11,985 years'.[20] And in a number of sources Manetho is said to have given the figure of 36,525 years for the entire duration of the civilization of Egypt from the time of the gods down to the end of the last dynasty of mortal kings.[21]

A rather different total of around 23,000 years has been handed down to us by the Greek historian Diodorus Siculus who visited Egypt in the first century BC and spoke there with priests and chroniclers. According to the stories he was told: 'At first Gods and Heroes ruled Egypt for a little less than 18,000 years . . . Mortals have been kings of their country, they say, for a little less than 5000 years.'[22]

Time bridge

An overview of all the available chronologies in context of other related documents such as the Pyramid Texts and the Edfu Building Texts leaves two distinct impressions. Despite the conflicts and confusions over the precise numbers of years involved, and despite the endless proliferation of names and titles and honorifics and epithets:

- It is clear that the ancient Egyptians thought in terms of very long periods of time and would never have accepted the Egyptological view that their civilization 'began' with the First

Above: The megalithic architecture of the Sphinx Temple, at dawn, with the squat, massive form of the Valley Temple in the background. Many of the blocks used in the construction of the Valley Temple weigh in excess of 200 tons each. Modern engineers are unable to explain how – or why – such enormous blocks were put into position.
Below: The lower courses at the western end of the Second Pyramid were hewn out of solid bedrock, with the upper courses later built on top. It is possible that the original 'foundation platform' might be much older than the rest of the Pyramid.

21.

22.

Above: Overview of the Giza necropolis with the Great Sphinx and its causeway in the foreground. The causeway, which has a bearing of fourteen degrees south of due east, is not to be confused with the modern road running to the right (north) of the Sphinx. *Right*: Aerial overview of Giza Pyramid Plateau. *Left*: The so-called 'solar boat', 143 feet long, that was found buried in a rock-hewn trench beside the southern face of the Great Pyramid. There is much to suggest that this magnificent boat was originally used on the Nile by the Horus-Kings of Egypt in astronomical rituals that mimicked the apparent passage of the sun across the Milky Way – the celestial counterpart of the River Nile.

Pyramid Plateau, Giza.

23.

24.

Above: The Second Pyramid, viewed from the top of the Great Pyramid one month before the Spring Equinox, with the sun setting a little to the south of due west. *Below*: Overview of the Giza Pyramids from the south-east.

25.

Above: Step-Pyramid of Zoser at Saqqara – supposedly the oldest massive construction in Egypt. However, recent carbon-dating evidence from organic compounds in the mortar of the Great Pyramid (see Appendix 5) suggests that the Great Pyramid may be older than the Pyramid of Zoser, a state of affairs that throws orthodox Egyptological chronology into confusion. *Below*: The 'Bent' and 'Red' Pyramids of Dhashour in silhouette.

28.

Above: These inscriptions, more than 4000 years old, were carved on the walls of the tomb-chamber of Unas, last Pharaoh of the Fifth Dynasty. Belonging to a larger body scripture now known as the 'Pyramid Texts', they contain complex astronomical nota that have been badly misunderstood by Egyptologists, and references to the remote 'F Time', *Zep Tepi*, when the Gods established their Kingdom in Egypt. *Below*: The 'Shabaka Stone' photographed in the British Museum. Inscribed with hieroglyphic te this relic is a vital source for the reconstruction of the lost epoch of the 'First Time'.

29.

Above: The Abydos King List at the Temple of Seti I in Abydos, with Pharaoh Seti I showing his young son Rameses II a list of all the Pharaohs of Egypt who had ruled before them. On the opposite wall is a list of the Gods who ruled in Egypt, going back to the remote 'First Time'. Like the Pyramid Texts, the Shabaka Texts, and the Edfu Building Texts, the list indicates that the civilisation of ancient Egypt was seen as a legacy handed down by the 'gods' thousands of years before the beginning of the recognised historical period. *Below*: 'Osiriform' sarcophagus lid in Cairo Museum showing Isis in the form of a kite being impregnated by the mummified Osiris. The fruit of this union was Horus, archetype for all the 'Horus-Kings' of ancient Egypt. *Overleaf*: Relief at Abydos showing Osiris, the paramount deity of the First Time, mummified and seated, being attended to by his son Horus. In his left hand, Horus holds the *ankh*, symbol of immortal life.

Dynasty of Pharaohs.

- It is clear that they were aware of an 'influence' at work in their history – a continuous, unbroken influence that had extended over many thousands of years and that was wielded by an élite group of divine and semi-divine beings, often associated with leonine symbolism, who were called variously 'Gods and Heroes', the 'Spirits of the Dead', the 'Souls', the 'Sages', the 'Shining Ones', the 'Ancestors', the 'Ancestor-Gods of the Circle of the Sky', the 'Followers of Horus', etc., etc.

It is clear, in other words, that the ancient Egyptians envisaged a kind of 'time bridge', linking the world of men to the world of the gods, today to yesterday and 'now' to the 'First Time'. It is clear, too

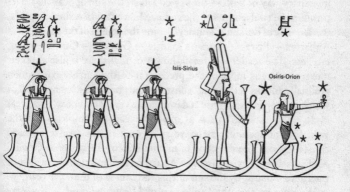

55. It is clear that the ancient Egyptians were aware of an 'influence' at work in their history – a continuous, unbroken influence that extended over many thousands of years and that was wielded by an élite group of divine and semi-divine beings.

that responsibility for maintaining this 'bridge' was attributed to the 'Followers of Horus' (by this and many other names). And it is clear that the 'Followers' were remembered as having carried down intact the traditions and secrets of the gods – always preserving them, permitting not a single change – until finally sharing them with the first dynasties of Egypt's mortal kings.

Following the vernal point

The etymology of the ancient Egyptian term *Shemsu Hor*, 'Followers of Horus', was studied by the Alsatian scholar R. A. Schwaller de Lubicz who concluded: 'The term *Shemsu Hor* . . . literally means . . . "those who follow the path of Horus", that is, the "Horian way", also called the solar way . . . These Followers of Horus bear with them a knowledge of "divine origin" and unify the country with it . . .' [23]

The 'solar way' or 'path of Horus' is, of course, the ecliptic – that imaginary way or path in the sky on which the sun appears to travel through the twelve signs of the zodiac. As we saw in earlier chapters, the *direction* of the sun's 'journey' during the course of the solar year is Aquarius → Pisces → Aries → Taurus → Gemini → Cancer → Leo, etc., etc. The reader will recall, however, that there is also another, more ponderous motion, the precession of the earth's axis, which gradually rotates the 'ruling' constellation against the background of which the sun is seen to rise at dawn on the vernal equinox. This great cycle, or 'Great Year', takes 25,920 solar years to complete, with the vernal point spending 2,160 years in each of the twelve zodiacal constellations. The direction of motion is Leo → Cancer → Gemini → Taurus → Aries → Pisces → Aquarius, etc., etc., i.e. the reverse of the route pursued by the sun during the course of the solar year.

We suggest that the 'Followers of Horus' *followed* – in a very precise, astronomical sense – not only the annual path of the sun, eastwards through the zodiac, but also, for thousands of years, the vernal point's relentless precessional drift westwards through the same twelve constellations. We also suggest that this shadowy brotherhood, whose members were said to have carried the 'knowledge of divine origin' (which they would later use to 'unify the country'), may have interrelated on an extremely selective basis with the more primitive inhabitants of the Nile Valley in the prehistoric and Predynastic periods, interbreeding with chosen women and recruiting new generations from amongst the brightest and the best of their offspring – but leaving little or no trace of their presence in the archaeological record. We suggest, too, that around the beginning of the third millennium BC something happened in the cosmic order of the night sky – something long preordained and expected by their astronomers – that caused the 'Followers' to launch their grand attempt to initiate and 'unify' the historical civilization of Egypt. Last but not least, we suggest that whoever they really may have been, it was the 'Followers' – the Sages, the Builder Gods – who provided this nascent civilization with the injection of advanced technical knowledge, engineering, architectural and organizing skills necessary for the completion of the vast celestial 'temple' that we know today as the Giza necropolis . . .

In the next chapters we will test some of these hypotheses.

Chapter 14

Space–Time Co-ordinates

'The mind has lost its cutting edge, we
hardly understand the ancients.'

Gregoire de Tours, sixth century AD

In astronomical terms the 'vernal point' is the 'address' that the sun
occupies on the spring equinox – its particular position on that
particular day against the background of the zodiacal constellations
that encircle the ecliptic (i.e. the perceived 'path' of the sun). As a
result of a cosmic coincidence these twelve prominent constellations
are distributed in the heavens in the plane of the ecliptic (i.e. in the
plane of the earth's orbit around the sun) and, furthermore, are spaced
out more or less evenly around it. The vernal point, however, is not
fixed. Because of the phenomenon of precession, as we have seen in
earlier chapters, it gradually sweeps around the whole 'dial' of the
zodiac at a precise and predictable rate.

Between 3000 BC and 2500 BC, the epoch in which Egypt appears to
have received the sudden spark of genius that initiated the most
brilliant achievements of the Pyramid Age, the vernal point was
stationed on the immediate right (i.e. 'west') bank of the Milky Way,
drifting almost imperceptibly slowly past the small group of stars,
known as the Hyades, which form the head of Taurus[1] – the Bull of
the Sky.

What this means is that the vernal point had arrived in that region
of the sky dominated by the adjacent constellations of Taurus and
Orion, and particularly by the three stars of Orion's belt. Moreover, as
we have seen in Part I, the three great Pyramids of Giza – which stand
on the west bank of the Nile – were designed to serve as terrestrial
models, or 'doubles' of those three stars.

Now here is the interesting thing. If we regard the Giza Pyramids (in relation to the Nile) as part of a scaled-down 'map' of the right bank of the Milky Way, then we would need to extend that 'map' some 20 miles to the south in order to arrive at the point on the ground where the Hyades-Taurus should be represented. How likely is it to be an accident that two enormous Pyramids – the so-called 'Bent' and 'Red' Pyramids of Dahshur – are found at this spot? And how likely is it to be an accident, as was demonstrated in *The Orion Mystery*, that the site plan of these monuments, i.e. their pattern on the ground, correlates very precisely with the pattern in the sky of the two most prominent stars in the Hyades? [2]

We suggest none of this is accidental, that the 'celestial signal' which 'sparked off' the incredible Pyramid-building programme of Egypt's Fourth Dynasty was provided by the precessional drift of the vernal point into the Hyades-Taurus region, and that the 'Hyades Pyramids' of Dahshur were therefore naturally built first.

Such a theory provides a motive for the vast enterprise of Fourth-Dynasty Pyramid construction (involving some 25 million tons of stone blocks – more than 75 per cent of all the stone that was quarried and shaped into Pyramids during the Pyramid Age).[3] In addition, it accords fully with archaeological evidence which suggests that the two superb Pyramids at Dahshur were built by Sneferu (2572–2551 BC), the founder of the Fourth Dynasty and the father of Khufu. In other words the Bent and the Red Pyramids were indeed built *before* any of the great Pyramids of Giza[4] – which is exactly what one would expect if the drift of the vernal point into the Hyades-Taurus was the trigger that set the whole enterprise in motion.

And there is something else.

Journey in time

The Hyades-Taurus region, together with its terrestrial analogue, is identified in the Pyramid Texts as the starting point for the Horus-King's 'quest' – i.e. that great dualistic journey, enacted both in the sky and on the ground, that we described in Part III. As the reader will recall, the texts specifically and unambiguously instruct Horus in his solar form, i.e. the sun's disc, to position himself at this starting point and thence to 'go to Horakhti', i.e. to voyage eastwards towards the constellation of Leo. And we have seen how the sun actually does this, sailing along the ecliptic path during the solar year in the direction Taurus A Gemini A Cancer A Leo.

This order of the constellations therefore appears to define 'forward' movement in time and, at one level, the identifiable astronomical events described in the texts do indeed unfold in the 'normal' forward direction of the solar year (after being stationed near Taurus, and then crossing the Milky Way, the sun reaches Leo later in the year – i.e. *later in time*). Moreover this same 'normal' forward motion also appears to be mirrored in the ritual performed by the Horus-King on the ground: i.e. *after* crossing the river Nile it is inevitable that the initiate will arrive at the breast of the Great Sphinx somewhat later in time.

But in the Pyramid Texts, and in the arrangement of the Giza monuments – as in so much else that has come down to us from ancient Egypt – everything may not be quite what it seems. An awareness of the effects of precession on the part of the 'Followers of Horus' (and the later priests of Heliopolis) would have included an intense focus on the stellar background at the vernal equinox and an understanding that the sun's 'journey' towards Horakhti-Leo, *as calibrated at this 'governing moment' of the year*, would by definition have been a journey *backwards* in time through a succession of 'world-ages' – i.e. from the Age of Taurus, *circa* 3000 BC (when the sun on the vernal equinox rose against the stellar background of the constellation of Taurus) to the Age of Leo, *circa* 10,500 BC, when the sun on the vernal equinox rose against the background of the celestial lion.

So when we read in the Pyramid Texts that the 'Followers of Horus' are urging the Horus-King to travel from Taurus to Leo it is possible that they may have had in mind something rather complex and clever. It is possible, in other words, that as well as offering the sun's annual path through the constellations as a kind of 'treasure trail' for the initiate to follow on his way to the breast of the Sphinx, they may also have offered him knowledge of its slow *reverse motion at the vernal equinox* – perhaps as his cue to embark on a different kind of journey, *against the flow of precession* and back to the 'First Time'.

This is more than speculation. As we saw at the end of Part III, the

Horus-King's journey to the breast of the Sphinx was undertaken *at the summer solstice* during the Pyramid Age (because in that epoch it was at the summer solstice that the great conjunction of the sun with Horakhti-Leo occurred). We also saw, however, that the initiate who had correctly followed the 'treasure trail' set out in the texts, and who had reached the Sphinx in the pre-dawn on the summer solstice, would immediately have become aware of a curious 'dislocation' between sky and ground. He would have noticed, in particular, that the Sphinx gazed due east but that his celestial counterpart – Horakhti-Leo – was rising at a point on the horizon located some 28 degrees north of due east. He would also have noticed that the three great Pyramids of Giza precisely straddled the meridian but that their terrestrial counterparts, the three stars of Orion's belt, hung low in the south-eastern portion of the pre-dawn sky, far to the left of the meridian.

Given the profoundly astronomical character of his religious frame of reference he might well have felt a numinous urge to 'put sky and ground together again' – i.e., so to arrange matters that the Sphinx would be gazing *directly* at Leo in the pre-dawn, whilst, at the same moment, the three stars of Orion's belt would straddle the meridian in the precise pattern 'specified' by the meridional layout of the Pyramids. If that could somehow be brought about then the monuments would truly represent 'an image of heaven'[5] – as the old Hermetic doctrines teach – and the land of Egypt 'which once was holy, a land which loved the gods and wherein alone the gods deigned to sojourn on earth', might once again become, as it was before, 'the teacher of Mankind'.[6]

But how could the Horus-King hope to unite sky and ground?

The only way would be if he were equipped to use precession – presumably just as an intellectual tool – to *travel backwards in time*.

For as the reader will recall there *was* a time when a unique celestial conjunction involving the moment of sunrise, the constellation of Leo, and the meridian-transit of the three stars of Orion's belt, did indeed occur. That time, of course, was near the beginning of the Age of Leo, at around 10,500 BC,[7] some 8000 years prior to the Pyramid Age.

Becoming equipped

The Utterances conventionally numbered 471, 472 and 473 in the ancient Egyptian Pyramid Texts contain information of an extraordinary nature. In view of the importance of this information, we set it out in full below:

> I am the essence of a god, the son of a god, the messenger of a god, [says the Horus-King]. The Followers of Horus cleanse me, they bathe me, they dry me, they recite for me the Spell [formula] for Him who is on the Right Way, they recite for me the Spell of Him who Ascends, and I ascend to the sky.
>
> I will go aboard this Bark of Re [the Solar Bark] . . . Every god will

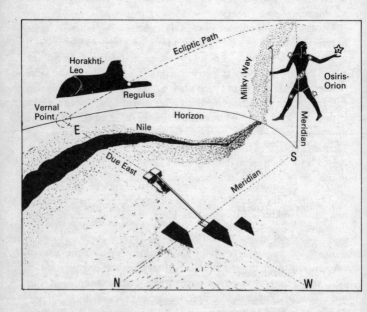

56. Artist's impression of the unique celestial conjunction that occurred at sunrise on the vernal equinox in the epoch of 10,500 BC.

rejoice at meeting me as they rejoice at meeting Re [the sun] when he ascends from the eastern side of the sky in peace, in peace.

The sky quivers, the earth quakes before me, for I am a magician, I possess magic . . . I have come that I may glorify Orion, that I may set Osiris at the head, that I may set the gods upon their thrones.

O Mahaf, Bull of the gods [Taurus-Hyades], bring me this [solar bark] and set me on yonder side . . . The reed-floats of the sky are set down for me by the day-bark that I [the solar Horus-King] may go up on them to Re at the Horizon. The reed floats of the sky are brought down to me by the night bark that I may go up on them to Horakhti at the horizon. I go up on the eastern side of the sky where the gods are born, and I am born as Horus, as Him of the Horizon . . . I have found the *Akhus* with their mouths equipped . . .

'Who are you?' say they [the *Akhus*], with their mouths equipped.

'I am an *Akhu* with my mouth equipped.'

'How has this happened to you,' say they, the *Akhus* with their mouths equipped, 'that you have come to this place more noble than any place?'

'I have come to this place more noble than any place because: The reed-floats of the sky were set down for Re [the sun disc and the emblem of the Horus-King] that Re might cross [the Milky Way] on them to Horakhti at the Horizon . . .' [8]

These Utterances appear to describe an important part of the Horus-King's initiatory journey – an ordeal of questions and answers based on astronomical science wrapped up in esoteric symbols. The inquisitors are the 'Followers of Horus', also known as the *Akhus* (the 'Venerables', the 'Shining Ones', the 'Transfigured Spirits', etc., etc.). Moreover, as we would expect, the Horus-King's cosmic journey begins in the Taurus-Hyades region of the sky, on the right bank of the Milky Way. and proceeds along the ecliptic path to end at Leo i.e. 'Horakhti', at the horizon. Here, at 'this place more noble than any place', the *Akhus* greet him – indeed he claims to have become an *Akhu* himself – and give him the final instructions or directions that he will need to complete his quest.

What we have to consider is the possibility that these final instructions might somehow have 'equipped' the Horus-King to make the necessary journey back in time, to the 'First Time', and into the cosmic Kingdom of Osiris when sky and ground were united in perfect harmony.

Unification

As the reader will recall from the previous chapter, the 'Followers of Horus' were said to have possessed 'a knowledge of divine origin' that was to be used to 'unify the country'. It is therefore presumably of relevance that large numbers of ancient Egyptian inscriptions and papyri make reference to an event known as 'the Uniting of the Two Lands' – an event that is eloquently related in the so-called Shabaka Texts (the 'Memphite Theology') which we have reviewed in Part III.

It is the scholarly consensus that the 'Unification of the Two Lands' was a political and economic 'federation' between southern and northern Egypt, resulting from the military conquest of the latter by the former, which supposedly occurred at around the year 3000 BC.[9] This conquest, as T. G. H. James informs us, 'was effected by a King known to history as Menes. No contemporary monument bears a royal name that can with certainty be read as Menes, but he is generally identified with King Narmer who is shown wearing both the red and white crowns [respectively of northern and southern Egypt] on a great palette [now in the Cairo Museum]. With the unification of the Kingdoms begins the historic period of Egypt.'[10]

Also sometimes referred to as 'King Scorpion' (after a symbol that appears on an archaic mace-head) we have already met Menes-Narmer.[11] We have noted, too, the strange Egyptological double standard by which he is accorded the status of a genuine historical figure whilst his predecessors – mentioned with equal prominence in the king-lists and Manetho – are dismissed as 'mythical beings'.

Indeed, Egyptologists speak with such immense confidence of 'the political consolidation of Egypt around 3000 BC' and of the 'unification under Narmer'[12] that one would suppose they were in possession of bundles upon bundles of ancient treaties, land deeds and historical records. The truth, however, as James half admits, is that nothing is known for sure about the supposed first Pharaoh of the First Dynasty. On the contrary, the whole of what we read about him, including his identification with 'Narmer', is scholarly speculation based on idiosyncratic interpretations of certain scenes – some of which depict battles – that are carved on the so-called 'Narmer Palette' and on certain votive mace-heads from Hierakonpolis (an ancient religious capital in southern Egypt).[13]

In short, Egyptology's case that 'the Unification of the Two Lands' refers to the political unification of northern and southern Egypt under Menes rests on three completely uninscribed artefacts which are carved with scenes that *might* bear such an interpretation – but that could also be interpreted in many other ways. These curious artefacts tell us precious little about Menes-Narmer himself,[14] let alone what his political and territorial aspirations – or those of anybody else – might have been *circa* 3000 BC in Egypt. Semi-legendary or semi-historical, Narmer (or Menes or 'King Scorpion' – take your pick) is thus the quintessential 'King Arthur' of Egyptology. And so, too, is his supposed 'Unification of Egypt' – which is also veiled in semi-mythical, semi-historical confusion, very much like the confederation of King Arthur's Round Table.[15]

Moreover the conclusion that Menes-Narmer was the first ruler to have been involved in the 'Unification of the Two Lands' clashes rudely with the beliefs of the ancient Egyptians themselves. Their records and traditions make it clear that there had been earlier 'Unifications' in the 'Time of the Gods' – all going back to the original Kingdom of Osiris, the 'Kingdom of the "First Time" ' which was torn asunder by Seth and then unified once again by Horus.

We do not think that this talk of 'Unification' was ever entirely to do with events that happened on the ground. Although we do not dispute that some form of political unification did indeed take place at around 3000 BC, we suspect that in dualistic Egypt a wider understanding of the whole issue will not be possible unless *events in the sky* are taken into account as well. Building on earlier work done by Egyptologist and archaeoastronomer Jane B. Sellers,[16] we suggest that the original notion of 'Unification' – to which all later attempts to 'Unify the Two Lands' were directly related – had something to do with the precessional drift of the stars . . .

High and far-off times

In her landmark study *The Death of Gods in Ancient Egypt* Sellers sets out persuasive astronomical and textual evidence to show that the prehistoric Egyptians – at least as far back as 7300 BC – had observed and tracked the slow precessionally induced changes that constantly relocate the cosmic 'address' of the constellation of Orion. And she argues that, although political unity was credited to Menes, there was a much older notion of the 'Unification' based not on events on earth but those observed in the sky . . .[17] Indeed, she goes so far as to claim that Menes merely brought to fruition a very ancient and archetypal vision of cosmic duality which so perfectly harmonized with the mentality of the ancient Egyptians 'as to appear both inevitable and perennial': 'A dual monarchy united under the rule of one was a form that came from the mists of distant antiquity. It was a form that had been created for gods in the heavens, and how inevitable it was that an imitation of the cosmic order should prevail for men on earth.'[18]

Sellers supports her case by drawing on the late Henri Frankfort's studies of ancient Egyptian kingship. Like her, the former Professor of Preclassical Antiquity at the University of London was firmly of the opinion that it was 'possible to view the unification of Egypt, not as the ephemeral outcome of conflicting ambitions, but as the revelation of a predestined order'.[19] And he was further convinced that 'the dual monarchy centred round Memphis realized a divine plan', that the social and state order established by Menes-Narmer was presented 'as part of the cosmic order',[20] and that Menes-Narmer, in establishing himself as sole ruler of Upper and Lower Egypt, was performing 'an act in harmony with the Egyptian tendency to understand the world in dualistic terms, "a series of pairs of contrasts balanced in unchanging equilibrium" . . .'[21]

What Sellers was able to add to this, as a result of her own powerful insights into ancient Egyptian cosmology and observational astronomy, was the notion that events taking place on the ground were somehow directly conditioned by observations of the sky – and also that what was observed in the sky was described more or less accurately in certain 'myths':

> I am postulating the creation of specific myths to deal with distressing alterations in the sky, followed by an artificial duality, or symmetry, imposed, not just on the deities, but on geographical centres of worship, and this duality remained a constant in Egyptian affairs throughout its history. It was harking back to a wonderful Golden Age, now lost, an age when the skies had had a magnificent balance, and the religion had been fresh and new . . .'[22]

The Golden Age to which Sellers is referring is, of course, *Zep Tepi*, the 'First Time'. And the 'distressing alterations in the sky' which she believes that certain myths were created to explain were caused by the phenomenon of precession – specifically the precessional drift of the great constellation of Orion away from the station that it had occupied at the 'First Time'.[23]

These are daring and dangerous steps for an otherwise orthodox Egyptologist to have taken. Nevertheless, as we shall see in the next chapters, Sellers could be wrong in understanding the myths – by which she means principally the Pyramid Texts and the Memphite Theology – merely as accounts fabricated by superstitious priests to 'explain' precessional drift. The possibility needs to be confronted square on that elements of these ancient traditions, and the monuments and rituals that are so inextricably linked to them, could have been deliberately contrived as vehicles to carry an elaborate and ingenious 'message' from a past epoch otherwise long forgotten to a specific epoch in the future – from the 'First Time' to an astronomically defined 'Last Time'[24] – perhaps even to the very epoch in which we ourselves live today. Perhaps both epochs thus linked together are susceptible to accurate dating and decoding if only the right key can be found. And perhaps we may yet be able to read and understand the great cosmic blueprint that the 'Followers of Horus' sought to implement . . .

Who knows what might result?

There might even come, to quote the words of Giorgio de Santillana, 'some kind of "Renaissance" out of the hopelessly condemned and trampled past, when certain ideas come to life again . . . We should not deprive our grandchildren of a last chance at the heritage of the highest and farthest-off times.'[25]

Chapter 15

When the Sky Joined the Earth

'My Kingdom is not of this world. . . .'

[John 18: 36)

'Great is the Cosmic Order, for it has not
changed since the time of Osiris, who put it
there . . .'

Ptahotep, a high priest of the Pyramid Age

According to the Creation narrative of the ancient Egyptians, Nut, the
Sky-goddess, and Geb, the earth-god, joined in sexual union, but
were then rudely separated by the intervention of Shu, the god of air,
atmosphere and dryness. Nevertheless the union did produce
offspring in the form of Isis and Osiris, Nepthys and Seth. And in due
course, as we have seen, Osiris became the ruler of the idealized
'Kingdom of the "First Time" ', was murdered by Seth, experienced
resurrection, and then finally ascended into the heavens where he
established the cosmic 'Kingdom' of the *Duat*. The reader will
remember that a crucial role in effecting his 'astral rebirth' was played
by Horus, his son by the widow Isis, the archetype for all the historical
Horus-Kings of ancient Egypt – who revenged himself on Seth and
later reunified the divided Kingdom.

It can thus be said that a kind of cosmic blueprint to establish – or
re-establish – a unified 'Kingdom of Osiris' on earth had been devised
from the outset by the 'gods' and thus long before the advent of
'historical' kingship by Menes-Narmer at the beginning of the third
millennium BC.

Separation

In the Shabaka Texts (which express the Memphite Theology) we read that the defeat of Seth by Horus was followed by a convocation of the gods, under the leadership of Geb, who sat in judgement over the two 'contenders'. Initially each one was given authority to rule over his own area: 'These are the words of Geb to Horus [of the north] and Seth [of the south]: "I have separated you" – Lower and Upper Egypt . . . Then Horus stood over one region and Seth stood over one region . . .'[1]

Later, however, as the reader will recall from Part III, Geb 'gave to Horus [Seth's] inheritance': 'Then Horus stood over the land. He is the uniter of this land . . . He is Horus who arose as king of Upper and Lower Egypt, who united the Two Lands in [the region of Memphis], the "place" where the Two Lands were united . . .'[2]

The curious phrase 'I have separated you' which Geb uttered, is symbolic of the 'separation' that he, too, had endured from his consort the sky-goddess, Nut. With this in mind, should we not consider the possibility that the notions of 'Upper Egypt' and and 'Lower Egypt' – though obviously relating at one level to the geographical south and north of the earthly country – might also at another level have been intended to suggest *ground and sky*?

Doubles

There is much in the Memphite Theology which supports the proposition that the areas which were traditionally regarded as the southern and northern sacred regions of Osiris – Abydos and Memphis – were not only meant to be considered in terrestrial terms but also in cosmic terms.

In particular, a metaphor is relayed around the imagery of the huge 'body' of Osiris 'drifting' with the waters of the Nile from his southern shrine at Abydos to reach his northern shrine in the 'land of Sokar' – i.e. the Memphite necropolis in general and in particular the Giza plateau where, in the form of the three great Pyramids, we suspect that the 'body' of Osiris lies outstretched upon the sand to the present day . . .

At any rate, this same basic imagery of Osiris lying on the western bank of the Nile near Memphis also crops up in the Pyramid Texts, which add a further clue: 'They [Isis and Nepthys] have found Osiris ... "when his name became Sokar". . .'[3] The term 'when his name became Sokar' does clearly seem to imply that the 'body' of Osiris merged with the land of Sokar i.e. the Memphite necropolis, and that his image – i.e. the 'astral' image of the Orion region of the sky – was somehow grafted onto it. The impression that this 'image' must have something to do with the Pyramids of Giza is then confirmed elsewhere in the Pyramid Texts. In the following passage, for example, the Horus-King addresses the 'Lower Sky' to which he 'will descend to the place where the gods are' and utters this powerful and cryptic declaration:

> If I come with my *ka* [double], open your arms to me; the mouths of the gods will be opened and will request that I ascend to the sky, and I will ascend.
>
> A boon which Geb (earth) and Atum grant: that this *Pyramid* and *Temple* be installed for me and for my double, and that this *Pyramid* and *Temple* be enclosed for me and for my double ...
>
> As for anyone who shall lay a finger on this *Pyramid* and this *Temple* which belong to me and to my double, he will have laid a finger on the Mansion [Kingdom] ... which is in the sky ...[4]

It is beyond the scope of this book to present a detailed treatise on the concept of the *ka* – the 'double', the astral or spiritual essence of a person or thing – and of its role in ancient Egyptian funerary beliefs. Much confusion has been generated around this important subject.[5] At the very least, however, it is certain that what confronts us in the *ka* is yet another example of the prevailing dualism in Egyptian thought. Moreover its use in context of the utterance quoted above reminds us that the 'image' of Osiris 'when his name became Sokar' – i.e. the Memphite Pyramid necropolis – should at all times be considered as having a cosmic or celestial 'double'. And it should be obvious, too, that this 'double' can only be the Osirian Kingdom in the *Duat* – which the Pyramid Texts declare to be 'the Place Where Orion Is'. Indeed as Margaret Bunson notes in her *Encyclopaedia of Ancient Egypt*: '*Kas* ... served as guardians of places ... Osiris was always called the *ka* of the Pyramids ...'[6]

Other passages from the Pyramid Texts support this general analysis:

> O Horus, this King is Osiris, this Pyramid of the king is Osiris, this construction of his is Osiris, betake yourself to it . . .[7]
>
> Awake [Osiris] for Horus . . . spiritualize yourself [i.e. become an astral being] . . . May a stairway to the sky be set up for you to the Place Where Orion Is . . .[8]
>
> Live, be alive, be young . . . beside Orion in the sky . . .[9]
>
> O Osiris-King, you are this great star, the companion of Orion, who traverses the sky with Orion, who 'sails' in the *Duat* with Osiris . . .[10]

Link-up

Strangely, despite the obvious sky–ground dualism and profoundly astronomical 'flavour' of the Texts, no scholar other than Jane B. Sellers[11] has ever given serious consideration to the possibility that references to the 'Unification' of the 'Upper' and 'Lower' Kingdoms of Osiris might have something to do with astronomy. Indeed the only Egyptologist even to get close to such an unorthodox way of thinking was Selim Hassan when he observed: 'the Egyptians held the idea of the existence of more than one sky, possibly superimposed . . . Certain lines in the Pyramid Texts strongly suggest that "Upper" and "Lower" Egypt each had its own particular sky . . . i.e. the two skies in opposition to the Two Lands of Upper and Lower Egypt.' [12]

In his monumental study of ancient Egyptian cosmology, Hassan also drew attention to an intriguing papyrus, now kept at the Louvre Museum in Paris,[13] which suggests that the 'Two Skies' in question were considered as being 'one for the earth and the other for the *Duat*'.[14] 'These plural skies', wrote Hassan, 'were superimposed one above the other.' [15]

Pursuing such lines of thought, we were to discover that similar ideas are depicted in the Coffin Texts. There reference is made to the 'Upper' and 'Lower' landscapes which are said to be bound to the 'Two Horizons' – one in the east (the sky) and one in the west (the earth i.e. the Memphite necropolis[16]): 'Open! O Sky and Earth, O eastern and western Horizons, open you chapels of Upper and Lower Egypt . . .' [17]

The language of all these texts is exotic, laden with the dualistic thinking that lay at the heart of ancient Egyptian society and that may have been the engine of its greatest achievements. In the Pyramid Age, as we have seen, the gigantic 'image' of Osiris appears to have been physically *defined* on the ground with the creation of the 'Lower' landscape of the Memphite Pyramids – a development referred to in the Pyramid Texts by means of the obvious metaphor 'When his name became Sokar'. Likewise, it should come as no surprise that the gigantic celestial 'image' of Osiris in the sky is referred to in the same texts by means of the same metaphorical device, i.e. 'When his name became Orion': 'Horus comes, Thoth appears . . . They raise Osiris from upon his side and make him stand up . . . when there came into being this his name of Orion, long of leg and lengthy of stride, who presides over "Upper" Egypt . . . Raise yourself, O Osiris . . . the sky is given to you, the earth is given to you . . .' [18] Selim Hassan, again

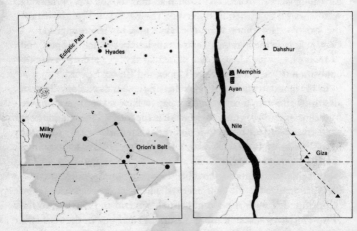

57. (Left) The sky-*Duat* of Osiris 'in his name of Orion'.
(Right) The ground-*Duat* of Osiris 'in his name of Sokar'.

almost but not quite getting the point, comments as follows: 'this line shows that Osiris was given the dominion of heaven and earth.'[19]

Yet clearly there is more to say. These 'dominions' were by no means vague and general but were defined in the sky by the pattern of Orion's stars, and were defined on the ground – in the land of 'Sokar' (i.e the Memphite necropolis) – by the pattern of the Pyramids.

We wonder whether the first major 'station' of the quest-journey of the Horus-King, reached after he had been prompted to 'find the astral body of Osiris', might not have been the initiate's dawning awareness that the body in question was a *duality* that could only be approached by linking Orion with the pattern of the Great Pyramids in the Memphite necropolis.

Riding the vernal point

The reader will remember that the starting point of the Horus-King's 'journey in the sky' was when the sun's position along the zodiac (during the solar year) was close to the Hyades, at the 'head' of the constellation of Taurus, standing, as it were, on the banks of the Milky Way.

If we now transpose this sky image to the ground then the Horus-King would have to place himself near the 'Bent' and the 'Red' Pyramids of Dahshur some 20 miles south of Giza (but nevertheless still very much part of the extensive Memphite necropolis). As we saw in the last chapter, the trigger for the construction of these two Fourth-Dynasty monuments appears to have been the slow precessional drift of the vernal point into the Hyades-Taurus region of the sky in the third millennium BC. Indeed it is more than possible that by building those Pyramids (which map the two brightest stars in the Hyades) Pharaoh Sneferu (2575–2551 BC) was deliberately laying down a marker for the position of the vernal point in his epoch.

If he was doing that, as all the evidence seems to suggest, then it is probable that such a highly initiated Horus-King would also have known that by metaphorically 'boarding' the solar bark *at the spring equinox*, and crossing the Milky Way, he would effectively be 'sailing back in time' – against the flow of precession – riding the vernal point towards the distant constellation of Leo.

But why, then, all this parallel emphasis in the texts on Orion-Osiris moving from somewhere in the distant 'south' to his final resting place in the Memphite necropolis?

Secret spell

We suspect that for thousands of years before the Pyramid Age, hundreds of generations of Heliopolitan astronomer-priests had kept the constellation of Orion continuously under observation, paying particular attention to its place of meridian-transit – i.e. the altitude above the horizon at which it crossed the celestial meridian. We think that careful records were kept, perhaps written, perhaps orally encoded in the ancient 'mythological' language of precessional astronomy.[20] And we suppose that note was taken of Orion's slow precessional drift – the effect of which was that *the constellation would have seemed to be slowly drifting northwards along the west 'bank' of the Milky Way*.

It is our hypothesis that the mythical image of the vast body of Osiris slowly being carried to the north, i.e. 'drifting' on the waters of the Nile, is a specific piece of astronomical terminology coined to describe the long-term changes being effected by precession in Orion's celestial 'address'. In the Memphite Theology, as the reader will recall, this drift was depicted as having commenced in the south, symbolically called Abydos (in archaeological terms the most southerly 'shrine' of Osiris), and to have carried the 'body' of the dead god to a point in the north symbolically called Sokar, i.e. the Memphite necropolis (the most northerly 'shrine' of Osiris). As we saw in Part III, the Shabaka Texts tell us that when he reached this point:

> Osiris was drowned in his water. Isis and Nepthys looked out, beheld him, and attended to him. Horus quickly commanded Isis and Nepthys to grasp Osiris and prevent his [submerging]. They heeded in time and brought him to land. He entered the hidden portals in the glory of the Lords of Eternity. Thus Osiris came into the earth at the Royal Fortress [Memphis], to the north of the land to which he had come [Abydos].[21]

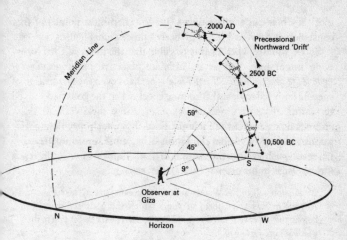

58. The effect of Orion's slow precessional slide up the meridian between 10,500 BC and 2500 BC is that the constellation would literally have appeared to be 'drifting' very slowly northwards along the course of the Milky Way.

In the light of what we now know it is hard to imagine that the reference to Osiris coming 'into the earth' (or down to earth?) could signify anything other than the *physical construction* of the 'body of Osiris on the ground' on the west banks of the Nile – in the form of the great Pyramid-fields of the sprawling Memphite necropolis. Since Osiris is Orion the desire to achieve such an effect would more than adequately explain why the three Pyramids of Giza should have been arranged in the pattern of the three stars of Orion's belt. Moreover, since we know that the stated goal of the Horus-King's quest was not only to find the astral 'body' of Osiris but to find it as it was in the 'First Time', we should not be surprised by the fact that the Pyramids, as we saw in Part I, are set out on the ground in the pattern that they made at the beginning (i.e. 'southernmost point') of that constellation's upward (i.e. 'northerly') precessional half-cycle.

So we wonder whether it is possible that the quest of the Horus-King might have had as its ultimate objective *the acquisition of knowledge concerning the 'First Time'* – perhaps even the acquisition of specific knowledge *from* that remote epoch when the gods had walked the earth?

Several passages in the Pyramid Texts invite such speculation. For example, we are told that the Horus-King must 'travel upstream' – i.e. must push against the natural drift of 'time' – in order to reach Orion-Osiris in his proper 'First Time' setting:

> Betake yourself to the Waterway, fare upstream [south], travel about Abydos in this spirit-form of yours which the gods command to belong to you; may a stairway [road] to the *Duat* be set up for you to the Place Where Orion Is . . .[22]
>
> They have found Osiris . . . 'When his name became Sokar' [Memphite necropolis] . . . Wake up [Osiris] for Horus . . . raise yourself . . . fare southward [upstream] to the lake, cross over the sea [sky], for you are he who stands untiring in the midst of Abydos . . .[23]
>
> Betake yourself to the Waterway, fare upstream . . . traverse Abydos. The celestial portal to the Horizon is open to you . . . may you remove yourself to the sky, for the roads of the celestial expanses which lead up to Horus are cleaned for you . . . for you have traversed the Winding Waterway [Milky Way] which is in the north of the sky as a star crossing the sea which is beneath the sky. The *Duat* has grasped your hand at the Place Where Orion Is . . .[24]

Likewise there is a striking passage in the Coffin Texts which refers to some secret 'spell' or formula to allow the deceased to use the 'path of Rostau' on the land and in the sky (i.e. the path to the Giza necropolis on land and to Orion's belt in the sky) in order to 'go down to any sky he wishes to go down to':

> I have passed on the path of Rostau, whether on water or on land, and these are the paths of Osiris [Orion], they are in the limit of the sky. As for him who knows the spell [formula] for going down into them, he himself is a god in the suite of Thoth [meaning he is as wise as Thoth, 'the controller of the stars'[25]] [and] he will go down to any sky he wishes to go down to . . .[26]

Special numbers

We suspect that the phrase to 'go down to any sky' suggests an awareness – and recording – of precessionally induced changes in the positions of the stars over long periods of time. And we also note its implication that if the chosen initiate was equipped with the correct numerical spell then he would be able to work out – and visualize – the correct positions of the stars in any epoch of his choosing, past or future.

Once again Sellers stands out amongst Egyptologists for being the first to have entertained such apparently outlandish notions. 'It is possible', she writes, 'that early man encoded in his myths special numbers; numbers that seemed to reveal to initiates an amazing knowledge of the movement of the celestial spheres.' [27]

Such numbers, she argues, appear to have been derived from a sustained, scientific study of the cycle of precession and a measurement of its rate and, puzzlingly, turn out to be extremely 'close to the calculations made with today's sophisticated procedures'. Intriguingly, too, there is evidence not only 'that these calculations were made, and conclusions drawn', but also that 'they were transmitted to others by secret encoding that was accessible only to an élite few':[28] In short, Sellers concludes, 'ancient man calculated a special number that he believed would bring this threatening cycle [of precession] back to its starting point . . .' [29]

The 'special number' to which Sellers is referring to is 25,920 (and multiples and divisions of it) and thus represents the duration, in solar years, of a full precessional cycle or 'Great Year'.[30] She shows how it can be derived from a variety of simple combinations of other numbers – 5, 12, 36, 72, 360, 432, 2160, etc., etc. – all of which are in turn derived from precise observations of precession. *Most crucially of all, she shows that this peculiar sequence of numbers occurs in the ancient Egyptian myth of Osiris* where, notably '72 conspirators' are said to have been involved with Seth in the murder of the God-King.[31]

As was shown in *Fingerprints of the Gods*, the sun's perceived motion through the signs of the zodiac at the vernal equinox proceeds at the rate of one degree every seventy-two years. From this it follows that a movement of the vernal point through 30 degrees will take 2160 years to complete, 60 degrees will take 4320 years, and a full 360-degree cycle will require 25,920 years.[32]

Curiously enough, as the reader will recall from Part I, the Great Pyramid itself incorporates a record of these precessional numbers – since its key dimensions (its height and the perimeter of its base) appear to have been designed as a mathematical model of the earth's polar radius and equatorial circumference on a scale of 1:43,200. The number 43,200 is, of course, exactly 600 times 72. What we have in this remarkable monument, therefore, is not just a scale model of a hemisphere of the earth but also one in which the scale involved incorporates a 'special number' derived from one of the key planetary motions of the earth itself – i.e. the rate of its axial precession.

In short it seems that secret knowledge is indeed available in the myth of Osiris and in the dimensions of the Great Pyramid. With this secret knowledge, if we wanted to fix a specific date – say 1008 years in the future – and communicate it to other initiates, then we could do so with the 'special number' 14 (72 × 14 = 1008). We would also have to specify the 'zero point' from which they were to make their calculations – i.e the present epoch – and this might be done with some kind of symbolic or mathematical marker to indicate where the vernal point presently is, i.e. moving out of Pisces and into Aquarius.

A similar exercise could likewise be carried out in reverse. By following the 'eastwards' direction along the ecliptic path we can 'find' (calculate, work out) where the vernal point was at any epoch in the past. Thus if today we wished to use the precessional code to direct attention towards the Pyramid Age we would need to confide to other initiates the 'special number' of 62.5 (72 × 62.5 = 4500 years ago = approximately 2500 BC). Again, we could rule out any ambiguity as to the zero date from which the calculations were to be made if we could find a way to indicate the present position of the vernal point.

We have seen that this is what Sneferu appears to have done with the two Pyramids at Dahshur, which map the two sides of the head of the celestial bull – the 'address' of the vernal point in his epoch. And in a sense, though with a great deal more specificity and precision, this could also be exactly what the builders of the Great Pyramid were doing when they deliberately targeted the southern shafts of the King's and Queen's Chambers on the meridian-transits of such significant stars as Orion and Sirius in the epoch of 2500 BC. To be clear about this, it seems to us well worth investigating the possibility that by setting up such obvious and precise 'time markers' they were trying to provide an unambiguous *zero point* – circa 2500 BC – for calculations that could only be undertaken by initiates steeped in the mysteries of precession, who were equipped by their training to draw out the hidden portents concealed in certain 'special numbers'.

We note in passing that if the Horus-King could have been provided with the 'special number' 111.111, and had used it in the way described above, it would have led him back to (72 × 111.111 years =) 7,999.99 years before the specified 'ground zero', i.e. to almost exactly 8000 years before 2500 BC – in short, to 10,500 BC.

We know this seems like wishful numerology of the worst sort – i.e. 'factoring in' an arbitrary value to a set of calculations so as to procure spurious 'corroboration' for a specific desired date (in this case the date of 10,500 BC, twelve and a half thousand years before the present, that we have already highlighted in Chapter 3 in connection with the Sphinx and the Pyramids of Giza). The problem, however, is that the number 111.111 may well *not* be an arbitrary value. At any rate, it has long been recognized that the main numerical factor in the design of the Great Pyramid, and indeed of the Giza necropolis as a whole, is the prime number 11 – a prime number being one that is only divisible by itself to produce the whole number 1. Thus 11 divided by 11, i.e. the ratio 11:11, produces the whole number 1 (while 11 divided by anything else, i.e. any other ratio, would, of neccessity, generate a fraction).

What is intriguing is the way that the architecture of the Great Pyramid responds to the number 11 when it is divided, or multiplied, by other whole numbers. The reader will recall, for example, that its side length of just over 755 feet is equivalent to 440 Egyptian royal cubits – i.e. 11 times 40 cubits.[33] In addition, its height-to-base ratio is 7:11.[34] The slope ratio of its sides is 14:11 (tan 51 degrees 50').[35] And the slope ratio of the southern shaft of the King's Chamber – the shaft that was targeted on Orion's belt in 2500 BC – is 11:11 (tan 45 degrees).[36]

Arguably, therefore, the ratio 11:11, which integrates with our 'special number' 111.111, could be considered as a sort of mathematical key, or 'stargate' to Orion's belt. Moreover, as we shall see, a movement of 111.111 degrees 'backwards along the ecliptic from 'ground-zero' at the Hyades-Taurus, the head of the celestial bull, would place the vernal point 'underneath' the cosmic lion.

Is it not precisely such a location, underneath the Great Sphinx, that the Horus-King is urged to investigate as he stands between its paws 'with his mouth equipped' and faces the questions of the *Akhus* whose initiations have led him this far? Indeed, does it not seem probable that the 'quest-journey' devised by the 'Followers of Horus' was carefully structured so as to sharpen the mind of the initiate by requiring him to piece together all the clues himself until he finally arrived at the realization that somewhere underneath the Great Sphinx of Giza was something (written or pictorial records, artefacts, maps, astronomical charts) that touched on 'the knowledge of a divine origin', that was of immense importance, and that had been concealed there since the 'First Time'?

In considering such questions, we are reminded of the Hermetic doctrines which transmit a tradition of the wisdom god Thoth who was said to have 'succeeded in understanding the mysteries of the heavens [and to have] revealed them by inscribing them in sacred books which he then hid here on earth, intending that they should be searched for by future generations but found only by the fully worthy'.[37] Do the 'sacred books of Thoth', or their equivalent, still lie in the bedrock beneath the Great Sphinx of Giza, and do the 'fully worthy' still seek them there?

Seekers after truth

Other questions, too, have been raised implicitly and explicitly in the foregoing chapters:

1 Were the Great Sphinx and the great Pyramids of Giza designed to serve as parts of an immense three-dimensional 'model' of the sky of the 'First Time'?
2 Could other features of the necropolis also be part of this model?
3 If so, then has enough survived for us to compare the model with computer simulations of the skies above Giza in previous epochs

and thus arrive at an accurate archaeoastronomical *dating* for the 'First Time', i.e. for the true 'genesis' of the extraordinary civilization of Egypt?

4 By looking at simulations of the ancient skies would we not, to use the language of the Egyptian funerary texts, be 'going down to any sky we wished to go down to'?

5 Is it an accident that so many of these texts have survived for thousands of years, or could their compilers have *intended* them to survive and carefully designed them in such a way that human nature would ensure their copying and recopying down the ages (a process that has been promiscuously resumed in the last century and a half, since the decipherment of the ancient Egyptian hieroglyphs, with the Coffin Texts, the Pyramid Texts, the Book of the Dead, etc., etc., now translated and reprinted in dozens of modern languages and editions – and even available on CD-ROM)?

6 In other words, is it not possible in our readings of the texts, and in our analysis of the rituals to which they were linked, that we have stumbled upon a *message* of primordial antiquity that was composed not just for the Pyramid Age, and not just for the Horus-Kings of ancient Egypt, but for all 'seekers after the truth' – from any culture, in any epoch – who might be 'equipped' to put texts and monuments together and to view the skies of former times?

Chapter 16

Message in a Bottle?

'We have reached this fascinating point in
our evolution . . . we have reached the time
when we know we can talk to each other
across the distances between the stars . . .'

Dr John Billingham, NASA Ames Research
Center, 1995

Together with the ancient texts and rituals that are linked to them,
could the vast monuments of the Giza necropolis have been designed
to transmit *a message* from one culture to another – a message not
across space, but across time?

Egyptologists reply to such questions by rolling their eyes and
hooting derisively. Indeed they would not *be* 'Egyptologists' (or at any
rate they could not long remain within that profession) if they reacted
with anything other than scorn and disbelief to suggestions that the
necropolis might be more than a cemetery, that the Great Sphinx
might significantly predate the epoch of 2500 BC, and that the
Pyramids might not be just 'royal tombs'. By the same token, no self-
respecting Egyptologist would be prepared to consider, even for a
moment, the outlandish possibility that some sort of mysterious
'message' might have been encoded into the monuments.

So whom should we turn to for advice when confronted by what we
suspect may be a message from a civilization so far distant from us in
time as to be almost unknowable?

Anti-cipher

The only scientists actively working on such problems today are those
involved in the Search for Extraterrestrial Intelligence – SETI for

short. They endlessly sweep the heavens for messages from distant civilizations and they have therefore naturally had to give some thought to what might happen if they ever did identify such a message. According to Dr Philip Morisson of the Massachusetts Institute of Technology:

> To begin with we would know very little about it. If we received it we would not understand what we're getting. But we would have an unmistakable signal, full of structure, full of challenge. The best people would try to decode it, and it will be easy to do because those who have constructed it would have made it easy to decode, otherwise there's no point. This is anti-cryptography: 'I want to make a message for you, who never got in touch with any symbols of mine, no key no clue, nevertheless you'll be able to read it . . .' I would have to fill it full of clues and unmistakable clever devices . . .[1]

In his book, *Cosmos*, Professor Carl Sagan of Cornell University makes much the same point – and does so, curiously enough, with reference to the ancient Egyptian hieroglyphic system. He explains that the 'Egyptian hieroglyphics are, in significant part, a simple substitution cipher. But not every hieroglyph is a letter or syllable. Some are pictographs . . .' When it came to translation, this 'mix of letters and pictographs caused some grief for interpreters . . .' In the early nineteenth century, however, a breakthrough was made by the French scholar Champollion who deciphered the famous 'Rosetta Stone', a slab of black basalt bearing identical inscriptions in Egyptian hieroglyphics and in Greek. Since Champollion could read the Greek, all he needed was some kind of 'key' to relate specific hieroglyphs to specific Greek words or letters. This key was provided by the constant repetition in the Greek text of the name of Pharaoh Ptolemy V and an equal number of repetitions in the Egyptian text of a distinctive oblong enclosure – known as a cartouche – containing a repeated group of hieroglyphs. As Sagan comments:

> The cartouches were the key . . . almost as though the Pharaohs of Egypt had circled their own names to make the going easier for Egyptologists two thousand years in the future . . . What a joy it must have been [for Champollion] to open this one-way communication channel with another civilization, to permit a culture that had been

mute for millennia to speak of its history, magic, medicine, religion, politics and philosophy.[2]

Professor Sagan then offers a comparison that is highly apposite to our present inquiry. 'Today,' he says:

> we are again seeking messages from an ancient and exotic civilization, this time hidden from us not only in time, but in space. If we should receive a radio message from an extraterrestrial civilization, how could it possibly be understood? Extraterrestrial intelligence will be *elegant, complex, internally consistent and utterly alien*. Extraterrestrials would, of course, wish to make a message sent to us as comprehensible as possible. But how could they? Is there in any sense an interstellar Rosetta Stone? We believe there is a common language that all technical civilizations, no matter how different, must have. That common language is science and mathematics. The laws of Nature are the same everywhere.[3]

It seems to us that if there is indeed a very ancient 'message' at Giza then it is likely to be expressed in the language of science and mathematics that Sagan identifies – and for the same reason. Moreover, given its need to continue 'transmitting' coherently across thousands of years (and chasms of cultural change), we think that the composer of such a message would be likely to make use of the Precession of the Equinoxes, the one particular 'law of Nature' that can be said to govern, and measure – and identify – long periods of terrestrial time.

Durable vehicles

The Pyramids and the Great Sphinx at Giza are, above all else, as elegant, as complex, as internally consistent and as utterly 'alien' as the extraterrestrial intelligence that Sagan envisages (alien in the sense of the tremendous, almost superhuman scale of these structures and of their uncanny – and in our terms apparently unnecessary – precision).

Moreover, returning briefly to Dr Philip Morisson's remarks quoted earlier, we think that the Giza necropolis also qualifies rather well for the description 'packed full of clues and unmistakable clever devices'.[4] Indeed, it seems to us that a truly astonishing quantum of ingenuity was invested by the Pyramid builders to ensure that the four fundamental aspects of an 'unmistakable' message were thoroughly elaborated here:

1 the creation of durable, unequivocal markers which could serve as beacons to inflame the curiosity and engage the intelligence of future generations of seekers;

2 the use of the 'common language' of precessional astronomy;

3 the use of precessional co-ordinates to signal specific time-referents linking past to present and present to future;

4 Cunningly concealed store-rooms, or 'Halls of Records' that could only be found and entered by those who were fully initiated in the 'silent language' and thus could read and follow its clues.

In addition, though the monuments are enabled to 'speak' from the moment that their astronomical context is understood, we have also to consider the amazing profusion of funerary texts that have come down to us from all periods of Egyptian history – all apparently emanating from the same very few common sources.[5] As we have seen, these texts operate like 'software' to the monuments' 'hardware', charting the route that the Horus-King (and all other future seekers) must follow.

We recall a remark made by Giorgio de Santillana and Hertha von Dechend in *Hamlet's Mill* to the effect that the great strength of myths as vehicles for specific technical information is that they are capable of transmitting that information independently of the knowledge of individual story-tellers.[6] In other words as long as a myth continues to be told true, it will also continue to transmit any higher message that may be concealed within its structure – even if neither the teller nor the hearer understands that message.

So, too, we suspect, with the ancient Egyptian funerary texts. We would be surprised if the owners of many of the coffins and tomb walls onto which they were copied had even the faintest inkling that specific astronomical observations and directions were being duplicated at their expense. What motivated them was precisely what the texts offered – the lure of immortal life. Yet by taking that lure did they not in fact guarantee a kind of immortality for the texts themselves? Did they not ensure that so many faithful copies would be made that some at least would be bound to survive for many thousands of years?

We think that there were always people who understood the true 'science of immortality' connected to the texts, and who were able to read the astronomical allegories in which deeper secrets, not granted to the common herd, lay concealed. We presume that these people were once called the 'Followers of Horus', that they operated as an invisible college behind the scenes in Egyptian prehistory and history, that their primary cult centre was at Giza-Heliopolis, and that they were responsible for the initiation of kings and the realization of blueprints. We also think that the timetables they worked to – and almost everything of significance that they did – was in one way or another written in the stars.

Hints and memories

The powerfully astronomical character of the Giza necropolis, although ignored by Egyptologists, has been recognized by open-minded and intuitive researchers throughout history. The Hermetic Neoplatonists of Alexandria, for example, appear to have been acutely sensitive to the possibility of a 'message' and were quick to discern the strong astral qualities of the textual material and the monuments.[7] The scholar Proclus (fifth century AD) also acknowledged that the Great Pyramid was astronomically designed – and with certain specific stars in mind. Indeed, in his commentary on Plato's *Timaeus* (which deals with the story of the lost civilization of 'Atlantis'), Proclus reported strangely that 'the Great Pyramid was used as an observation for Sirius'.[8]

Vague memories of an astronomically constructed 'message' at Giza appear to have filtered down to the Middle Ages. At any rate the Arab chroniclers in this period spoke of the Great Pyramid as 'a temple to the stars' and frequently connected it to the Biblical 'Flood' which they dated to *circa* 10,300 BC.[9] Also of relevance is a report written by the Arab geographer Yakut al Hamawi (eleventh century AD) to the effect that the star-worshippers of Harran, the Sabians (whose 'holy books' were supposedly the writings of Thoth-Hermes) came at that time on special pilgrimages to the Pyramids at Giza.[10] It has also been pointed out that the very name of the Sabians – in Arabic *Sa'Ba* – almost certainly derived from the ancient Egyptian word for star, i.e. *Sba*.[11] And the reader will recall from Part I that as far back as the early second millennium BC – i.e. almost *three thousand years* before Yakut al Hamawi left us his report connecting the Sabians to the Pyramids – pilgrims from Harran are known to have visited the Sphinx which they worshipped as a god under the name *Hwl*.[12]

In the seventeenth century, the British mathematician Sir Isaac Newton became deeply interested in the Great Pyramid and wrote a dissertation on its mathematical and geodetic qualities based on data that had been gathered at Giza by Dr John Greaves, the Savillian Professor of Astronomy at Oxford.[13] Later, in 1865 the Astronomer Royal of Scotland, Charles Piazzi Smyth, launched an investigation into the Great Pyramid which he was convinced was an instrument of prophecy that incorporated a Messianic 'message'. It was Piazzi Smyth who first accurately measured and demonstrated the intense polar and meridional alignments of the monument, the precision of which he assigned to sightings of the ancient Pole star, Alpha Draconis.[14]

In the first half of the twentieth century, a succession of eminent astronomers – such as Richard Proctor, Eugene Antoniadi, Jean Baptiste Biot and Norman Lockyer – made persistent attempts to draw attention to the astronomical qualities of the Giza monuments. Their efforts, however, had little impact on professional Egyptologists who by this time felt that they had got the whole intellectual business of the necropolis 'wrapped up' (it was a cemetery), did not understand astronomy at all (and claimed that the ancient Egyptians didn't either), and routinely ganged up to debunk, deride or simply ignore any astronomical 'theories' which diverged from their consensus.

Despite this hostile intellectual climate, we are of the opinion at the end of our own research that the big question is no longer *whether* the monuments of Giza were designed to express key astronomical and mathematical principles, but *why*.

Once again, the clue may lie in the narrow star-shafts of the Great Pyramid.

The language of the stars

The first major breakthrough in understanding the function of the Great Pyramid's shafts was made in the summer of 1963 by the American astronomer Virginia Trimble and the Egyptologist-architect, Dr Alexander Badawy. It came about because they decided to follow up Badawy's 'hunch' that the shafts might not be 'ventilation channels' as Egyptologists supposed,[15] but might instead prove to have a symbolic function related to the astral rituals of the Pyramid builders. Virginia Trimble was able to buttress her colleague's intuition by showing that the shafts from the King's Chamber had pointed, in the epoch of 2500 BC, to major star systems that were of crucial importance to the Pyramid builders. As readers will recall from Part I, the northern shaft had been targeted on Alpha Draconis – the Pole Star in the Pyramid Age – and the southern shaft had been targeted on Orion's belt.[16]

Today Virginia Trimble is a senior professor of astronomy at UCLA and the University of Maryland and is also the Vice-President of the American Astronomical Society. Her views, as well as being enlightened by a comprehensive grasp of astronomy, accord fully with common sense:

> Which constellations the Egyptians saw in the sky is still something of a mystery . . . but they had one constellation that was an erect standing man, Osiris, the god. And the one constellation that looks like a standing man to everyone is Orion, and the identification between a deceased Pharaoh and the god Osiris made Orion immediately a candidate for a shaft whose sole purpose was to enable the soul of the Pharaoh to communicate between earth and sky . . .[17]

When we met Virginia Trimble we immediately realized we were in the presence of an acute and formidable thinker. Alexander Badawy had passed away in the late 1980s yet she remained undaunted. She had concluded that the shafts were astronomically aligned, she said, and that they had an astronomical function, because logic and evidence dictated that this was the case.

Trimble's views have won general acceptance amongst senior astronomers. To give one recent example, Dr Mary Bruck of Edinburgh, writing in the *Journal of the British Astronomical*

Association in 1995, had this to say about the shafts: 'Their alignments are . . . compatible with the hypothesis that they indicate the culmination of certain important stars around the 25th century BC . . . The addition of a Sirius shaft [southern shaft of the Queen's Chamber] to the Orion one strongly supports the claim that they have an astronomical significance.' [18]

Thought-tools

We suggest that one of the major objectives of the unseen academy, whose members were known as the 'Followers of Horus', was to 'fix' the epoch of 2500 BC (i.e. 4500 years before the present) by using the Great Pyramid, its precisely angled shafts, and the stars of Orion's belt. We suggest that they envisaged those stars rather like the gauge of a gigantic sliding scale set across the south meridian. Once this 'thought-tool' was in place all they needed to do in order to determine a date either in the past or in the future was mentally to 'slide' the belt up or down the meridian from the 'zero point' targeted by the southern shaft of the King's Chamber.

We also suggest that a second and somewhat similar 'thought-tool' was attached to the ecliptic (the apparent annual path of the sun through the twelve constellations of the zodiac). Here the gauge was the vernal point. By mentally sliding it to the left (east) or to the right (west) of a 'fixed' marker on the ecliptic the 'Followers of Horus' would once again have been able to determine and denominate either a past date or a date in the future . . .

In our own epoch, *circa* AD 2000, the vernal point is poised to enter the sign or 'Age' of Aquarius. For a little over 2000 years it has been passing through Pisces (160 BC to AD 2000) and before that it was in Aries (2320 BC to 160 BC). In the Pyramid Age the vernal point slowly swept through Taurus (4480 BC to 2320 BC). Going further back we reach the 'Ages' of Gemini (6640 BC to 4480 BC) and then Cancer (8800 BC to 6640 BC). After six 'Great Months' we reach the Age of Leo (10,960 BC to 8800 BC).

Now imagine that we find an ancient document at Giza which states that it was composed when the vernal point was in the sign of the Ram – i.e. when the sun on the spring equinox rose against the stellar background of the constellation of Aries. Armed with this information all that we can do is *roughly* bracket the document's date as being somewhere between 2320 BC and 160 BC. What we need in order to arrive at a more precise chronology is some means to 'fine-tune' the vernal point. It is here that the specific utility of the sliding scale at the meridian becomes apparent because if the ancient document not only stated which zodiacal sign housed the vernal point but also advised that the lowest star of Orion's belt crossed the meridian at an altitude of 50 degrees above the horizon then we would be able, using precession, to calculate with great accuracy that the date in question must be very near 1400 BC.[19]

The Pyramid Age occurred when the vernal point was in Taurus and, as we have seen, the fine-tuning permitted by the 45-degree angle of the Great Pyramid's 'Orion shaft' draws particular attention to the date of 2500 BC. With this date, 4500 years before the present, we can use precession to calculate the exact position of the vernal point – which, as the reader will recall, was near the head of the Hyades-Taurus at that time, close to the right (i.e. west) bank of the Milky Way.

The reader will also not have forgotten that this is the 'address' given in the Pyramid Texts as the starting point for the cosmic journey of the solar Horus-King. It is here that he receives his instructions to board the solar-bark and 'sail' across the Milky Way towards the 'horizon' to meet up with Horakhti. His direction of travel is, therefore, eastwards, i.e. to the left of the vernal point. In terms of the chronology of the 'Great Year' of precession (as distinct from the solar year), this means that the Horus-King is now poised to travel back in time towards the age of Leo-Horakhti and to a specific spot on the ecliptic path – 'The Splendid Place of the "First Time"' ... 'the place more noble than any place'.[20]

But where is that place? How is the Horus-King (initiate, seeker) to find it in the 2160-year, 30-degree swathe that the constellation of Leo occupies on the ecliptic?

The answer is that he would have to use the gauge of Orion's belt at the meridian to fine-tune the exact place of the vernal point and hence also to arrive at an exact date. In his mind's eye he would have to slide the belt 'down' the meridian to its 'First Time' and then see how far to the east that operation had 'pushed' the vernal point along the ecliptic.

Wherever that place was would be the celestial destination that the 'Followers of Horus' were urging him to reach.

And it would, of course, have its counterpart on the ground at Giza, in the vicinity of the lion-bodied Sphinx.

Chapter 17

The Place of the 'First Time'

'Know that we would be universal scientists
if it were given to us to inhabit the sacred
land of Egypt . . .'

Manetho, Egyptian high priest, third century
BC

'I have come to this place more noble than
any place . . .'

Pyramid Texts

The epoch of the 'First Time', *Zep Tepi*, was frequently referred to as
the 'First Time of Horus', the 'First Time of Re' and the 'First Time
of Osiris'.[1] The implication of this terminology is that the position of
the (vernal) sun along the ecliptic path, which denoted the 'First
Time', was also seen to be marked – perhaps 'controlled' would be a
better word – by the position of Osiris-Orion at the meridian.

As we have seen, the ancient brotherhood of astronomer-priests
who designed the Great Pyramid, and who were later responsible for
the compilation of the Pyramid Texts, were well aware of Orion's
slow precessional drift 'upwards' – 'northwards' in the allegorical
language of the texts – when the constellation was sighted at the
meridian over long periods of time. They also knew that they were
'fixing' a specific location to which the 'body of the god' had drifted
(and a specific date in time – 2500 BC in our calendar) when they
targeted the meridian at 45 degrees with the southern shaft of the
King's Chamber. They knew, in other words, that the belt stars would
rise to higher altitudes above the horizon (i.e. drift further 'north') in
future epochs and, conversely, that they had been at lower altitudes

(i.e. 'further south') in previous epochs. The reader will recall from Chapter 1 that the lowest ('southernmost') point in the entire precessional cycle of Orion's belt – the 'First Time of Osiris' in allegorical terms – occurred in 10,500 BC. Most mysteriously, it is the precise disposition of these stars in the sky at that date that is frozen on the ground in the form of the three great Pyramids of Giza.

It was the mystery of this perfect meridian-to-meridian match, together with the equinoctial alignment of the lion-bodied Sphinx (and the vast antiquity of that monument as indicated by geology) that provoked us to undertake the present investigation. For while we did not dispute the orthodox Egyptological dating of the Pyramids to the epoch of 2500 BC, we had a strong intuition that their layout in the image of Orion's belt some 8000 years earlier was most unlikely to have come about by chance.

We are now satisfied that chance was not involved. After factoring-in the data preserved in the vast storehouses of ancient Egyptian funerary 'software', it seems to us obvious that what was created – or rather *completed* – at Giza in 2500 BC was an entirely deliberate work of sky–ground dualism. It was a model (on a lavish scale intended to do justice to its cosmic original) of the 'kingdom' established by Osiris in the sky-*Duat* in the remote epoch 'when his name became Orion' – i.e. in his 'First Time'. It was also, for all time, the 'Kingdom of Osiris' on the ground – 'when his name became Sokar' (in the lower *Duat*, i.e. the Memphite necropolis).

It may have been the case that the ground-plan of the three great Pyramids was *physically established* in 10,500 BC – perhaps in the form of low platforms. Or it may have been that precise astronomical records from that epoch were preserved and handed down to the astronomer-priests of Heliopolis by the 'Followers of Horus'. Either way, we are still reasonably certain that the Pyramids themselves were largely built in 2500 BC when Egyptologists say they were. We are also sure, however, that the site was already vastly ancient by then and had been the domain of the 'Followers' – the Sages, the 'Senior Ones' – for the previous 8000 years.

We think the evidence suggests a continuous transmission of advanced scientific and engineering knowledge over that huge gulf of time, and thus the continuous presence in Egypt, from the

Palaeolithic into the Dynastic Period, of highly enlightened and sophisticated individuals – those shadowy *Akhus* said in the texts to have possessed 'a knowledge of divine origin'.

Fine-tuning Leo

The basis for this conjecture, above and beyond the astronomical alignments of the Giza necropolis, is the geological condition of the Sphinx which we have described in Part I. To state matters briefly: *the signs of intense precipitation-induced weathering visible to this day on the great monument itself, and on the rock-hewn trench surrounding it, are consistent with an age of more than 12,000 years.*

The genesis date indicated by astronomy for the site as a whole is 10,500 BC. That is what the *layout* of the Pyramids says, even if they themselves are younger. And that, too, as we saw in Chapter 3, is what is proclaimed by the due-east orientation of the Sphinx. Its astronomical and leonine symbolism does not make any sense unless it was built as an equinoctial marker for the Age of Leo.

But *when*, exactly, in the Age of Leo? The constellation spans 30 degrees along the ecliptic and housed the sun on the vernal equinox from 10,960 BC to 8800 BC – a period of 2160 years. So when in that period?

There is no way to answer this question on the basis of the alignments of the Sphinx alone, or on the basis of what one may deduce from its alignments and its geology viewed together. What is needed is precisely what the 'Followers of Horus' provided us with – a thought-tool with which to fine-tune the date. That thought-tool is the sliding scale of Orion's belt and the date that it fine-tunes for the Great Sphinx is 10,500 BC.

But it also does something else. As the scale 'slides' down the meridian it also 'pushes' the vernal point steadily eastwards along the ecliptic, bringing it to rest in 10,500 BC (the 'bottom of the scale') *at a specific stellar address that can be identified by precessional calculations.*

In terms of the sky–ground dualism of the initiatory quest of the Horus-King, it is obvious that the vernal point's 'stellar address' in 10,500 BC – i.e. its precise whereabouts on the ecliptic within the constellation of Leo – is likely to have a terrestrial analogue. Once we know what's what with the sky, in other words, we should know where to look on the ground.

And would it be entirely unreasonable to suppose that what we would find there, if we had calculated *exactly* where to look, might turn out to be a physical entrance into that mythical 'place more noble than any place', the 'Splendid Place of the "First Time" '?

Setting stars

As though to reward such conjectures, like a one-armed bandit coughing up the jackpot, all the bells and lights of the Giza necropolis start ringing and flashing at once when the sliding scale of Orion's belt is pushed down to its 'First Time' in 10,500 BC.

We already know from Chapter 3 that what the principal monuments seem to model is an unusual astronomical conjunction that occurred at the spring equinox in that distant epoch. Not only did the Great Sphinx gaze at his own celestial counterpart in the sky but also the moment of sunrise (at the point on the horizon targeted by the Sphinx's gaze) coincided, to the second, with the meridian-transit of Orion's belt (which is what the three Pyramids model).

If these were the only correspondences they would already be too detailed to be attributed to coincidence. But there is a great deal more. For example, immediately south of the third and smallest of the three great Pyramids is a group of three 'satellite' pyramids. Egyptologists generally refer to them as the 'tombs' of queens of the Pharaoh Menkaure. Since they contain no inscriptions, nor the slightest trace of human remains or funerary equipment, such an attribution can never be anything more than a matter of opinion. However these 'satellite' pyramids do have an unambiguous astronomical alignment: they form a row running east-west – the equinox sunrise-sunset direction.

The British geometrician and pyramid researcher, Robin Cook, has recently shown that these three satellite pyramids bear a designed relationship to the Giza necropolis as a whole.[2] They appear to be located on the boundary of a circle, or artificial 'horizon', the focus of which is the Pyramid of Khafre and the circumference of which envelops the whole necropolis. An angle of 27 degrees west of south[3] –

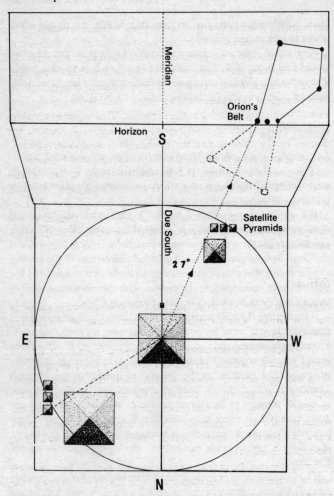

59. Epoch of 10,500 BC: setting of the three stars of Orion's belt in line with the three satellite pyramids on the southern rim of the Horizon of Giza.

corresponding to an azimuth of 207 degrees[4] – seems to be defined by a straight line extending from the meridian axis of the Pyramid of Khafre to these three 'satellite' pyramids of Menkaure.[5] In general the satellites give the impression of being 'reduced models' of the three Great Pyramids. What is notably different however, is that the latter lie at an angle of 45 degrees to the meridian, while the former run from east to west at right-angles to the meridian. This apparent architectural anomaly, together with their curious location at azimuth 207 degrees on the artificial 'horizon' of Giza, begs an obvious question: are we again looking at datable sky event frozen in architecture?

The computer confirms that we are. In 10,500 BC, on the real horizon of Giza, the lowest of the three stars of Orion's belt, *Al Nitak*, set at 27 degrees west of south – i.e. at azimuth 207 degrees. Moreover, the belt stars at that moment would have formed an axis running east-west – the alignment that is mimicked by the three satellite pyramids.

Sirius

Another bit of the 10,500 BC 'jackpot of correspondences' concerns the star Sirius, which symbolizes the very heart of the ancient Egyptian mystery.

All stars, including our own sun (and our solar system with it) move through space. Because of the vast distances involved, however (hundreds and often thousands of light-years), this 'proper motion' registers barely perceptible effects on the *positions in the sky* of the majority of stars as viewed from earth. Where these stars are concerned the only significant factor is precession (which, as we know, is a perceived 'motion' that is actually caused by a wobble on the axis of the earth).

Sirius is one of the major exceptions to this rule. As many readers will be aware, it is the brightest star in the sky. It is also one of the *nearest* stars to earth, being only 8.4 light-years away. Because of this proximity it registers a very large 'proper motion' in space relative to our own solar system – large enough to bring about observable changes in its celestial address, *over and above those caused by precession*, within just a few thousand years.

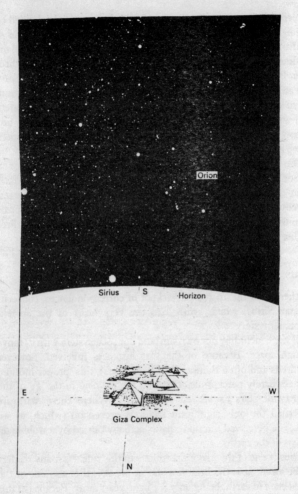

60. Artist's impression of the 'First Time' of Sirius, in the epoch of 10,500 BC, when the bright star of Isis would have been seen to be resting exactly on the horizon.

To be specific about this, the proper motion of Sirius is estimated to be in the range of 1.21 arc-seconds per year (about 1 degree every 3000 years). This means that for an epoch as far back as 10,500 BC, the change in its celestial co-ordinates resulting from proper motion could exceed 3 full degrees of arc, i.e about six times the apparent diameter of the moon.[6]

Once this rapid and noticeable rate of movement is taken into account alongside the effects of precession, computer simulations indicate a rather intriguing state of affairs. Calculations show that when Sirius reached its 'First Time' – i.e. its lowest altitude above the horizon – viewers at the latitude of Giza (30 degrees north) would have seen it resting exactly on the horizon. Moreover it was from this latitude, *and this latitude only*, that such a conjunction of star and horizon could be witnessed. The implication is that a special co-relationship exists between the latitude of Giza and the star Sirius at its 'First Time'.[7]

Because of its large proper motion there is uncertainty over when exactly the 'First Time' of Sirius would have occurred. There is no doubt, however, that it would have been somewhere between 11,500 and 10,500 BC.[8] We wonder, therefore, whether the decision to establish the sacred site of Giza at 30 degrees north latitude could have been connected to this 'First Time' of Sirius? And we recall that in 1993 Rudolf Gantenbrink's robot camera discovered a mysterious 'door' inside the Great Pyramid, more than 200 feet along the narrow southern shaft of the Queen's Chamber.[9] The shaft in which the 'door' was found was, of course, targeted on the meridian-transit of Sirius in 2500 BC.

Cross-quarter causeways

Amongst the strangest and most unaccountable features of the Giza necropolis are the massive causeways that link each of the three great Pyramids with the Nile Valley below. Today only fragments of their floorings remain, but as late as the fifth century BC at least one causeway, that of the Great Pyramid, was still almost intact. We know this because it was seen and described by the Greek historian Herodotus (484–420 BC) – who reflected that its construction almost matched, in engineering prowess and architectural splendour, that of the Great Pyramid itself.[10]

Recent archaeological research has confirmed that the information provided by Herodotus is correct. Moreover, we now know that the roofs of the causeways were spangled on their undersides with patterns of stars[11] – highly appropriate symbolism if, as we believe is the case, these grand and curious corridors were designed to serve as *Viae Sacrae* – ceremonial 'roadways' which initiates would follow on their way to the 'Pyramid-stars' of Rostau-Giza.[12]

The causeway from the Third Pyramid (the Pyramid of Menkaure) is directed due-east,[13] like the gaze of the Sphinx, and thus conforms to the general north-south and east-west grid structure of the Giza necropolis. By contrast the two causeways linked to the other two Pyramids definitely do *not* conform to that grid structure. As a result of the work of geometrician John Legon, who has undertaken a

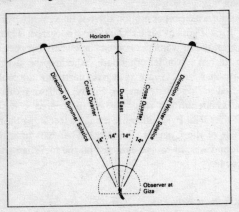

61. The course of the sun throughout the year as viewed from the latitude of Giza. A full range of 56 degrees is defined between summer solstice at 28 degrees north of east and winter solstice at 28 degrees south of east (with the equinox, of course, at due east). The 'cross-quarter' sunrises therefore occur at 14 degrees north of east and 14 degrees south of east respectively, thus dividing the sun's range along the horizon into four equal parts.

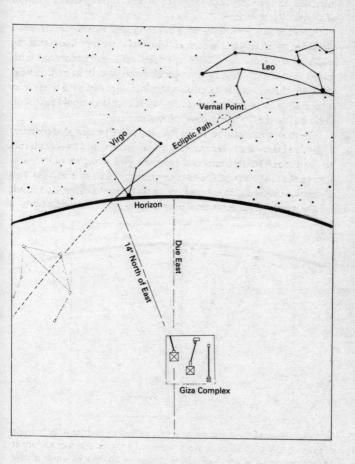

62. The Khufu causeway runs 14 degrees north of east in perfect alignment with the cross-quarter sunrise that falls between the spring equinox and the summer solstice (and thus also, on the sun's 'return journey', between the summer solstice and the autumn equinox).

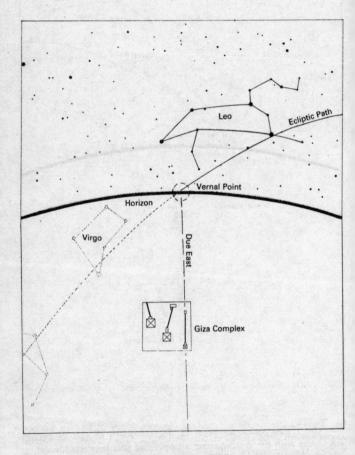

63. The Menkaure causeway runs due east in perfect alignment with sunrise on the spring equinox and on the autumn equinox.

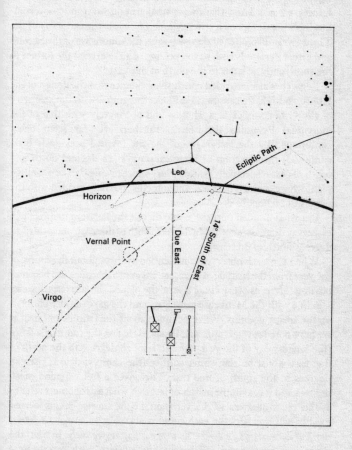

64. The Khafre causeway runs 14 degrees south of east in perfect alignment with the cross-quarter sunrise that falls between the winter solstice and the spring equinox (and thus also, on the sun's 'return journey', between the autumn equinox and the winter solstice).

detailed analysis of the site-plans and grids provided by modern Egyptologists (such as Selim Hassan, Reisner, Holscher, Ricke and Lauer), we now know that this anomalous nonconformity nevertheless incorporates its own strict symmetry: 'while the causeway of the Third Pyramid is aligned due east-west, the causeways of the Second and Great Pyramids both have a bearing of 14 degrees – the former to the south and the latter to the north of due east.'[14]

Legon has also provided conclusive evidence that the design of the Khufu and Khafre causeways is in fact integrated with the geometry of the Giza complex as a whole – and not merely with that of the individual Pyramids themselves. Furthermore, far from being conditioned by the *topography* of the site (as had previously been supposed) the direction of these causeways (14 degrees north and south of east respectively) shows every sign of being part of a 'unified plan' whose 'hidden purpose' and impetus 'possibly resided with the priests of Heliopolis'.[15]

But what 'hidden purpose' could dictate the decision to direct one causeway due east, another 14 degrees south of due east, and a third 14 degrees north of due east?

When sunrise is observed conscientiously throughout the course of the year from the latitude of Giza, the answer to this question becomes obvious. Here, as everywhere else on the planet, the sun rises due east – in line with the Menkaure causeway (and the gaze of the Sphinx) – on the spring equinox. What is unique about the latitude of Giza, as we have noted several times previously, is that on the summer solstice (the longest day of the year) the sun rises 28 degrees to the north of due east whilst on the winter solstice (the shortest day) it rises 28 degrees to the south of due east. This gives a full variation of 56 degrees and it is a simple matter of fact that what astronomers refer to as the 'cross-quarters' of this variation, i.e the sunrise-points located exactly half way between each equinox and solstice, are at *14 degrees north of due east and 14 degrees south of due east respectively*. In short the three causeways signal and bracket the equinox with two gigantic 'arrows' pointed at the cross-quarter sunrises and a third arrow (the Menkaura causeway) pointed at the equinox sunrise itself. In this fashion the sun's range throughout the year along the eastern horizon

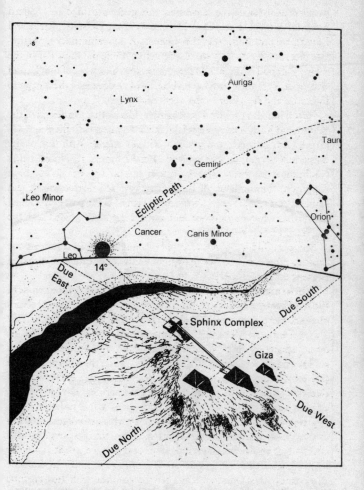

65. Epoch of 10,500 BC: the rising of Leo on the cross-quarter sunrise between the winter solstice and the spring equinox. This sunrise occurs at 14 degrees south of east, the point on the horizon targeted by the Khafre causeway.

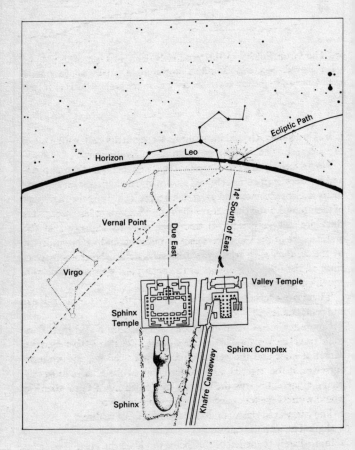

66. Epoch of 10,500 BC: gaze of the Sphinx on the cross-quarter sunrise between the winter solstice and the spring equinox. Note the profile of the constellation of Leo with only its head, back and shoulders protruding above the sky-horizon and compare with the profile of the Sphinx, as viewed from the south.

67. The Great Sphinx in the 'ground-horizon' of Giza, with only its massive head, back and shoulders protruding into view above ground level. Once again the images in the sky and on the ground 'lock' at 10,500 BC.

is architecturally divided into four equal segments each with a range of 14 degrees – i.e. into its astronomical 'cross-quarters'.

Now a focus on the cross-quarter days, together with the equinoxes and solstices, is an extremely well-documented phenomenon amongst many ancient astronomically minded peoples (dictating the alignment of their temples and the dates of their most important festivals).[16] It is therefore not surprising to find such a focus expressed in the architecture of the Giza necropolis. Neither should we be surprised by the *accuracy* with which the causeways define the cross-quarters since all the other alignments of the necropolis were achieved with equally high precision.

There is one feature of the layout, however, that is truly exceptional and remarkable.

Computer reconstructions of the ancient skies reveal that if we could travel back in time to the cross-quarter day that fell between the winter solstice and the vernal equinox in 10,500 BC, and position ourselves at the 'top', i.e. the western end, of the Khafre causeway gazing along it towards the edge of the 'Horizon' of Giza, then we would witness the following celestial events at dawn:

1 The sun would rise at 14 degrees south of east in direct alignment with the causeway;[17]

2 Immediately to the left of this point would be the great constellation of Leo-Horakhti, with only its massive head and shoulders protruding above the horizon line (*it would, in other words, appear to be partially sunk, or 'buried' in the 'Horizon of the Sky'*).

Now let us look down from the sky to the ground. Following the south-easterly direction of the causeway from the same viewpoint we note that it sinks down with the general slope of the Giza plateau and passes just to the south of the southern edge of the Sphinx enclosure. The Sphinx itself – Hor-em-Akhet – stands *partially sunk, or 'buried'* in that enclosure (and thus in the 'Horizon of Giza') with only its massive head and shoulders protruding out of the groundline.

Once again the images of sky and ground match perfectly at 10,500 BC and in no other epoch . . .

Treasure map

We said earlier that in the architectural-astronomical system of the Pyramid builders the position of the vernal point along the ecliptic which denoted the 'Splendid Place of the "First Time"' was considered to be 'controlled' by the position of Osiris-Orion at the meridian: 'slide' Orion's belt up from its location at 2500 BC and the vernal point is 'pushed' westwards around the ecliptic (and forward in time) in the direction Taurus → Aries → Pisces → Aquarius; 'slide' it down and the vernal point is pushed 'east', i.e. back in time, in the direction Taurus → Gemini → Cancer → Leo. So in 10,500 BC, with the belt stars fully 'slid down' to their lowest possible altitude above the horizon, how far around the ecliptic has the vernal point been 'pushed? We know it is in Leo. But where in Leo?

Computer simulations show that it lay exactly 111.111 degrees east of the station that it had occupied at 2500 BC. Then it had been at the head of the Hyades-Taurus close to the right bank of the Milky Way; 8000 years earlier it lay *directly under the rear paws of the constellation of Leo.*

As we have hinted, this is a location that is likely to have a terrestrial 'double'. The three stars of Orion's belt have their terrestrial doubles in the form of the three Great Pyramids. The constellation of Leo-Horakhti has its terrestrial double in the form of Hor-em-Akhet, i.e. the Great Sphinx. The 'Horizon of the Sky' has its terrestrial double in the form of the 'Horizon of Giza'. And the Great Sphinx crouches literally *within* this 'Horizon'.

It was to the breast of the Great Sphinx, at the summer solstice in the Pyramid Age, that the quest of the Horus-King led. There he encountered the *Akhus*:

> 'How has this happened to you', say they, the *Akhus* with their mouths equipped, 'that you have come to this place more noble than any place?'
>
> 'I have come . . . because the reed floats of the sky were set down for Re [the sun-disc and cosmic 'double' of the Horus-King] that Re might cross [the Milky Way] on them to Horakhti at the Horizon' . . .[18]

In other words, the Horus-King has successfully understood and used the clues provided in the ritual. He has noted and followed the path of the sun during the solar year from its starting point – designated in the texts as being beside the Hyades-Taurus, i.e. the 'Bull of the Sky' – and thence across the Milky Way until the moment of its conjunction with Regulus, the heart-star of Leo. He has then taken this celestial treasure map, transposed its co-ordinates to the ground, made his way across the River Nile and ascended to the Giza plateau, coming eventually to the breast of the Sphinx.

We think that he received there the necessary clues or instructions to find the entrance to the terrestrial *Duat*, to the 'Kingdom of Osiris' on the ground – in short to the 'Splendid Place of the "First Time" ' where he would have to go in order to complete his quest. And we suggest that these clues were designed to encourage him to *track the vernal point*, just as we have done, to the location that it would have occupied in 10,500 BC when Orion's belt had reached the lowest point in its precessional cycle.

In other words it is our hypothesis that the Giza monuments, the past, present and future skies that lie above them, and the ancient funerary texts that interlink them, convey the lineaments of a message. In attempting to read this message we have done no more than follow the initiation 'journey' of the Horus-Kings of Egypt. And like the ancient Horus-Kings we, too, have arrived at a most intriguing crossroad. The trail of initiation has guided us, directed us and finally lured us to stand in front of the Great Sphinx and, like Oedipus, to confront the ultimate riddles: 'Where did we come from?' 'Where are we to go to?'

The gaze of the Sphinx urges us to see through the shadowy veil and seek the 'First Time'. But, having done that, it also provokes us to ask whether there might not in fact be something at Giza, *something physical*, that would give form to the site's strange aura of vast and exceptional antiquity.

We remember a passage from the Coffin Texts which invites us to consider the possibility that some great 'secret' of Osiris may remain hidden within or beneath the monuments of Rostau-Giza in a 'sealed' container: 'This is the sealed thing, which is in darkness, with fire about it, which contains the efflux of Osiris, and it is put in Rostau. It has been hidden since it fell from him, and it is what came down from him onto the desert of sand; it means that what belonged to him was put in Rostau . . .'[19]

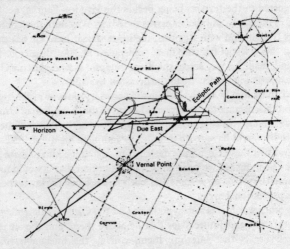

68. The Horus-King's treasure map: the heliacal rising of Leo on the spring equinox in 10,500 BC. The sun, marking the vernal point, lies below the horizon, some 12 degrees beneath the constellation's rear paws. When this image is transposed to the ground, the logic of the Horus-King's quest suggests the possibility of a hidden chamber deep in the bedrock of the Giza plateau, approximately 100 feet beneath the rear paws of the Sphinx.

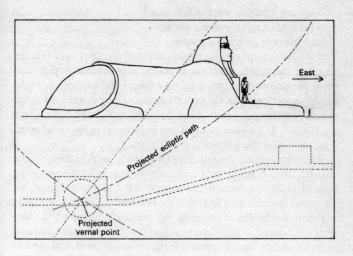

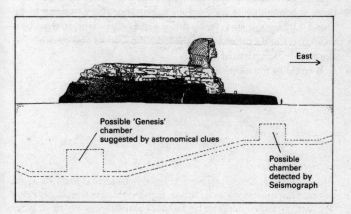

69. Possible locations of an underground system of passageways and chambers beneath the Great Sphinx suggested by astronomical correlations and by seismographic tests (see Part I of the present work).

What can it be that was put in Rostau?
What hidden thing with fire about it?
And where in darkness does it lie?

If we look at our computer simulation of the skies over Giza in 10,500 BC the answer appears to be staring us in the face. In that year, in the pre-dawn on the spring equinox, the constellation of Leo could be seen rising slowly in the east. By around 5 a.m. it was fully risen, exactly straddling due east – a lion in the sky, with its belly resting on the horizon. At the same moment, the sun – marking the vernal point – lay some 12 degrees beneath its rear paws.

When we translate this sky-image onto the ground, in the form of a colossal, leonine, equinoctial monument with its belly resting on the bedrock of the real physical environment of the 'Horizon of Giza', we do indeed find ourselves looking at the Horus-King's treasure map. It is a map, not buried in the earth but cunningly concealed in time, where 'X' almost literally 'marks a spot' directly under the rear paws of the Great Sphinx of Egypt at a depth, we would guess, of about 100 feet.

If we have read the message of the 'Followers of Horus' right, then there is something of momentous importance there, waiting to be found – by seismic surveys, by drilling and excavations, in short by a rediscovery and exploration of the hidden corridors and chambers of the earthly 'Kingdom of Osiris'.

It could be the ultimate prize.

Conclusion

Return to the Beginning

'I stand before the masters who witnessed
the genesis, who were the authors of their
own forms, who walked the dark, circuitous
passages of their own becoming . . . I stand
before the masters who witnessed the
transformation of the body of a man into the
body in spirit, who were witnesses to
resurrection when the corpse of Osiris
entered the mountain and the soul of Osiris
walked out shining . . . when he came forth
from death, a shining thing, his face white
with heat . . . I stand before the masters who
know the histories of the dead, who decide
which tales to hear again, who judge the
books of lives as either full or empty, who are
themselves authors of truth. And they are
Isis and Osiris, the divine intelligences. And
when the story is written and the end is good
and the soul of a man is perfected, with a
shout they lift him into heaven . . .'

Ancient Egyptian Book of the Dead (Normandi Ellis
translation)

The dictionary tells us that, separately from its modern usage, the
word 'glamour' has a traditional meaning roughly equivalent to
'magic spell' or 'charm', and is the Old Scottish variant of: 'grammar
. . . hence a magic spell, because occult practices were popularly
associated with learning.'

Is it possible that men and women of great wisdom and learning
cast a 'glamour' over the Giza necropolis at some point in the distant

past? Were they the possessors of as yet unguessed-at secrets that they wished to hide here? And did they succeed in concealing those secrets almost in plain view? For thousands of years, in other words, has the ancient Egyptian royal cemetary at Giza veiled the presence of something else – something of vastly greater significance for the story of Mankind?

One thing we are sure of is that unlike the hundreds of Fourth-Dynasty *mastaba* tombs to the west of the Sphinx and clustered around the three great Pyramids, the Pyramids themselves were never designed to serve primarily as burial places. We do not rule out the possibility that the Pharaohs Khufu, Khafre and Menkaure may at one time have been buried within them – although there is no evidence for this – but we are now satisfied that the transcendent effort and skill that went into the construction of these awe-inspiring monuments was motivated by a higher purpose.

We think that purpose was connected to the quest for eternal life wrapped up in a complete religious and spiritual system that the ancient Egyptians inherited from unknown predecessors and that they later codified in their eerie and other-worldly funerary and rebirth texts. We suggest, in short, that it was the goal of immortality, not just for one Pharaoh but for many, that the corridors and passages and hidden chambers and concealed gates and doorways of the Giza complex were ultimately designed to serve. Depicted in the *Book of What is in the Duat* as being filled with monsters, these narrow, claustrophobic, terrifying places, hemmed in on all sides by sheer stone walls, were in our view conceived as the ultimate testing ground for initiates. Here they would be forced to face and overcome their most horrible and debilitating fears. Here they would pass through unimaginable ordeals of the spirit and the mind. Here they would learn esoteric wisdom through acts of concentrated intelligence and will. Here they would be prepared, through practice and experience, for the moment of physical death and for the nightmares that would follow it, so that these transitions would not confuse or paralyse them – as they might other, unprepared, souls – and so that they might become 'equipped spirits' able to move as they wished through heaven and earth, 'unfailingly, and regularly and eternally'.[1]

Such was the lofty goal of the Horus-King's quest and the ancient

Egyptians clearly believed that in order to attain it the initiate would have to participate in the discovery, the unveiling, the *revelation*, of something of momentous importance – something that would bestow wisdom, and knowledge of the 'First Time', and of the mysteries of the cosmos, and of Osiris, the Once and Future King.

We are therefore reminded of a Hermetic Text, written in Greek but compiled in Alexandria in Egypt some 2000 years ago, that is known as the *Kore Kosmu* (or *Virgin of the World*).[2] Like other such writings, this text speaks of Thoth, the ancient Egyptian wisdom-god, but refers to him by his Greek name, Hermes:

> Such was all-knowing Hermes, who saw all things, and seeing understood, and understanding had the power both to disclose and to give explanation. For what he knew, he graved on stone; yet though he graved them onto stone he hid them mostly . . . The sacred symbols of the cosmic elements [he] hid away hard by the secrets of Osiris . . . keeping sure silence, that every younger age of cosmic time might seek for them.[3]

The text then tells us that before he 'returned to Heaven' Hermes invoked a spell on the secret writings and knowledge that he had hidden:

> O holy books, who have been made by my immortal hands, by incorruption's magic spells . . . free from decay throughout eternity remain, and incorrupt from time. Become unseeable, unfindable, for every one whose foot shall tread the plains of this land, until Old Heaven doth bring forth meet instruments for you . . .[4]

What instruments might lead to the recovery of 'unseeable and unfindable' secrets concealed at Giza?

Our research has persuaded us that a scientific language of precessional time and allegorical astronomy was deliberately expressed in the principal monuments there and in the texts that relate to them. From quite an early stage in our investigation, we hoped that this language might shed new light on the enigmatic civilization of Egypt. We did not at first suspect, however, that it would also turn out to encode specific celestial co-ordinates or that these would transpose onto the ground in the form of an arcane 'treasure map', directing the attention of seekers to a precise location in the bedrock deep beneath the Sphinx.

Nor did we suspect, until we met them, that others such as the Edgar Cayce Foundation and the Stanford Research Institute – see Part II – might already be looking there.

Osiris breathes

Throughout this investigation we have tried to stick to the facts, even when the facts have been very strange.

When we say that the Sphinx, the three Great Pyramids, the causeways and other associated monuments of the Giza necropolis form a huge astronomical diagram we are simply reporting a fact. When we say that this diagram depicts the skies above Giza in 10,500 BC we are reporting a fact. When we say that the Sphinx bears erosion marks which indicate that it was carved before the Sahara became a desert we are reporting a fact. When we say that the ancient Egyptians attributed their civilization to 'the gods' and to the 'Followers of Horus' we are reporting facts. When we say that these divine and human civilizers were remembered as having come to the Nile Valley in *Zep Tepi* – the 'First Time' – we are reporting a fact. When we say that the ancient Egyptian records tell us this 'First Time' was an epoch in the remote past, thousands of years before the era of the Pharaohs, we are reporting a fact.

Our civilization has had the scientific wherewithal to get to grips with the many problems of the Giza necropolis for less than two centuries, and it is only in the last two decades that computer technology has made it possible for us to reconstruct the ancient skies and see the patterns and conjunctions that unfolded there. During this period access to the site, and knowledge about it, has been monopolized by members of the archaeological and Egyptological professions who have agreed amongst themselves as to the origin, and age, and function of the monuments. New evidence which does not support this scholarly consensus, and which might actively undermine it, has again and again been overlooked, or sidelined, and sometimes even deliberately concealed from the public. This, we assume, is why everything to do with the shafts of the Great Pyramid

– their stellar alignments, the iron plate, the relics, and the discovery of the 'door' – has met with such peculiar and inappropriate responses from Egyptologists and archaeologists. And we assume that it explains, too, why the same scholars have paid such scant attention to the solid case that geologists have made for the vast antiquity of the Sphinx.[5]

The Giza monuments are a legacy for Mankind, preserved almost intact over thousands of years, and, outside the privileged circles of Egyptology and archaeology, there is today a broad-based expectation that they might be about to reveal a remarkable secret. That expectation may or may not prove to be correct. Nevertheless in an intellectual culture polarized by public anticipation and orthodox reaction, we feel it is only wise that future explorations at the necropolis should be conducted with complete 'transparency' and accountability. In particular the opening of the 'door' inside the southern shaft of the Queen's Chamber, the videoscopic examination of the northern shaft, and any further remote-sensing and drilling surveys conducted around the Sphinx, should be carried out under the scrutiny of the international mass media and should not again be subjected to bizarre and inexplicable delays.

We cannot predict what new discoveries will be made by such research, or even whether any new discoveries will be made. However, after completing our own archaeoastronomical investigation, and following the quest of the Horus-King, we are left with an enhanced sense of the tremendous mystery of this amazing site – a sense that its true story has only just begun to be told. Looking at the awe-inspiring scale and precision of the monuments we feel, too, that the purpose of the ancient master-builders was sublime, and that they did indeed find a way to initiate those who would come after – thousands of years in the future – by making use of the universal language of the stars.

They found a way to send a message across the ages in a code so simple and so self-explanatory that it might rightly be described as an anti-cipher.

Perhaps the time has come to listen to that clear, compelling signal that beckons to us out of the darkness of prehistory. Perhaps the time has come to seek the buried treasure of our forgotten genesis and destiny:

> Stars fade like memory the instant before dawn. Low in the east the sun appears, golden as an opening eye. That which can be named must exist. That which is named can be written. That which is written shall be remembered. That which is remembered lives. In the land of Egypt Osiris breathes . . .[6]

Appendix 1
The Scales of the World

'We three kings of Orion are;
Bearing gifts we traverse afar;
Field and fountain,
Moor and mountain,
Following yonder star.
Oh! Star of wonder, Star of might,
Star with royal beauty bright!
Westward leading,
Still proceeding,
Guide us to thy perfect light.
HE is the King of Glory.'

In her thesis on the astronomical content of ancient Egyptian funerary texts, Jane B. Sellers observes that Spell 17 of the *Book of the Dead*, which is drawn from extremely ancient sources, alludes in cosmic terms to the 'unification' or joining of the 'Two Lands':[1] 'Horus, son of Osiris and Isis . . . was made ruler in the place of his father, Osiris, on that day the Two Lands were united. It means the union of the Two Lands at the burial of Osiris . . .'[2]

Following this statement, Spell 17 also makes specific reference to the 'sun-god' and how he was not obstructed by the celestial river but rather 'passed on, having bathed in the Winding Waterway'.[3]

Sellers notes the conclusion of Yale astronomer-Egyptologist Virginia Lee Davis that the 'Winding Waterway' of the Pyramid Texts is to be equated with the Milky Way and that this feature of the sky 'divides' the cosmic landscape into two halves.[4] She then adds: 'I have contended that the joining of the two lands is a joining of sky to earth.'[5]

In fact, both Sellers and Davis arrive at the same conclusion, namely that the 'divider' of the celestial landscape is the Milky Way, and that which crosses it from one side to the other is the sun. Sellers also observes that the point of 'crossing' of the ecliptic path is near the V-shaped Hyades-Taurus constellation.[6]

If we seek to be precise about these matters we will discover that the point of crossing is in fact a little further east along the ecliptic path, marking a spot on the western shore of the Milky Way where today is found the M1 nebula, also known as the Crab Nebula.[7]

Sellers, oddly, does not pursue the logical sequence of events in Spell 17, namely that the sun continues along its journey, reaches the 'other side' (i.e. the eastern side) of the Milky Way, and thence heads towards the constellation of Leo. Indeed, Spell 17 bids the solar 'Horus', i.e. the sun-disc, to 'run, run to this' location: 'How well built is your House, O Atum, how well founded is your mansion, O Double Lion . . .'

Atum or Atum-Re, as was shown in *The Orion Mystery*, was originally venerated as a 'pillar' in Heliopolis which, as many researchers have concluded, was also seen as his 'phallus'.[8] A somewhat similar 'pillar', the so-called Djed pillar, was also associated with Osiris.[9] Bearing this in mind, Spell 17 makes a most telling statement: 'As for the Lion whose mouth is bright and whose head is shining, he is the Phallus of Osiris. Otherwise said, he is the Phallus of Re . . .'[10]

Earlier in Spell 17 we are specifically informed that Atum is:

> . . . in his sun-disc. Otherwise said he is Re when he rises in the eastern horizon of the sky.
>
> To me belongs yesterday, I know tomorrow.
>
> What does it mean? As for yesterday, that is Osiris. As for tomorrow, that is Re in which the foes of the Lord Of All were destroyed and Horus was made to rule. Otherwise said: That is the day of the 'We remain' festival, when the burial of Osiris was ordered by his father Re.
>
> The Battle-Ground of the gods was made in accordance with my command.
>
> What does it mean? It is the West. It was made for the souls of the gods in accordance with the command of Osiris, Lord of the Western Desert. Otherwise said: It means that this is the West, to which Re made every god descend and he fought for the Two [Lands] for it.
>
> I know that Great God who is in it.
>
> Who is he? It is Osiris . . .[11]

70. The Djed pillar of Osiris, flanked by Isis and Nepthys. Above it is the symbol of the Horian sun-god, probably marking the meridian-transit of the solar disc.

From this text we can see that a special 'land of the gods' was envisaged as having been established in the Western Desert at the time of the burial of Osiris – that is in the far-off epoch of the First Time. This was also the day on which Horus united the Two Lands and inherited this 'battle ground' or 'land of the gods'.

We have seen in earlier chapters how the Memphite Theology in the Shabaka Texts nominates the area in which these 'unification' events took place as Ayan near Memphis.[12] Oddly, the process of 'the Unification of the Two Lands' is also referred to in these same sources as 'the Balance of the Two Lands, in which Upper and Lower Egypt have been weighed . . .'[13]

In the present work we have brought forward additional evidence in support of Sellers's contention that the 'Two Lands' in question were indeed 'sky' and 'earth' and we have also shown that very specific parts of the sky and earth were meant – i.e. the 'Orion-Leo-Taurus' sky-region and the 'Giza-Heliopolis-Memphis' earth-region.

But how could these two sky-to-earth regions be 'balanced' and 'weighed'?

A state of perfect order

The point of 'balance' is defined on the ground as: '. . . Ayan, that was the division of the Two Lands . . . in the name of the "White Wall" [Memphis] . . .'[14]

We have seen how this terrestrial location corresponds to a point in the sky along the ecliptic path marking the spot on the western shore of the Milky Way where the M1 Crab Nebula is located.

A closer look at the Memphite Theology, however, reveals that while Ayan is envisaged as the pivot or 'balance point' of the Two Lands, the actual process of 'weighing' is described as taking place somewhere else – specifically in 'the land . . . [of the] burial of Osiris in the House of Sokar . . .'[15]

Since we have already demonstrated that 'the land of the House of Sokar' was Rostau, i.e. the Giza necropolis, we can conclude – by a simple transposition of sky–ground terminology – that the 'weighing' or 'balancing' of the land was somehow done at Giza, and most likely

Sun-boat on the back of the double-lion hieroglyph for
Aker. Below is a scene of revivification, showing the solar
path from east to west. Note the hawk's head beneath the
solar disc at the meridian.

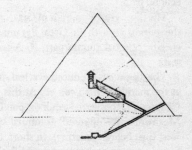

Great Pyramid, looking west

Osirian Djed pillar looking west with
'revivification' scene below. Compare this
to the schematic system of the Great
Pyramid. (Source: Papyrus of Pa-di-
amon, *circa* 1000 BC).

beside or within the Great Pyramid, the original 'House' of Sokar-Osiris.[16]

But why should the Great Pyramid have been seen as an 'instrument' by which the 'Two Lands' – sky and ground – could be 'balanced' at a specific spot, i.e. at Ayan-Memphis?

We must remind ourselves that the chronology and context of the 'unification' events was set way back in the cosmic landscape of the 'First Time'. Let us, therefore, transfer the imagery that now confronts us back to the epoch 10,500 BC, and see how the supposed 'perfect balance' was achieved at the cosmic 'Ayan', i.e. at the location, marked by the M1 Crab Nebula that we have already identified on the ecliptic path.

The three great Pyramids of Giza, of course, become Orion's belt at the meridian – with the Great Pyramid itself being represented by its specific celestial counterpart, *Al Nitak*, the lowest of the three belt stars.

The diagram reproduced overleaf shows Orion's belt with *Al Nitak* at the meridian in 10,500 BC. At this precise moment, as we saw in Chapter 17, the vernal-equinox point lay due east, just below Leo. Meanwhile the 'opposed' autumnal equinox point lay precisely due west (just below Aquarius). In short, this was a time when the 'Two Skies' – one on each side of the Milky Way – were in perfect balance, perfectly divided, just as the texts describe.

Much suggests that the 'Followers of Horus' envisaged the ecliptic path of the sun arching like the huge beam of a scale across the visible sky. One end of this beam was marked by Leo at the vernal-equinox point, and the other by Aquarius at the autumnal-equinox point. So, when *Al Nitak* came to rest at the celestial meridian on the vernal equinox in 10,500 BC the sky could rightly be said to have been in a state of perfect order.

Maat

Cosmic Order, in the symbolic terminology of the ancient Egyptians, was known as *Maat*. The same word also means 'justice' and 'law' – for example the justice that was exercised by the 'council of gods' of

Heliopolis when they judged in favour of Horus, after his conflict with Seth, and passed on to him the legacy of the Osirian throne.

The ancient Egyptian religious texts transmit details of one of the high rituals of the Osirian liturgy – the 'weighing of the soul' of the dead in the Great Judgement Hall of Osiris. This is a sort of archetypal 'Judgement of Solomon', with the weighing being done on the Great Scales of *Maat*.

The Papyrus of Ani in the British Museum provides us with a particularly vivid depiction of the Great Judgement Hall, and also of the Great Scales of *Maat*. These latter have a name – *Mekhaat* [17] – which means in other contexts 'the balance of the Earth'. [18]

The hieroglyphic determinative sign for the verb 'to weigh' shows a triangle, or builder's 'square', with a plumb-bob suspended from the

72. The Scales of *Maat*. (Source: British Museum papyrus 9901–3).

apex[19] – a sign which can also mean to 'balance the earth'.[20] The triangle distinctly recalls the profile or cross-section of a pyramid.

As we have seen in Part II of this book, a curious stone sphere, a length of wooden rod, and a bronze hook were found inside the Great Pyramid in 1872, sealed since the time of the construction of the monument in the shafts of the Queen's Chamber. Mr Henry Williams Chisholm, the Head of the Standards Department of the Board of Trade in London, carefully examined these relics in the year of their discovery and concluded that the sphere was most probably a standard weight and that the rod and hook might also have had functions connected with weighing and measuring. He published these conclusions in the prestigious journal, *Nature*, on 26 December 1872.

Similar views were held by the Astronomer Royal of Scotland, Charles Piazzi Smyth, who also examined the relics in 1872.[21]

And a certain Mr E. H. Pringle suggested in a letter to *Nature* that the stone sphere could have been a 'mason's plumb-bob' and that the 'bronze hook and the cedar rod may have formed part of the same tool'.[22]

A 'plumb-bob' of some sort must have been used to align the slopes of the shafts. And we have also seen how a 'plumb-bob' was used in the hieroglyphic sign meaning 'weighing' and, by extension, 'the balance'.

Perhaps the Great Pyramid – the terrestrial counterpart of the star *Al Nitak* – was seen as a weighing device or 'instrument' playing its part in some as yet unexplained attempt to restore the 'balance' or cosmic order of the world, i.e. *Maat*, as it was in the 'First Time'. Let us consider this possibility.

Juggling for balance

We saw in Chapter 3 that the Great Pyramid functions as a mathematical scale model of the northern hemisphere of the earth on a scale of 1:43,200.[23] By transposition and extension, therefore, it should be obvious that the monument can also serve as an architectural and mathematical representation of the northern hemisphere of the *sky*.[24]

Now if we look at a cross-section of the Great Pyramid, we notice that each of its two sets of 'star-shafts' – i.e. the northern and the southern in the King's and Queen's Chambers respectively – are theoretically intended to emerge at the same heights on the north and south faces of the monument. They appear to hang out like gigantic arms balancing, as it were, the whole geometrical scheme of the Pyramid. But there is something curious about the position of the two chambers from which these shafts emanate. The Queen's Chamber lies along the centre-line of the Pyramid. The King's Chamber, on the other hand, is offset somewhat to the south of the centre-line – almost as though the 'counterweight' on a huge set of scales had been slid to the left in order to achieve 'balance'.

The consequences of this curious architectural anomaly are as follows:

1 Queen's Chamber: the 'designed' average angle of the two shafts is 38 degrees 08', thus forming a right angle with the faces of the pyramid (51 degrees 52' + 38 degrees 08' = 90 degrees).[25]

2 King's Chamber: the 'designed' angle of the southern shaft is 45 00' and that of the northern shaft is 32 30'. This counteracts the effects of the offset of the chamber and restores the 'balance' of the general geometrical design.

The altitude of *Al Nitak* at the meridian in 2500 BC was 45 degrees – in line with the southern shaft of the King's Chamber. The reader will recall that the vernal point in this epoch was just over the Hyades-Taurus, whose terrestrial counterpart we have identified as the region of the Dahshur Pyramids.[26]

But let us see in what epoch *Al Nitak* would have crossed the meridian at 38 degrees 08' altitude – i.e. in alignment with the southern shaft of the *Queen's* Chamber?

Precessional calculations show that such an alignment would have occurred in *circa* 3850 BC – a date that is extremely close to that favoured by many earlier Egyptologists for the epoch of the 'Unification' which was supposedly sealed at Ayan-Memphis.[27] It is therefore surely of interest to note that in in 3850 BC the vernal point was positioned near the M1 Crab Nebula, the spot on the celestial landscape – and along the ecliptic path – that we have identified as the sky-counterpart of Ayan-Memphis.

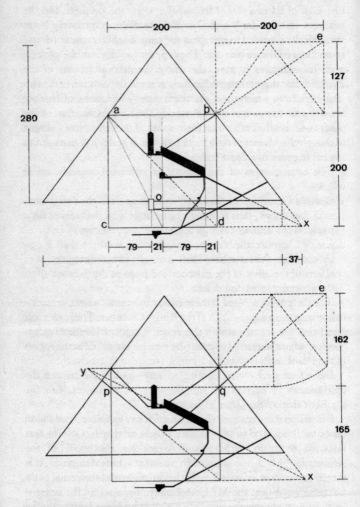

73. Cross-sections of the Great Pyramid showing the 'balancing' of the monument with the star-shafts.

Three Wise Men

In 10,500 BC the star *Al Nitak* in the belt of Orion was at the lowest altitude of its precessional cycle and Leo housed the vernal-equinox point. In our own epoch – the epoch of AD 2000 – the other extreme of the curious 'balancing mechanism' of Giza is about to be reached: *Al Nitak* today stands within a few arc seconds of the highest altitude that it will attain in its precessional cycle and the vernal point is about to drift into the constellation of Aquarius. Between the 'First Time' and the 'Last Time', in other words, the skies have reversed themselves – literally flipped left to right – with Aquarius now marking the vernal equinox and Leo marking the autumnal equinox.

We wonder whether it is possible that the sages of Heliopolis, working at the dawn of history, could somehow have created an archetypal 'device', a device designed to trigger off messianic events across the 'Ages' – the Pyramid Age when the vernal point was in Taurus, for example, the Christic Age in Pisces,[28] and perhaps even a 'New Age' in Aquarius?

We note in this connection that in *circa* 330 BC, when the vernal point was beginning its precessional drift into the 'Age of Pisces', the altitude of *Al Nitak* (viewed from the latitude of Giza) was 51 degrees 52' – the angle of slope of the Great Pyramid. At this time the conquests of Alexander the Great (356–323 BC), and the resulting merger of the Eastern and Western worlds, triggered great expectations of a messianic 'Return' in the East. First at Alexandria, then across the Levant, a general agitation began, as if triggered by some prophetic 'device', which culminated in the great messianic events of Christianity.[29]

The three stars of Orion's belt are depicted in the folklore of many countries as the heraldic 'Three Wise Men', or 'Kings', or 'Magi' from the East, who feature in the Christic nativity story.[30] Interestingly, as we saw in Part I, the star-worshipping Sabians of Harran – archetypal Magi – appear to have performed annual pilgrimages to Giza from at least as far back as the second millennium BC until as late as the eleventh century AD.[31] Interestingly, too, as seen from Harran – which is east of Bethlehem and at a higher latitude than Giza – the belt star *Al Nitak* would have culminated at the meridian at 51 degrees 52'

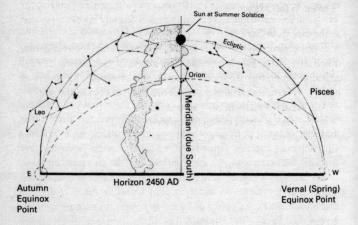

Autumn
Equinox
Point

Vernal (Spring)
Equinox Point

74. The sky as will be seen in 2450 AD at the 'Last Time' of Orion. Note the vernal (spring) equinox in the west.

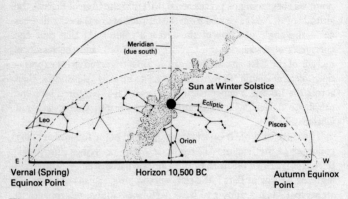

Vernal (Spring)
Equinox Point

Autumn Equinox
Point

The sky as was seen in 10,500 BC at the 'First Time' of Orion. Note the vernal (spring) equinox to the east.

in 4 BC, the generally accepted birth year of Christ. In that year also the 'birth star' Sirius would have risen and been brightly visible in the east as the sun set at dusk.[32]

Is there something – some ancient tradition, veiled, but still very much alive, that is subtly carrying blueprints and plans across the ages aimed at generating messianic fervour, and changing the course of history, at certain crucial moments which are 'written in the stars'?

And is such a moment now approaching?

Is the 'device' about to reactivate itself?

We shall return to these questions in our next book.

Appendix 2

Precession, Proper Motion and Obliquity

Determining the positions of the bright stars Regulus, Sirius and Alnitak in the remote past.

Unlike the fixed coordinates of latitude and longitude used by the cartographer to determine the position of a feature on a terrestrial map, the astronomer's charts have to be redrawn periodically owing to the continually changing coordinates of the stars. This is largely due to the effects of precession, with numerous other small quantities, which we shall investigate shortly, manifesting themselves over long periods of time.

The change in position of any given star is gradual and, what with the number of complex trigonometric and polynomial calculations to be performed, this was immensely frustrating to the archaeoastronomer seeking to determine the age of an architectural structure through a suspected alignment with a prominent celestial body in the pre-computer era. Fortunately, however, the vast majority of these effects can be allowed for in calculations performed by desktop computers running dedicated astronomical software.

Precession:

The Earth orbits the Sun in an almost invariable plane, known as the ecliptic, and its axis of rotation in space is currently inclined to the perpendicular of this plane (i.e. a line joining the north and south poles of the ecliptic) by an angle of about 23.4°. This angle, which varies slightly and somewhat unpredictably over large periods of time, is known as the obliquity and is the cause of our seasonal variations.

As Sir Isaac Newton was first to explain, the precession of the Earth can be best illustrated through drawing an analogy with a spinning top: with both the Sun and Moon exerting a gravitational influence on our planet's equatorial bulge (the so-called lunisolar precession) the Earth's axis describes a circle with a radius of almost 23.4° about the north pole of the ecliptic once in a period of just under 26,000 years.

A product of general precession (that is, the sum of lunisolar precession and planetary precession, the latter being due to the gravitational influences of the other members of the Solar System) is the slow westward movement of the spring and autumn equinoxes along the ecliptic on opposing sides of the celestial sphere by about 50.3" (arc-seconds) per annum, or 1° every 71.6 years.

This means that the vernal equinox, where the Sun crosses the celestial equator from south to north every spring, moves backwards through the zodiac (the band of sky immediately either side of the ecliptic at the rate of one constellation every 2100 years or so. At present the vernal (spring) equinox lies in the constellation of Pisces, bordering on Aquarius. Most authorities attribute the discovery of precession to Hipparchus in 130 BC, but there is strong evidence to support the theory that the ancient Egyptians were a society aware of its effects. A rigorous mathematical treatment of precession appears in Appendix II of *The Orion Mystery* (pages 242–249).

Nutation:

The slow precessional circle of the Earth's axis around the poles of the ecliptic is not perfectly circular, but wavy: it is subject to small periodic 'nods' to and fro (nutation means 'nodding'), the chief component of which has a period of 18.6 years and an amplitude close to 9 arc-seconds – too small to be perceived by the naked eye. The culprit is the Moon and the effect is due to its relative proximity, changing position with respect to the Sun and distance.

Aberration of starlight:

Another correction that has to be applied to the mean position of a star, which is also imperceptible to the naked eye, is due to the finite velocity of light and the Earth's orbital speed about the Sun of about 30 kilometres per second. This has the effect of displacing the position of a star by anything up to 20 arc-seconds, or 1/180th of a degree.

Proper motion:

All stars are travelling through space. Younger stars that have only recently (cosmically speaking) emerged from the stellar nurseries of gas and dust where they were born tend to move as a loosely bound cluster (the Pleiades or 'Seven Sisters' in the constellation of Taurus are one such example), gradually splitting up and changing direction with time under external gravitational influences.

The quantity we term proper motion is the motion of the star perpendicular to our line of sight and is usually split into two components. These are right ascension and declination, which are the two principal coordinates used on the celestial sphere which are analogous to latitude and longitude on the Earth. The movements are small owing to the immense distances of the stars, but the effects are cumulative and reveal themselves during the long periods of archaeoastronomical investigation.

The largest proper motion known belongs to a stellar body, Barnard's Star, which traverses the sky at a rate of 10.3 arc-seconds per year, or a degree every 350 years. The brightest star, Sirius, also has a relatively large proper motion in declination of about -1.21 arc-seconds per annum, travelling in a southerly direction with respect to the background stars covering a distance equivalent to the width of the Full Moon every 1500 years or so.

Refraction:

Next to long-term precession, this phenomenon introduces the largest displacement of a star's apparent position that the researcher is likely to encounter, yet the cause is close to hand and only noticeably effects objects that are close to the horizon. When observing a star at a very low altitude we are looking obliquely through a thick layer of atmosphere which has a slight lenticular effect, bending the light rays slightly and making the object appear higher in the sky that it really is. Refraction also makes celestial bodies rise earlier and set later than calculations would otherwise suggest. Even so, the largest displacement of a star close to the horizon is in the region of 0.6°, or slightly larger than the Full Moon.

Obliquity:

The present 23.4° inclination of the Earth's axis to the ecliptic is not fixed and for the last few centuries it has been decreasing slightly. If high precision is required, then the following empirical polynomial expression is valid for about 500 years, where T is the number of Julian centuries of 36,525 ephemeris days from the 1900.0 epoch:

$$\text{Obliquity} = 23.452294° - 0.0130125° \ T - 0.00000164° \ T^2 + 0.000000503° \ T^3$$

However, over longer periods of time, the formula begins to break down and other methods have to be employed. These largely rely on mathematical models of the Solar System as applied to the Earth/Moon system. The largest uncertainty in the computation of the obliquity by this method arises from the unpredictable changes of dynamical ellipticity of the Earth that can occur during an ice age. An intensely mathematical treatment of the matter is given by Laskar, Joutel and Boudin in the *Journal of Astronomy and Astrophysics*, na270, pp.522–533 (1993). From their findings, the apparent limits of the obliquity are 22° to 24.5°, though these values are far from certain.

Computing the positions of Regulus, Sirius and Alnitak in the past:

Applying corrections for the principal terms discussed above with a program called Sky Chart 2000.0 running on an Apple Macintosh computer, the following data was obtained at various dates for the stars Regulus, Sirius and Alnitak which reside in the constellations Leo, Canis Major and Orion, respectively:

	Regulus		Sirius		Alnitak	
Epoch:	Right Ascension	Declination	Right Ascension	Declination	Right Ascension	Declination
2000 AD	10h 08.4m	+11° 58'	06h 45.2m	−16° 43'	05h 40.8m	−01° 57'
2500 BC	05h 50.7m	+24° 10'	03h 28.0m	−20° 52'	02h 02.1m	−15° 03'
7500 BC	01h 12.2m	+07° 28'	23h 39.8m	−44° 22'	21h 45.1m	−42° 19'
10,500 BC	22h 34.5m	−10° 25'	20h 12.0m	−58° 43'	17h 58.3m	−50° 34'
Altitudes at culmination:						
2000 AD		+72.0°		+43.3°		+58.0°
2500 BC		+84.2°		+39.1°		+44.9°
7500 BC		+67.5°		+15.6°		+17.7°
10,500 BC		+49.6°		+01.6°		+09.5°
The Proper Motion taken is:	Right Ascension	Declination	Right Ascension	Declination	Right Ascension	Declination
	−0.017s	+0.003"	−0.038s	−1.211"	−0.000s	−0.002"

[Note: Sky Chart 2000.0 was written by Tim DeBenedictis and is available as shareware from Macintosh libraries or the internet via anonymous FTP from lpl.seds.arizona.edu]

Appendix 3

Correspondence with Mark Lehner
Concerning Chapter 5

The Egyptologist Mark Lehner was sent the first draft of Chapter 5 of this book, a chapter that largely concerns himself. His comments and corrections were taken into account, and the draft was rewritten in the form that is published herewith. When Dr Lehner was sent the revised draft he wrote us the following letter making further comments which we agreed to reproduce in full as an Appendix. Our own reply to Dr Lehner's letter is also appended.

From: Mark Lehner
To: Mr Robert G. Bauval and Mr Graham Hancock

November 16, 1995

Dear Graham and Robert,

Thank you for your letter of 12 November 1995 and for the second draft of your Chapter 5, 'The Case of the Psychic, the Scholar And the Sphinx'(!). It appears to be much more accurate than the first draft concerning the events of which I was a part.

I have the following observations to make and corrections to suggest (again open to the public):

p. 90: 'his pronouncements . . . spawned multi-million dollar industry . . . embroiled . . . with mainstream Egyptological research . . . first learned about . . . when reviewing . . . Mark Lehner.'

Do you mean to convey that Cayce alone (without theosophy, anthroposophy, freemasonry, astrology, sacred metrology, channeling, UFO aficionados, and Shirley MacClaine) spawned a multi-million dollar industry that fed directly into my involvement with Egyptology? That would be a little absurd.

p. 96: 'The equipment for RSI's work . . . Immediately afterwards the project was stopped.'

This is still not quite right. The drilling equipment was tested and used elsewhere, for example, west of the Second Pyramid, before it was brought down for the two holes in the Sphinx Temple. The project was not stopped immediately afterwards. RSI/SRI drilled two more holes in the southeast corner of the floor of the Sphinx and under the south forepaw of the Sphinx. Then the project kind of fizzled to an end because of the falling out between RSI and SRI and, as I remember, because the SRI team had been in Egypt for a couple of months or more and had other work.

p. 96: 'did not appreciate . . . led to . . . falling out between RSI and SRI.'

As I recall, although RSI did not appreciate particularly the Cayce involvement, the falling out between RSI and SRI was over fiduciary issues. Why don't you contact SRI and ask them?

p. 97: 'Adding to the intrigue . . . yet another project financed by the Edgar Cayce Foundation.'

You do want to hang on to that intrigue! No, this was not yet another project. The down-hole immersion acoustical sounding was done in the last days of SRI's fieldwork at the Sphinx in 1978, not 1982, not another project. I do not have, at present, a copy of this *Venture Inward* but if it says this is another project in 1982, it is wrong. All that I describe in the quote you excerpted happened the last few days of the 1978 project.

p. 98: 'a survey, as the reader will recall, ... abrupt halt ... Antiquities Organization.'

You seem inclined to see 'abrupt halts'. You should not cite me to verify this point because I was not at these events, but my impression is that Schoch, West, and Dobecki were not thwarted in their first season of work at the Sphinx. Permission for such work is granted or denied by a large committee of the Supreme Council for Antiquities (formerly Egyptian Antiquities Organization).

p. 99: 'Pulling Away. When, exactly, Professor Lehner began to pull away from the influence of the Edgar Cayce Foundation and crossed over into the mainstream of professional Egyptology and its orthodoxy is not especially clear.'

Are you suggesting, based on your own understanding of how belief systems operate, that there are definite lines where 'now you believe' and 'now you don't'? You seem particularly interested in this question. The way you frame it reminds me of the US Congressional hearings on the Watergate cover-up conspiracy: 'What did the President know, and when did he know it?' 'What did Lehner believe, and when did he not believe it?!'

Let me offer some biography to use if you so choose.

I already had doubts when I went to Egypt in 1973, since Cayce's ancient history did not agree much with anthropology courses I took at the University of North Dakota. But as I indicated in my last letter,

I did indeed have hopes that evidence could be found of past events bearing some agreement with Cayce's story.

During my two years at the American University in Cairo I majored in anthropology, and took my first courses in Egyptian archaeology and prehistory. I also spent most of my free time at Giza, and I visited other ancient sites and archaeological projects. I did not 'find footprints of the gods'. By becoming acquainted with a vast amount of previous archaeological research with which the Cayce community and like-minded Egypt-enthusiasts are only minimally familiar, I found the 'footprints' of people – their tool marks, names, family relationships, skeletons, and material culture.

In 1974 I read social psychologist Leon Festinger's work on 'cognitive dissonance', in particular his book, *When Prophecy Fails*. Festinger deals with people reacting to conflict between a *revealed* belief system and empirically derived information, that is, physical evidence. In his work, I recognized many attributes of the Cayce worldview, my own belief, and my growing doubts.

When I returned to Virginia Beach I would outline in lectures and conversations the real achaeological evidence surrounding the Sphinx and the Pyramids and its conflict with the Cayce picture of Egypt. I spoke to my good friends and supporters, like Hugh Lynn and Joseph Jahoda (are your two unnamed ARE men supposed to remain as mysterious as 'The Scholar'?), about my doubts, and how the Cayce community and belief system fits many aspects discussed by Festinger and other social scientists.

In these talks I began to suggest to the Cayce community that they look at the Egypt/Atlantis story as a myth in the sense that Joseph Campbell popularized, or that Carl Jung drew upon in his psychology of archetypes. Although the myth is not *literally true*, it may in some way be literarily *true*. The Cayce 'readings' themselves say, in their own way, that the inner world of symbols and archetypes is more 'real' than the particulars of the physical world. I compared Cayce's Hall of Records to the Wizard of Oz. Yes, we all want the 'sound and fury' and powerful wizardry to be real, without having to pay attention to the little man behind the curtain (ourselves). In archaeology, many dilettantes and New Agers want to be on the trail of a lost civilization, aliens, yes, 'the gods', without having to pay attention to the real people behind time's curtain and without having to deal with the difficult subject matter upon which so-called 'orthodox' scholars base their views.

(An aside: So a John West can blast Egyptologists for suppressing the sacred science inherent in Egyptian culture without being able to read Egyptian language – a little like saying one knows Shakespeare's real meaning without reading English. Another pyramid theorist said, in an animated dinner conversation, 'Where's the evidence? The pyramid stands out there with no evidence of how the ancient Egyptians could have built it.' I ticked off four Egyptological titles – all in English – devoted to ancient Egyptian tools, technology, stone building, and materials and industries. Although he had published a widely acclaimed book with a new theory on the pyramids, he admitted to not having read a single one of these basic works. It would be so much more fun and challenging if such theorists did actually read and absorb such primary sources, and then launched the dialogue.)

These ideas were on my mind as I joined my first 'mainstream' excavation in 1976. They are reflected in my statement that the Hall of Records is worth looking for, but not in a tangible way. You know, like the Holy Grail.

In 1977–78 I had the opportunity not only to work with the SRI project at Giza, but also to work with Zahi Hawass in excavations of ancient deposits neglected by earlier archaeologists in the northeast corner of the Sphinx floor – just beside the north forepaw, and on the floor of the Sphinx Temple. We recovered pottery, parts of stone tools, and other material directly on the floor, filling deep crevasses and nooks and crannies – material in contexts that only make sense as left by the Old Kingdom Sphinx and pyramid builders.

Such findings, and the negative results of the SRI project, sealed it for me. That is, I knew there was an extremely low probability that Cayce's story of Egypt and the Giza monuments (and his ancient 'history' involving Atlantis, etc.) reflected real events.

My interest in the Cayce-like genre of literature as having anything to do with the archaeological record was gone, although I am still interested in this genre as a social and literary phenomenon. My encounters with bedrock reality were far more fascinating. I was excited by the process of reconstructing the past from empirical evidence. I put aside my interest in the dynamics of beliefs, and in general questions of philosophy and religion, as I spent the next decade doing archaeological fieldwork for projects at various places in Egypt. At Giza, my interest and research was no longer premised on Cayce or any similar point of view. In 1982 I carried out the research and writing for an Egyptological monograph on the tomb of Hetepheres (published in 1985 by the German Archaeological Institute). Cayce ideas had nothing to do with this work.

Meanwhile Hugh Lynn Cayce (until he died), Charles Thomas Cayce and other members of the Cayce community remained very close friends. Some (but not all) were still interested in contributing to research at Giza. Their support of the Pyramids Radiocarbon Dating Project was a way to do something useful for the archaeology of the pyramids, as well as to *test* their ideas about the origin and date of the Great Pyramid and Sphinx.

I remember a very personal moment in 1983 when I was working for an expedition at Abydos, the cult center of Osiris in Upper Egypt. The tombs of Egypt's earliest pharaohs were sunk into a spur of low desert far to the west of the cultivation, near the base of the great cleft in the high cliffs, probably seen by the ancients as symbolizing the entrance to the Netherworld. Many centuries later, one of the tombs of a real man who ruled as one of the First Dynasty kings was outfitted as the Tomb of Osiris. Over subsequent centuries hundreds of pilgrims left pottery offerings, resulting in mounds of millions of shards that masked the site, prompting its Arabic name, Umm el-Qa-ab, 'Mother of Pots'. One evening near sunset I walked from the dig house to Umm el-Qa-ab. I stood on the mounds above these tombs and wondered if the ancient pilgrims really believed the god Osiris himself was buried here, and if 'those who sit near the temple' (as a Zen proverb would say) – the local priests – knew they had simply outfitted one of the First Dynasty tombs of a pharaoh to 'symbolize' the burial of Osiris. I thought of my own pilgrimage that brought me to Egypt in the first place, and the myth of the Hall of Records. I realized that this was part of a worldview that had moved far away from me, like a chunk of ice that had separated from a continent and was now melting in a distant sea.

Sorry to be so long-winded. But Graham, I agree with your statement in your last letter that readers should be in possession of the facts to evaluate the opinions of academic authorities.

Sincerely,

Mark Lehner

PS Details: It probably does not matter much for a popular readership, but the difference between an Assistant Professor – my title at the Oriental Institute – and Professor is significant in the tenure-track world. I resigned my fulltime post, but I am still a Visiting Assistant Professor at the University of Chicago and Oriental Institute, I return every other year to teach.

cc: Bruce Ludwig
        Douglas Rawls

To: Mark Lehner
From: Graham Hancock

8 December 1995

Dear Mark,

Thank you for your further letter of 16 November 1995 in response to our revised draft of Chapter 5. We greatly appreciate your openness.

If you have no objections, we propose to publish the revised draft of Chapter 5 as you have seen it and to publish your 16 November 1995 letter in full as an appendix to our book. We consider this to be a fair and reasonable way to present the whole matter to the public. If we don't hear back from you in the next couple of weeks we will assume this is OK with you.

Merry Christmas and a happy New Year!

Warm best wishes,

Graham Hancock

PS We remember one Egyptological title (not four) that you 'ticked off' during a certain 'animated dinner conversation'. The one title was Clarke and Engelbach's *Ancient Egyptian Construction and Architecture*. We've both read it since and weren't overly impressed. Robert Bauval, as you know, is a construction engineer by training and spent twenty years actually *building* enormous buildings in the Middle East. In my opinion – Clarke and Engelbach notwithstanding – this gives him a rather good basis from which to engage in 'fun and challenging' dialogue about the construction logistics of the Great Pyramid. There's no substitute for real experience no matter how many 'primary sources' we 'read and absorb'. (And by the way, in what sense are Clarke and Engelbach a primary source? Were they present when the Pyramid was built? Did they build it?)

Appendix 4

Harnessing Time with the Stars: The Hermetic Axiom 'As Above So Below' and the Horizon of Giza

An observer at Giza, as anywhere else on the globe where the horizontal view is not obstructed, will perceive the landscape as a huge circle whose edge is the horizon with himself at the centre – hence the term 'Horizon' used by the ancients when referring to the Giza necropolis. Making apparent contact with the horizon is the *celestial landscape*, the latter perceived as a huge circular dome or hemisphere.

The 'below', earth-landscape, is steadfast. The 'above', sky-landscape, however, appears to rotate in perpetual motion around an imaginary axis which passes through the two poles of the earth and extends to the 'celestial poles' in the sky. The apparent rotation of the sky makes the celestial orbs – the stars, the sun, the moon and the planets – rise in the east, culminate at the meridian (an imaginary loop running due north-south directly over the observer's head) and set in the west.

Observations of sunrise through the year will fix four distinct points, sometimes called the colures, on the ecliptic path of the sun around the twelve zodiacal constellations. These are the two equinoxes (spring and autumn), and the two solstices (summer and winter). Today these take place in the following zodiacal signs:

1 Spring equinox (21 March) with the sun in Pisces.
2 Summer solstice (21 June) with the sun in Taurus.
3 Autumn equinox (22 September) with the sun in Virgo.
4 Winter solstice (21 December) with the sun in Sagittarius.

The table below shows in which zodiacal signs the four 'colures' fell for a variety of different epochs:

EPOCH	10,000 BC	5000 BC	3000 BC	1000 BC	2500 AD
S. Equinox	Leo	Gemini	Taurus	Aries	Aquarius
S. Solstice	Scorpio	Virgo	Leo	Cancer	Taurus
A. Equinox	Aquarius	Sagittarius	Scorpio	Libra	Leo
W. Solstice	Taurus	Pisces	Aquarius	Capricorn	Scorpio

Strictly speaking, the term 'colures' denotes the two great circles of the celestial sphere which are at right angles to each other, pass through the poles and intersect the two equinox points and the two solstice points respectively.

The diurnal or daily apparent motion of sun is from east to west. The annual or yearly apparent motion is much slower from west to east against the background of the starry landscape through a path known as the ecliptic, or zodiacal circle (containing the twelve zodiacal signs). Also because of the phenomenon of the precession of the equinoxes, the four points on the colures (the two equinoxes and the two solstices) will appear to drift westwards at the very slow rate of 50.3 arc-seconds per year (a full circuit in approximately 25, 920 years).

These apparent cyclical motions of the sky are, of course, caused not by the sky itself moving but by the earth's own spin on its axis in one day, its orbital revolution around the sun in one year, and its slow wobble-like motion in one Great Year (of 25,920 'solar' years). As we have already said, the most noticeable effect of the letter is that the four points on the colures which mark the two equinoxes and the two solstices on the ecliptic, will drift in clockwise direction along the great ecliptic or 'zodiacal' circle.

Every day there is a moment when these four points on the colures find themselves in precise alignment with the four cardinal points of the terrestrial globe defined by the directions due east, due south, due west and due north on the circle of the horizon. This is when it can be said that the sky and earth are a 'reflection' of each other. In archaic terminology, this is when the 'Hermetic' axiom of 'as above so below' can be most faithfully expressed.

At this exact moment the colure containing the two solstice points will be looping above the head of the observer from north to south, and thus becomes the prime meridian of the observer. The colure which contains the two equinox points will loop from east to west and will intersect the horizon at due east to due west, and thus define the parallel of the observer. Again, using archaic terminology, this is when the observer is at the 'centre of the visible universe'.

A simple yet quite precise way of knowing when this idealistic 'as above so below' conjunction takes place is to make use of a bright star that sits on the colure containing the two solstice points. The choice of a bright star on the colure as near to the winter solstice point as possible, will permit the observer to lock the sky in the most favourable condition possible: the precise moment of the rising of the vernal (spring) point in the east. This is simply achieved by waiting for the star in question to transit the south meridian. When this happens, the winter solstice point is due south, and all the other colures lock to the remaining cardinal directions.

The effect of the precession of the vernal point, however, will cause the chosen star to change position with time. After a century or so the star can no longer be used.

The Great Pyramid is often said to be perfectly set to the four cardinal points. What seems more likely, as we shall see, is that it is set perfectly to the four colure points when they transit the cardinal directions. The setting-out of the Pyramid, therefore, is not merely directional but also, and perhaps more especially, dependent on 'time'.

In 1934 the French astronomer E.M. Antoniadi correctly noted that the 'astronomical character of the pyramids (of Giza) is established by the following facts:

1. They are almost exactly, and intentionally, on the thirteth parallel of the latitude North.

2. They are marvellously orientated on the cardinal points.

3. Their inclined passageways were, with their closing, colossal meridian instruments, by far the largest ever constructed.' [1]

These confirmed facts, and also the fact that the Great Pyramid is a near-perfect mathematical model of the celestial dome or hemisphere, make this monument a material and earthly representation of the sky-landscape. When linked to a specific star, however, the element of 'time' is introduced into the equation.

We recall that the ancient builders fixed the main north-south axis of the Great Pyramid to the south meridian transit of the bright star Alnitak, the lowest of the three stars in Orion's belt. We also recall that the general layout of the three Pyramids of Giza is at 45 degrees to the meridian axis and that this peculiarity, in turn, is reflected in the sky-image of the three stars in Orion's belt as they appeared in c.10,500 BC. This was no arbitrary date, however, because it denoted the lowest point or 'First Time' in the precessional cycle of Orion. To the ancients, Orion was 'Osiris', and the latter, too, had a 'First Time' or genesis.

Computer reconstructions of the ancient skies of 10,500 BC show that the star Alnitak was located precisely on the colure containing the two solstice points, and nearer to the winter solstice. If an observer was there to 'lock' the perfect 'as above so below' condition in 10,500 BC, the image of the sky containing the star Alnitak would convert into a 'hologram' on the ground precisely in the manner we find at Giza today. That such a perfect sky-to-earth correlation cannot be the result of some incredible 'coincidence' is confirmed by the equinoctial rising of Leo, which took place in precisely the same epoch of 10,500 BC and precisely when the star Alnitak transited the south meridian. This brought the vernal (spring) equinox point in perfect alignment with the Great Sphinx, the terrestrial counterpart of the image of Leo. The conclusion thus seems inevitable: the ancients appear to have established a global prime-meridian at Giza locked into the time frame of 10,500 BC.

All this implies, however, that the ancients were somehow

attempting to 'navigate' not only in distance ('space') but also in 'time'. What did they have in mind? How can 'time' be navigated?

Hypothetically at least, a time-related apparatus locked into the colures of 10,500 BC would present the 'reincarnated' Horus-king with a subliminal landscape or 'magical theatre', at the height of his extensive initiation, to work out intuitively how far in time his 'soul' had travelled from its point of genesis. In Parts III and IV of this book we have shown how the Horus-king may have used the phenomenon of the precession of the equinoxes to perform such a task by inducing his mind to undertake a journey or quest to find his 'ancestors' using the subliminal architectural setting or 'cosmic ambiance' of Giza as some sort of 'star-memory' device. Today we use a computer to re-create the ancient skies on a television monitor. We are suggesting that the Horus-king initiate could perform this task intuitively with the 'computer' of his mind and the 'monitor' of his inner perception. This conclusion does not present a problem to us. We have found that by fully familiarising ourselves with the apparent motions of the skies and by constantly reconstructing ancient skies with the aid of computers, images, coordinates and epochs subliminally enter the mind and become logged in the memory. We have discovered for ourselves that these 'flies' are easily retrieved at will without the mechanistic aid of the computer. Hypothetically then, with such 'star-memory' logged in the mind, should we suddenly find ourselves flung into a future 'time zone', say AD 6000, we could relatively easily 'work out' how far ahead in time we have moved.

By extension of such rhetoric, therefore, it could be said that the function of the Giza blueprint is to provide a virtually indestructable 'holographic' apparatus for the use of 'reincarnated' or 'reborn' entities of the Horian lineage in order to induce 'remembrance' of a 'divine' genetic origin in Egypt in the time-frame of 10,500 BC. The ultimate function, however, appears to have been to perpetuate the 'immortality' of their souls into 'time' – in short, the ultimate *gnostic* experience entailing the release of the spiritual part of the living entity from its material, inert, part. To put it in other terms, 'living' man is the result of a holographic union between matter and spirit. It would very much appear that the 'Followers of Horus' understood the cosmic mechanism to somehow reseparate the two.

Such questions, we are well aware, lead us into the misty realm of metaphysics, extrasensory perception and psychic thinking from which we have tried to steer clear. Nonetheless, we must respond to our intuitive feeling that a form of metaphysical thinking very much like this was used to those mysterious 'Followers of Horus' who set their initiatory and 'astronomical' academy at Heliopolis – and whose genius resulted in the construction of the amazing 'holographic' star/stone (spirit/matter) apparatus of Giza. All references in the ancient texts to this mysterious brotherhood suggest that we are dealing not with 'priests' but with high adepts who fully understood the working of the human psyche and the subliminal techniques needed to evoke 'remote memory' through deep-felt inner perceptions of 'time'. The esoteric teachings and initiations into such cosmic mysteries using the skies are certainly not prosaic ones, as Egyptologists maintain, to develop and refine calendrical systems for 'land irrigation' and 'religious ceremonies', but far more subtle: somehow to reach and harness the extrasensory capabilities of the human mind in order to link up to the invisible and immaterial, yet very perceptible, 'flux of time'.

The questions, for those looking for 'scientific' explanations, can be formulated in another way: Do we humans carry 'remote memory files' locked in our genes? And if so, can it not be possible that such 'files' could be retrieved by using the correct subliminal keys?

More provocative still: is our 'consciousness' umbilically linked to 'time' such that it merely passes through biological matter, ourselves, like a thread passing through pearl's and stones?

It has long been appreciated by students of intellectual history that monumental architecture and archetypal imgaes can serve as powerful subliminal devices to evoke dormant 'memory' in the minds of those who are made receptive through initiation. The murals and panels of gothic cathedrals or the painted ceilings such as those in the Sistine Chapel are but obvious examples of such powerful mind-games – aptly called 'silent poetry' by the fourth century BC poet, Simonides of Ceos. These ancient memory-aids, and the techniques refined for using them, which are loosely termed 'mnemotechnics' today, were the subject of a major thesis by Dame Frances A. Yates in 1966 entitled *The Art of Memory*. In this book Yates shows that powerful cerebral techniques were taught in ancient Greece which were rooted in the so-called 'Egyptian hermetic tradition'.[2] Recently, the author Murry Hope, in a thesis entitled *Time the Ultimate Energy*, tackled the complex subject of 'time travel' as a form of energy, and suggested that pre-dynastic Egyptian adepts may have understood and harnessed 'time' through a yet-to-be discovered ability to break away from the confines of biological 'time' and into another mental realm of time-perception. Murry Hope termed this realm 'Outer Time'. Likewise, in another recent study, *From Atlantis to the Sphinx*, the author and philosopher Colin Wilson boldly proposes that the ancients may have cultivated powerful extrasensory capabilities through 'a different knowledge system' based on intuitive thinking (as opposed to rationalistic or 'solar' thinking) in order to enter higher states of consciousness. Such higher consciousness might have been the key into altered perceptions of 'time'.

That such untapped abilities to perceive dilated time-fields might be an intrinsic part of human mental machinery was very seriously investigated by one of America's most prestigious scientific foundations, the Stanford Research Institute in California – better known as SRI International. In 1972 SRI International was recruited as main consultant for the so-called remote viewing programmes run by the CIA and other government agencies including the US navy, the US army and the US Defence Intelligence Agency (DIA). These programmes were managed by a highly respected physicist, Dr Hal Puthoff, who sought out and employed renowned psychics (called 'remote viewers' in SRI jargon) to 'locate' enemy military targets and installations using extrasensory capabilities.

The reader will recall that SRI International (which has been described as 'America's second largest think-tank') was also, in 1973, involved in high-tech archaeological projects in Egypt and, at least on one occasion, worked in participation with the Edgar Cayce Foundation (ECF) in a series of remote sensing projects at Giza (see Chapter Five).

Many 'remote viewers' involved in the remote viewing programmes, such as the psychic Ingo Swann and Nel Riley, the latter a sergeant in the US army, openly claimed to have the inner abilities to undertake a form of 'time travel' into any remote locations on the globe. Such claims are in many ways reminiscent of those made by the Edgar Cayce adepts who maintain that, when in an altered state of consciousness such as deep trance or hypnosis, thay can 'remember' past lives i.e. 'time travel' mentally to remote locations. Cayce himself, who is dubbed America's best-known medium and psychic, claimed to have had a previous life in Egypt in 10,500 BC – a claim which at one time, as we have seen in Chapter Five, was considered worthy of investigation by Egyptologist Mark Lehner in the early 1970s within the framework of his scientific research at Giza.

Appendix 5

Carbon-dating the Great Pyramid: Implications of a little-known Study

The evidence presented in this book concerning the origins and antiquity of the monuments of the Giza necropolis suggests that the genesis and original planning and layout of the site may be dated, using the tools of modern computer-aided archaeoastronomy, to the epoch of 10,500 BC. We have also argued, on the basis of a combination of geological, architectural and archaeoastronomical indicators, that the Great Sphinx, its associated megalithic 'temples', and at least the lower courses of the so-called 'Pyramid of Khafre', may in fact have been built at that exceedingly remote date.

It is important to note that we do not date the construction of the Great Pyramid to 10,500 BC. On the contrary, we point out that its internal astronomical alignments – the star-shafts of the King's and Queen's Chambers – are consistent with a *completion* date during ancient Egypt's 'Old Kingdom', somewhere around 2500 BC. Such a date should, in itself, be uncontroversial since it in no way contradicts the scholarly concensus that the monument was built by Khufu, the second Pharaoh of the Fourth Dynasty, who ruled from 2551–2528 BC.[1] What places our theory in sharp contradiction to the orthodox view, however, is our suggestion that the mysterious structures of the Giza necropolis may all be the result of an enormously long-drawn-out period of architectural elaboration and development – a period that had its genesis in 10,500 BC, that came to an end with the completion of the Great Pyramid come 8000 years later in 2500 BC, and that was guided throughout by a unified master-plan.

According to orthodox Egyptologists, the Great Pyramid is the result of only just over 100 years of architectural development, beginning with the construction of the step-pyramid of Zoser at Saqqara not earlier than 2630 BC, passing through a number of 'experimental' models of true Pyramids (one at Meidum and at two Dashour, all attributed to Khufu's father Sneferu) and leading inexorably to the technological mastery of the Great Pyramid not earlier than 2551 BC (the date of Khufu's own ascension to the throne). An evolutionary 'sequence' in pyramid-construction thus lies at the heart of the orthodox Egyptological theory – a sequence in which the Great Pyramid is seen as having evolved from (and thus having been preceded by) the four earlier pyramids.[2]

But suppose those four pyramids were proved to be not earlier but *later* structures? Suppose, for example, that objective and unambiguous archaeological evidence were to emerge – say, reliable carbon-dated samples – which indicated that work on the Great Pyramid had in fact begun some 1300 years *before* the birth of Khufu and that the monument had stood substantially complete some 300 years before his accession to the throne? Such evidence, if it existed, would render obsolete the orthodox Egyptological theory about the origins, function and dating of the Great Pyramid since it would destroy the Saqqara → Meidum → Dashour → Giza 'sequence' by making the technologically-advanced Great Pyramid far older than its supposed oldest 'ancestor', the far more rudimentary step-pyramid of Zoser. With the sequence no longer valid, it would then be even more difficult than it is at present for scholars to explain the immense architectural competence and precision of the Great Pyramid (since it defies reason to suppose that such advanced and sophisticated work could have been undertaken by builders with no prior knowledge of monumental architecture).

Curiously, objective evidence *does* exist which casts serious doubt on the orthodox archaeological sequence. This evidence was procured and published in 1986 by the Pyramids Carbon-dating Project, directed by Mark Lehner (and referred to in passing in his correspondence with us, see Appendix III above). With funding from the Edgar Cayce Foundation, Lehner collected fifteen samples of ancient mortar from the masonry of the Great Pyramid. These samples of mortar were chosen because they contained fragments of organic material which, unlike natural stone, would be susceptible to carbon-dating. Two of the samples were tested in the Radiocarbon Laboratory of the Southern Methodist University in Dallas Texas and the other thirteen were taken to laboratories in Zurich, Switzerland, for dating by the more sophisticated accelerator method. According to proper procedure, the results were then calibrated and confirmed with respect to tree-ring samples.[3]

The outcome was surprising. As Mark Lehner commented at the time:

> The dates run from 3809 BC to 2869 BC. So generally the dates are . . . significantly earlier than the best Egyptological date for Khufu . . . In short, the radiocarbon dates, depending on which sample you note, suggest that the Egyptological chronology is anything from 200 to 1200 years off. You can look at this almost like a bell curve, and when you cut it down the middle you can summarize the results by saying our dates are 400 to 450 years too early for the Old Kingdom Pyramids, especially those of the Fourth Dynasty . . . Now this is really radical . . . I mean it'll make a big stink. The Giza pyramid is 400 years older than Egyptologists believe.[4]

Despite Lehner's insistence that the carbon-dating was conducted according to rigorous scientific procedures[5] (enough, normally, to qualify these dates for full acceptance by scholars) it is a strange fact that almost no 'stink' at all has been caused by his study. On the contrary, its implications have been and continue to be universally ignored by Egyptologists and have not been widely published or considered in either the academic or the popular press. We are at a loss to explain this apparent failure of scholarship and are equally unable to understand why there has been no move to extract and carbon-date further samples of the Great Pyramid's mortar in order to test Lehner's potentially revolutionary results.

What has to be considered, however, is the unsettling possibility that some kind of pattern may underly these strange oversights.

As we reported in Chapter 6, a piece of wood that had been sealed inside the shafts of the Queen's Chamber since completion of construction work on that room, was amongst the unique collection of relics brought out of the Great Pyramid in 1872 by the British engineer Waynman Dixon. The other two 'Dixon relics' – the small metal hook and the stone sphere – have been located after having been 'misplaced' by the British Museum for a very long while. The whereabouts of the piece of wood, however, is today unknown.[6]

This is very frustrating. Being organic, wood can be accurately carbon-dated. Since this particular piece of wood is known to have been sealed inside the Pyramid at the time of construction of the monument, radiocarbon results from it could, theoretically, confirm the date when that construction took place.

A missing piece of wood cannot be tested. Fortunately, however, as we also reported in Chapter 6, it is probable that another such piece of wood is still *in situ* at some depth inside the northern shaft of the Queen's Chamber. This piece was clearly visible in film, taken by Rudolf Gantenbrink's robot-camera *Upuaut*, that was shown to a gathering of senior Egyptologists at the British Museum on 22 November 1993.[7]

We are informed that it would be a relatively simple and inexpensive task to extract the piece of wood from the northern shaft. More than two and a half years after that screening at the British Museum, however, no attempt has been made to take advantage of this opportunity. The piece of wood still sits there, its age unknown, and Rudolf Gantenbrink, as we saw in Chapter 6, has not been permitted to complete his exploration of the shafts.

Appendix 6

The Door inside the Great Pyramid; Tunnels and Chambers under the Great Sphinx

Further developments to September 1996

Since the first English-language edition of this book went to press in February 1996 there have been a number of significant developments concerning the opening of the door in the Great Pyramid at the end of the southern shaft of the Queen's Chamber (see in particular Chapter 7) and the search for tunnels and chambers under the Great Sphinx (see in particular Chapters 2 and 5). We anticipate that there will be further developments – quite possibly of major historical significance – which we will cover in a future book. It is our intention, meanwhile, to monitor this 'running story' and to update our readers in a series of appendices that will be published in future editions of *Keeper of Genesis*.

The update presented herewith covers the period from March to end-August 1996.

The Great Pyramid

At the end of 1995, as reported in Chapters 6 and 7, the position of the Egyptian Antiquities Organization regarding the 'door' at the end of the southern shaft of the Queen's Chamber was apparently one of official disinterest. The reader will recall that Dr Nur El Din, Chairman of the EAO (now renamed the Supreme Council of Antiquities) had declined Rudolf Gantenbrink's offer to donate the robot to the Egyptian government and to train an Egyptian technician to operate it: 'Thank you for your offer to train the Egyptian technician . . . Unfortunately we are very busy for the time being, therefore we will postpone the matter . . .'[1] Similarly Dr Zahi Hawass had declared: 'I do not think this is a door and nothing is behind it.'[2]

In March 1996, however, Dr Hawass changed his mind, declaring in the *Egyptian Gazette* that Gantenbrink's find was of huge interest and that the door would be opened in September 1996 by a multinational team led by the Egyptian geologist (and NASA consultant) Dr Farouk El Baz. Rudolf Gantenbrink would not be involved and 'another robot' – not *Upuaut* – would be used to explore the shaft. Participating in the exploration would be a 'Canadian' contingent.[3]

The Canadian element, 'Amtex', is headed by Peter Zuuring, a wealthy Dutch-Canadian businessman, who told us that he had shown the Egyptians how the door could be opened 'relatively inexpensively . . . We're working with Spar Aerospace to design a miniature arm with tools that could first tap the door, knock it and try to lever things a little bit to see if there's anything loose. But I think ultimately we'll go straight through.'

In two conversations, Zuuring told us that he thought it unlikely that the project could start as early as September 1996: the following year, he said, 1997, was far more likely. The objective, which might take some time, was to raise the huge sum of US $10 million to promote a staged 'live opening' of the door on international television networks. 'I'm working with a private guy who is a personal friend of Hawass and we are absolutely going to drum this thing to death. Whatever the event we are going to stage, it will be televised live.'[4]

The Great Sphinx

In 1993–4 (see Chapters 2 and 5) Dr Zahi Hawass appeared to be adamantly opposed to the notion that the Sphinx might be far older than ancient Egypt – and thus the work of a lost civilization. The reader will recall that the EAO official was particularly incensed by the NBC television film, *The Mystery of the Sphinx*, that was made about the work of John Anthony West. In addition Hawass had been personally responsible for expelling John West and his research team from the Sphinx enclosure. The team included the geologist Robert Schoch, a Professor at Boston University, and the seismologist Thomas Dobecki (who was to identify a large rectangular chamber concealed in the bedrock at a depth of about 20 feet beneath the front paws of the Sphinx).

The NBC documentary linked the Sphinx to Altantis and suggested that the chamber that Thomas Dobecki's seismograph had detected beneath its paws might contain some sort of 'time capsule' of Atlantean wisdom and history. Hawass called these claims: 'American hallucinations. West is an amateur. There is absolutely no scientific base for any of this. We have older monuments in the same area. They definitely weren't built by men from Atlantis. It's nonsense and we won't allow our monuments to be exploited for personal enrichment. The Sphinx is the soul of Egypt.'[5]

An article in the Egyptian press responding to the NBC film quoted Dr Hawass on his further reasons for expelling John West and his team from the Sphinx enclosure: 'I have found that their work is carried out by installing endoscopes in the Sphinx's body and shooting films for all phases of the work in a propaganda . . . but not in a scientific manner. I therefore suspended the work of this unscientific mission and made a report which was presented to the permanent commission who rejected the mission's work in the future.'[6]

The NBC film was produced by Boris Said (see Chapter 2) and partially financed by investments from members of the Association for Research and Enlightenment (ARE). Headquartered in Virginia Beach in the US (see Chapter 5), the ARE is a multi-million dollar organization that exists to promulgate the teachings and prophecies of the American psychic Edgar Cayce, who died in 1945. Prominent amongst Cayce's pronouncements were many statements – some of which were reported in the NBC film – to the effect that the Sphinx had been built in 10,500 BC by the survivors of Atlantis who had concealed beneath it a 'Hall of Records' containing all the wisdom of their lost civilization and the true history of the human race. Cayce prophesied that this Hall of Records would be rediscovered and opened between 1996 and 1998. He connected the opening to the second coming of Christ and asserted that the contents of the Hall would not be shared with the general public until many years after it had first been entered by 'three who would make of the perfect way of life'.[7]

In 1995 John West and Professor Robert Schoch of Boston University (in cooperation with the prestigious Princeton Engineering Anomalies Research Laboratory, better known as PEAR) put in an application to the Egyptian authorities to resume their research. Their application was ignored.

At the end of March 1996 the Egyptian authorities granted a one-year licence to a new team to conduct surveys around the Sphinx and the Giza necropolis using seismic equipment and ground-penetrating radar. This team, which claimed academic sponsorship from Florida State University (and reportedly involved the participation of four geologists from that university), was largely financed, through the Schor Foundation of New York, by Dr Joseph Schor, an American multimillionaire. Dr Schor is a life-member of the ARE and was one of the two ARE members who met us at Virginia Beach with Charles Thomas Cayce in May 1994 (see Chapter 5). Later that month he wrote to us of his great personal interest in corroborating 'the Cayce records which indicated that the culture which led to the building of the Pyramids dates from 10,400 BC.' He also stated his wish 'to further delineate that civilization.'[8]

On 11 April 1996, when we informed Joseph Schor that we intended to write about these matters in the London *Daily Mail*,[9] he threatened us with a libel action and stated: 'We do not work for the Edgar Cayce group . . . The major purpose of the Schor Foundation and the Florida State University is to aid in the preservation and restoration of the Pyramids and Sphinx. In addition we are surveying the underground of the Giza Plateau to find faults and chasms that might collapse. This will increase the safety of the plateau because chasms and faults can be collapsed or roped off for the protection of tourists and plateau personnel.'[9]

On 14 April 1996 Dr Zahi Hawass gave a rather different account, mentioning hidden tunnels around the Pyramids and the Sphinx.' He made no mention of the question of public safety but hinted that excavation of the tunnels would reveal many clues regarding the establishment of the Giza pyramids.'[10]

Nor did that question appear to be the main thrust of a short video, *Secret Chamber*, in which Dr Hawass took part. Filmed on location in Cairo in November and December 1995, the video was produced and written by Boris Said and, according to him, financed to the tune of US $100,000 by Joseph Schor. In this video, as we reported at the end of Chapter 5, Dr Hawass is shown scrambling into a tunnel under the Sphinx. When he reaches the bottom he turns to face the camera and whispers to the viewer: 'Even Indiana Jones will never dream to be here. Can you believe it? We are now inside the Sphinx, in this tunnel. This tunnel has never been opened before. No one really knows what's inside this tunnel but we are going to open it for the first time.'[11]

The narrator of the video drives home an interesting point: 'Edgar Cayce, America's famous "Sleeping Prophet", predicted that a chamber would be discovered beneath the Sphinx – a chamber containing the recorded history of human civilization. For the first time ever we'll show you what lies beneath this great statue – a chamber which will be opened, live, for our television cameras.'[12]

In July 1996, after worldwide protest over the activities of the Schor Foundation and Florida State University at the Sphinx, Dr Hawass claimed on South African radio that he had halted the project: 'I found that their work is not following the correct steps . . . I wrote a letter to them saying that they cannot do work again because they are not really following the correct work.'[13]

That same month, however, rumours began to circulate that the team had identified nine further tunnels or chambers under the Giza plateau. In all of them, apparently, their remote-sensing equipment had identified objects made of metal.

By the end of August 1996, despite Hawass's statement, team members still appeared confident that their project would go ahead and Boris Said was reputed to be negotiating with major television networks in the US for an exclusive documentary on the Sphinx.

The Edgar Cayce legacy

As we saw in Chapter 5, Edgar Cayce (known in America as the 'Sleeping Prophet' because he gave his psychic 'readings' in a trance-like state) believed himself to be a re-incarnated priest called Ra-Ta, a survivor of Atlantis who had settled in Egypt in 10,500 BC. Throughout the 1930s, until his death in 1945, he used the contacts made through his 'readings' to 'pick up players' – artists, bankers, businessmen, university professors and even politicians – who were all convinced that in their 'past lives' they too had played a role in the unfolding drama of Atlantis.[14]

One of these players, perhaps the most active the ARE would know, was Cayce's eldest son, Hugh Lynn (1907–1983), a graduate of Harvard University who took over the management of the newly founded ARE in 1931 when he was just 24 years old. With youthful enthusiasm, he vowed that one day an 'ARE sponsored expedition' to Giza would vindicate his father's prophecies concerning the Hall of Records.[15]

Perhaps Hugh Lynn had been inspired by the so-called 'Baraize Expedition' to the Sphinx which was already well underway in 1930 when the ARE was founded. Led by the then Director of the Egyptian Antiquities Department, a French archaeologist named Emile Baraize, this expedition stripped off the ancient skin of 'repair blocks' from the lower parts of the body of the Sphinx. While removing some of the blocks from the rump of the statue, Baraize came across the entrance to a tunnel. Then, for some extraordinary reason, he resealed the mouth of the tunnel with rock and cement and never reported the matter. With Baraize at the time was a young Arab boy called Mohamad Abdel Mawgud – whose descendants still live at Giza.[16]

The Baraize expedition ran from 1926 to 1936. But it was not until 1972 that Hugh Lynn Cayce, by then in his sixties, finally set in motion the plan that he had long ago conceived for getting the ARE into mainstream archaeology at Giza. His first move was to recruit a 'college dropout named Mark Lehner' (the ARE President thought he recognised the young man from a past life), and then arrange for him to take a post-graduate degree at the American University in Cairo. Today the Visiting Professor of Egyptology at the University of Chicago's prestigious Oriental Institute, we saw in Chapter 5 how Lehner became the ARE's 'man' at Giza, participating during the 1970s and 1980s in almost every important project undertaken around the pyramids and the Sphinx.

Despite a number of setbacks experienced by the ARE as a result of these projects, an official biography reports that Hugh Lynn Cayce 'had no sense of defeat . . . He would stay with the search as long as it took, building alliances with other groups and individuals. One of the latter was the Egyptian Chief Inspector at Giza, Hawass, who he had met through Lehner in 1975. In 1980, Hawass, accommodated the ARE by conducting an excavation in front of the Sphinx temple . . .'[17]

In October 1980 Mark Lehner made contact with Mohamad Abdel Mawgud, the 'young Arab boy' (by now in his sixties) who had seen Emile Baraize seal up the tunnel under the Sphinx in 1926. Together with Ahmed Al Fayed, Abdel Mawgud's son, Lehner was permitted by Zahi Hawass to remove the seal and enter the tunnel. But again, apparently, nothing was found. The tunnel reached a 'dead end' in the bedrock underneath the Sphinx.[18]

Soon afterwards Ahmed Al Fayed went to settle in Virginia Beach and in due course joined the staff of the ARE. Hawass also travelled to the USA at about this time to expand his formal education in Egyptology. As Hugh Lynn Cayce's biographer reports: 'If Zahi Hawass was to advance within the [Egyptian] government to further his own career and open doors for Hugh Lynn's project, he could do it best on the wings of higher education at an American Ivy League college.' Just before he died Hugh Lynn Cayce was to explain how: 'I got him [Zahi Hawass] a scholarship at the University of Pennsylvania in Egyptology, to get his Ph.D. I got the scholarship through an ARE person who happens to be on the Fulbright scholarship board. He [Hawass] had aided Mark [Lehner] to work on the Sphinx and I am very appreciative.'[19]

Interviewed on South African radio in July 1996 Hawass responded to an earlier interview given by ourselves in which we had mentioned his apparent connections with the Edgar Cayce Foundation. He accused us of lying, stated that we were merely claiming these things to make ourselves famous, and insisted that he discredited Edgar Cayce, adding emphatically: 'The Edgar Cayce theory is wrong.' The interviewer (John Robbie of Radio 702, Johannesburg) then read out on the air the passage quoted above from Hugh Lynn Cayce's biography in which the former ARE President claims to have been instrumental in obtaining a Fulbright scholarship for Hawass. Hawass replied: 'That's not true. I met him, I lectured to the Edgar Cayce Foundation many times. He was such a nice man. I never believed his theories. He never supported a fellowship for me to study outside at all. He just once attended a dinner that I invited him to in Cairo with one of the Fulbrights . . . but he did not support any study. The Egyptian government supported my studies for five years and the Fulbright supported my studies at the University of Pennsylvania for two years. It had no support from such an organization like that.'

Hawass was then asked about *Secret Chamber*, the short video referred to above made by Boris Said in November and December 1995 and financed by Joseph Schor. The interviewer pointed out that this video makes positive reference to Edgar Cayce and his prophecies and includes an appearance by Zahi Hawass in which the Egyptian official stated that a tunnel under the Sphinx is about to opened. 'How come you're involved with that?' asked the interviewer.

HAWASS: This is not true! I'm a public figure and I get interviews every day! Every day if you come to my office you will see almost three TVs from all over the world. I . . . my interviews always explain my discoveries. This video is talking about the tunnel that I found inside the Sphinx based on my work. It is not by the work that is done here, it's by Florida University. It is not by Cayce or anything! And we found even that Florida University are not following the scientist's steps therefore I wrote a letter two months ago that those type . . . even the universities, the universities are not following the exact steps that they supposed to do.

INTERVIEWER: It seems a coincidence . . . it seems a coincidence, Dr Zahi, that the Cayce prophecy talks about tunnels under the Sphinx. You've discredited it. You've banned various researchers according to *Keeper of Genesis* – people like John West who are trying to do work on this theory – and now you seem to be taking it over yourself. Is that true?

HAWASS: No! I'm not taking over myself . . . If there is evidence, actual evidence from an institution, to tell us there is something under the Sphinx we'll excavate it. But all of it is just hallucination! We cannot run after hallucinations at all.

INTERVIEWER: But in that video, where you are actually filmed in a tunnel under the Sphinx, you indicated that this might lead to something very, very exciting . . . I saw that myself, Zahi!

HAWASS: If I did found . . . I told you! I excavated this tunnel. And I did excavate it and I'm excavating it. If it leads to something important, we'll announce it. You know what I'm saying? I'm not denying that . . . Maybe it will lead to something exciting.

The interviewer asked Dr Hawass why he had not taken legal action against us, the authors of *Keeper of Genesis*, 'because they make some serious accusations against you.' Hawass replied: 'You know, if I make legal action against them I will make them famous. But I will never, err, make them famous.'[20]

On 15 August 1996, in an interview with the *Egyptian Gazette* in Cairo, Dr Hawass made an oddly similar remark concerning the Japanese team from Waseda University, led by Professor Sakuji Yoshimura, who in 1988 had used advanced technology to identify a hidden chamber inside the Great Pyramid and another beneath the left forepaw of the Great Sphinx. 'I believe these teams were not serious enough,' stated Dr Hawass, 'and their equipment was not well tooled. The members of these teams were merely interested in acquiring fame.'[21]

Mars and Giza:
Strange connections and synchronicity

In our research we have stumbled across a tangled web of clues, connections and overlapping interests appearing to suggest that American scientists with links to NASA may have quietly involved themselves, since at least the 1970s, in covert 'expeditions' to unveil the secrets of the great pyramids and the Great Sphinx of Giza. The story, oddly enough, appears to be running in parallel with research stemming from the existence of curious pyramidial structures (and a gigantic Sphinx-like 'Face') that were photographed on Mars by NASA spacecraft during the 1970s.

In 1971 NASA's Mariner 9 probe took the first ever photographs of strange 'pyramid' structures on Mars on a region of the planet known to astronomers as Elysium. Dr James Hurtak, a graduate in remote sensing technology (and an acquaintance of Mark Lehner's) was one of the earliest researchers to show interest in the Elysium 'pyramids' – which were officially dismissed by NASA as 'tricks of light'. In 1975, despite NASA's apparent indifference, Hurtak predicted that further finds of similar structures, including a sphinx-like monument, would be made on Mars and that they would all prove to be connected in a great cosmic blueprint to the Giza monuments in Egypt.[22]

Hurtak is an active campaigner against the secrecy of the US military and related agencies with regard to UFO 'cover-ups' and other similar issues. He also claims to have had close links with researchers at California's prestigious Stanford Research Institute, America's second largest scientific think-tank (which has an annual budget from the US government of over $300 million). The SRI's projects have included the 'Remote Viewing Programme' (started in 1972), funded by the CIA as an intelligence-gathering exercise, which recruited top psychics to 'remote view' enemy military installations and other sites.

In 1973, as we saw in Chapter 5, the Egyptian Antiquities Organisation (EAO) granted an official licence to the SRI, permitting it to conduct surveys around the Great Sphinx at Giza using ground-penetrating radar and seismographs. The local sponsor of this project was Cairo's Ain Shams Univesity. We recall that in the same year Hugh Lynn Cayce sent Mark Lehner to the American University in Cairo with funds raised by ARE members.

In 1976 a second NASA probe, Viking 1, went into Mars orbit. In the region known as Cydonia it photographed several more pyramidial structures (including the five-sided 'D&M Pyramid') and the famous 'Face'. Complete with its distinctive Sphinx-like headdress, this latter feature has been calculated from the NASA images to be 1.6 miles in length from crown to chin, 1.2 miles wide, and just under 2,600 feet high. NASA has argued officially that it is nothing more than a small mountain, naturally weathered. But how many mountains have their left and right sides so intricately similar? Image analysts say that the 'bilateral symmetry' of the Face, mimicking a natural, almost human appearance, is most unlikely to have come about by chance. And this impression is confirmed by other characteristics that have subsequently been identified under computer enhancement. These include 'teeth' in the mouth, bilaterally crossed lines above the eyes, and regular lateral stripes in the headpiece – suggestive, to some researchers at least, of the *nemes* headdress of ancient Egyptian pharaohs.[23]

Back in Egypt in 1977, a year after the Viking images had first reached the Earth, Mark Lehner made contact with NASA's Dr Lambert T. Dolphin, leader of the Stanford Research Institute project at the Sphinx. The reader will recall from Chapter 5 that Lehner was by then already well acquainted with Zahi Hawass.

Later in 1977 Lambert Dolphin travelled to Virginia Beach to negotiate funding from the Edgar Cayce organization for a proposed new SRI project at Giza. The purpose of this project was to use the latest remote sensing technology to search for hidden chambers around and under the Sphinx – with Lehner again 'participating as the Edgar Cayce Foundation's "man in Cairo".' Several underground 'cavities' were detected by this Sphinx Exploration Project.

In 1978 Mark Lehner proposed a project on the Sphinx to the American Research Centre in Egypt. The project, again partially financed by the Edgar Cayce group, was approved and went ahead with Lehner as its Field Director. Soon afterwards a US registered company called Recovery Systems International (RSI) appeared on the scene. As we saw in Chapter 5, it undertook core drillings in front of the Sphinx to investigate the promising underground cavities previously pinpointed by SRI.

In 1983 Hugh Lynn died and the management of the Edgar Cayce group was handed to his son, Charles Thomas Cayce. In the same year 'The Independent Mars Project' was set up in the United States by Richard Hoagland, a former NASA consultant, and Lambert Dolphin. Meanwhile in 1987 Dr Zahi Hawass completed his education in the United States and returned to Egypt to be appointed as the EAO's Director-General of the Giza Plateau.

In March 1996 Dr Hawass announced that the Egyptian scientist Farouk El Baz (whose name, meaning Hawk, translates into ancient Egyptian as Horus) had been chosen to lead a team to open the secret door inside the Great Pyramid at the end of the southern shaft of the Queen's Chamber. The reader will recall that Amtex, the Canadian company participating in the project, claim to be 'working with Spar Aerospace' to devise a tool to open or 'go straight through' the door. Spar Aerospace are better known for manufacturing hydraulic arms used in NASA Space Shuttles. As we noted at the beginning of this appendix, Dr El Baz, a graduate of Cairo's Ain Shams university, is a NASA consultant. He has been involved for many years with studies of geological formations on the Moon and on Mars and he is a one-time personal friend of astronauts Buzz Aldrin and Neil Armstrong. It was El Baz, nicknamed the King by his NASA colleagues, who in 1969 chose the spot for the Apollo 11 Moon landing. El Baz is the founder of the Centre of Remote Sensing at Boston University and presently serves as its Director.[24]

Also in March 1996 the EAO granted a one-year renewable licence for the project at the Sphinx – see above – financed by Joseph Schor. Project members include Boris Said, Thomas Dobecki, and four senior geologists from Florida State University, who began work with a million dollars worth of ground-penetrating radar and seismic equipment at their disposal. It was reported to us that team members had consulted with Dr James Hurtak and Richard Hoagland in August 1996.

References

Chapter 1

1 Selim Hassan, *Excavations at Giza*, Government Press, Cairo, 1946, Vol. VI, Part I, pp. 34–5
2 Ibid.
3 E. A. Wallis Budge, *An Egyptian Hieroglyphic Dictionary*, Dover Publications Inc., New York, 1978, Vol. I, p. 469.
4 Selim Hassan, *The Sphinx: Its History in the Light of Recent Excavations*, Government Press, Cairo, 1949, p. 76. See also Veronica Seton-Williams and Peter Stock, *Blue Guide Egypt*, A. & C. Black, London, 1988, p. 432.
5 Zahi Hawass and Mark Lehner, 'The Sphinx: Who Built It and Why', *Archaeology*, September–October 1994, p. 34. See also E. A. Wallis Budge, *Hieroglyphic Dictionary*, op.cit., Vol. II, p. 752.
6 We have many surprising survivals from the ancient Egyptian language in the English language. For example the small species of greyhound that we know as the 'Whippet' derives its name from the ancient Egyptian canine deity *Upuaut*, the 'Opener of the Ways'. Normandi Ellis in her excellent *Awakening Osiris*, Phanes Press, Grand Rapids, 1988, cites other examples: '*armen*/arm; *heku* (magic utterance)/hex; *neb* (spiralling force of the universe)/nebulous; *Satis* (goddess of the flood, or meaning enough)/satisfy; *aor* (magic light)/aura'.

Chapter 2

1 I. E. S. Edwards, *The Pyramids of Egypt*, Pelican Books, London, 1949, p. 106.

2 Ahmed Fakhry, *The Pyramids*, University of Chicago Press, Chicago, 1969, p. 159.

3 Mark Lehner, 'Computer Rebuilds the Ancient Sphinx', *National Geographic*, Vol. 179, No. 4, April 1991; Mark Lehner, 'Reconstructing the Sphinx', *Cambridge Archaeological Journal*, Vol. 1, No. 1, April 1992.

4 *National Geographic*, April 1991, op.cit.

5 Ibid.

6 Ibid.

7 *Cambridge Archaeological Journal*, op.cit., pp. 10 and 11.

8 Ibid., p. 9.

9 Ibid., p. 20.

10 John Anthony West, *Serpent in the Sky: The High Wisdom of Ancient Egypt*, Quest Books, Wheaton, Ill, 1993, p. 231.

11 Ibid., p. 232.

12 American Association for the Advancement of Science, Chicago, 7 February 1992, debate: 'How Old is the Sphinx?'

13 *Cambridge Archaeological Journal*, op.cit., p. 6.

14 For a fuller discussion of the dating issue see Graham Hancock, *Fingerprints of the Gods*, William Heinemann Ltd, London, 1995, and Crown Publishers, New York, 1995, p. 51.

15 Hassan, *The Sphinx*, op.cit., p. 75.

16 *Cambridge Archaeological Journal*, op.cit., p. 6

17 E. A. Wallis Budge, 'Stela of the Sphinx' in *A History of Egypt*, London, 1902, Vol. IV, p. 80 ff.

18 Ibid., pp. 85–6.

19 James Henry Breasted, *Ancient Records of Egypt*, Histories and Mysteries of Man Ltd, London, 1988, Volume II, p. 324.

20 Ibid.

21 Ibid.

22 *National Geographic*, April 1991, op.cit.

23 Gaston Maspero, *The Passing of Empires*, New York, 1900.

24 James Henry Breasted, *Ancient Records*, op.cit., Vol. I, pp. 83–5.

25 Gaston Maspero, *The Dawn of Civilization*, SPCK, London, 1894, p. 247.

26 Gaston Maspero, *A Manual of Egyptian Archaeology*, p. 74.

27 Hassan, *The Sphinx*, op.cit., p. 91.

28 American Association for the Advancement of Science, 1992, debate 'How Old is the Sphinx?', op.cit.

29 *Archaeology*, September–October 1994, op.cit., pp. 32–3.

30 Ibid., p. 34.
31 R. A. Schwaller de Lubicz, *Sacred Science*, Inner Traditions International, Rochester Vt, 1988, p. 96.
32 John Anthony West, *Serpent*, op.cit., pp. 1–2.
33 Ibid., p. 186.
34 Ibid., p. 187.
35 Ibid., p. 226.
36 Ibid., p. 225.
37 Ibid., p. 226.
38 Ibid., p. 227.
39 Ibid.
40 Ibid.
41 Ibid., pp. 226–7.
42 Ibid., p. 228.
43 Interviewed in NBC television documentary *Mystery of the Sphinx*, 1993.
44 John Anthony West, *Serpent*, op.cit., p. 227.
45 Quoted in *An Akhbar El Yom*, 8 January 1994.
46 John Anthony West, *Serpent*, op.cit., p. 229.
47 *Boston Globe*, 23 October 1991.
48 *Los Angeles Times*, 23 October 1991.
49 John Anthony West, *Serpent*, op.cit., p. 229.
50 Ibid.
51 Ibid.
52 Ibid.
53 Ibid., p. 229.
54 Ibid., p. 230.
55 Ibid., p. 229.
56 *Mystery of the Sphinx*, op.cit.
57 Ibid., and *KMT*, Vol. V, No. 2, Summer 1994, p. 7.

Chapter 3

1 For block weights see I. E. S. Edwards, *The Pyramids of Egypt*, op.cit., p. 215; John Anthony West, *Serpent*, op.cit., p. 242; John Anthony West, *The Traveller's Key to Ancient Egypt*, Harrap Columbus, London, 1989, pp. 143–5; *Mystery of the Sphinx*, op.cit.; Dr Joseph Davidovits and Margie Morris, *The Pyramids: An Enigma Solved*, Dorset Press, New York, 1988, p. 51.
2 *Mystery of the Sphinx*, op.cit.

3 Interviewed in ibid.
4 See for example I. E. S. Edwards, *Pyramids of Egypt* op.cit., p. 220;
   John Baines and Jaromir Malek, *Atlas of Ancient Egypt*, Time-Life
   Books, 1990, pp. 138–9.
5 The most thorough study is provided in Peter Hodges (Julian Keable
   ed.), *How the Pyramids Were Built*, Element Books, 1989.
6 Ibid., p. 11.
7 Ibid., pp. 11–13.
8 Ibid., p. 13.
9 Jean Kerisel, a prominent soils engineer in France and also President of
   the Franco-Egyptian Society, did an extensive study on the hauling of
   large blocks using human labour and wooden sledges. Kerisel kindly
   made this study – *La Grande Pyramide et ses Derniers Secrets* – available
   to us prior to its publication (due 1996). The basis of his calculation is
   that the pressure on the soil cannot exceed 1.5 tons/sq.m. for ramps
   made of compacted soil (probably covered with stone slabs) with slopes
   not exceeding 8 per cent. The friction coefficient has been calculated at
   15 per cent using soaked lime as the lubricant. Kerisel noted that a
   greater pressure than 1.5 tons would cause the lubricant to seep away
   and thus the friction coefficient would increase, making hauling even
   more difficult. The average speed has been worked out to be 0.3
   metres/second with a 13-kilogram traction force produced by each
   man. Thus the hauling of a 70-ton block would require (70,000 × 0.15
   × 1/13 =) 807 men and would take some 9.25 hours for a ramp of one
   kilometre. Kerisel worked out that if the traction was much higher than
   13 kg/man – even for a short period of time – the result would be
   serious back injuries. Thus, assuming at least 1 clear metre distance
   between each standing man, 807 men in 6 rows would need a ramp
   space of 134.5 metres long and 6 metres wide. The problem, of course,
   is greatly increased for blocks of 200 tons within the confined working
   conditions of the Sphinx and Valley Temples – a task almost impossible
   to imagine with such primitive techniques.
10 Robert Schoch's evidence presented in *Mystery of the Sphinx*, op.cit.
11 *KMT* Vol. V, op.cit., p. 7.
12 *The Sacred Sermon* (Hermetica, *Libellus III*), translated by G. R. S.
   Mead in *Thrice Great Hermes: Studies in Hellenistic Theosophy and
   Gnosis*, Samuel Weiser Inc., North Beach, Maine, 1992, Book II, p. 51.
13 British Museum Manuscript 25,619, pp. 15–19.
14 W. M. Flinders Petrie, *The Pyramids and Temples of Gizeh*, Histories
   and Mysteries of Man Ltd, London, 1990, pp. 50–1.
15 Chassinat, *Monuments et Mémoires*, Fondation Piot, Volume XXV,

p. 57.

16 Thor Heyerdahl, *The Ra Expeditions*, Book Club Associates, London, 1972, p. 15.

17 Ibid., pp. 15–17.

18 Graham Hancock, *Fingerprints of the Gods*, op.cit. Robert Bauval and Adrian Gilbert, *The Orion Mystery*, William Heinemann Ltd, London, 1994.

19 Gaston Maspero, *The Dawn of Civilization*, op.cit., pp. 366–7. See also Peter Tompkins, *Secrets of the Great Pyramid*, Harper & Row, New York and London, 1978, p. 17 and W. M. Flinders Petrie, *Pyramids and Temples*, op.cit., p. 13.

20 W. M. Flinders Petrie, *Pyramids and Temples*, op.cit., p. 13.

21 The supposed discoverer was Archimedes.

22 For further discussion see *Fingerprints of the Gods*, op.cit., Chapter 48.

23 Ibid.

24 Piazzi Smyth, *The Great Pyramid*, Bell Publishing Co., New York, 1990, pp. 79–80.

25 Ibid., p. 80.

26 J. H. Cole, Paper No. 39, 'The Determination of the Exact Size and Orientation of the Great Pyramid of Giza', *Survey of Egypt*, Cairo, 1925. See also I. E. S. Edwards, *The Pyramids of Egypt*, op.cit., p. 87.

27 Ibid.

28 I. E. S. Edwards, *The Pyramids of Egypt*, op.cit., p. 208.

29 See discussion in Flinders Petrie, *Pyramids and Temples* op.cit., pp. 83–4.

30 See *Fingerprints of the Gods*, op.cit., pp. 330–8, *The Orion Mystery*, op.cit., pp. 41–5.

31 I. E. S. Edwards, *The Pyramids of Egypt*, op.cit., p. 93.

32 We are grateful to James Macaulay for this suggestion.

33 Joseph R. Jochmans, *The Hall of Records*, unpublished manuscript, 1985, p. 175. See also Hodges, *How the Pyramids Were Built*, op.cit., p. 122.

34 Flinders Petrie, *Pyramids and Temples*, op.cit., p. 19.

35 Ibid.

36 Vyse and Perrings figures quoted in Edwards, *The Pyramids of Egypt*, op.cit., p. 88.

37 Ibid., pp. 88–96.

38 Ibid., p. 88.

39 Herodotus, *The History*, David Grene transl., University of Chicago Press, 1988, 2:124, pp. 185–6.

40 Cited in Jochmans, *The Hall of Records*, op.cit., pp. 176–7.

41 R. Cook, *The Pyramids of Giza*, Seven Islands, Glastonbury, 1992, p. 52.
42 Jean Kerisel, 'The Pyramid of Cheops: Further Research' (October and December 1992), extract from his paper in the *Revue Française d'Egyptologie*, 1993, p. 4.
43 Ibid, p. 6.
44 Ibid.
45 Ibid, p. 7.
46 Personal communication.
47 A. Badawy, 'The Stellar Destiny of the Pharaoh and the so-called Air Shafts in Cheops' Pyramid', *Mitt. Inst. Orient. zu Berlin*, Band 10, 1964, pp. 189–206.

Chapter 4

1 See, for example, I. E. S. Edwards, *The Pyramids of Egypt* op.cit., pp. 209–10.
2 For further discussion see *The Orion Mystery*, op.cit.
3 For example, see E. M. Antoniadi, *L'Astronomie Egyptienne*, Paris, 1934, p. 119.
4 See *The Orion Mystery*, op.cit., pp. 97–104.
5 Ibid.
6 Ibid., pages 105–37.
7 Ibid.
8 Ibid.
9 Ibid., pp. 179–96.
10 See *The Orion Mystery*, op.cit., p. 192.
11 Using the rigorous formula of precession corrected for nutation, aberration of starlight, proper motion (from the most recent Yale Bright Star Catalog) and parallax, gives *circa* 10,500 BC as the epoch that Orion's belt reached its lowest altitude (9 degrees 25' measured at the south meridian, i.e. declination 50 degrees 35').
12 Giving a full precessional cycle of 25,920 years.
13 For a detailed discussion see Giorgio de Santillana and Hertha von Dechend, *Hamlet's Mill*, Godine, Boston, 1977.
14 Ibid., p. 59.
15 See *Fingerprints of the Gods*, op.cit., pp. 454–8.
16 For a discussion see J. Norman Lockyer, *The Dawn of Astronomy*, MIT Press, 1973, pp. 60–1 ff.
17 From *Hermetica*, Sir Walter Scott transl., Shambhala, Boston, 1993,

Asclepius III:24b, p. 341.

18 From the eleventh division of the *Duat*, in the 'Book of What is in the Duat', Sir E. A. Wallis Budge transl., in *The Egyptian Heaven and Hell*, Martin Hopkinson & Co, London, 1925, p. 240.

19 Ibid., the twelfth division of the *Duat*, p. 258.

20 Ibid., p. 70.

21 For a discussion see *The Orion Mystery*, op.cit., pp. 179–84; *Fingerprints of the Gods*, op.cit., p. 380 ff.

22 Ibid. See also E. A. Wallis Budge, *The Gods of the Egyptians*, Dover Publications Inc., New York, 1969.

Chapter 5

1 The tradition that important 'records' were brought to Egypt 'after the flood' i.e. after 10,000 BC, goes back to at least the third century BC. It is found, for example, in *The Book of Sothis* (commented upon by the Byzantine historian Georgios Synecellus who lived in the ninth century AD) and which some scholars attribute to the Egyptian scribe, Manetho (See Garth Fowden, *The Egyptian Hermes*, Princeton University Press, New Jersey 1993, pp. 29–33). The idea is also planted in the *Kore Kosmou* (Excerpt XXIII of the Hermetic writings) of the first and second century AD (See *Hermetica*, op.cit., p. 461). In the *Kore Kosmou* (section 8) the goddess Isis claims that Thoth deposited in a secret place the 'sacred books' which contained 'the secret things of Osiris . . . these holy symbols of the cosmic elements' and then cast a spell that these books shall remain 'unseen and undiscovered by all men who shall go to and fro on the plains of this land until the time when Heaven, grown old, shall beget organisms [i.e. humans] worthy of you . . .'

2 Andrew Tomas, *From Atlantis to Discovery*, Robert Hale, London 1972, p. 109.

3 Ibn Abd Alhokim and the Arab Manuscripts of Ibn Khurradhbih and Lohfat, cited by Joseph R. Jochmans, *The Hall of Records*, unpublished manuscript, 1985, p. 174. See also John Greaves, *Pyramidographia*, 1646, translation from the Arabic of Ibn Alhokim.

4 Peter Tompkins, *Secrets of the Great Pyramid*, Allen Lane, 1972, p. 6.

5 The famous Westcar Papyrus in the (east) Berlin Museum suggests that a secret chamber or chambers were concealed in the 'horizon' of Cheops – i.e. the alleged builder of the Great Pyramid (See *The Orion Mystery*, op.cit., Appendix 3). The term 'Horizon', however, could mean either the Great Pyramid itself or the whole necropolis of Giza, thus including

the Sphinx. Spell 1080 of the Coffin Texts (*c.* 2000 BC) speaks of a secret 'sealed thing' belonging to Osiris of Rostau (Giza) and spell 1087 suggests that it was 'writing material' linked to Heliopolis (Djedu, the 'Pillar City'), and hidden somewhere in the desert sands.

6 These Coptic traditions were recorded by the Arab chroniclers Al Qodai, Al Masudi and Al Maqrizi, cited in Jochmans, *The Hall of Records*, op.cit., p. 210.

7 The so-called 'Old Charges' of Freemasonry speak of a certain Hermenes (obviously Hermes, i.e. Thoth) who preserved the 'crafts' by carving their knowledge on sacred pillars or obelisks (see Fred L. Pick and G. Norman Knight, *The Pocket History of Freemasonry*, Frederick Muller Ltd., London 1983, p. 32). It is generally accepted that much of the 'Egyptian' esoteric strain in Freemasonry, Rosicrucianism and, to a certain extent, the Theosophists, comes from the so-called Hermetic Tradition that developed in Europe in the late Italian Renaissance but drew its source from the Greek and Coptic texts known as the Hermetic writings (see Frances A. Yates, *Giordano Bruno and the Hermetic Tradition*, University of Chicago Press, Chicago 1991; also *The Rosicrucian Enlightenment*, Ark Paperbacks, London 1986, p. 212).

8 Harmon Hartzell Bro, *Edgar Cayce: A Seer Out Of Season*, Signet Books, New York 1990, pp. 43–4. Cayce's life-long secretary was Gladys Davis, described as 'an attractive honey-blonde', whom Cayce believed to be his 'reincarnated' daughter, Iso, from Atlantean times (Ibid., p. 245).

9 Edgar Evans Cayce, Gail Cayce Schwartzer and Douglas G. Richards, *Mysteries of Atlantis Revisited: Edgar Cayce's Wisdom for the New Age*, Harper & Row, San Francisco 1988, p. xxi.

10 Ibid. p. 119. We have had the pleasure of meeting with the author, Douglas G. Richards, in July 1995 at the Edgar Cayce Foundation in Virginia Beach.

11 Ibid. p. 120.

12 Edgar Cayce 'Reading' on the Great Pyramid No. 5748–6. This 'reading' was given at his home on Arctic Crescent, Virginia Beach, Va., on 1 July 1932 at 4.10 p.m. EST.

13 'Reading' 378–16. See Mark Lehner, *The Egyptian Heritage: Based on the Edgar Cayce Readings*, A.R.E. Press, Virginia Beach 1974, p. 99.

14 'Reading' No. 5748–6. *The Egyptian Heritage*, op.cit., p. 119.

15 'Reading' No. 294–151. See Thomas Sugrue, *There is a River: The story of Edgar Cayce*, A.R.E. Press, Virginia Beach, 1988, p. 393. See also Harmon Hartzell Bro, *A Seer Out Of Season*, op.cit., p. 247.

16 Mark Lehner, *The Egyptian Heritage*, op.cit., p. 92. See also Harmon

Hartzell Bro, *A Seer Out Of Season*, op.cit., p. 133.

17 Edgar Evans Cayce, etc., *Mysteries of Atlantis*, op.cit., p. 121.

18 Ibid, p. 131.

19 Confirmed by Douglas G. Richards, in a documented conversation by telephone in September 1995 (Richards is co-author with Edgar Evans Cayce and Gail Cayce Schwartzer of *Mysteries of Atlantis Revisited*, op.cit.). When we questioned Mark Lehner directly on this matter he replied in writing (pp. 1–2 of letter dated 15 October 1995): 'I believe I probably am the "scholar" in question. It was never expected that the outcome of the ECF's support of my Year Abroad at The American University in Cairo would be that I would become a "respected Egyptologist". ARE-affiliated people supported my stint in Egypt because Hugh Lynn Cayce asked them to. Neither he nor I were sure where it would lead. I think Hugh Lynn helped me to go to Egypt because we both had some sense of destiny about it in line with the common New Age notion that it was "meant to be".'

20 Edgar Evans Cayce, etc., *Mysteries*, op.cit., p. 131. In his letter of 15 October 1995 Mark Lehner commented on our draft text, which was supplied to him without footnotes: 'I do not know the reference for your note [20] but I suspect that rather than a prospectus written before I went to Egypt as a student at AUC, this summary was written in hindsight several years later than 1973.'

21 Edgar Evans Cayce, etc., *Mysteries*, op.cit., p. 132.

22 Mark Lehner, *The Egyptian Heritage*, op.cit., back cover text.

23 Ibid., p. v.

24 In his letter to us of 15 October 1995 Mark Lehner commented as follows: 'Neither I nor the Edgar Cayce Foundation had anything to do with the first two seasons of the SRI programme at the pyramids and elsewhere in Egypt. This is not clear in your text. The SRI "Science and Archaeology" Project picked up the work of Alvarez who used cosmic rays (before I arrived in Egypt) to analyze the Second Pyramid for undiscovered chambers. I met the SRI team in 1977 about the time they did preliminary resistivity measurements on the Sphinx. SRI was in the business of looking for hidden chambers at Giza well before I or the Edgar Cayce Foundation met up with them.'

25 L. T. Dolphin, E. Moussa et. al., 'Applications of Modern Sensing Techniques to Egyptology', Menlo Park, Calif., SRI International, September 1977.

26 Ibid. See also Zahi Hawass 'Update' to Sir W. M. Flinders Petrie's *The Pyramids and Temples of Gizeh*, Histories and Mysteries of Man Ltd, London 1990, p. 102.

27 Edgar Evans Cayce, etc., *Mysteries*, op.cit., p. 132.
28 Mark Lehner's letter to us of 15 October 1995, p. 3.
29 Cited in Jochmans, *The Hall of Records*, op.cit., p. 221a. Confirmed in documented telephone conversation with project financier, 16 February 1995. Confirmed also by Mark Lehner in his letter to us dated 15 October 1995, p. 3.
30 Mark Lehner's letter to us, 15 October 1995, p. 3.
31 Ibid.
32 Ibid.
33 Ibid.
34 See also Part I of the present work for further details of Mark Lehner's ARCE project on the Sphinx.
35 Edgar Evans Cayce, etc., *Mysteries*, op.cit., pp. 142–3. The discovery of the granite was also confirmed to us by Mark Lehner in his letter, op.cit., p. 4.
36 *Venture Inward*, May–June 1986, p. 57.
37 Ibid.
38 See American Research Center in Egypt (ARCE) Newsletter No. 112, Fall 1980, p. 20 ('The American Research Center Gratefully acknowledges the support of the Edgar Cayce Foundation for the work of the Sphinx Project'). See also ARCE Newsletter No. 131, 1985, p. 44 (Mark Lehner of the ARCE wrote: 'We would like to acknowledge the financial sponsorship of . . . Bruce Ludwig of TRW Realty in Los Angeles . . . the Edgar Cayce Foundation . . . Joseph and Ursula Jahoda of Astron Corporation in Falls Church, Va., . . . Matthew McCauley of McCauley Music in Los Angeles . . .'). Mr Zahi Hawass, University of Pennylvania, is specifically acknowledged as advisor and assistant to the project 'and we look forward to continued collaboration'. The Edgar Cayce Foundation also funded (with US$17,000) a project at Giza in 1983–4, which involved an attempt to apply Carbon-14 dating to the mortar (which contains certain organic compounds) used in the Great Pyramid. This project was arranged by Mark Lehner through the ARCE's director, Dr Robert J. Wenke. We have met Joseph Jahoda several times at the Edgar Cayce Foundation in Virginia Beach in 1994–5 (see below), and also Matthew McCauley once at the Movenpick Hotel in Giza, Cairo, with Dr Mark Lehner in March 1995 while researching this book.
39 Edgar Evans Cayce, etc., *Mysteries*, op.cit., p. 138.
40 *Smithsonian*, vol. XVII, No. 1, April 1986. In his letter to us, op.cit., pp. 4–5, Mark Lehner commented: 'By the time I started the Mapping

Project, Cayce support of my work was phasing out. I stopped accepting their support after the Pyramids Radiocarbon Project [see footnote 38 above and 44 below for fuller details] because my interests and theirs were becoming too divergent. I would have to check the date of their last contribution, but if they did contribute to the mapping project it was a very minimal percentage of total financial support. The primary financial sponsors have been the Yale Endowment for Egyptology, Bruce Ludwig and David Koch. Koch and Ludwig have supported the excavations that we started in 1988.'

41 *Archaeology*, op.cit., Sept–Oct 1994, p. 41.

42 The ARE Magazine, *Venture Inward*, 'The Search for Ra-Ta', by A. Robert Smith, January–February 1985, p. 7.

43 Ibid., p. 6.

44 The Edgar Cayce Foundation had commissioned and funded a Carbon–14 dating project of the Giza monuments directed by Mark Lehner in 1983–4. Apparently small charcoal samples were extracted from the ancient mortar in the core's joints. The results gave a wide range of dates for the Great Pyramid – between 3809 BC to 2853 BC – which is a few centuries earlier than the c. 2600 BC date assigned by Egyptologists, but very far from the 10,500 BC date given in the Cayce Readings. Although many doubts have been raised concerning the validity of the results (see *Venture Inward* issues May–June 1986 and November–December 1986), this, and other archaeological evidence Mark Lehner came across at Giza, appears to have undermined his beliefs in Cayce's readings. For further details of the carbon-dating see Appendix 5

45 *Venture Inward*, May–June 1986, p. 56.

46 Ibid., p. 57.

47 Ibid.

48 *KMT Magazine*, Spring issue 1995, p. 4.

49 Ibid. In his letter to us, op.cit., p. 5, Lehner elaborated: 'I am happy that my professional work developed out of a more personal quest – call it what you will, philosophical, spiritual, ethical. Rather than look only for agreement with notions I had already conceived before coming to Giza – that is, what I wanted to be true – I looked for ways to test these and, later, other ideas about ancient Egyptian cultural development. I found few resemblances between the physical evidence and Cayce-derived ideas of an earlier civilization at Giza. But I did find the pyramids to be very human monuments. Because there is such an

abundance of evidence of real people and an Egyptian society building the Sphinx and the Pyramids, it seems culturally chauvinistic to ascribe these monuments to a different, conveniently lost, civilization on the basis of "revealed" information and ambiguous patterns. My work is still part of a lifelong quest for meaning. I would not change the path that led me to Giza even if I could.'

50 Charles Piazzi Smyth, *Our Inheritance in the Great Pyramid*, W. Isbister, London 1880 edition (reprinted recently by Bell Publishing Co., New York 1990 under the title *The Great Pyramid*). For the connection of the Petries with Piazzi Smyth, see H. A. Bruck and Mary Bruck, *The Peripatetic Astronomer: The Life of Charles Piazzi Smyth*, Adam Hilger, Bristol 1988, pp. 28, 123–6, 133–6. It seems William Matthew Flinders Petrie's father, William, almost married the daughter of Piazzi Smyth, Henrietta. She was to marry eventually, however, Professor Baden-Powell (the father of the founder of the Boy Scouts). William Petrie was later introduced by Mrs Piazzi Smyth to Anne Flinders, whom he married – hence the name Flinders Petrie. 'So Mrs (Piazzi) Smyth,' wrote Flinders Petrie, 'was the agent by whom scouting and Egyptian archaeology took their present form' (see *Seventy Years in Archaeology*, Sampson Low, Marston & Co. Ltd, London, 1931, p. 4).

51 *Al Akhbar Al Yom* weekly of 8 January 1994, front page article entitled 'Stealing of Egypt's Civilization'. Translation by Fouad Nemah of the official Egyptian Translation Bureau.

52 *Mystery of the Sphinx* was a Magic Eye North Towers Production (Executive Producer: Boris Said; Producer: Robert Watts; Directed by Bill Cote of BC Video NY).

53 Ibid.

54 Mark Lehner's letter, op.cit., p. 5: 'Yes, this sounds like the fine people of the Cayce community, some of the nicest and most positive individuals I have known.'

55 As a result of receiving this letter, which clarified many points, we were pleased to revise the present chapter extensively into the form that appears herewith.

56 Mark Lehner's letter, op.cit., p. 1.

57 CNN News reports October 1995; Middle East News Agency (MENA) 25 October 1995. At time of writing (November 1995) Zahi Hawass is the Director of the Giza necropolis for Egypt's Supreme Council of Antiquities and thus has overall responsibility for all excavations taking place on the site.

Chapter 6

1 Robert Bauval and Adrian Gilbert, *The Orion Mystery*, op.cit., Mandarin paperback edition, 1995, epilogue pp. 237–50. Also discussed recently in *Amateur Astronomy and Earth Sciences*, 'Operation Dixon' issue 1, November 1995 (Chief Editor: Dave Goode).

2 Interviewed by film maker and producer Jochen Breitenstein in Los Angeles in April 1993. Footage shown on Sat. 1, Spiegel Reportage, 15 August 1995 (*Gantenbrinks Reise in das Reich der Pharaonen*).

3 *The Times*, London, 28 January 1995, p. 18. Article by Simon Seligman.

4 Sat. 1, Spiegel Reportage, op.cit., 15 August 1995.

5 Peter Tompkins, *Secrets of the Great Pyramid*, op.cit., p. 61.

6 Where, after some difficulty, we were able to arrange to view it on 7 November 1995.

7 Bernd Scheel, *Egyptian Metalworking and Tools*, Shire Egyptology, Bucks, 1989, p. 17. For a more detailed discussion see A. Lucas, *Ancient Egyptian Materials and Industries*, Histories & Mysteries of Man Ltd, London 1989, pp. 235–43.

8 A very interesting discussion is found in Zecharia Sitchin, *The Stairway to Heaven*, Avon Books, New York, 1980, pp. 253–79.

9 Joseph R. Jochmans, *The Hall of Records*, op.cit., pp. 194–5.

10 Ibid., p. 195.

11 See Zecharia Sitchin, *The Stairway to Heaven*, op.cit., p. 266.

12 Ibid., pp. 266, 271–2, 274.

13 I. E. S. Edwards, *The Pyramids of Egypt*, Pelican Books, London, 1949, pp. 95–6.

14 Colonel Howard Vyse, *Operations carried out at the Pyramids of Gizeh: With an account of a Voyage into Upper Egypt and Appendix*, James Fraser of Regent Street, London 1837, vol. 1, p. 275.

15 Ibid., p. 276.

16 Ibid.

17 W. M. Flinders Petrie's *The Pyramids and Temples of Gizeh*, Leadenhall Press, London, 1883 edition, pp. 212–13.

18 El Sayed El Gayer and M. P. Jones, 'Metallurgical Investigation of an Iron Plate found in 1837 in the Great Pyramid at Gizeh, Egypt' in *Journal of the Metallurgy Society*, Vol. XXIII (1989) pp. 75–83.

19 Ibid. See also Robert G. Bauval, 'Investigation on the origin of the Benben Stone: was it an iron meteorite?' in *Discussions in Egyptology* Vol. XIV, 1989, pp. 5–17.

20 El Sayed El Gayer and M. P. Jones, op.cit., p. 82.

21 Ibid.

22 Ibid.

23 Ibid., p. 123 (letter to the editor of JHMS titled 'Comment on the Iron Plate from Gizeh paper').

24 Letter to Robert Bauval dated 2 November 1993, ref. EA/AJS/JAC.

25 *The Orion Mystery* op.cit., Chapter 3.

26 Ibid., Heinemann edition 1994, pp. 204–11. See also a very interesting publication by Sydney Aufrere, *L'Univers Mineral dans la pensee Egyptienne*, Institut Français D'Archéologie Orientale du Caire, pp. 433–41.

27 *The Ancient Egyptian Pyramid Texts*, R. O. Faulkner transl., Oxford University Press, 1969, lines 1983–4.

28 Ibid., lines 11–13.

29 Ibid., lines 1713–17.

30 Ibid., lines 820–2.

31 Ibid., line 904.

32 Ibid., lines 1014–16.

33 Ibid., line 852.

34 Ibid., line 907.

35 Dr Zahi Hawass calls him 'the father of modern Egyptology' (see Zahi Hawass 'Update' to Sir W. M. Flinders Petrie's *The Pyramids and Temples of Gizeh*, op.cit., p. 98; see also Jean Vercoutter, *The Search for Ancient Egypt*, Thames & Hudson, London 1992, pp. 152–5). A good account of Petrie's involvement with the Great Pyramid is given in Peter Tompkins, *Secrets of the Great Pyramid*, op.cit., pp. 96–107.

36 Charles Piazzi Smyth, *Our Inheritance in the Great Pyramid*, op.cit., pp. 535–634.

37 H. A. Bruck and Mary Bruck, *The Peripatetic Astronomer*, op.cit., p. 229.

38 Ibid., p. 38.

39 *The Orion Mystery*, op.cit., Heinemann edition, 1994, epilogue. Also see Charles Piazzi Smyth, *Our Inheritance*, op.cit., pp. 427–31.

40 Charles Piazzi Smyth, *Our Inheritance*, op.cit., pp. 427–31.

41 Ibid.

42 Ibid.

43 No one knew of this attempt by the Dixons to probe the shafts with an iron rod until Rudolf Gantenbrink, in early 1992, explored the northern shaft of the Queen's Chamber with a robot mounted with a mini-video camera. The rod still lies there, inside the shaft, at about 8 metres from the entrance and runs to the 'corner', some 24 metres up the shaft. Gantenbrink could not take his robot round the corner but he managed to see, with the video camera, that it runs for a further two metres or so

and then turns sharply back on track. What lies at the end is still unknown.

44 The Dixons, who were iron structural contractors from Newcastle, were building a bridge across the Nile near Cairo. The iron rod they used seems to have been purpose made to probe the shaft. It was cut in lengths of approximately 12 feet then assembled together with sleeve-joints as the rod was pushed within the shaft. It seems to have been stuck at the upper end, forcing the Dixons to abandon it.

45 *Nature*, 26 December 1872, p. 147.

46 Letter from John Dixon to Piazzi Smyth dated 23 November 1872.

47 *The Graphic*, 7 December 1872, p. 530. Also *Nature*, 26 December 1872 p. 146. Piazzi Smyth mentions these relics, and describes how they were found, in his book, *Our Inheritance*, op.cit., and also refers to the articles in *The Graphic* and in *Nature* in the 1874 edition of his book, pp. 155 and 364.

48 The last mention before they re-emerged in 1993, as far as we know, was in a letter written by a certain Mr E. H. Pringle dated 20 June 1873 (see *Nature* of 31 July 1873, p. 263). It is possible, however, that some other publication mentioned them in more recent times.

49 Aubrey Noakes, *Cleopatra's Needles*, H. F. & G. Witherby Ltd, London, 1962, p. 16.

50 Ibid., pp. 26–7.

51 Ibid., p. 26. See also Martin Short, *Inside the Brotherhood*, Grafton Books, London, 1989, p. 119.

52 R. M. Hadley, 'The Life and Works of Sir Erasmus Wilson (1809–1884)' in *Medical History* journal, Vol. III, 1959, pp. 215–47.

53 Ibid., p. 238.

54 Fred L. Pick and G. Norman Knight, *The Pocket History of Freemasonry*, Muller, 1977, pp. 44–5. See also Frances A. Yates, *The Rosicrucian Enlightenment*, op.cit., pp. 193–205.

55 *Illustrated London News*, 21 September 1878, p. 286.

56 *Independent*, London, 6 December 1993. See also Martin Short, *Inside the Brotherhood*, op.cit., p. 120.

57 Letter to Robert Bauval dated 28 October 1993.

58 *Independent*, 6 December 1993, p. 3.

59 *Independent*, 13 December 1993.

60 *Beaconsfield Advertiser* ('Row erupts over "missing" relics') 12 January 1994, p. 3.

61 Telephone conversation with Dr I. E. S. Edwards.

62 The video films were shown at the British Museum by R. Gantenbrink on 22 November 1993. Also shown on Sat. 1, Spiegel Reportage, op.cit.,

on 15 August 1995.

Chapter 7

1 J. P. Goidin and G. Dormion, *Kheops: Nouvelle Enquête*, Editions Recherche sur les Civilisations, Paris, 1986. See also Jean Vercoutter, *The Search for Ancient Egypt*, op.cit., p. 195.

2 Jean Vercoutter, op.cit.

3 For a more detailed discussion see *Fingerprints of the Gods*, op.cit., pp. 320–3. The shafts were concealed yet, in a curious manner, their position was obvious once a logical correlation was made with those in the King's Chamber above – as Waynman Dixon finally did in 1872 (see I. E. S. Edwards, *The Pyramids of Egypt*, op.cit., 1982 edition, p. 123). Once the openings were found, then natural curiosity would urge a deeper probe into the shafts. Dixon, in fact, frantically probed inside these shafts with metal rods in the hope of finding relics or a 'chamber', but his technology was not yet sufficiently developed to 'see' what he was doing.

4 Presented to the German Archaeological Institute in Cairo and dated March 1991.

5 This was the original title given to the documentary made by Rudolf Gantenbrink which was broadcast on the A & E channel in the USA (title changed to *The Great Pyramid*) on 8 January 1995. A shortened version was broadcast in Germany on Sat. 1 on 15 August 1995.

6 *Smithsonian*, Vol. XVII, No. 1, April 1986. Uli Kapp also assisted Mark Lehner in the Giza Mapping Project in 1985 (ARCE Newsletter 131, 1985, p. 44).

7 Documented information provided to authors.

8 I. E. S. Edwards, *The Pyramids of Egypt*, op.cit., p. 123.

9 Documented information provided to authors.

10 A curious letter was mailed by the inspector Muhammad Shahy to Rudolf Gantenbrink dated 5 August 1993 – i.e. five months after the discovery. Shahy (better transliterated as Sheeha) wrote: 'I'm in troubles now because of your project . . . I shall face questioning soon.' The young inspector was also worried that he could not write a report on this project because 'there is no reference here' (this letter was shown to the authors by R. Gantenbrink). We have been unable to make contact with Mr Muhammad Shahy.

11 The statue went missing on the 19 January 1993, when it was supposed to be displayed to President Mubarak and his guest, Libya's President,

Muammar Gaddafi, on a table near the Sphinx. It may have been stolen by the same smuggling gang that was rounded up in March 1995 (see *The Times* of London 12 and 13 March 1995).

12 Documented information from R. Gantenbrink and Jochen Breitenstein.

13 Gantenbrink has, in fact, entered the history books. His name is found in I. E. S. Edwards, *The Great Pyramid*, op.cit., 1993 edition, p. 151 and also in various education manuals on the Great Pyramid. Should a major find be made when the 'door' is opened – even though, as now seems likely, not by him – it will be entirely because of his efforts and bold imagination.

14 All articles appeared between 17 and 19 April 1993.

15 Several major international journals (*Stern*, *Der Spiegel*, etc.) also published articles and pictorials.

16 Not published in the press but mentioned in *Ancient Skies* magazine No. 3/1993, 17. Jahrgang, p. 4.

17 Reuters wire, Cairo 16 April 1993.

18 *Sunday Telegraph*, 1 January 1995.

19 Ibid.

20 Ibid.

21 Ibid.

22 Documented conversation with the authors.

23 Ibid.

24 Reported to us by R. Gantenbrink in September 1995.

25 Sat. 1, Spiegel Reportage, 15 August 1995. See also *Los Angeles Times*, 30 August 1993.

Chapter 8

1 *Kore Kosmou* (Excerpt XXIII–29) in *Hermetica*, op.cit. p. 473.

2 Ibid, p. 457.

3 From the Second Division of the *Book of What is in the Duat*, E. A. Wallis Budge transl., *The Egyptian Heaven and Hell*, Martin Hopkinson & Co. Ltd, London, 1925, Vol. 1, page 41. See also Third Division, ibid., p. 56.

4 *The Orion Mystery*, op.cit., 1994 edition, Chapter 4. There are thousands of references to 'stars' 'star-souls', 'the sun-god', 'the sky', 'the Milky Way' etc., that make the Pyramid Texts obvious candidates for a proper astronomical investigation into their content and hidden meaning. The intense concept of 'time' – especially the 'time' of the

'sky gods' and of a cosmic 'Creation' – that is found in these texts strongly suggests that the science of precession is also an important factor to apply on such an esoteric codex. The best translation is given by R. O. Faulkner, *The Ancient Egyptian Pyramid Texts*, OUP, 1969.

5 Giorgio de Santillana and Hertha von Dechend, *Hamlet's Mill*, op.cit., p. 132.

6 Ibid, p. 373.

7 For a useful discussion on the *Duat*, see Selim Hassan, *Excavations at Giza*, op.cit., Cairo, 1946, pp. 276–319.

8 A great deal of confusion has resulted from a failure to understand that the *Duat* is a fixed location in the sky (obviously encompassing Orion, Canis Major, Taurus and Leo) which has its counterpart on the land and, as the case may be, underneath the land. Access to it was deemed possible by either ascending to the sky or by going underground.

9 Selim Hassan, *Excavations at Giza*, op.cit., p. 277. See also *The Orion Mystery*, op.cit., p. 76.

10 *Excavations at Giza*, op.cit., p. 277.

11 Ibid., pp. 277–8.

12 Ibid, p. 279.

13 Although their actual composition may long pre-date the third millennium BC. See *The Orion Mystery*, op.cit., pp. 69–70.

14 Observation stations may have been spread in a sort of 'triangle' extending from Heliopolis, Memphis and Giza. It seems likely that this whole region was somehow considered the original 'land of the gods', with its epicentre at Giza.

15 The conjunction of summer solstice sunrise, the rising of Sirius and the start of the flood occurred in 3400 BC and throughout the early Pyramid Age, when the Pyramid Texts were most certainly compiled.

16 *The Orion Mystery*, op.cit., pp. 119–24.

17 The Milky Way appeared rising due east at the summer solstice pre-dawn along with Orion and Sirius in the third millennium BC.

18 *Pyramid Texts*, op.cit., lines 343–57.

19 Ibid., line 508 and Utterance 317.

20 Ibid., line 1760.

21 E. A. Wallis Budge, *The Egyptian Book of the Dead*, Dover Publications Inc., New York, 1967, p. cxxiii.

22 R. O. Faulkner, *The Book of the Dead*, British Museum Publications, London 1972, p. 90. Also see R. O. Faulkner 'The King & the Star-Religion in the Pyramid Texts' in *Journal of Near Eastern Studies*, 1966, Vol. XXV, p. 154 footnote 7. Dr Virginia Lee Davis also makes the link between the Milky Way and the 'Winding Waterway' in

Archaeoastronomy, Vol. IX, JHA xvi, 1985, p. 102. The archeoastronomer and Egyptologist, Jane B. Sellers, also arrives at the same conclusion as V. L. Davis (J. B. Sellers, *The Death of Gods in Ancient Egypt*, Penguin Books, London, 1992, p. 97).

23 *Pyramid Texts*, op.cit., line 2061.

24 Ibid., line 1717.

25 Ibid., line 882.

26 R. T. Rundle Clark, *Myth and Symbol in Ancient Egypt*, Thames & Hudson, London, 1978, pp. 263–5. Clark explains how the Pharaoh's role was to re-enact and commemorate events that were believed to have happened in a blissful golden age called 'Tep Zepi' [*Zep Tepi*].

27 Ibid.

28 Ibid p. 27.

29 *Pyramid Texts*, op.cit., Utterance 600. Here the 'pyramids' are also placed amidst the landscape of 'Creation' at the first sunrise of the world.

30 R. T. Rundle Clark, *Myth and Symbol*, op.cit., page 264.

31 Ibid.

32 Henri Frankfort, *Kingship and the Gods*, The University of Chicago Press, 1978, pp. 24–35.

33 *Hamlet's Mill*, op.cit., pp. 86–7.

34 British Museum No. 498. The Shabaka Stone is fixed on the south wall of the ground floor of the 'Egyptian' wing. It measures some 135 × 92 cm. (approx. 4 × 3 feet) and is badly damaged at the centre – apparently due to it being used as a grinding millstone before its discovery by archaeologists. It contains 62 columns of hieroglyphic inscriptions. Miriam Lichtheim, who gives a full translation, wrote that 'the language is archaic and resembles that of the Pyramid Texts' (Miriam Lichtheim, *Ancient Egyptian Literature* Vol. 1: The Old and Middle Kingdoms, University of California Press, Los Angeles, 1975, pp. 3–57).

35 Miriam Lichtheim, *Ancient Egyptian Literature*, op.cit., Vol. 1, p. 52. A variation to Osiris's death is that he was killed by his brother, Seth, and his body cut into fourteen pieces.

36 Ibid. Ayan must have been a sacred location immediately north of the city walls of Memphis. It is the present-day location of the village of Mit Rahin.

37 Where Ayan existed there remain, today, the vestiges of a ruined Graeco-Roman fort which must have been built in the Egyptian style (as the broken columns which still can be seen there attest) and which, curiously enough, is known by the locals as the 'prison of Joseph' (the

Biblical patriarch who was kept in the 'round tower' by Pharaoh – see Genesis 39:21). It can be reached along the narrow canal road opposite and north of the Memphis Museum.

38 Miriam Lichtheim, *Ancient Egyptian Literature*, op.cit., Vol. 1, p. 53.
39 About 15 kilometres south of the outskirts of the Maadi suburbs of Cairo.
40 Miriam Lichtheim, *Ancient Egyptian Literature*, op.cit., Vol. 1, p. 53.
41 E. A. Wallis Budge, *The Egyptian Heaven and Hell*, op.cit., Vol. III, p. 131.
42 I. E. S. Edwards, *The Pyramids of Egypt*, op.cit., 1993 edition, p. 10.
43 R. T. Rundle Clark, *Myth and Symbol*, op.cit., p. 108.
44 James H. Breasted, *Ancient Records of Egypt*, Part II, Histories & Mysteries of Man Ltd, London, 1988, pp. 320–4.
45 Ibid., p. 323. On line 7 of the stela.
46 Miriam Lichtheim, *Ancient Egyptian Literature*, op.cit., Vol. 1, p. 53.
47 *Pyramid Texts*, op.cit., line 1717.
48 *Orion Mystery*, op.cit, 1994 edition, pp. 116–19.
49 Selim Hassan, *Excavations at Giza*, op.cit., pp. 278, 285.
50 Ibid., p. 265.
51 Ibid.
52 Ibid., pp. 302, 315.
53 Ibid., p. 338.
54 Ibid., p. 265.
55 Ibid.
56 Ibid., p. 263.
57 Ibid., p. 265.
58 Ibid.
59 Ibid.
60 Ibid.
61 Mark Lehner, *The Egyptian Heritage*, op.cit.
62 Ibid, p. 119.
63 J. B. Sellers, *The Death of Gods in Ancient Egypt*, op.cit., p. 164.
64 R. O. Faulkner, *The Ancient Egyptian Coffin Texts*, Aris & Phillips Ltd, Wiltshire, Vol. III, p. 132, Spell 1035.
65 Ibid. Vol. I, p. 190, Spell 241.
66 Ibid. Vol. I, p. 185, Spell 236.
67 J. B. Sellers, *The Death of Gods*, op.cit., pp. 164–5.
68 Ibid.
69 *The Orion Mystery*, op.cit., 1994 edition, pp. 116–9.

Chapter 9

1 James H. Breasted, *Ancient Records*, op.cit., Part II, pp. 320–4.

2 *Innu* means 'pillar' thus Heliopolis was, quite literally, the 'City of the Pillar'. All that can be seen there today is an obelisk of Sesostris I (12th Dynasty *c.* 1880 BC) and a few remains of a temple.

3 I. E. S. Edwards, *The Pyramids of Egypt*, op.cit., 1993 edition, pp. 284–6.

4 Herodotus, *The Histories*, Book II, 2–8. See Penguin Classics translation, 1972, p. 130.

5 Aristotle, *De Caelo*, II, 12, 292a. See translation in R. A. Schwaller de Lubicz, *Sacred Science*, Inner Traditions International, New York 1982, p. 280.

6 E. M. Antoniadi, *L'Astronomie Egyptienne*, Paris, 1934, pp. 3–4.

7 *Diodorus of Sicily*, The Library of History, Book V, 57 and Book I, 81.

8 Proclus Diadochus, *Commentaries on the Timaeus*, IV. See translation in R. A. Schwaller de Lubicz, *Sacred Science*, op.cit., p. 286.

9 *The Orion Mystery*, op.cit., pp. 182–4, 287 note 7.

10 R. T. Rundle Clark, *Myth and Symbol in Ancient Egypt*, op.cit., pp. 38–9.

11 Edouard Naville, 'Le nom du Sphinx dans le livre des morts' in *Sphinx*, Vol. V, 188, p. 193.

12 Edouard Naville, 'Le Sphinx III' in *Sphinx*, Vol. XXI, 1924, p. 13.

13 Ibid., p. 12.

14 Ibid.

15 Ibid.

16 Edouard Naville, 'Le nom du Sphinx dans le livre des morts', op.cit., p. 195.

17 Selim Hassan, *The Sphinx: Its History in the Light of Recent Excavations*, Government Press, Cairo, 1949, p. 129.

18 Ibid.

19 A spell from the ancient Egyptian *Book of the Dead*, op.cit.

20 *Pyramid Texts*, op.cit., lines 2081–6.

21 Selim Hassan, *The Sphinx*, op.cit., p. 70, fig. 13. See Also E. Naville in 'Sphinx III', op.cit., p. 19.

22 Zahi Hawass and Mark Lehner 'The Sphinx: Who built it, and why?' in *Archaeology*, September–October 1994, p. 34.

23 Ibid.

24 George Hart, *A Dictionary of Egyptian Gods and Goddesses*, Routledge & Kegan Paul, London, 1988, p. 46.

25 Rosalie David, *Ancient Egyptian Religion, Beliefs and Practices*,

Routledge & Kegan Paul, London, 1982, p. 46.

26 Ibid.

27 George Hart, *Dictionary of Egyptian Gods and Goddesses*, op.cit., p. 94. Hart also says that 'the element "Akhti" can be a dual form of the noun "Akhet", "Horizon"; there may be a play on words when the king is said to be given power over the "Two Horizons" (i.e. east and west) as Horakhti'.

28 Quote from Jane B. Sellers, *The Death of Gods*, op.cit., p. 89. For further details, see Hermann Kees, *Ancient Egypt: A Cultural Topography*, University of Chicago Press, 1977.

29 Often sitting down on a throne, holding the royal staff.

30 George Hart, *Dictionary*, op.cit., p. 94.

31 Lewis Spence, *Egypt*, Bracken Books, Myths & Legends Series, London 1986, p. 291.

32 Selim Hassan, *The Sphinx*, op.cit., p. 94.

33 Egypt Exploration Society Report, First General Meeting, 1883, p. 8.

34 Ibid.

35 Ahmed Fakhry, *The Pyramids*, University of Chicago Press, 1961, p. 164. See *Pyramid Texts*, op.cit., lines 1085, 926. See also E. A. Wallis Budge, *An Egyptian Hieroglyphic Dictionary*, Dover Publications Inc., New York, 1978, Vol. I, p. 500b.

36 Selim Hassan, *Excavations at Giza*, op.cit., figs. 18, 39, 40, 41, 46, 66.

37 Selim Hassan, *The Sphinx*, op.cit., p. 76.

38 Ibid.

39 James H. Breasted, *Ancient Records*, op.cit., Part II, pp. 320–4.

40 Ibid.

41 Lewis Spence, *Egypt*, op. cit., p. 158.

42 Ibid.

43 Selim Hassan, *The Sphinx*, op.cit., p. 104.

44 Lewis Spence, *Egypt*, op.cit., p. 157.

45 E. A. Wallis Budge, *An Egyptian Hieroglyphic Dictionary*, op.cit., Vol. I, pp. 418b, 500b, 501b.

46 Lewis Spence, *Egypt*, op.cit., p. 84.

47 Ahmed Fakhry, *The Pyramids*, op.cit., p. 164.

48 Ibid.

49 J. Malek, *In the Shadow of the Pyramids*, Orbis, London 1986, p. 10.

50 *Pyramid Texts*, op.cit., p. 323.

51 George Hart, *Dictionary of Egyptian Gods and Goddesses*, op.cit., p. 88.

52 *Pyramid Texts*, op.cit., lines 525–7.

53 Ibid., lines 928–9.

54 Ibid., lines 352–3.

55 Ibid., lines 928–9.
56 Ibid., line 1961.
57 Ibid., line 820.
58 Ibid., line 151.
59 Ibid., lines 927–30.
60 Ibid., line 458.
61 Ibid., line 965.
62 E. C. Krupp, *In Search of Ancient Astronomies*, Chatto & Windus, 1980, pp. 186–90. Krupp wrote: 'The Nile, with its annual flooding, made civilisation possible in Egypt . . . even more compelling was the fact that the heliacally rising Sirius (the dawn rising) and the rising of the Nile coincided, approximately, with the summer solstice.' Interestingly, *Pyramid Texts* lines 1131 and 1172 speak of the 'Great Flood' which is in the sky as seen in the east of the sky at dawn. This matches the actual celestial picture in *c.* 2800–2500 BC, when the Milky Way would rise due east on the pre-dawn of the summer solstice.
63 *Pyramid Texts*, lines 360–3.
64 Ibid., line 2047.
65 Ibid., lines 1131–2.
66 Ibid., line 362.

Chapter 10

1   R. T. Rundle Clark, *Myth and Symbol in Ancient Egypt*, op.cit.
2   Ibid., p. 121.
3   Ibid., pp. 121–2.
4   Ibid., p. 122.
5   E. A. Wallis Budge, *The Literature of Funeral Offerings*, Kegan Paul Ltd, London, 1909, p. 2.
6   *Pyramid Texts*, op.cit., lines 1703, 1710–20.
7   Ibid., line 1730.
8   Ibid., line 1860.
9   R. A. Schwaller de Lubicz, *Sacred Science*, op.cit., p. 175.
10 *Pyramid Texts*, op.cit., line 632. See also *The Orion Mystery*, op.cit., pp. 132, 136.
11 *The Orion Mystery*, op. cit., pp. 220–5.
12 O. Neugebauer and R. Parker, *Egyptian Astronomical Texts*, Brown University Press, Lund Humphries, London, 1964, Vol. I, p. 70. For a summarized discussion see *The Orion Mystery*, op.cit., Appendix 4.
13 Ibid.

14 Ibid. The first rising of a star after a prolonged period of invisibility is at dawn, about one hour before sunrise. Sirius has its heliacal rising today in early August. In *c*. 3000 BC this occurred in late June. The 'shift' from a fixed point such as the summer solstice is about seven days every millennium. See R. A. Schwaller de Lubicz, *Sacred Science*, op.cit., p. 175.

15 *Pyramid Texts*, op.cit., Utterances 606, 609.

16 The ecliptic passes a few degrees north of the Hyades and thus just 'west' or on the 'right' bank of the Milky Way as viewed at the meridian. In *c*. 2500 BC the vernal point would have been located there.

17 Dr Virginia Lee Davis seems to be convinced about this in *Archaeoastronomy*, Vol. IX, JHA xvi, 1985, p. 102. So is the archeoastronomer and Egyptologist, Jane B. Sellers, in *Death of Gods*, op.cit., p. 97.

18 *Pyramid Texts*, op.cit., line 2172.

19 Ibid., line 2045.

20 Ibid., lines 1704–7.

21 Ibid., line 1541.

22 Ibid., line 1345.

23 Ibid., lines 343–6.

24 Ibid., lines 525–7.

25 Ibid., lines 928–9.

26 Among all modern Egyptologists it is only Schwaller de Lubicz, as far as we know, who realized the immense implications of the stellar-solar conjunction in Leo during the Pyramid Age – a conjunction that could hardly have gone unnoticed by the ancients since it occurred not only at the summer solstice but also at the heliacal rising of Sirius. Lubicz wrote: 'It is significant also that tradition had already related the heliacal rising of Sirius with the beginning of the Nile's flooding and with the constellation of Leo; indeed since the foundation of the calendar to the beginning of our era, in Egypt the sun was always situated in the constellation of Leo at the date of the heliacal rising of Leo' (*Sacred Science*, op. cit., p. 176). The tradition which Schwaller is alluding to is also confirmed by several Greek and Roman chroniclers who passed through Egypt in ancient times. Harpollon, for example, who visited Egypt in the fifth century, commented that: 'Lions were a symbol of the inundation in consequence of the Nile rising more abundantly when the sun was in Leo. Those who anciently presided over sacred works made the waterspouts and passages of fountains in the form of lions . . .' (Harpollon Book I, 21). The same is stated by Plutarch, who came to Egypt in the first century AD. Plutarch is distinguished for being the

only scholar in antiquity to have compiled a full coherent account of the Osiris and Isis myth. He held a high position as a magistrate in Boeotia and also belonged to the priesthood of Delphi. In about AD 50 he compiled his celebrated *De Iside et Osiride* (*On Isis and Osiris*) after consulting Egyptian priests in Egypt, who also told him of the astral rituals of the summer solstice: 'Of the stars, the Egyptians think that Sirius, the Dog Star, is the star of Isis, because it is the bringer of water [i.e. the Nile's flood]. They also hold the lion in honour, and they adorn the doorways of their shrines with gaping lions' heads, because the Nile overflows "when for the first time the Sun comes in conjunction with [the constellation] of Leo" . . .' (see quote in R. A. Schwaller de Lubicz, *Sacred Science*, op.cit., p. 91).

27 Richard H. Allen, *Star Names: Their Lore and Meaning*, Dover Publications Inc., New York, 1963, pp. 255–6. It is the brightest star in Leo, a constellation known as the 'Domicilium Solis' ('House of the Sun'). Allen makes this curious comment but gives no reference: 'The great androsphinx [of Giza] is said to have been sculptured with Leo's body and the head of the adjacent Virgo . . .' (ibid., p. 253).

28 Memphis.

29 For a full discussion on the 'solar boats' see Selim Hassan, *Excavations at Giza*, op.cit., pp. 1–156. There are various boat 'pits' at Giza, two of which contained actual boats (one fully assembled in a museum south of the Great Pyramid). Rudolf Gantenbrink has remarked that the size (and shape) of the Grand Gallery in the Great Pyramid would be an ideal store for such a boat.

30 Probably somewhere within the Sphinx Temple. This idea was, in fact, suggested by the German Egyptologist, Adolf Erman, who wrote: 'Rosetau, the gate of the ways, led direct to the underworld. It is possible that part of this shrine has survived in the so-called temple of the Sphinx . . .' (*A Handbook of Egyptian Religion*, Archibald Constable & Co. Ltd, 1907, p. 15).

31 R. O. Faulkner, *The Ancient Egyptian Coffin Texts*, op.cit., Vol. III, p. 132, Spell 1035.

32 Ibid., p. 109.

33 *Pyramid Texts*, op.cit., lines 1128–34.

34 Ibid., lines 924–5.

35 Ibid., line 1328.

36 Ibid., line 1657.

37 Seventh Division, *Book of What is in the Duat*, E. A. Wallis Budge transl., *Egyptian Heaven and Hell*, op.cit., Vol. I, p. 143.

38 Robin Cook, *The Pyramids of Giza*, op.cit., p. 42.

39 *Pyramid Texts*, op.cit., lines 1710–18.

40 E. A. Wallis Budge, *An Egyptian Hieroglyphic Dictionary*, op.cit., Vol. I, p. 580a.

41 Selim Hassan, *Excavations at Giza*, op.cit., p. 184.

42 E. A. Wallis Budge, *Dictionary*, op.cit., Vol. 1, p. 579b.

43 Selim Hassan, *Excavations at Giza*, op.cit., p. 184.

44 Adolf Erman, *A Handbook of Egyptian Religion*, op.cit., 1907, p. 15.

45 *Coffin Texts*, op.cit., Vol. III, p. 134.

46 I. E. S. Edwards, *The Pyramids of Egypt*, op.cit., 1993 edition, p. 286.

47 The causeway of the Pyramid of Unas at Saqqara has a small part of the original roof on the ceiling of which are carved five-pointed stars. The ceiling was painted blue and the stars probably gold or yellow.

48 Jean Kerisel (*La Grande Pyramide et ses Derniers Secrets*, scheduled for publication 1996) discusses this matter at length. The table is about 10 metres below the floor-level of the Sphinx enclosure.

49 Kerisel appeared on the BBC documentary, *The Great Pyramid: Gateway to the Stars*, shown on 6 February 1994.

50 Jean Kerisel, *La Grande Pyramide*, op.cit., pp. 196–8.

51 *Pyramid Texts*, op.cit., lines 1195–9.

52 The 'Herald of the Year' mentioned in the *Pyramid Texts* implies the star Sirius which follows Orion. The latter, by necessity, must be near the 'Field of Offerings'.

53 See fig. 11 in R. A. Schwaller de Lubicz, *Sacred Science*, op.cit., p. 97. See also various diagrams of so-called 'Sphinx stelae' shown in Selim Hassan, *The Sphinx*, op.cit.

54 Kerisel has recently obtained a scientific licence from the Egyptian Antiquities Department to explore the subterranean chamber of the Great Pyramid and test a hunch he's had for many years that somewhere under the chamber is an access to a hidden chamber itself connected, perhaps, by tunnel with the valley or even the Sphinx area. In July 1995 Kerisel managed to use a high-precision drill to make tiny boreholes into the wall of the horizontal passageway that leads to the chamber but so far nothing has been found.

55 Robert Bauval, 'The Seeding of the star-gods: A fertility ritual inside Cheops's Pyramid?' in *Discussions In Egyptology*, Vol. XVI, 1990, pp. 21–9.

56 *The Orion Mystery*, op.cit., p. 221. The 'ritual' was graphically recreated in the BBC documentary *The Great Pyramid: Gateway to the Stars*, shown in February and September 1994.

57 *Pyramid Texts*, op.cit., line 632.

58 E. A. Wallis Budge, *Dictionary*, op.cit., Vol. II, p. 654b.

59 *Smithsonian Contributions to Astrophysics*, Vol. X, No. 2, 5000 and 10,000 Year Star Catalogs, by Gerald S. Hawkins and Shoshana K. Rosenthal, Washington, DC, 1967, p. 154. For 2500 BC the declination for Regulus is given as +24.1 degrees. Thus for latitude 30 degrees the rising point would be very close to 28 degrees. The sun's declination at the summer solstice in *c*. 2500 BC was very near this point, at 23.98 degrees. Since the apparent angular width of the sun is about 0.5 degrees, both Regulus and the sun would have occupied the same 'place' in the eastern horizon at the summer solstice in *c*. 2500 BC.

60 James H. Breasted, *Ancient Records*, op.cit., Part II, pp. 321–2.

61 'Egyptians of the New Kingdom were . . . in the dark concerning it [the Sphinx] and it is extremely doubtful if there ever was a single person living in Egypt at this period, who knew as much of the true history of the Sphinx as we do to-day . . .' (Selim Hassan, *The Sphinx*, op.cit., p. 75).

62 James H. Breasted, *Ancient Records*, op.cit., Part II, p. 323.

Chapter 11

1 T. G. H. James, *An Introduction to Ancient Egypt*, British Museum Publications Ltd, 1987, p. 37.

2 Ibid., p. 38.

3 *Boston Globe*, op.cit., 23 October 1991.

4 Labib Habachi, *The Obelisks of Egypt*, The American University Press, Cairo, 1988, p. 40.

5 Ibid.

6 Nicholas Grimal, *A History of Ancient Egypt*, Blackwell, Oxford, 1992, p. 12.

7 Ibid.

8 W. B. Emery, *Archaic Egypt*, Penguin, London, 1987, p. 23.

9 Michael A. Hoffman, *Egypt Before the Pharaohs*, Michael O'Mara Books Ltd, London, 1991, p. 12.

10 Ibid.

11 W. B. Emery, *Archaic Egypt*, op.cit., p. 32 ff.

12 *Cambridge Ancient History*, Volume I, p. 250.

13 Henri Frankfort, *Kingship and the Gods*, University of Chicago Press, 1978, p. 90.

14 I. E. S. Edwards, *The Pyramids of Egypt*, op.cit., 1993 edition, p. 286: 'The high priest of the centre of the sun cult at Heliopolis bore the title "Chief of the Astronomers" and was represented wearing a mantle

adorned with stars.'

15 Giorgio de Santillana and Hertha von Dechend, *Hamlet's Mill*, op.cit., p. 58.

Chapter 12

1 See for example C. W. Ceram, *Gods, Graves and Scholars*, Book Club Associates, London, 1971, p. 26 ff.

2 See Sarva Daman Singh, *Ancient Indian Warfare*, Motilal Banarsidass, Delhi, 1989, p. 7 ff.

3 Labib Habachi, *The Obelisks of Egypt*, op.cit., p. 39.

4 Ibid.

5 Cited in ibid., pp. 39–40.

6 For a detailed discussion see E. A. E. Reymond, *The Mythical Origin of the Egyptian Temple*, Manchester University Press, Barnes and Noble Inc., New York, 1969.

7 John Anthony West, *Traveller's Key to Ancient Egypt*, op.cit., p. 412.

8 E. A. E. Reymond, *Mythical Origin of the Egyptian Temple*, op.cit., p. 4.

9 Ibid.

10 Ibid., p. 8 ff.

11 Letter to Robert Bauval dated 27 January 1993: 'I believe it [the mound] represented the primaeval mound on which life first appeared.'

12 E. A. E. Reymond, *Mythical Origin of the Egyptian Temple*, op.cit., pp. 28, 39, 46, 48, etc., etc.

13 Ibid., p. 42.

14 Ibid., p. 41.

15 Ibid., p. 44.

16 Ibid., pp. 27 and 31.

17 Jeremy Black and Anthony Green, *Gods, Demons and Symbols of Ancient Mesopotamia*, British Museum Press, London, 1992, pp. 163–4.

18 Donald A. Mackenzie, *Myths and Legends of India*, The Mystic Press, London, 1987, p. 141 ff; Veronica Ions, *Indian Mythology*, Hamlyn, London, 1983, pp. 120–1.

19 E. A. E. Reymond, *Mythical Origin of the Egyptian Temple*, op.cit., pp. 106–7.

20 Ibid., p. 55.

21 Ibid., p. 90.

22 Ibid., p. 113.

23 Ibid., pp. 109 and 127.

24 Ibid., p. 77.

25 Ibid., p. 112.

26 Ibid., p. 273.

27 Cited in R. A. Schwaller de Lubicz, *Sacred Science*, op.cit., pp. 103–4. See also Henri Frankfort, *Kingship and the Gods*, op.cit., p. 90.

28 E. A. E. Reymond, *Mythical Origin of the Egyptian Temple*, op.cit., p. 59.

29 R. T. Rundle Clark, *Myth and Symbol in Ancient Egypt*, op.cit., p. 37.

30 *P. dem Berlin*, 13603. For the ancient traditions asserting that Heliopolis was originally founded in remote pre-Dynastic times see J. Norman Lockyer, *The Dawn of Astronomy*, op.cit., p. 74.

31 E. A. E. Reymond, *Mythical Origin of the Egyptian Temple*, op.cit., p. 122.

32 Ibid., pp. 121–2.

33 Margaret Bunson, *The Encyclopaedia of Ancient Egypt*, New York, Oxford, 1991, p. 110.

34 Ibid., p. 45.

35 E. A. Wallis Budge, *An Egyptian Hieroglyphic Dictionary*, op.cit., Vol. II, p. 958.

36 Flinders Petrie, *Royal Tombs* II, Pl.v,3, cited in E. A. E Reymond, *Mythical Origin of the Egyptian Temple*, p. 136.

37 E. A. E. Reymond, *Mythical Origin of the Egyptian Temple*, op.cit., p. 257. See also p. 262.

38 Ibid., p. 262.

39 Ibid., p. 114; see also R. T. Rundle Clark, *Myth and Symbol*, op.cit., p. 37 ff.

40 *Encyclopaedia Britannica*, 9:393.

41 *The Orion Mystery*, op.cit., p. 188.

42 Ibid., p. 17.

43 Ibid., pp. 203–4.

44 Ibid., p. 17.

45 R. T. Rundle Clark, *The Legend of the Phoenix*, University of Birmingham Press, 1949, p. 17.

46 *The Orion Mystery*, op.cit., p. 212 ff.

47 R. T. Rundle Clark, *Myth and Symbol*, op.cit., p. 246.

48 Robert K. G. Temple, *The Sirius Mystery*, Destiny Books, Rochester, Vt, 1987, p. 186.

49 E. A. Wallis Budge, *Hieroglyohic Dictionary*, op.cit., Vol. II, pp. 828–32.

50 Ibid., Vol. I, p. 11b.

51 Mark Lehner, *The Egyptian Heritage*, op.cit., p. 119.

52 E. A. Wallis Budge, *Hieroglyphic Dictionary*, op.cit., p. 11b.

Chapter 13

1 See for example W. B. Emery, *Archaic Egypt*, op.cit., p. 22.
2 *Manetho*, W. G. Waddell trans., Heinemann, London, 1940, p. 3, note 1.
3 R. A. Schwaller de Lubicz, *Sacred Science*, op.cit., p. 86; Lucy Lamy, *Egyptian Mysteries*, Thames & Hudson, London, 1986, pp. 68–9; Jane B. Sellers, *The Death of Gods in Ancient Egypt*, op.cit., p. 94.
4 *Sacred Science*, op.cit., p. 86.
5 Ibid.
6 Jane B. Sellers, *The Death of Gods*, op.cit., p. 94.
7 E. A. Wallis Budge, *Hieroglyphic Dictionary*, op.cit., Vol. I, pp. 22–3.
8 Ibid.
9 *Sacred Science*, op.cit.
10 Henri Frankfort, *Kingship and the Gods*, op.cit., p. 93.
11 Later known as Buto and Hierakonpolis respectively.
12 Frankfort, *Kingship*, op.cit., p. 94.
13 Ibid.
14 *The Ancient Egyptian Pyramid Texts*, R. O. Faulkner, transl., op.cit., lines 478 and 1717, pp. 94 and 253 respectively; Frankfort, *Kingship*, op.cit., pp. 93–5; R. T. Rundle Clark, *Myth and Symbol*, op.cit., pp. 122–3.
15 E. A. E. Reymond, *Mythical Origin of the Egyptian Temple*, op.cit., p. 122.
16 John Anthony West, *Serpent in the Sky*, op.cit., p. 1.
17 *Manetho*, op.cit., p. xi.
18 Ibid., p. 3.
19 Ibid., p. 5.
20 Ibid., p. 15.
21 Ibid., p. 227.
22 *Diodorus Siculus*, C. H. Oldfather transl., Harvard University Press, 1989, Vol. I, p. 157.
23 R. A. Schwaller de Lubicz, *Sacred Science*, op.cit., p. 111.

Chapter 14

1 Skyglobe 3.6.
2 *The Orion Mystery*, op.cit., p. 140 ff.
3 *The Orion Mystery*, op.cit., pp. 29 and 281, note 1. Details are as follows: Sneferu, about 9 million tons (two Pyramids at Dahshur) plus

three Giza Pyramids (about 15 million tons) plus Abu Roash and Zawayat Al Aryan (about 1 million tons) = 25 million tons, i.e. about 75 per cent of the total volume of 'Pyramid Age' Pyramids (estimated at around 30 million tons).

4 See for example Ahmed Fakhry, *The Pyramids*, op.cit.

5 *Hermetica*, op.cit., *Asclepius III*, 24b, p. 341.

6 Ibid., 25, p. 343.

7 See in particular Chapter 4.

8 *Pyramid Texts*, op.cit., Utterances 471–3, pp. 160–1.

9 T. G. H. James, *Introduction to Ancient Egypt*, op.cit., p. 41.

10 Ibid.

11 See discussion in W. B. Emery, *Archaic Egypt*, op.cit., p. 42 ff.

12 *The Age of the God Kings*, Time-Life, 1987, p. 56 ff.

13 See discussion in W. B. Emery, *Archaic Egypt*, op.cit., p. 42 ff.

14 Even his name is put into doubt. According to Dr Jaromir Malek, for example, the name of Menes 'could be completely fictitious and based on a word-play which was misunderstood as a royal name by the later compilers of king-lists' (Jaromir Malek, *In the Shadow of the Pyramids*, Orbis, London, 1986, p. 29). As for his other name, Narmer, this, too, is plagued with confusion and doubt. On the so-called votive mace-heads and palettes found at Hierakonpolis there is shown the image of a chieftain or 'king' and on the front of his face are shown certain hieroglyphic signs, in some cases forming the syllables 'Nar-Mer' and in others showing a scorpion. This has led Egyptologists to conclude that the Menes of the king-lists is this Narmer or 'King Scorpion' (ibid., pp. 28–9). To overcome the obvious confusion of having this presumed 'last king of Predynastic Egypt' bearing three names, Egyptologists have arrived at the unsatisfactory conclusion that the name 'King Scorpion' on the votive mace-head 'is almost certainly wrong' and that it must be regarded as some sort of 'large ceremonial image'. Consequently 'if King "Scorpion" is thus refuted,' proposed Dr Malek, then 'the likeliest candidate for identification with the figure on the mace-head is Narmer' (ibid., p. 29).

15 W. A. Fairservis Jr, 'A Revised View of the Narmer Palette', in *Journal of the American Research Center in Egypt*, XXVIII, 1991, pp. 1–20.

16 Jane B. Sellers, *The Death of Gods in Ancient Egypt*, op.cit., pp. 93–4.

17 Ibid., p. 90.

18 Ibid., p. 94.

19 Henri Frankfort, *Kingship and the Gods*, op.cit., pp. 18–19.

20 Ibid., p. 33.

21 Ibid., p. vi.

22 Sellers, *Death of Gods*, op.cit., p. 93.

23 Ibid., pp. 93 ff, 115 ff and 192 ff. Having determined that the ancient Egyptians made use of the phenomenon of precession, Sellers then focused, to the exclusion of all else, on the idea that the ancients were tracking the heliacal rising of Orion at the spring equinox. With this in mind she based all her observations in the eastern horizon at the time of the spring equinox. This led her to make precessional calculations which bracketed the 'Golden Age' between 7300 BC and 6700 BC, the two epochs marking the beginning and end of Orion's heliacal rising with the spring equinox (e.g. pp. 28 and 43). Although the core of her thesis that the key to the ancient mystery is to be found in the tracking of Orion's precessional drift is spot on, her conclusion that the measurements are to be made at the rising in the east of Orion at the spring equinox is a curious error of judgement. For what is most surprising about Sellers's analytical approach is that, while she correctly puts all the emphasis of her thesis on Orion and its precessional drift, she makes absolutely no reference to the most obvious astronomical 'Orion marker' in ancient Egypt: the 'Orion' star-shaft in the Great Pyramid. Indeed, Sellers completely ignores the Pyramids or any other structure in Egypt, and instead centres her attention only on the textual material. The fact is that the Pyramid builders and the compilers of the Pyramid Texts were not tracking Orion in the eastern horizon but high in the southern skies, at the meridian.

24 Precessional calculations show that we live in the astronomical 'Last Time' of Orion, with the belt stars in our epoch approaching the highest altitude at the meridian that they will ever attain in their precessional cycle.

25 Giorgio de Santillana and Hertha von Dechend, *Hamlet's Mill*, op.cit., p. 11.

Chapter 15

1 Miriam Lichtheim, *Ancient Egyptian Literature*, Vol. I: The Old and Middle Kingdoms, p. 52.

2 Ibid., pp. 52–3.

3 *Pyramid Texts*, op.cit., lines 1256–7, p. 200.

4 Ibid., 1278, p. 202.

5 For a brief review see Bunson, *The Encyclopaedia of Ancient Egypt*, op.cit., p. 130.

6 Ibid.

7 *Pyramid Texts*, op.cit., 1657, p. 247.

8 Ibid., Utterance 610, p. 253.

9 Ibid., lines 2180–1, p. 305.

10 Ibid., lines 882–3, p. 155.

11 Sellers, *Death of Gods*, op.cit., pp. 90–3.

12 Selim Hassan, *Excavations at Giza*, op.cit., pp. 194 ff.

13 Pap. Louvre 3292.

14 Ibid., and see *Excavations at Giza*, op.cit., p. 194.

15 *Excavations at Giza*, op.cit., p. 195.

16 The following point made by E. A. E. Reymond in *The Mythical Origin of the Egyptian Temple*, op.cit., p. 57, is of obvious relevance. Referring to the content of Papyrus dem. Berlin 13603 he notes: 'Heliopolis was regarded as the centre of creation. The primordial aspect of Heliopolis is not described; however, there is a clear allusion to the theory according to which Heliopolis existed before the Earth was created. From the primaeval Heliopolis, so it is explained in our text, the Earth-God created the Earth, which received the name *Mn-nfr*, Memphis.'

17 *The Ancient Egyptian Coffin Texts*, R. O. Faulkner transl., Aris & Phillips, Warminster, Vol. III, Spell 1065.

18 *Pyramid Texts*, op.cit., Utterance 477, p. 164.

19 Hassan, *Excavations at Giza*, op.cit., p. 198.

20 It is this 'language' – a great, archaic, world-wide system – that is the principal focus of Giorgio de Santillana's and Hertha von Dechend's ground-breaking study *Hamlet's Mill*, op.cit.

21 Lichtheim, *Ancient Egyptian Literature*, op.cit., Vol. I, pp. 55–6.

22 *Pyramid Texts*, op.cit., lines 1716–17, p. 253.

23 Ibid., lines 1256–61, p. 200.

24 Ibid., 798–803, p. 144.

25 See, for example, Lewis Spence, *Ancient Egyptian Myths and Legends*, Dover Publications, New York, 1990, p. 106.

26 *Coffin Texts*, op.cit., Spell 1035, Vol. III, p. 132. Interestingly, the Spell directly links the acquisition of knowledge concerning past and former skies to the desired attainment of immortal life and existence: 'As for him who does not know this spell, he shall be taken into the infliction of the dead . . . as one who is non-existent . . .'

27 Sellers, *Death of Gods*, op.cit., p. 192.

28 Ibid., p. 193.

29 Ibid.

30 For a fuller discussion see *Fingerprints of the Gods*, op.cit., pp. 256 ff.

31 Ibid., and see Sellers, *Death of Gods*, op.cit., p. 193.

32 Ibid., and see Sellers, *Death of Gods*, op.cit., pp. 192–209.

33 As pointed out in Chapter 10, the Egyptian royal cubit measures 20.6 inches.
34 Mary Bruck, 'Can the Great Pyramid be Astronomically Dated?', in *Journal of the British Astronomical Association*, 105, 4, 1995, p. 163.
35 Ibid., p. 164.
36 Ibid., p. 163.
37 Garth Fowden, *The Egyptian Hermes*, Cambridge University Press, 1987, p. 33. The reference is to the *Hermetica*, op.cit., the *Kore Kosmu*, 5 and 6, pp. 459–61.

Chapter 16

1 Interviewed in *The Search for Extraterrestrial Life*, Discovery Channel, June 1995.
2 Carl Sagan, *Cosmos*, Book Club Associates, London, 1980, p. 296.
3 Ibid.
4 Indeed, what we appear to be looking at here is a veritable 'Hermetic language' making use of architecture and astronomy.
5 Of which the earliest surviving are the Pyramid Texts *circa* 2300 BC. Egyptologists accept, however that these texts are themselves transcripts (or translations?) of even earlier texts that are now lost to history, and that the scribes who initially wrote them down in Egyptian hieroglyphs often did not understand the words they were copying. According to E. A. Wallis Budge, for example: 'Several passages bear evidence that the scribes who drafted the copies from which the cutters of the inscriptions worked did not understand what they were writing . . . The general impression is that the priests who drafted the copies made extracts from several compositions of different ages and having different contents . . .' In consequence, Budge concludes: 'The Pyramid Texts are full of difficulties of every kind. The exact meanings of a large number of words found in them are unknown . . . the construction of the sentence often baffles all attempts to translate it, and when it contains wholly unknown words it becomes an unsolved riddle.' See E. A. Wallis Budge, *From Fetish to God in Ancient Egypt*, Dover Publications, New York, 1988, pp. 321–2.
6 *Hamlet's Mill*, op.cit., p. 312.
7 Proclus was a Neoplatonist who studied at Alexandria. His keen interest in the astronomy of the Great Pyramid, described in his *Commentaries on the Timaeus*, shows that scholars of the time, many of whom were Neoplatonists, understood the monument to be related to the stars.

Proclus's ideas formed the basis of the nineteenth-century astronomer Richard Proctor's thesis, *The Great Pyramid: Observatory, Tomb and Temple* (published by Chatto & Windus, London, 1883), who argued that the Grand Gallery was used as a sighting device for the stars.

8 James Bonwick, *Pyramids: Facts and Fancies*, Kegan Paul, 1877, p. 169.

9 William R. Fix, *Pyramid Odyssey*, Mercury Media Inc., Urbanna, Va, 1978, pp. 52–3. The Copts apparently took the 'traditional' date for the Biblical Flood as 10,000 BC.

10 In the geographical dictionary *Mo'gam-el-Buldan*, cited in Hassan, *Excavations at Giza*, op.cit., p. 45.

11 Ibid.

12 Ibid., p. 34. Hassan notes that an alternative name for the Sphinx, apparently bestowed upon it by these incomers, was *Hwron*.

13 See Peter Tompkins, *Secrets of the Great Pyramid*, op.cit., pp. 30–1.

14 Piazzi Smyth, *The Great Pyramid*, op.cit., page 368 ff.

15 Alexander Badawy, 'The Stellar Destiny of the Pharaoh', op.cit.; Virginia Trimble, 'Astronomical Investigations concerning the so-called Air Shafts of Cheops Pyramid', in *Mitt. Inst. Orient. zu Berlin* Band 10, pp. 183–7.

16 And see *The Orion Mystery*, op.cit.

17 Interviewed on Arts and Entertainment Channel, 8 January 1995.

18 Mary Bruck, 'Can the Great Pyramid be Astronomically Dated?', op.cit., pp. 164 and 162.

19 Skyglobe 3.6.

20 *Pyramid Texts*, op.cit., line 932, p. 161.

Chapter 17

1 R. T. Rundle Clark, *Myth and Symbol in Ancient Egypt*, op.cit., p. 264.

2 Robin Cook, *The Pyramids of Giza*, op.cit., p. 60.

3 Plus or minus 1 degree.

4 Plus or minus 1 degree.

5 Derived geometrically from scaled plan of Giza.

6 Sirius has a proper motion of 1.21 arc seconds per year. For 13,000 years this would give 4.36 degrees of motion. But the motion is oblique to the meridian, giving some 3 degrees decrease in declination.

7 Calculations using the rigorous formula for precession corrected for nutation, aberration of starlight, proper motion (from the most recent Yale Bright Star Catalogue) and parallax was done by astronomer Adrian Ashford in August 1995. In *circa* 11,850 BC Sirius would theoretically be

at the lowest point in its cycle, with a declination of −60 degrees, thus just on the south horizon. In 10,500 BC it would have had a declination of nearly −59 degrees, thus shining brightly approximately 1 degree over the south horizon as seen from Giza.

8 Ibid.

9 See Part II of the present work for a discussion.

10 Herodotus, *The History*, op.cit., II:124, p. 185. See also I. E. S. Edwards, *The Pyramids of Egypt*, op.cit., 1982 edition, p. 147.

11 Surviving examples of star-spangled causeway ceilings can be seen at the Pyramid of Unas (Fifth Dynasty) at Saqqara.

12 Many passages in the *Pyramid Texts*, op.cit., speak of 'roads' to the stars and to the sky where the deceased will become a god. For example, Utterance 667a, line 1943: 'You have your tomb O King, which belongs to [Osiris] . . . He opens for you the doors of the sky, he throws open for you the doors of the firmament, he makes a road for you that you may ascend by means of it into the company of the gods . . .'

13 John Legon, 'The Giza Ground Plan and Sphinx' in *Discussions in Egyptology* 14, 1989, p. 55.

14 Ibid. Although the bearing of the Khafre causeway at 14 degrees south of east is not in dispute, there has been some disagreement amongst scholars over the direction of the Khufu causeway – most traces of which have been long ago obliterated. Some authorities believe it proceeded straight on the 14-degree bearing it takes from the Mortuary Temple of the Great Pyramid, others believe that it started with this bearing and then changed direction, before reaching the Valley Temple of the Great Pyramid. To give some indication of the range of opinion on this matter see George Goyon, *Le Secret des Batisseurs des Grandes Pyramides: Kheops*, Pygmalion, Gerard Watelet, Paris, 1990, p. 140: 'contrary to what some have long believed, the direction [of the Khufu causeway] stays uniform and does not change direction in the valley below.' Zahi Hawass in *The Pyramids of Ancient Egypt*, The Carnegie Series on Egypt, Pennsylvania, 1990, p. 22, also shows a straight causeway on the 14-degree bearing, but points out on page 18: 'scholars disagree over the exact course of the causeway, but it led to Khufu's Valley Temple, the ruins of which lie under the present-day village of Nazlet-el-Sammam.'

15 John Legon, *The Giza Ground Plan*, op.cit., p. 60.

16 For a general discussion, see Richard Heinberg, *Celebrate the Solstice*, Quest Books, Wheaton, Ill, 1993, pp. 11–14.

17 We note with interest that this 'cross-quarter' alignment appears to have been of major importance at Heliopolis. In *The Dawn of*

Astronomy, op.cit., p. 77, the British astronomer J. Norman Lockyer, who was able to survey the site of ancient Heliopolis before it was obscured by the modern suburb that now covers it, noted in passing that the principal mound on the site had a bearing of 14 degrees south of east – i.e. the identical bearing to the Khafre causeway. Lockyer also reminds us of ancient Egyptian traditions that Heliopolis was founded by the *Shemsu Hor*, the 'Followers of Horus', long before the beginning of Dynastic history (ibid., p. 74).

18 *Pyramid Texts*, op.cit., Utterances 471–3, pp. 160–2.

19 *Coffin Texts*, op.cit., Spell 1080, Vol. III, p. 147.

Conclusion

1 From the Eleventh Division of the *Duat*, '*The Book of What is in the Duat*', E. A. Wallis Budge trans., in *The Egyptian Heaven and Hell*, op.cit., p. 240.

2 Translated as 'The Virgin of the World' by G. R. S. Mead in *Thrice Great Hermes: Studies in Hellenistic Theosophy and Gnosis*, op.cit., Book III, p. 59 ff. Translated by Sir Walter Scott as the *Kore Kosmu* in *Hermetica*, op.cit., p. 457 ff.

3 'The Virgin of the World', G. R. S. Mead transl., pp. 60–1.

4 Ibid., p. 61.

5 See Part I of the present work.

6 The quotation is from the Normandi Ellis's translation of the *Ancient Egyptian Book of the Dead*, *Awakening Osiris*, Phanes Press, Grand Rapids, MI, 1988, p. 43, and is drawn from Chapter XV of the *Ancient Egyptian Book of the Dead*, Papyrus of Ani.

Appendix 1

1 J. B. Sellers, *The Death of Gods in Ancient Egypt*, op.cit., p. 157–9.

2 R. O. Faulkner, *The Book of the Dead*, op. cit., p. 49.

3 Ibid.

4 J. B. Sellers, *The Death of Gods*, op.cit., p. 97.

5 Ibid., p. 159.

6 Ibid., page 97.

7 The M1 Crab Nebula is the remnant of a great supernova explosion which occurred in *c.* 4500 BC, roughly when the vernal point occupied this specific place in the sky. However, the supernova was about 5500

light-years away and its light only started reaching our planet in *c.* AD 1000. It was recorded by the Chinese and, apparently, by the North American Indians. No one seems to have recorded it in Europe or the Middle East, which is very odd, since Christians, at that time, fervently awaited a 'sign' from heaven to announce the 'Second Coming' of Christ.

8 *The Orion Mystery*, op.cit., p. 200. See also Robert G. Bauval 'Investigation on the origin of the Benben Stone: was it an iron meteorite?' in *Discussions in Egyptology*, Vol. XIV, 1989, pp. 5–17.

9 R. T. Rundle Clark, *Myth and Symbol in Ancient Egypt*, op. cit., p. 235.

10 R. O. Faulkner, *The Book of the Dead*, op.cit., Spell 17.

11 Ibid.

12 See also Miriam Lichtheim, *Ancient Egyptian Literature*; op.cit., Vol. I p. 53.

13 Ibid.

14 Ibid. The 'White Wall' probably refers to the Tura limestone walls of the royal palace and the boundary wall of Memphis.

15 Ibid., p. 54.

16 Most Egyptologists would contest this point, but we feel that the evidence is overwhelming in favour of a direct cultic connection between Osiris and the Great Pyramid. An interesting article touching upon this idea can be read in Steuart Campbell, 'The Origin and Purpose of the Pyramids' in the *New Humanist*, December 1990 issue, pp. 3–4, who wrote that 'the Great Pyramid might have been intended as a dwelling place for the spirit of Osiris'. The French Antiquarian and Freemason, Alexandre Lenoir (see 'A dissertation on the Pyramids of Egypt' in FMR No. 39, 1989) was also to claim that 'all considered it [the Great Pyramid] may be the tomb of Osiris'.

17 E. A. Wallis Budge, *An Egyptian Hieroglyphic Dictionary*, op.cit., Vol. I, p. 285b.

18 Ibid.

19 Ibid., Vol. II, pp. 614b, 622a, 688a.

20 Ibid., p. 614a.

21 Charles Piazzi Smyth, *Our Inheritance in the Great Pyramid*, Bell edition, 1990, p. 429.

22 *Nature*, 31 July 1873.

23 The reader will also recall that 43,200 is 20 × 2160, the 'special' number denoting a precessional or zodiacal age. See Chapter 3 of the present work.

24 This pertinent point was raised very recently by the eminent astronomer, Dr Mary Bruck: 'Can the Great Pyramid be astronomically

dated?' in *The Journal of the British Astronomical Society*, 105, 4, 1995, pp. 161–4.

25 See J. Legon, 'The air-shafts in the Great Pyramid' in *Discussions in Egyptology* 27, 1993, pp. 33–44. See Robin Cook, 'The stellar geometry of the Great Pyramid' in *Discussions in Egyptology* 29, 1994, pp. 29–36. Rudolf Gantenbrink, who remeasured the angles of the shafts recently, gave a higher 'adjusted' value of 39.6 degrees for the southern shaft of the Queen's Chamber. None the less, the 'designed' intention to have the shafts come out at the same level very much seems to be the case for the Great Pyramid.

26 *The Orion Mystery*, op.cit., pp. 222–3.

27 Ibid., p. 34.

28 Hence the 'Fish' symbol amongst the early Christians, denoting the 'new age' of Christianity marked by the vernal equinox in Pisces. The vernal point is now poised to enter the new age of Aquarius.

29 When Alexander the Great liberated Egypt from Persian rule, he was hailed by the Egyptian priests as a divine hero and the returned 'son of Ammon' – and by his Macedonian followers as 'son of Zeus'. Both titles stand, of course, for 'son of god'. After his death a 'cult of Alexander' was established in Alexandria which spread with almost messianic fervour across the Fertile Crescent. For the three centuries preluding the Christian era, Alexander (who had died at the age of thirty-three in 323 BC) was the archetype of the conquering martyred 'hero-king' and 'son of god' of quasi-solar pedigree who had unified the known world on the basis of a divine blueprint or mission. It was thus that, in the closing years of the last century BC, the whole Roman world, sickened by the endless civil and foreign wars, placed much hope for the return of a 'saviour-king' modelled on Alexander who would unite the empire and usher in a new golden age. This hope was very much pinned on Augustus Caesar (Octavian) by the Roman poet Virgil in *c.* 42 BC in his famous *Eclogues* ('see how Olympian Caesar's star has climbed the sky, the star to gladden all our corn with grain . . . your children's children will enjoy the fruits . . .'). In 12 BC Augustus Caesar was declared head of the Roman (thus 'world') religion and given the title of Pontifex Maximus – a title later to denote the Catholic pontiffs or 'Popes' of Rome. Ironically, in 4 BC – the assumed year that Christ was born – Augustus adopted Tiberius (second Emperor of Rome who ruled from AD 14 to AD 37, thus in the ministry of Jesus) and declared him his heir. Yet by the most unexpected twist of fate Virgil's prophecy was eventually to be fulfilled not by 'Divine Augustus' but by a Jewish 'saviour-king', the Christos or Christ, fostered four centuries later by

Rome itself under the rule of Constantine the Great (see Ian Wilson, *Jesus, the Evidence*, Pan Books, London, 1984, pp. 134–44). It may well be that Virgil's 'star of Caesar' influenced the unknown author of the gospel of Matthew ('We have seen his star and come to pay him homage . . .' Matthew 2:1–9) who used the astral prophesy for the birth of Jesus. Not unexpectedly, many of the great Italian Hermetic philosophers of the late Renaissance (Bruno, Pico della Mirandola, Campanella, etc.) often presented Virgil as a 'Gentile prophet' of Christianity and the 'Egyptian' Hermes Trismegistos (i.e. the Egyptian god Thoth) in par with the Old Testament prophet Moses (see Frances A. Yates, *Giordano Bruno*, op.cit.). Many of these Hermetic 'Cabala' philosophers adamantly believed that the 'Egyptian' astral magic as found in the ancient texts was the agency or 'device' for great world-changing events (ibid. et al.). It can be thus argued that in the first century of our era the scene was set in the collective subconscious by astrologer-prophets of old to bring about a messianic event. In our next book, we will explore how such powerful 'Hermetic devices' were activated throughout the ages and also, as the case may be, may be about to be galvanized in present times.

30 Richard H. Allen, *Star Names*, op.cit., p. 316.
31 Selim Hassan, *Excavations at Giza*, op.cit., p. 45.
32 Worked on Skyglobe 3.6.

Appendix 4

1 E.M. Antoniadi, *L'Astronomie Egyptienne*. Paris, 1934, p. 119.
2 Frances A. Yates, *The Art Of Memory*, University of Chicago Press, 1966.

Appendix 5

1 E.g. John Baines and Jaromir Malek, *Atlas of Ancient Egypt*, Time-Life Books, 1990, p. 36, 156 ff.
2 Ibid. See also Ahmen Fakry, *The Pyramids*, University of Chicago Press, 1969, and Kurt Mendelssohn, *The Riddle of the Pyramids*, Thames and Hudson, London, 1986.
3 *Venture Inward*, Virginia Beach, May-June 1986, p. 13.
4 Ibid.
5 Ibid., p. 12–14.

6 See Chapter 6 for fuller details concerning the Dixon relics.

7 Those present included Dr Vivian Davies, Keeper of Egyptian Antiquities at the British Museum, and Dr I. E. S. Edwards, author of the standard text *They Pyramids of Egypt*.

Appendix 6

1 *Sunday Telegraph*, 1 January 1995.

2 Sat 1, Spiegel Reportage, 15 August 1995.

3 *Egyptian Gazette*, 31 March 1996.

4 Documented conversations with Peter Zuuring.

5 *Serpent*, op.cit., p. 229.

6 *Al Akhbar El Yom*, 8 January 1994.

7 Edgar Cayce Reading Ref No 3976–15, in *Earth Changes* circulating file, Edgar Cayce Foundation, 1993, p. 38.

8 Schor's May 94 letter.

9 See *Daily Mail*, London, 2 and 3 May 1996.

10 *Egyptian Gazette*, 14 April 1996.

11 *Secret Chamber*, Magical Eye Productions, 1996.

12 Ibid.

13 Hawass interview, John Robbie Show.

14 Harmon Hartzell Bro, *A Seer Out Of Season: The Life of Edgar Cayce*, Signet Books, 1990, p. 242.

15 Quote from a senior ARE researcher in a letter to Charles I. Cayce dated 12 June 1996.

16 *Venture Inward*, Jan/Feb 1985, Vol 6, p. 9.

17 A.R. Smith, *Hugh Lynn Cayce: About My Father's Business*, Donning Co., Norfolk, Virginia, 1988, p. 249.

18 *Venture Inward*, op.cit.

19 A.R. Smith, op.cit., p. 250.

20 John Robbie Show, Radio 702 Johannesburg, 17 July 1996.

21 *Egyptian Gazette*, Cairo, 15 August 1996.

22 Dr James Hurtak, *The Keys of Enoch*, California, 1976. See also the video *UFO: Evidence of the use of Extraterrestrial Technology*, Labyrinth Media, UK.

23 Richard C. Hoagland, *The Monuments of Mars*, North Atlantic Books, Berkeley, California, 1992, p. 363. See also Plates 38 and 39.

24 *Omni Magazine*, 'Interview with Farouk El Baz', 1990, p. 75.

Selected Bibliography

Allen, Richard H., *Star Names: Their Lore and Meaning*, Dover Publications Inc., New York, 1963.

Ancient Egyptian Book of the Dead (trans. R. O. Faulkner), British Museum Publications, 1989.

Ancient Egyptian Pyramid Texts (trans. R. O. Faulkner), Oxford University Press, 1969.

Antoniadi, E. M., *L'Astronomie Egyptienne*, Paris, 1934.

Aristotle, *De Caelo*, see translation in Schwaller de Lubicz, R. A., *Sacred Science*, Inner Traditions International, New York, 1982.

Baines, John and Malek, Jaromir, *Atlas of Ancient Egypt*, TimeLife Books, 1990.

Bauval, Robert and Gilbert, Adrian, *The Orion Mystery*, William Heinemann Ltd, London, 1994.

Black, Jeremy and Green Anthony, *Gods, Demons and Symbols of Ancient Mesopotamia*, British Museum Press, London, 1992.

Bonwick, James, *Pyramids: Facts and Fancies,* Kegan Paul, 1877.

Breasted, James Henry, *Ancient Records of Egypt*, Histories and Mysteries of Man Ltd, London, 1988.

Bro, Harmon Hartzell, *Edgar Cayce: A Seer Out of Season*, Signet Books, New York, 1990.

Bunson, Margaret, *The Encyclopaedia of Ancient Egypt*, New York, Oxford, 1991.

Cayce, Edgar Evans, Cayce Schwartzer, Gail, and Richards, Douglas G., *Mysteries of Atlantis Revisited: Edgar Cayce's Wisdom for the New Age*, Harper & Row, San Francisco, 1988.

Ceram, C. W., *Gods, Graves and Scholars*, Book Club Associates, London, 1971.

Cook, Robin, *The Pyramids of Giza*, Seven Islands, Glastonbury, 1992.

David, Rosalie, *Ancient Egyptian Religion, Beliefs and Practices*, Routledge & Kegan Paul, London, 1982.

Davidovits, Dr Joseph and Morris, Maggie, *The Pyramids: An Enigma Solved*, Dorset Press, New York, 1988.

Diodorus Siculus (trans. C. H. Oldfather), Loeb Classical Library, London, 1989; Harvard University Press, 1989.

Edwards, I. E. S., *The Pyramids of Egypt*, Pelican Books, London, 1949.

Emery, W. B., *Archaic Egypt*, Penguin Books, London, 1987.

Fakhry, Ahmed, *The Pyramids*, University of Chicago Press, 1969.

Faulkner, R. O., *The Book of the Dead*, British Museum Publications, London, 1972.

Fix, William R., *Pyramid Odyssey*, Mercury Media Inc., Urbanna, Va., 1978.

Flinders Petrie, W. M., *The Pyramids and Temples of Gizeh*, Histories and Mysteries of Man Ltd, London, 1990.

Fowden, Garth, *The Egyptian Hermes*, Princeton University Press, New Jersey, 1993.

Frankfort, Henri, *Kingship and the Gods*, The University of Chicago Press, 1978.

Goidin, J. P. and Dormion, G., *Kheops: Nouvelle Enquête*, Editions Recherche sur les Civilisations, Paris, 1986.

Goyon, George, *Le Secret des Batisseurs des Grandes Pyramides: Kheops*, Pygmalion, Gerard Watelet, Paris, 1990.

Grimal, Nicholas, *A History of Ancient Egypt*, Blackwell, Oxford, 1992.

Habachi, Labib, *The Obelisks of Egypt*, The American University Press, Cairo, 1988.

Hancock, Graham, *Fingerprints of the Gods*, William Heinemann Ltd, London 1995, and Crown Publishers, New York, 1995.

Hart, George, *A Dictionary of Egyptian Gods and Goddesses*, Routledge & Kegan Paul, London, 1988.

Hassan, Selim, *Excavations at Giza*, Government Press, Cairo, 1946.

——*The Sphinx: Its History in the Light of Recent Excavations*, Government Press, Cairo, 1949.

Heinberg, Richard, *Celebrate the Solstice*, Quest Books, Wheaton Ill., 1993.

Herodotus, *The History* (trans. David Grene), University of Chicago Press, 1988.

Heyerdahl, Thor, *The Ra Expeditions*, Book Club Associates, London, 1972.

Hoffman, Michael A., *Egypt before the Pharaohs*, Michael O'Mara Books Ltd, London, 1991.

Ions, Veronica, *Indian Mythology*, Hamlyn, London, 1983.

James, T. G. H., *An Introduction To Ancient Egypt*, British Museum Publications Ltd, 1987.

Keable, Julian (ed.), *How The Pyramids Were Built*, Element Books, Dorset, 1989.

Kees, Hermann, *Ancient Egypt: A Cultural Topography*, University of Chicago Press, 1977.

Krupp, E. C., *In Search of Ancient Astronomies*, Chatto & Windus, London, 1980.

Lamy, Lucy, *Egyptian Mysteries*, Thames and Hudson, London, 1986.

Lehner, Mark, *The Egyptian Heritage: Based on the Edgar Cayce Readings* ARE Press, Virginia Beach, Norfolk, Va., 1974.

Lichtheim, Miriam, *Ancient Egyptian Literature*, University of California Press, 1975.

Low, Sampson, *Seventy Years In Archaeology*, Marston & Co. Ltd, London, 1931.

Lucas, *Ancient Egyptian Materials and Industries*, Histories & Mysteries of Man Ltd, London, 1989.

Mackenzie, Donald A., *Myths and Legends of India*, The Mystic Press, London, 1987.

Malek, Jaromir, *In the Shadow of the Pyramids*, Orbis, London, 1986.

Maspero, Gaston, *The Passing of Empires*, New York, 1900.

——*The Dawn of Civilization*, SPCK, London, 1894.

Noakes, Aubrey, *Cleopatra's Needles*, H. F. & G. Witherby Ltd, London, 1962.

Piazzi Smyth, Charles, *Our Inheritance in The Great Pyramid*, W. Isbister, London, 1880 edition. (Reprinted recently by Bell Publishing Co.,

New York, 1990, under the title *The Great Pyramid*.)

Pick, Fred L. and Knight, G. Norman, *The Pocket History of Freemasonry*, Frederick Muller Ltd, London, 1983.

Reymond, E. A. E., *The Mythical Origin of the Egyptian Temple*, Manchester University Press, Barnes and Noble Inc., New York, 1969.

Rundle-Clark, R. T., *Myth and Symbol in Ancient Egypt*, Thames and Hudson, London, 1991.

——*The Legend of the Phoenix*, University of Birmingham Press, 1949.

Sagan, Carl, *Cosmos*, Book Club Associates, London, 1980.

Santillana, Giorgio de and Dechend, Hertha von, *Hamlet's Mill*, David R. Godine, Boston, 1977.

Scheel, Bernd, *Egyptian Metalworking and Tools*, Shire Egyptology, Bucks, 1989.

Schwaller de Lubicz, R. A., *Sacred Science*, Inner Traditions International, Rochester, Vt; 1988.

Sellers, J. B., *The Death of Gods in Ancient Egypt*, Penguin Books, London, 1992.

Seton-Williams, Veronica and Stock, Peter, *Blue Guide: Egypt*, A&C Black, London, 1988.

Short, Martin, *Inside the Brotherhood*, Grafton Books, London, 1989.

Singh, Sarva Daman, *Ancient Indian Warfare*, Motilal Banarsidass, Delhi, 1989.

Sitchin, Zecharia, *The Stairway To Heaven*, Avon Books, New York, 1980.

Spence, Lewis, *Egypt*, Bracken Books, Myths & Legends Series, London, 1986.

——*Ancient Egyptian Myths and Legends*, Dover Publications, New York, 1990.

Sugrue, Thomas, *There is a River: The Story of Edgar Cayce*, ARE. Press, Virginia Beach, Norfolk, Va., 1988.

Temple, Robert K. G., *The Sirus Mystery*, Destiny Books, Rochester, Vt, 1987.

The Ancient Egyptian Pyramid Texts (trans. R. O. Faulkner), Oxford University Press, 1969.

Tomas, Andrew, *From Atlantis to Discovery*, Robert Hale, London, 1972.

Tompkins, Peter, *Secrets of the Great Pyramid*, Allen Lane, London, 1972.

Vercoutter, Jean, *The Search for Ancient Egypt*, Thames and Hudson,

London, 1992.

Vyse, Colonel Howard, *Operations carried out at the Pyramids of Gizeh in 1837: With an account of a Voyage into Upper Egypt and Appendix*, James Fraser of Regent Street, London 1837.

Wallis Budge, E. A., *An Egyptian Hieroglyphic Dictionary*, Dover Publications Inc., New York, 1978.

——*A History of Egypt*, London, 1902.

——*The Gods of the Egyptians*, Dover Publications Inc., New York, 1969.

——*The Egyptian Book of the Dead*, Dover Publications Inc., New York, 1967.

——*The Literature of Funeral Offerings*, Kegan Paul Ltd, London, 1909.

——*From Fetish to God in Ancient Egypt*, Dover Publications, New York, 1988.

West, John Anthony, *Serpent in the Sky: The High Wisdom of Ancient Egypt*, Quest Books, Wheaton, Ill., 1993.

——*The Traveller's Key to Ancient Egypt*, Harrap Columbus, London, 1989.

Yates, Frances A., *Giordano Bruno and the Hermetic Tradition*, University of Chicago Press, 1991.

Index

Page numbers in bold indicate illustrations

THE SIGN AND THE SEAL

Graham Hancock

The explosively controversial international bestseller
A quest for the lost ark of the covenant, *The Sign and the Seal*
shatters the greatest secret of the last 3,000 years.

'Graham Hancock's obsession has led him to give up nine years
of his life to tracking down the exact location of the Ark of the
Covenant . . . The obsession is well worth sharing. The
excitement is nail biting.' *Sunday Express*

'Highly readable.' *The Times*

'Hancock's book will probably be as popular as the Raider's film.
Added to the Holy Grail excitement of his quest, he has invented
a new genre: an intellectual whodunit by a do-it-yourself sleuth.'
Guardian

'Part travelogue, part sensation, part unravelling, a fascinating
story.' *Catholic Herald*

'It should cause widespread discussion and it deserves to.'
Daily Telegraph

'Eat your heart out, Harrison Ford.' *Gerald Seymour*

FINGERPRINTS OF THE GODS

Graham Hancock

In a drastic re-evaluation of man's past, using the high-tech tools of modern archaeology, geology and astronomy, Graham Hancock's extraordinary book exposes the eerie network of connections between:

- The Great Sphinx and pyramids of Egypt
- The Andean temples of Tianhuanaco
- The Mexican Pyramids of the Sun and Moon
- The lost continent that lies beneath Antarctica
- Ancient knowledge of spherical geometry and astro-navigation
- The myths and legends of humanity that have remained strangely consistent across geographical and social divides
- New theories about the causes of the ice-ages

His new evidence reveals not only the clear fingerprints of an unknown civilisation that flourished during the last ice-age, but also horrifying conclusions about the type and extent of planetary catastrophe that would have had to occur in order to obliterate almost all traces of it.

'500 pages of inspired story-telling' *The Times*

'One of the intellectual landmarks of this decade'
Literary Review

OTHER TITLES OF INTEREST